HISTORY

OF

TENNESSEE

From the Earliest Time to the Present; Together with an Historical and a Biographical Sketch of the County of Knox and the City of Knoxville, Besides a Valuable Fund of Notes, Original Observations, Reminiscences, Etc., Etc.

ILLUSTRATED

Nashville:
THE GOODSPEED PUBLISHING CO.,
1887.

This volume was reproduced from
An 1887 edition located in the
Library of Mr. John E. Ladson, Jr
Vidalia, Georgia

All rights reserved. No part of this publication may be reproduced,
stored in a retrieval system, transmitted in any form,
posted on to the web in any form or by any means
without the prior written permission of the publisher.

Please direct all correspondence and orders to:

www.southernhistoricalpress.com
or
SOUTHERN HISTORICAL PRESS, Inc.
PO BOX 1267
375 West Broad Street
Greenville, SC   29601
southernhistoricalpress@gmail.com

Originally published: Nashville, 1887
Reprinted with New Material by:
Southern Historical Press, Inc.
Greenville, SC
New Material Copyright 1988 by
The Rev. Silas Emmett Lucas, Jr.
Easley, SC
ISBN #0-89308-125-6
All rights Reserved.
Printed in the United States of America

PREFACE.

THIS volume has been prepared in response to the prevailing and popular demand for the preservation of local history and biography. The method of preparation followed is the most successful and the most satisfactory yet devised—the most successful in the enormous number of volumes circulated, and the most satisfactory in the general preservation of personal biography and family record conjointly with local history. The number of volumes now being distributed appears fabulous. Within the last four years not less than 20,000 volumes of this class of works have been distributed in Kentucky, and the demand is not half satisfied. Careful estimates place the number circulated in Ohio at 50,000; Pennsylvania, 60,000; New York, 75,000; Indiana, 35,000; Illinois, 40,000; Iowa, 35,000, and every other Northern State at the same proportionate rate. The Southern States, with the exception of Kentucky, Virginia and Georgia, owing mainly to the disorganization succeeding the civil war, yet retain, ready for the publisher, their stories of history and biography. Within the next five years the vast and valuable fund of perishing event in all the Southern States will be rescued from decay, and be recorded and preserved—to be reviewed, studied and compared by future generations. The design of the present extensive historical and biographical research is more to gather and preserve in attractive form while fresh with the evidences of truth, the enormous fund of perishing occurrence, than to abstract from insufficient contemporaneous data remote, doubtful or incorrect conclusions. The true perspective of the landscape of life can only be seen from the distance that lends enchantment to the view. It is asserted that no person is competent to write a philosophical history of his own time—that, owing to conflicting circumstantial evidence that yet conceals the truth, he can not take that luminous, correct, comprehensive, logical and unprejudiced view of passing events that will enable him to draw accurate and enduring conclusions. The duty, then, of a historian of his own time is to collect, classify and preserve the material for the final historian of the future. The present historian deals in fact, the future historian, in conclusion; the work of the former is statistical, of the latter, philosophical.

To him who has not attempted the collection of historical data, the obstacles to be surmounted are unknown. Doubtful traditions, conflicting statements, imperfect records, inaccurate private correspondence, the bias or untruthfulness of informers, and the general obscurity which envelops all events combine to bewilder and mislead. On the contrary, the preparation of statistical history by experienced, unprejudiced and competent workers in specialties; the accomplishment by a union of labor of a vast result that would cost one person the best years of his life and transfer the collection of perishing event beyond the hope of research; the judicious selection of important matter from the general rubbish; and the careful and intelligent revision of all final manuscript by an editor-in-chief, yield a degree of celerity, system, accuracy, comprehensiveness and value unattainable by any other method. The publishers of this volume, fully aware of their inability to furnish a perfect history, an accomplishment vouchsafed only to the dreamer or the theorist, make no pretension of having prepared a work devoid of blemish. They feel assured that all thoughtful people, at present and in future, will recognize and appreciate the importance of their undertaking and the great public benefit that has been accomplished.

In the preparation of this volume the publishers have met with nothing but courtesy and assistance. They acknowledge their indebtedness for valuable favors to the Governor, the State Librarian, the Secretary of the State Historical Society and to more than a hundred of other prominent citizens of Nashville, Memphis, Knoxville, Chattanooga, Jackson, Clarksville and the smaller cities of the State. It is the design of the publishers to compile and issue, in connection with the State history, a brief yet comprehensive historical account of every county in the State, copies of which will be placed in the State Library. In the prosecution of this work they hope to meet with the same cordial assistance extended to them during the compilation of this volume.

THE PUBLISHERS.

NASHVILLE, July, 1887.

CONTENTS.

KNOX COUNTY.

	PAGE.
KNOX COUNTY	797
Attorneys, List of	819
Business at Knoxville, Early	841–844
Banking	866–867
Business Houses, Later	851–855
Boundary, etc	797
Cavett Massacre, The	804
Commerce, Early	807
County Officers	814
Casteel Massacre, The	805
Courts, The	815
Commerce, Extent of	851
Education	875–883
Finances, etc	813
Indians, Dealings with the	800–806
Industries, Early	846–849
Insurance	867
Incorporation	873–874
Knox County Organized	808–809
Knoxville	839
Knoxville Since the War	849
Lodges	868–870
Military Record	825–839
Massacres by the Indians	806
Minerals, etc	797–798
Manufacturers	856–866
Medical Society, The	870–871
Mayors, Catalogue of	874–875
Public Buildings	809–813
Poor Farm, The	811–812
Press of Knoxville, The	871–873
Postoffice Building	875
Railroads	808
Retail Trade at Present	855
Religion	883–908
Soil, Fertility of the	797
Streams, Drainage, etc	798
Settlement, etc	799–806

BIOGRAPHICAL APPENDIX.

	PAGE.
KNOX COUNTY	909

KNOX COUNTY.*

KNOX COUNTY is situated very near the center of the valley of East Tennessee. Its shape is very irregular, having no two sides parallel. Beginning on the north and passing around it to the right it is bounded by the counties of Union, Grainger, Jefferson, Sevier, Blount, Loudon, Roane and Anderson. It contains an area of about 576 square miles. The surface of the greater portion of the county consists of a series of parallel ridges and valleys extending from the northeast to the southwest. Along the northwest boundary runs Flint or Chestnut Ridge. It receives its former name from the character of the rock forming it, which is a kind of chert, resembling true flint. The latter name is derived from the chestnut timber which abounds there. On the west side, in a divide of the ridge, lies a short section of a narrow valley known as Raccoon Valley. On the east side it slopes gradually into Bull Run Valley, which receives its name from Bull Run Creek, a tributary of the Clinch which flows through it. On the east side of this valley Copper Ridge rises somewhat abruptly, and beyond the ridge is Beaver Creek Valley, which is one of the richest in the county, and was one of the earliest settled. It is divided through the middle by the creek whose name it bears. Lying between Beaver and Black Oak Ridges is the section of a valley known as Hind's Valley, the lower half of which is watered by Hickory Creek, a tributary of the Clinch. The soil of this valley is generally light and thin, but is well adapted to grass, and is capable of improvement. The fertile section bounded by Black Oak and Webb's Ridges is known as Grassy Valley. It, unlike the others, does not slope gradually from northeast to southwest, but is crossed transversely by small ridges and depressions. Black Oak Ridge constitutes the watershed between the waters of the Tennessee and the Clinch. Poor Valley lies between Webb's Ridge and McAnnally's Ridge. As its name indicates its soil is poor, consisting of the washings of the shale and dolomite, which make up the ridges. The largest valley in the county is the Central or Knoxville Valley, otherwise known as Rocky Valley or New Market Valley, which constitutes the valley of the Tennessee River. The soil is composed of the shale, chert, limestone and dolomite, which have washed down from the surrounding ridges on a clay sub-soil, the whole

---

*Much matter connected with the history of Knoxville is found in other chapters of this work, and to avoid repetition is here omitted. The facts concerning the settlement of the county have been taken from Ramsey, Haywood and other publications. For other matters the writer is indebted to Dr. Thomas W. Humes, Prof. W. G. McAdoo, Col. J. H. Crozier and many other citizens of Knoxville.

of which is mixed with more or less iron which gives it a reddish color. This constitutes the most fertile portion of the county, and is made up of excellent farming lands. A part of the county southeast of the French Broad and Tennessee Rivers constitutes what is known as the Knobby region, in which the parallelism incident to the other sections is broken up. It consists of a vast group of red-topped hills of remarkable uniformity of size and shape rising above the plane of the valley from 200 to 400 feet, and separated from each other by rough, irregular ravines. The formation is described by State Geologist Safford as red ferruginous, sandy, fossiliferous, limestone, interstratified with calcareous strata of floggy limestone. The soil of the valleys, which are very narrow, is exceedingly fertile, and produces good crops of corn, oats and wheat. The creeks from this region on account of its peculiar configuration are small. They are Hind and Mill Shoal emptying into the French Broad; Baker, Hodge and Knob, tributaries of the Tennessee, and Stock Creek flowing into Little River.

The Holston River enters the county from the east and flows in a generally southwest course to a point about four miles above Knoxville, where it unites with the French Broad to form the Tennessee. The French Broad enters the county at a point near where the line between the counties of Sevier and Blount intersects the Knox County line, and continues in a nearly due west course until its junction with the Holston. The Tennessee, from its origin to the point where it leaves the county, makes several curves of greater or less size, but its general direction is to the southwest. This portion of the Tennessee and extending to Kingston, previous to 1874, was known as the Holston. The tributaries of the Holston are Big Flat Creek, into which flows Little Flat Creek, Rosebury Creek and Doak Creek on the right bank, and Swan Pond, Turkey and Sinking Creek on the left bank. The Tuckahoe empties into the French Broad on the right bank, while Love Creek, First Creek, Second Creek, Third Creek and Lyon Creek are tributaries of the Tennessee from the north.

Probably the first white persons to set foot in what is now Knox County were the troops under Cols. Evan Shelby and John Montgomery, upon their return from the Chickamauga expedition* in May, 1779, and it was undoubtedly the beauty of the scenery, the fertility of the soil, and the many other natural advantages of this region, which they now saw for the first time, that induced many of them, a few years later, to make it their home. In March of the next year, the heroic Col. Donelson with his party, passed down the Holston River, on their way to the Cumberland

---

*See page 79.

settlement. On the second day of the month they passed the mouth of French Broad River, and about 12 o'clock of that day one of the boats was sunk upon an island supposed to have been Dickinson's Island about two miles above Knoxville. This misfortune delayed the entire party and they camped upon the bank of the river opposite the island until the next morning when they resumed their journey.* A year or two later corn having become scarce among the settlers on the Nolachucky, Jeremiah Jack and William Rankin, of Greene County, descended the river in a canoe for the purpose of bartering with the Indians for corn. On their return they landed and camped one night on the north bank of the French Broad about a mile above its mouth, and so well pleased was Mr. Jack with the place, that upon his immigration to the present Knox County in 1787, he selected this spot as his future residence.

In August, 1783, James White, Robert Love, F. A. Ramsey and others for the purpose of locating land warrants, explored the country as low as the confluence of the Holston and Tennessee Rivers. They crossed the French Broad at War Ford, and continued on the south side of that stream until they reached the mouth of Dumplin Creek, when they recrossed, and explored the county between the French Broad and Holston. They then crossed the latter stream a few miles above where Knoxville now stands, and continued through the Grassy Valley to the mouth of the Holston. It was upon this tour that Gen. White and Col. Ramsey saw the lands which they soon after entered and occupied.

In 1785 the Government of Franklin formed two new counties out of the county of Greene, known as Sevier and Caswell, the latter of which probably contained what is now Knox County. Settlements were made in that year on both sides of the French Broad and on the Holston. Adam Meek made the first settlement on the head of Beaver Creek in Quaker Valley. He had no neighbor to the west of him and so sparsely settled was the county to the east that he at first obtained his meal from the neighborhood of Greeneville. He was a surveyor from Mecklenburg County, N. C., and had previously explored the country and made surveys on the frontier. Like most other pioneers he built his first cabin of round poles with a covering of bark and grass. During the Indian troubles he frequently retired at evening with his family to a deep sink three-quarters of a mile from his cabin, and there spent the night. Very soon after settlements were made at the head of Flat Creek and Bull Run, and in the fork between the Holston and French Broad a colony was formed at Greene's, afterward Manifold's Station, and near it located James Cosby, James Beard, Bowman and Gibson. At the same

*See page 129.

time Col. James White settled on the north bank of the French Broad, about four miles above its mouth, opposite Cozby and Greene. Capt. Thomas Gillespie located three miles below on the north side of the river. In 1787 Jeremiah Jack opened the second plantation above the mouth of the French Broad. During the same year Robert Armstrong planted corn and raised a crop on the Holston, a little above the mouth of Swan Pond Creek, on which he settled the next year. At the same time Devereaux Gilliam occupied the plantation embracing the point between the French Broad and Holston, while Archibald Rhea, Sr., settled immediately opposite, on the south bank of the French Broad. These settlements between the rivers being almost isolated were less annoyed by the Indians, than those south or north of them. On one occasion, however, a party of warriors crossed the river to Capt. Gillespie's cabin, while the captain was away from home, and finding Mrs. Gillespie alone entered the house. One of them then taking out a scalping knife was at the point of scalping an infant which lay in the cradle, when Mrs. Gillespie sprang to the door, and looking in the direction of the clearing where the Captain had the day before been at work and where the fires were still burning, called for help. The Indians thinking that the men were near by dashed out of the house and into the adjacent canebrakes while Mrs. Gillespie with the child in her arms fled in the direction from which, she knew her husband, who had gone to Dumplin Creek twelve miles away, would return. After proceeding several miles she met the Captain, who took her and the child upon the horse, and carried them back to Manifold's Station. He then reinforced himself with three men, and returned in haste to his home. The savages had plundered it of its contents, and while some were carrying off the spoils, one was busily engaged in setting fire to the house. He was fired upon by the Captain, who had outridden his companions, but being partly obscured by the smoke, escaped. The property however, was recaptured and the Indians were driven across the river. Thereafter these settlements suffered but little from Indian aggressions except the stealing of horses, which frequently occurred. The population of this section now rapidly increased, the two rivers making it easy of access by boats and canoes. Among those who came were James Anderson, Moses Brooks and George McNutt, who removed from the Nolachucky and settled on the north side of the Holston above Knoxville. The year before James White had removed from his first location in the fork, and with James Conner, an old neighbor from Iredell County, N. C., had begun a settlement on the present site of Knoxville. Their cabin stood on the west side of First Creek about one hundred rods from its mouth. It afterward constituted one corner of White's Fort, which consisted of a quadrangular plat of ground containing a quarter of an acre, on each corner of which was a strong cabin. Between these corners stockades were placed eight feet high, impenetrable to small arms, and having port holes at convenient height and distance. This fort became a central point for immigrants, and a rendezvous for rangers and scouts. Attracted by the beauty and healthfulness of the location, immigrants came in large numbers.

While Col. White was establishing this settlement, John Adair built a station five miles to the north, and by an act of the Legislature of North Carolina passed in December, 1789, his house was made a depot for supplies for the use of the Cumberland Guards, when called upon to conduct families through the wilderness to the Cumberland settlements. At the same time Adair was appointed commissary.

The country now began to be reached by wagons. Settlers were pushing on to the West, and in quick succession Well's, Bennett's, Byrd's, Hackett's and Cavett's Stations were formed. Campbell's Station was settled by several emigrants from Virginia, prominent among whom was Col. David Campbell. The settlements, however, were subject to frequent interruptions from hostile Indians, both Cherokees and Creeks, but more especially the latter, and even those who located in the immediate vicinity of Knoxville were not altogether exempt from incursions by these savage tribes. Numerous treaties of peace were made, only to be broken, usually by the Indians, but it must be confessed, on more than one occasion, by irresponsible whites. During all of 1788 the Indians were troublesome along the frontier, and did the settlers as much harm as they could. At last Gen. Joseph Martin was compelled to raise troops for their protection. He had been appointed to the command on the resignation of Col. Evan Shelby, in 1784. He collected soldiers from all the four counties west of the Alleghanies, and some were sent from Virginia. They rendezvoused at the present site of Knoxville, and then crossed the Holston and marched by the way of the Little Tennessee and the Hiwassee to the Chickamauga town, and burned every house there. They then, after inflicting other injuries upon the Indians, returned to their homes. Shortly afterward, on October 15, a body of not less than 200 or 300 Indians, Cherokees and Creeks, captured Gillespie's Station, on Little River, within eight or ten miles of Knoxville, and took several prisoners. Gen. Sevier immediately started in pursuit, overtook them and recaptured the prisoners. He also succeeded in taking several Indians, who were afterward exchanged for white captives that had been carried into the Nation.

During the next two years the Indians directed their attention to the Cumberland settlements, and although occasional depredations were committed, the pioneers along the Holston enjoyed comparative quiet.

On the 2d of July, 1791, a treaty of peace and perpetual friendship was concluded between Gov. Blount and the Cherokee chiefs, who met at the treaty ground on the present site of Knoxville.* But notwithstanding this treaty the hostility of the Indians was very distressing throughout the greater part of 1791 and the four or five years succeeding. On the 10th of May, 1792, as two sons of a Mr. Wells, in Hind's Valley, within twelve miles of Knoxville, were picking strawberries, six Indians came up, tomahawked and scalped them before his eyes, but went off without making further attempts upon the family. At about the same time several warriors came to Col. Campbell's and fired upon him and another man who was plowing at his side, but fortunately neither was injured. During this year the settlers on the more exposed parts of the frontier were compelled to seek safety at the forts, and except in cases of necessity did not venture far from them. On the 12th of September, while a Mr. Gillespie and two sons were at their home after some corn, they were attacked by the Indians. Gillespie and the elder son were killed and the younger son taken prisoner. The latter was held by the Indians until the following month, when he was ransomed by James Carey for 250 pounds of leather and a horse. During the latter part of this year the lower Cherokees formally declared war against the United States, and fearing that their attack might be directed against the Holston settlement, the militia colonel of Knox County issued orders to his captains similar to the following:

KNOXVILLE, September 11, 1792.

Sir: You are hereby commanded to repair with your company to Knoxville, equipped to protect the frontier; there is imminent danger. Bring with you two days' provisions, if possible; but you are not to delay an hour on that head.

I am, sir, yours, JAMES WHITE.

CAPT. THOMAS GILLESPIE.

The militia thus summoned paraded at various points designated, and were distributed to the more exposed stations. It was soon learned, however, that the expedition of the Indians had been directed against the Cumberland settlement, and Gov. Blount disbanded most of the troops. How inadequately the frontiers of Knox County were protected at this time is apparent from the following list of the stations and their strength on December 22, 1792: Gamble's Station—William Reagan, lieutenant, men thirteen (on furlough, five; at station, eight). Black's Station—Joel Wallace, ensign; men, four. Henry's Station—George

---
*See page 93.

Huffacre, corporal; men, six. Well's Station—Richard Dearmond, corporal; men, six. Ish's Station—Matthew Karr, sergeant; men, eight. Campbell's Station—none. Lowe's Station—none. Manifee's Station—Captain Samples; men, fourteen. Raccoon Valley Station—Sergt. Finley and one man. Total at stations, forty-seven.

With this small force it is little to be wondered at that the Indian aggressions continued. On the 12th of November, 1792, a party of fifteen Cherokees attacked the home of Ebenezer Byram in Grassy Valley, about eight miles from Knoxville, in which were only two men with their families. The Indians had surrounded the house, before they were discovered, and forced open a window and pointed their guns into it; but by a well directed fire from the two men two of the savages were wounded and the remainder put to flight. On the 22d of the following January the Indians killed and scalped John Pates on Crooked Creek, about sixteen miles from Knoxville, and on the 29th they stole several horses from Gamble's Station. These continued aggressions created great excitement, and the local militia without orders assembled for the purpose of marching to the nearest Indian towns and retaliating upon them. The Governor, however, assisted by Col. White and others succeeded in restraining them from entering the Indian territory, and quiet was restored. But the Indians continued their depredations. On the 16th of March fourteen horses were stolen from Flat Creek within sixteen miles of Knoxville, and two days later two young men named Clements, living below Knoxville, were killed and scalped. On May 25 Thomas Gillam and his son James were killed and scalped by the Indians in the Raccoon Valley about eighteen miles from Knoxville. Capt. Beard with fifty mounted infantry started immediately in pursuit, and on the 12th of June came upon the *Hanging Maw's family and other Indians ordered to the place by the Government. These were immediately attacked, and several were killed, among whom were two or three chiefs and the Hanging Maw's wife. As these Indians had assembled to confer with Maj. King and other agents of the United States, this attack of Beard's was an atrocious violation of the faith of the Government, and a general war with the Cherokees was thought to be inevitable. Another invasion of the Indian country by Col. Doherty and Col. McFarland occurred later in the season, and served still further to incite the savages to murderous attacks. No general movement of the Cherokees in the direction of the Holston was made, however, until September of this year. On Wednesday, the 25th of that month, the expected incursion was made by a large body of Creeks and Cherokees variously estimated

---

*A Cherokee chief.

at from 900 to 1,500, including 100 horsemen, under the leadership of John Watts and Double Head. They crossed the Tennessee below the mouth of the Holston, and marched all night toward Knoxville, expecting to reach there before daylight on the morning of the 25th, but some detention at the river prevented. A further delay was occasioned by Double Head, who insisted upon taking every cabin as they passed. A dispute also arose over the question of killing all of the inhabitants of Knoxville or only the men, and before the plan of procedure was adjusted daylight was at hand. They were then at the head of Sinking Creek in Grassy Valley, having passed Campbell's Station in which twenty families were stationed, and which, in their haste to reach Knoxville, they had left undisturbed. In sight of them was the station of Alexander Cavett, in which besides himself and family were two men, in all thirteen persons. Disappointed in their hopes of plunder, and not daring to risk an attack upon Knoxville in daylight, they determined to wreak their vengeance upon this defenseless family. They accordingly marched to the house and surrounded it. The three men within resolved to sell their lives as dearly as possible, and opened fire upon the assailants, killing one Creek, one Cherokee, and wounding three more. The Indians then offered to spare their lives if they would surrender, and to immediately exchange them for Indian prisoners amongst the whites. These terms they accepted, but no sooner had they left the house than Double Head and his party fell upon them, and treacherously put them to death. This station was only eight miles from Knoxville, and the firing was heard by the people of that place.

The action taken by them at this time is but an illustration of the heroic character of the early pioneers of Tennessee. The following account is taken from the semi-centennial address of Rev. Dr. Thomas W. Humes: "At that time Knoxville could muster but forty fighting men, but these forty were no cravens to fly at the approach of danger even though it presented itself in the terrible shape in which it then menanced them. Here was their homes, their families, their all, and with an alacrity and zeal worthy of the crisis they prepared to defend their firesides. A knowledge of Indian cunning induced them to conclude that the approach of the savages to the town would not be made by the main western road but in a more northern and circuitous direction, and they determined to meet them on the ridge over which the road now passes to Clinton about one mile and a half from town, and then, by a skillful arrangement of their little company, check their march, and if possible alarm and intimidate them. Leaving the oldest two of their number (John McFarland and Robert Williams) to mold bullets in the blockhouse which stood on the spot now (1842) occupied by the Mansion House, and which contained 300 guns belonging to the United States, the other thirty-eight proceeded, under the command of Col. James White, to station themselves on the south side of the ridge we have mentioned with an interval of twenty feet between the men. Orders were given to reserve their fire until the Indians were brought within range of every gun when at a given signal, they were to pour in upon them a well directed volley, and before the savages could recover from their surprise secure their own retreat to the block-house, and there with their wives, mothers, and children around them sell their lives at a fearful price or scatter from the port-holes a shower of leaden hail among the besiegers that would drive them from their banquet of blood. Happily neither of these contingences awaited them."

After burning Cavett's Station the Indians returned southward, and within a few days Gen. Sevier with 600 or 700 men started in pursuit.* They marched into the Indian country, burned several towns, and administered a decisive blow to the savage inhabitants.

While this campaign had the effect to render the Indians more cautious it did not put a stop to their marrauding expeditions. On the 23d of the following December, while two men, Roger Oats and Nicholas Ball, were bringing in a load of corn to Well's Station for the support of its inmates, they were attacked and killed by the Indians and their horses taken away.

On the evening of the 24th of April, 1794, Dr James Cozby, who, as has been stated, lived south of the French Broad about eight miles from Knoxville, observed, in the gathering darkness, a party of twenty Indians stealthily approaching his house. He was an old Indian fighter, and at once prepared to defend himself and family, consisting of his wife, and several children only one of whom could shoot, from the port holes in the house. A constant watch was kept, and as there was a cleared space about the house, any near approach of a savage could be seen. Cozby, in a loud voice, gave several commands as if addressing a body of soldiers. The Indians thus deceived hesitated to make the attack, and after lingering in the vicinity until near daybreak withdrew. In the morning it was found that they had gone to the house of William Casteel, two miles away, and murdered the entire family, except one daughter whom they had left for dead, but who afterward recovered.

After this atrocious murder it was with the greatest difficulty that Gov. Blount restrained the inhabitants south of the French Broad from an immediate invasion of the Indian territory. In this he was assisted

---

* See page 95.

by the civil officers of Knox County, who met in committee on the 20th of June at the house of James Beard, and prepared an address to the people advising them to acquiesce in the design of the Government to obtain peace by negotiation rather than by arms.

One of the last murders committed by the Indians in Knox County was that of George Mann, living twelve miles above Knoxville, which occurred on the night of the 25th of May, 1795. Hearing some noise about his stable he left the house to discover its cause, and upon his return was intercepted by the Indians who fired upon him, dangerously wounding him. He fled to a cave a short distance away, but was pursued, dragged from his hiding place and slain. His wife, hearing the Indians in pursuit of her husband, locked the door and sat in silent expectation of their return. She did not have long to wait, however. Hearing their approaching footsteps she seized a rifle, which she had learned to use, and leveled it at the door. The savages approached in single file, and the foremost pushed the door partly open. Instantly she pulled the trigger, and two Indians, wounded by the single shot, fell to the ground. The others, gathering them up, fled, and she and her children were safe. On only one occasion after this were the inhabitants aroused by an Indian alarm. On July 27, 1795, it was learned that a party of Creeks to the number of about a thousand were marching through the Cherokee country toward the Holston settlements. Gen. White was ordered out with one-half of the Knox County militia to oppose them, while the Cherokee women and children were removed to the north side of the Tennessee. The Creeks, however, advanced only to Will's Town, from which point they were turned back, and from that time the Holston settlements were undisturbed by Indian hostilities.

About two years later two white men, Micajah and Wiley Harp came to Knox County, and during their short residence there proved themselves as barbarous as their red-skinned brethren. They settled on Beaver Creek where they made a crop in 1797, and during that season furnished the butcher in Knoxville, John Miller, with hogs, sheep and cattle which they stole from their neighbors. Finally they took several fine horses from Edward Tiel, who lived about one mile northeast of Knoxville. With some of his neighbors he started in pursuit, and captured them in the Cumberland Mountains, but while bringing them home they were allowed to escape, and afterward they committed several murders. The first was that of a youth named Coffin, whom they killed on Copper Ridge while on his way to mill. They murdered one Ballard, mistaking him for Hugh Dunlap, who had at one time attempted to arrest them. They also killed a man by the name of Bradbury. After about a year they removed west of the Cumberland Mountains, where they became a terror to the inhabitants.

Meanwhile the immigration to East Tennessee had continued. In July, 1795, a census of the territory was taken at which time Knox County, which then included an area several times as great as at present, had a population of 11,573, of whom 2,365 were slaves. During the same month occurred two events of importance in the county: the opening of a wagon road from Knoxville to Nashville, and the arrival in Knoxville of two wagons from South Carolina by the way of Warm Springs.

Up to this time no regular postoffices had been established. In the Knoxville *Gazette* of October, 1792, John Chisolm advertised that he would establish a post route from Knoxville to Greene Court House, thence to Jonesboro, and to Abingdon, Va., returning by the way of Sullivan Court House and Hawkins Court House, to Knoxville, once in every twenty-one days, provided that $250 were subscribed for that purpose. During the year 1795 a bi-monthly mail to Knoxville was established under provision of the postoffice department, and George Roulstone was appointed postmaster. To this office was sent all the mail for much of the country to the east and all of the country west of Knoxville. In a list of letters published as remaining on hand at this office January 1, 1797, are letters directed to Nolachucky, to Buncombe, to Jonesboro, to Blount County, to Jefferson County, to Powell's Valley, to Nashville, to Sumner County, to Palmyra, to Bledsoe's Lick and other points equally remote.

In 1797 the rivers began to be used as channels of commerce, mainly for the shipment of produce. On February 27 of that year two boats carrying five tons each, from the South Fork of the Holston in Virginia, reached Knoxville. They were loaded with flour and whisky, and had traveled a distance of about 300 miles.

In 1826 the first steamboat arrived. It was known as the "Atlas," and was under the command of Capt. Conner, to whom was extended an enthusiastic reception by the citizens of the town. It afterward proceeded as far as the fork of the French Broad and Holston, where another ovation was tendered by Dr. J. G. M. Ramsey, and his neighbors. A company was immediately formed for the purchase of a steamboat to ply upon the river, and W. B. A. Ramsey was dispatched to Cincinnati to contract for the building of a small boat, which arrived a few months later and was christened the "Knoxville." This boat remained upon the Tennessee until 1838, when, under the name of the "Indian Chief," it was used in the transfer of the Cherokees west of the Mississippi.

Upon the reception of the "Atlas" at Mecklenburg, Dr. Ramsey delivered an address, in which he pointed out the fact that New Orleans was too far away to become a profitable market for East Tennessee, and advocated the construction of a great macadamized road to Charleston, S. C. In 1828 he went to Charleston to spend the winter, and while there succeeded in interesting several prominent men in the project. At about this time the opening, and successful operation of the Baltimore & Ohio Railroad attracted the attention of the public to that method of transportation, and the question of building a railroad through East Tennessee connecting Charleston with the northwest, began to be discussed. It finally resulted in the holding of a great commercial convention, or rather railroad convention in Knoxville, July 4, 1836, at which time plans were perfected for the building of a road from Cincinnati to Charleston by the way of Cumberland Gap. Before anything of importance had been accomplished, however, the financial panic of 1837 put an end to the work, and it was never resumed. A portion of the delegates to the convention, not satisfied with its action, withdrew and formed an organization for the building of a road to Charleston by another route.* This finally resulted in the completion of the East Tennessee & Georgia Road in 1856. In 1852 the East Tennessee & Virginia Road was chartered, and completed six years later. At about the same time the Knoxville & Kentucky, and the Knoxville & Charleston Railroads were chartered, and in January 1853 the county court ordered an election to vote upon the proposition to subscribe $100,000 to each of these roads. The measure carried, and six per cent bonds were ordered to be issued. The work of construction progressed very slowly, and at the beginning of the war only a few miles of road had been completed.

On June 11, 1792, Gov. Blount issued an ordinance defining the limits of the counties of Greene and Hawkins and laying off two new counties, Knox and Jefferson. At the same time he appointed Charles McClung, James Mabry, Alexander Outlaw and Joseph Hamilton to survey and mark the dividing line between these counties. Courts of pleas and quarter sessions were ordered to be held in Knox County at Knoxville, and in Jefferson County at the house of Jeremiah Matthews. Five days later, the Governor commissioned the following justices of the peace for Knox County: James White, John Sawyers, Hugh Beard, John Adair, George McNutt, Jeremiah Jack, John Kearns, James Cozby, John Evans, Samuel Newell, William Wallace, Thomas McCulloch, William Hamilton, David Craig and William Lowry, all of whom appeared before Judge David Campbell and took an oath to support the Constitution of the United States, and also an oath of office. In a like manner, on the 25th

---

*See page 342.

of June, Robert Houston was commissioned by the Governor and qualified as sheriff, and was ordered to make proclamation for the opening of a county court at the house of John Stone in the town of Knoxville. Charles McClung had already received his commission as clerk of the court, and on Monday, the 16th of July, 1792, the first court was held by James White, Samuel Newell, David Craig and Jeremiah Jack, James White being elected chairman. But little business was transacted at this term. Robert Houston gave bond for the performance of his official duties in the sum of $12,500, with John Chisolm, James White, Jeremiah Jack, James Cozby and Robert Armstrong as his sureties. William Meeks, James Anderson, Benjamin Pride, James Neely, John Liddy, Joseph Hart, George Caldwell, William Gray and James Blair produced commissions as constables, and Luke Bowyers, Alexander Outlaw, Joseph Hamilton, Archibald Roane, Hopkins Lacy, John Rhea and James Reese qualified, and were admitted to practice law. William Henry was given permission to build a mill on Rosebury's Creek, and Alexander Cunningham obtained leave to keep a public ferry at his landing opposite Knoxville. Roads were ordered to be laid out from Knoxville to Col. Alexander Kelley's mill to David Craig's on Nine Mile Creek, to the ford on the Clinch River, and to Campbell's Station. Stone's house at which this court was held stood on the southwest corner of Gay and Cumberland Streets. At about this time, temporary buildings for a courthouse and a jail were erected. The former stood on the south side of Main Street, a little east of Gay. Soon after its erection it was set fire to by a lawyer, it is said, and was entirely destroyed. The jail proved less satisfactory than the courthouse, for at the second term of the court, the sheriff appeared and protested against it, and on January 26, 1793 commissioners were appointed to contract for the building of a new jail, which was to be sixteen feet square; the logs to be one foot square; the lower floor to be laid of logs of that size laid double and crosswise; the loft to be laid also of logs covered crosswise with oak plank one and a half inches thick, and well spiked down. This building was erected at the corner of Gay and Main Streets, on the lot afterward occupied by the Bank of East Tennessee. It is said that it proved to its builder as did the gallows prepared for Mordecai, to Haman, he being its first occupant. After the burning of the courthouse, a new one was not erected for several years, but instead a building was rented from Col. James White for that purpose, for which he received $30 yearly.

At the January term, 1793, the county court fixed the rates of taxation for that year at 10 cents on each 100 acres of land, and $16\frac{2}{3}$ cents on each poll, and a justice was appointed for each captain's company, to take a list of the taxables and taxable property. At the same time the following ordinary rates were fixed: Diet, 16 cents; corn per gallon, 10 cents; oats, same; fodder per bundle, 3 cents; whisky per one half-pint 8 cents; brandy per one-half pint, 12 cents; rum, 16 cents; wine, 16 cents; beer per quart, 8 cents; cider, the same; lodging per night, 6 cents, and pasturage per day, 8 cents.

On April 25, 1796, was begun the first county court, held under the State constitution, at which time the following justices of the peace, commissioned by Gov. Sevier, were present: James White, Joseph Greer, John McClellan, John Adair, George McNutt, John Hackett, David Campbell, John Manifee, Nicholas Gibbs, John Sawyers, Samuel Doak, James Cozby, Samuel Flanniken, Jeremiah, Jack and William Doak. All the county officers tendered their resignations, which were accepted, but they were immediately re-appointed by the court, and qualified under the new constitution.

On the 4th of February, 1797, Charles McClung, Francis A. Ramsey, John McClellan, John Adair and James Cozby, were appointed commissioners for the purpose of fixing on a site and contracting for the building of a courthouse. A lot fronting on Main Street, and extending from Gay to Prince, was donated as a site by Col. James White, and a building 30x40 feet, and two stories high, was erected. It was built of rough fragments of rock cemented with mortar, and did not present a very handsome exterior. Its aggregate cost was $5,803.19 and to meet this expenditure one-half of the county revenue from 1797 to 1807 was appropriated to that purpose. In 1812, by an act of the Legislature, the county court was given permission to sell a portion of the courthouse lot to the Bank of Tennessee, and accordingly a lot fronting on Main Street, and extending seventy feet from the corner of Gay was sold for $5. In November, 1801, the General Assembly passed an act authorizing Knox County to levy a special tax, not exceeding $12\frac{1}{2}$ cents on each 100 acres of land, for the purpose of building a prison and stocks, and Charles McClung, Robert Houston and Joseph Greer were appointed commissioners to let the contract. This jail was completed about 1807, at a cost of $4,569.56, and stood near the site of the one it superseded, at the corner of Gay and Main Streets. In July, 1818, Robert Craighead was appointed to sell this jail and lot, and to ascertain for what sum a suitable lot could be obtained. No further action was taken, however, until two years later, when a new brick jail was erected near the southeast corner of the square bounded by Main, Walnut, Hill and Locust Streets. This building was used for many years.

In 1836 the new State constitution went into effect, and several changes in the management of county affairs took place. Heretofore the county officers had been elected by the county court, now all but two or three were to be chosen by the people. The first officers thus elected were Moses M. Swan, clerk of the county court; George M. White, clerk of the circuit court; Samuel Love, trustee; William Dunlap, sheriff, and William R. Bowen, register. Prior to this time too, the county had been divided for local government and civil affairs, according to the militia companies, designated by the names of the captains. It was now divided into seventeen civil districts, and so continued until 1851, when the Eighteenth District was formed from portions of Districts Nos. 3 and 4, and the Nineteenth, from fractions of Districts Nos. 8 and 9. In 1857 a new district, No. 5, was formed from fractions of the 4th, 6th, and 7th, the greater part of original Fifth District having been cut off at the formation of Union County. These were the divisions of the county prior to the civil war.

In January, 1839, six commissioners, George M. White, William Baker, David Campbell, D. P. Armstrong, James Park and William S. Kennedy, were appointed to decide whether the old courthouse should be repaired, or a new one should be built. At the following April term they reported unanimously in favor of the last proposition, and the last three named commissioners were authorized to contract for and to superintend the construction of the new building. At the same time an appropriation of $10,000, in payments of not less than $2,000, was made to defray the expenses. The contract was let for $9,570, and by December, 1842, the building was tendered to the commissioners who refused to receive it on the grounds that it was not completed according to agreement. The matter was then referred to a board of arbitrators composed of James H. Cowan, Thomas Rodgers and G. M. Hazen, who sustained the commissioners, and a small reduction was made in the contract price.

In 1839 provision was also made for the purchase of a poor farm, and John Mynatt, Thomas D. Hall, and Lewis Lutterell were appointed to locate it. Accordingly a tract of 188 acres was purchased from Robert and James McCampbell for $950, and buildings were erected for the reception of paupers. Previous to that time these unfortunate persons had been farmed out to the lowest bidder, and, as was to have been expected, they often suffered cruel treatment at the hands of those to whom they were assigned. The management of the farm has remained substantially the same since its establishment. It is under the immediate direction of a superintendent, who is controlled by a committee from the county court. The average number of inmates is seventy, and the total cost to the county is about $3,000 annually. In 1875 a workhouse was established to which are sentenced persons convicted of misdemeanor, and those who are unable to pay their fines. These convicts are employed in building pikes, and since the work began about twenty-five miles have been completed. The annual cost to the county is about $10,000.

In October 1856 it was determined to build a new jail, and $10,000 was appropriated for that purpose to be expended under the direction of Ebenezer Alexander, C. W. Jones and William Craig. This building was completed the following year upon the site of the old jail. It became so badly damaged during the war, that a new one again became necessary, and in July 1866 David F. Dearmond, M. D. Bearden, and Charles Morrow were appointed to contract for it. Accordingly a new lot was purchased from William K. Eckles at a cost of $4,000, and the contract let for the new building for $18,000. This is the sixth and last jail erected by the county.

Previous to 1872, except a short time during and after the war, when a temporary bridge was used, the Tennessee River, then the Holston, was crossed at Knoxville by means of a ferry. In that year W. A. A. Conner John L. Moses, Alfred Caldwell, John Tunnell, Julius Ochs and M. Nelson were appointed to contract for the building of a bridge, and $75,000 was appropriated for that purpose. This was afterward increased until the aggregate appropriations amounted to $160,000 for which eight per cent bonds were issued. The bridge was completed in 1874, the entire cost being $163,653.65. This structure, however, was doomed to sudden destruction. On May 1, 1875 during a violent wind storm, it was blown down and entirely destroyed. In 1879 a contract was entered into between George W. Saulpaw, by the terms of which he was given the use of the old piers so long as he should keep open a bridge upon them. He at once began the erection of a bridge, which was opened March 2, 1880. Soon after S. B. Luttrell purchased a one-half interest in it, and the following year became the sole proprietor.

As soon as the county had somewhat recovered from the effects of the war the subject of building a new courthouse began to be agitated, but prior to 1883 all propositions to appoint commissioners for that purpose were voted down by the county court. In that year, however, W. S. Smith, Robert Hardin, J. W. Fowler, B. J. Hartley, M. D. Sullivan and J. T. Doyle were appointed to ascertain at what cost the Franklin House Square (the square bounded by Main, Prince, Hill and Gay streets) could be obtained as a site for the proposed new courthouse. They reported the cost at $26,000, and it was accordingly purchased for that sum. In 1885 the erection of the new building was begun under the supervision of S. R. Rodgers, R. A. Sterling H. Clapp, A. G. French, and G. W. Mabry with Stephenson and Getaz as the architects. The corner-stone was laid in July of that year, and the building was occupied for the first time on the 28th of September, 1886. It is built of brick, marble and iron, with terra cotta decoration, and, with possibly one exception, is the finest structure of the kind in the State. It is two stories high with a basement. On the first floor are the criminal courtroom, the county courtroom, grand jury room, witnesses-room, and offices for the chairman and clerk of the county court, trustees, register and district attorney. On the second floor are rooms for the chancery, circuit, and supreme court, and offices for the clerk and master, chancellor, clerk of the circuit court, and clerk of the supreme court.

The total cost of the building, including fence and pavement, was $136,000.

The present financial condition of the county, is as follows:

Bonded indebtedness, funded bonds issued since October 1, 1881, and outstanding, October 1, 1886	$261,200 00
Old bonds outstanding, not funded	18,500 00
Total	$279,700 00
Bonds redeemed since October 1, 1886	$12,250 00
Loans still outstanding, January 1, 1887	267,500 00
Unpaid county warrants	33,036 22
Balance due on courthouse	90,262 30
Total indebtedness of the county	$390,798 52

The assets are as follows:

1,000 shares in the Knoxville & Ohio Railroad	$100,000 00
Old courthouse	15,000 00
Eleven shares in Kingston Pike	375 00
Farm in the Fifth Civil District	5,000 00
Farm in the Fourth Civil District	700 00
Poor farm	3,000 00
Workhouse bail bonds	2,300 00
Notes good	700 00
Total	$127,075 00

The total collections for county purposes during 1886 amounted to $44,785.30, and the expenditures to $43,731.02. The aggregate collections and disbursements for all purposes were $137,209.91 and $134,360.49 respectively.

During the past eighteen years five new civil districts have been created. In July, 1869, the Twentieth was formed from portions of the Fifth and Sixth, and one year later a part of the Fifteenth was added to the Fourteenth, which was then divided forming the Twenty-first. In January, 1878, a part of the Sixteenth was united into the Twenty-second, and in October, 1879, the Twenty-third was formed from a part of the Seventeenth. In January, 1886, a suburb of Knoxville known as the West End was constituted the Twenty-fourth Civil District.

The following is a list of the officers of Knox County from its organization.

Sheriffs— Robert Houston, 1792–1802; John Love, 1802–03; Joseph Love, 1803–14; John Calloway, 1814–26; George M. White, 1826–34; William Dunlap, 1834–38; Samuel McCammon, 1838–50; William Craig, 1850–56; William P. Crippin, 1856–62; William H. Swan, 1862–64; Marcus D. Bearden, 1864–70; V. F. Gossett, 1870–74; M. D. Swan, 1874–76; Alexander Reeder, 1876–80; C. B. Gossett, 1880–82; Homer Gilmore, 1882–86; J. K. Lones, 1886.

Clerks of the county court—Charles McClung, 1792–1834; George M. White, 1834–36; Moses M. Swan, 1836–44; George W. C. Cox, 1844–56; William Craig, 1856–66; William Rule, 1866–71; J. S. A. Blang, 1871–74; J. F. J. Lewis, 1874–86; John W. Conner, 1886.

Trustees—Samuel Newell, 1793–94; Charles McClung, 1794–1806; John Hillsman, 1806–12; Robert Houston, 1812–30; Samuel Love, 1830–38; George W. C. Cox, 1838–44; William McCammon, 1844–52; Samuel McCammon, 1852–54; Hiram Barry, 1854–68; H. L. W. Mynatt, 1868–70; James S. Boyd, 1870–72; B. F. Bearden, 1872–76; W. A. Anderson, 1876–78; W. H. Swan, 1878–82; B. F. Bearden, 1882–84; J. A. Swan, 1884.

Registers—Thomas Chapman, 1792–1803; Samuel G. Ramsey, 1803–17; J. G. M. Ramsey, 1817—; J. G. M. Ramsey, 1829–36; W. R. Bowen, 1836–40; Henry B. Newman, 1840–48; J. C. Luttrell, 1848–56; A. S. Hudiburg, from January to March, 1856; R. H. Campbell, 1856–60; T. J. Burkhart, 1860–64; A. T. Cottrell, 1864–68; R. L. Hall, 1868–69; L. H. Bowlus, 1869–70; Charles Morrow; 1870–82; W. R. Carter, 1882.

Clerks of the circuit court—F. A. Ramsey, 1810–20; William Swan, 1820–36; George M. White, 1836–52; M. L. Hall, 1852–64; Stephen H. Smith, 1864–66; W. R. McBath, 1866–70; E. W. Adkins, 1870–82; W. B. Ford, 1882.

Clerks of the criminal court—H. C. Tarwater, 1870–73; W. H. Swan, 1873–74; George L. Maloney, 1874–82; W. F. Gibbs, 1882.

Clerks and masters of the chancery court— W. B. A. Ramsey, 1832–48; Hugh L. McClung, 1848–57; Samuel A. White, 1857–59; David A. Deaderick, 1859–70; M. L. Patterson, 1870–82; S. P. Evans, 1882.

As has been stated the court of pleas and quarter sessions of Knox County was organized July 16, 1792. At this time as well as for many years after, this court besides transacting public business, had original jurisdiction in minor civil and criminal cases, and appellate jurisdiction in all cases from justices' courts. The first case tried was that of William Burden *vs.* William Cavanaugh on appeal. The jury were John Coulter, William Rhea, Joseph Black, William Trimble, Samuel Doak, Moses Justice, Andrew Boyle, Samuel Boyle, Robert Gamble, Joseph Weldon, John McIntire and Pearson Brock, who returned a verdict for the Defendent. It was therefore considered by the court "that the Plaintiff take nothing by his plaint aforesaid, but for his falce clamour be in mercy, and the said Defendent go hence without day, and recover against the said Plaintiff his costs by him about his defence in this behalf expended."

This court continued to try causes of minor importance until the adoption of the constitution of 1834 when this part of its duties was transferred to the circuit court.

On March 13, 1793, Gov. Blount issued an ordinance creating Knox and Jefferson Counties a judicial district by the name of Hamilton, and during the following October the superior court was organized by David Campbell, who appointed Francis A. Ramsey clerk of the law court, and Samuel Mitchell clerk and master in equity. The former continued in his position until the discontinuance of the court in 1810. The latter was succeeded in 1797 by Joseph Greer, who, the year before, had been chosen one of the presidential electors. He continued as clerk and master until 1810.

During the first two or three terms of this court the transactions were unimportant. The first trial for a capital offense was begun and held in accordance with the following proclamation:

WILLIAM BLOUNT, GOVERNOR IN AND OVER THE TERRITORY OF THE UNITED STATES OF AMERICA SOUTH OF THE RIVER OHIO,

To David Campbell, John McNairy and Joseph Anderson, judges in and for said territory Greeting:

I do authorize you, any two or either of you, to hold a court of oyer and terminer and general jail delivery at Knoxville, to commence on the first day of August next, and to continue the same by adjournment from day to day, not **exceeding** three days, for the trial of a Creek Indian, apprehended on suspicion of being guilty of the murder of John Ish, a citizen of the United States, resident in this Territory, to hear, try and determine to give judgment and award execution thereon.

Given under my hand and seal at Knoxville this 29th day of July, 1794.
By the Governor,
WILLIAM BLOUNT.

HUGH L. WHITE.

Judge Anderson issued an order to Robert Houston, sheriff of Knox County, who returned a *venire facias* of forty men, from whom the following grand jury was chosen: John Patterson, foreman; Andrew Hannah,

Oliver Wallace, William Richie, Samuel Hindman, Moses Brooks, George Walker, David Walker, George Stout, Willam Trimble, Jeremiah Jeffrey, John Steel, William Lea, Robert Kirkpatrick, Thomas Milliken, Thomas Richie, George Hayes and James Cunningham. The jury immediately returned an indictment for murder against Abongphohigo, an Indian of the Creek Nation, late of the town of Zookcaucaugee or Punk Knob on Oakfuskey River. John Rhea was appointed to defend him, and John Carey was sworn as interpreter. The jury was composed of Andrew W. Campbell, William Sharpe, Nicholas Neal, Thomas Robison, Joseph Brooks, Alexander Cole, M. Pruett, James Milliken, Thomas Inglis, James Walker, John Kerr and Thomas Bounds. The trial lasted only one day, and a verdict of guilty was promptly returned. Four days later the prisoner was executed by the sheriff of Knox County.

Some of the penalties imposed by the laws at that time would now be considered barbarous. At the October term, 1795, of the superior court, Michael Johnson, of Jefferson County, was found guilty of stealing a horse of the value of $50, and for this offense received the following sentence. "It is ordered that the said Michael Johnson shall stand in the pillory one hour, and shall be branded, whipped on his bare back with thirty-nine lashes well laid on, and at the same time shall have both his ears nailed to the pillory and cut off, and shall be branded on the right cheek with the letter H of the length of three-fourths of an inch, and of the breadth of one-half inch, and on the left cheek with the letter T of the same dimensions as the letter H in a plain and visible manner, and that the sheriff of Knox County see this sentence put into execution on Tuesday, the 20th inst., between the hours of 12 and 2 o'clock in the afternoon." This penalty was deemed too light, and two or three years later the crimes of horse stealing, burglary, arson, etc., were made punishable by death. In 1797, at the April term of the superior court, Robert Parker, of Grainger County, was convicted of stealing 500 Spanish milled dollars from Thomas Humes, and was executed on the 28th of the same month. As there was no appeal from the decisions of this court, punishment for crime was promptly administered.

The custom of granting benefit of clergy under the old English common law, a rare occurrence in America, still obtained in this court, and through it many criminals escaped the severe penalties of the law. As the statutes provided that for a second offense benefit of clergy should not be granted, to prevent a repetition of the plea, it was customary to brand upon the thumb, the criminal pleading its protection. The following examples serve to illustrate this custom. April 22, 1797, Caleb Carter was convicted of carrying away by force of arms from one Jonathan

Boggle—"one straight coat pattern of the value of $8, one silk handkerchief of the value of $2, and $1.50 in cash. Being asked if he had aught to say why sentence of death should not be pronounced upon him, prayed the benefit of clergy, which was granted him. Therefore the sentence of the law pronounced by the court is that he be branded upon the brawn of the thumb with the letter T." At the same term of the court Benjamin Stephens was tried on an indictment for "stealing from Patrick Ninny, of Jefferson County, one piece of gingham containing six yards, at the price of five shillings per yard, the whole piece being equal in value to four Spanish milled dollars." He was found guilty, and had he not plead the benefit of clergy would have been sentenced to death. He took the advantage of that plea, however, and was simply branded upon the thumb. At the next term of the court Hugh Washburn also escaped the death penalty by pleading the benefit of clergy. To what persons the benefit of clergy might be granted in this court is not now known, but it is certain that it was restricted to a certain class. Considering the severity of the punishment, however, and the comparative insignificance of many of the offenses, it is not to be wondered at that the courts were willing to grant that plea without a too rigid examination as to the petitioner's right to its protection.

On January 1, 1831, with the opening of the penitentiary, a new penal code went into effect, and the whipping post, pillory, and branding iron as instruments of punishment, were abandoned. The first representatives to the penitentiary from Knox County were Abraham and Silas Conley convicted of stealing property to the value of $2 and $3 respectively, for which they were sentenced to one year's imprisonment.

In 1810 circuit courts were established, and the superior court of law and equity was superseded by the supreme court of errors and appeal. The latter court was organized at Knoxville on May 28, 1810, by Hugh L. White and George W. Campbell, judges of the supreme court, and William Cocke, judge of the first circuit. Thomas Emmerson was chosen clerk and so continued until 1816, when he was succeeded by Hugh Brown, who filled the office for many years. The circuit court was organized about the same time as the supreme court by James Trimble, judge of the second circuit, who appointed F. A. Ramsey as clerk. In 1816 Judge Trimble was succeeded by Edward Scott, who continued upon the bench continuously until 1844. The chancery court was not organized until April, 1832. The first chancellor was William B. Reese, who continued until the reorganization of the courts under the new constitution in 1836, when he was elected to the supreme bench, and was succeeded by Thomas L. Williams.

Of the attorneys admitted to practice at the first session of the court of pleas and quarter sessions, Alexander Outlaw was at that time the most prominent. He had taken a conspicuous part in the organization of the county of Franklin, and had represented the county of Caswell in the Assembly in 1786. He afterward took an equally important part in the formation of the State constitution, and among the early legislators, as a representative from Jefferson County. In 1799 he was chosen speaker of the Senate.

John Rhea was several years younger than Outlaw, and not so well known. He afterward attained considerable distinction, and was a member of Congress for a period of eighteen years. Hopkins Lacy became clerk of the Territorial Assembly, and upon the organization of the courts under the constitution of 1796, was chosen attorney-general of Washington District. Archibald Roane had been engaged in the practice of his profession for some time, and in 1796 he was under one of the judges of the superior court, a position which he held until elected governor in 1801.

In March, 1793, several lawyers practicing in the courts of East Tennessee inserted a notice in the *Knoxville Gazette* stating that thereafter they would not appear in court in any case unless the fees had been paid in advance, whereupon William Tatham published the following, which is so unique as to deserve representation here:

FIAT JUSTITIA.

Having adopted the above motto as early as I had the honor of admission to the bar I have covenanted with myself that I will never knowingly depart from it, and on this foundation I have built a few maxims which offered my reflection in satisfaction.

1. I will practice law because it offers me opportunity of being a more useful member of society.
2. I will turn a deaf ear to no man because his purse is empty.
3. I will advise no man beyond the comprehension of his case.
4. I will bring none into law whom my conscience tells me should be kept out.
5. I will never be unmindful of the cause of humanity and this comprehends, the widows and fatherless and those in bondage.
6. I will be faithful to my client but never so unfaithful to myself as to become a party to his crime.
7. In criminal cases I will not underrate my own abilities for if my client proves a rascal his money is better in my hands, and if not I hold the option.
8. I will never acknowledge the omnipotence of the Legislature to consider their acts to be law beyond the spirit of the constitution.
9. No man's greatness shall elevate him above the justice due to my client.
10. I will not consent to compromise when I conceive a verdict essential to my client's future reputation or protection, for of this he cannot be a complete judge.
11. I will advise the turbulent with candor, and if they will go to law against my advice, they must pardon me for volunteering against them.
12. I will acknowledge every man's right to manage his own case if he pleases.

The above are my rules of practice, and although I will not at any critical juncture promise to finish my business in person if the public interest should require my removal from hence I will do everything in my power for those who like them, and endeavor to leave it in proper hands if I should be absent.

Knoxville, Tenn. WILLIAM TATHAM.

The fate of this candid and upright, and it may be added eccentric attorney is not known, but it is probable that his hopes of political preferment were unrecognized.

In 1794 Willie Blount, John Cocke, William Cocke and W. C. C. Claiborne were admitted to practice in the courts of Knox County. All were men of distinguished ability, and prominent in the affairs of the State. Only the first named was a resident of Knoxville. He served as a judge of the supreme court for a few months in 1796, but never attained much prominence as a jurist.

Other attorneys were admitted to practice as follows: Ephraim Dunlap, 1792; David Greer, John Sevier, Jr., John Lowry and Samuel Mitchell, 1793; John McKee, 1795; John Gray, D. W. Breazeale, Hugh L. White,* John Wilkinson and Benjamin Seawell, 1796; George W. Campbell,* Jenkin Whiteside* and John F. Jack, 1798; James Porter, John Kennedy and Edward Scott,* 1799; Pleasant M. Miller,* 1800; John Williams, James Trimble* Samuel Love, Andrew White, and Thomas Dardis, 1803; Thomas Emmerson, J. D. Barnard, William Thompson, N. W. Williams, Luke Lea, William McNutt and Enoch Parsons, 1805; William Brown, Joel Casey and George W. Gibbs, 1806. Only a part of the above named persons were residents of Knoxville, and several who attained distinction in the profession have received sufficient mention elsewhere. D. W. Breazeale, who has been almost entirely forgotten, resided at Knoxville and for a number of years had an extensive practice. Enoch Parsons has also dropped out of remembrance, although for one time he figured quite conspicuously in political affairs. In 1819 he was a candidate for governor against McMinn, receiving about 8,000 votes. He afterward removed to Alabama, where he again became candidate for governor. He and his brother Peter, also a lawyer, married daughters of John Kain, who lived about seven or eight miles above Knoxville near where McMillian's Station now is.

With the exception of Judge White, the most prominent personage in Knoxville during the earlier part of the century, was undoubtedly Col. John Williams.† He was born in Surrey County, N. C., in 1778. He removed to Knoxville and became an attorney in the courts of the State in 1803. He was possessed of a fine person, and graceful, courtly

---

*See Chapter XII.

†The sketches of Col. John Williams and Judge Thomas L. Williams were furnished by Col. John H. Crozier.

and dignified manners, but his complaisant and benevolent countenance made him accessible to his humblest acquaintances. These qualities made him very popular with all classes. Soon after his arrival in Tennessee he married a daughter of Gen. James White, one of the most prominent, popular and wealthy citizens of the State. He industriously and devotedly practiced his profession until the beginning of the war in 1812, when he raised a regiment of volunteers and marched to Florida. Returning home he was appointed colonel of the Thirty-ninth Regiment United States Volunteers. Having recruited his regiment to 600 men, on the application of Gen. Jackson, then commanding the army against the Creek Indians, Col. Williams marched to his relief, and with his regiment took an active part in the battle of the Horseshoe. At the termination of the war, in 1815, he was elected to the United States Senate. He was re-elected in 1817 and served until 1823, when he was defeated by Gen. Jackson, who was a candidate for the presidency. Col. Williams was supposed to be indifferent or hostile to Gen. Jackson's election as President, but such was his popularity he could have defeated any candidate except Gen. Jackson. Soon after he became a candidate for the State Senate, from Knox County, but was not successful. He was then appointed minister to Guatemala, by President Adams. At the end of one year he returned and made a successful canvass for the State Senate. This was the last time he offered his service to the public, but no citizen in the State in a private station, exercised a greater influence on its politics and civil affairs. He was an ardent friend and promoter of every enterprise for the public welfare, and at the time of his death was a director in the Cincinnati & Charleston Railroad. From his retirement from the State Senate in 1829, up to his death, which occurred in 1837, he devoted himself assiduously to the practice of his profession.

About 1810 William C. Mynatt was admitted to the bar, and was soon after elected attorney-general. He continued in that office until 1818, when he was succeeded by William E. Anderson. He remained in the practice of his profession for a number of years, but was somewhat too fond of ardent spirits to achieve success. Later he became the proprietor of the Mansion House. He had a keen sense of the humorous, and is said to have been "a fellow of infinite jest." He was a contemporary of Thomas D. Arnold, a man of great eccentricity, of whom many amusing incidents are told. Arnold was born in Knox County in 1791. He studied law with John Cocke, and served under him as private in the war of 1812. He was a stanch Whig, and in 1830, after a third canvass defeated Pryor Lea for Congress. At the expiration of his term he moved to Greene County, and there, in 1840, was again elected to Congress. He died about 1869.

Pryor Lea was also a native of Knox County, born in 1794. He received his education in Greenville College, studied law and was admitted to practice in 1817. He served with Gen. Jackson in the Creek war in 1813, and was clerk of the Lower House of the General Assembly in 1816. In 1824, he was appointed United States District Attorney, and in 1826 was elected to Congress, where he remained two terms. In 1837 he removed to Jackson, Miss., and ten years later to Goliad, Tex., where he recently died.

Richard G. Dunlap became a member of the Knoxville bar about 1822. He was the eldest of seven sons of Hugh Dunlap, one of the first merchants of Knoxville, and is said to have been the first white child born in the town. He was a man of fine appearance and polished manners but of a somewhat pompous bearing. He soon removed to Texas, and in 1840 was sent as a minister from that republic to the United States. He afterward resided at New Orleans, where he died. Several of his brothers also rose to prominence: Hugh G. and William C. both became circuit court judges in West Tennessee, and the latter served two terms in Congress; James T. became comptroller of the treasury, a position he held for four years.

The Andersons, Isaac, William E., Robert M. and James, were another remarkable family of this period. They were all remarkable for their size and commanding presence and their great strength both physical and intellectual. Isaac became a prominent Presbyterian divine; William E. served as attorney-general of this judicial circuit from 1818 to 1825, when he removed to Nashville; Robert M. was admitted to the bar about 1820, and continued to practice at Knoxville until 1837. In that year the Twelfth Judicial Circuit was formed and he was elected to preside. As the new circuit did not include Knox County, he removed to New Market. He continued upon the bench until his death. The fourth brother, James, was a very respectable magistrate of Knox County.

Judge Thomas L. Williams, who was elected chancellor in 1836, was also a member of a remarkable family. He was a brother of Col. John Williams, mention of whom has been made, and a twin brother of Hon. Lewis Williams, who was a representative in Congress from North Carolina for twenty-seven consecutive years. Judge Williams, when a young man, came to Knoxville and began the practice of his profession. He was an impressive and eloquent speaker, and soon became a leading member of the bar. He never offered his services to the public for preferment but once, when he was elected to the Legislature. This was in the earlier part of his life. He was several times elected chancellor, and continued in office nearly twenty years or to within two or three years of his death. As chancellor he was very popular with the bar, and his decisions were generally acquiesced in by the lawyers. In fact his decisions were so generally correct that they were seldom reversed or modified by the supreme court. When such did occur, it was because some technical rule of equity intervened to prevent the appearance of a decree that was according to right and justice. An able judge of the supreme court who was studying one of Judge Williams' decrees once said: "Judge Williams is an excellent chancellor—I think I may say the best in the State, but I have one complaint against him. He will throw hard cases on the supreme court. Here is a case, which he has decided, according to the right, but a technical rule of equity compels the court to reverse his decree."

Judge Williams died at the residence of his sister, near Nashville, in 1857. The supreme court was in session at the time, and resolutions highly complimentary to his honesty and uprightness as a citizen, and his ability as a judge, were adopted by the bar.

In 1833 Knoxville was credited with eighteen lawyers. At this time John R. Nelson was attorney-general. He had previously been deputy sheriff of the county, and while occupying that office, had managed to obtain some knowledge of the law. He was then chosen to represent the county in the Lower House of the General Assembly, and while a member of that body was elected to the office of attorney-general. Here he had opportunity to display his strong native ability, and contrary to the expectation of his friends he made an excellent prosecutor. He resigned his office in 1835, but still continued to practice, and attained to considerable prominence as a criminal lawyer. Physically he was a man of great strength and vigor, but was somewhat given to over indulgence in eating and drinking. He was succeeded in the office of attorney-general by John H. Crozier, who was appointed to fill out the unexpired term. Col. Crozier is still living near Knoxville. He has now retired from practice, but for half a century he was one of the leading advocates of East Tennessee. He is a man of fine intellect, an orator of uncommon brilliancy and a conversationalist of rare powers. In 1836 he was a candidate before the Legislature for the office which he was then filling by appointment. Inexperienced in political intrigue, he would not consent to any exchange of votes in his behalf, and was consequently defeated, his successful opponent being Reuben B. Rodgers. In 1837 he was elected to the Legislature without opposition, and in 1844 was an elector on the Whig ticket. The following year he was elected to Congress and re-elected in 1847. From 1851 to 1854 he was appointed commissioner upon the supreme bench to decide cases in which Judge McKinney was incompetent.

One of the contemporaries of Col. Crozier was Samuel R. Rodgers who served as chancellor for a short time at the close of the war. He was a man of good ability, but was scarcely aggressive enough to achieve the highest distinction as an advocate. Upon the bench, however, he displayed conspicuous ability. In manner he was mild and amiable, and was highly esteemed by the community in which he lived. Samuel B. Boyd, who was another contemporary of those mentioned above, soon after receiving his license to practice, removed to Alabama where he resided for several years. He then returned to Knoxville, and remained until his death. He was throughly educated, and possessed strong native ability.

Samuel B. Kennedy became a member of the Knoxville bar about 1830, but he soon after removed to Mississippi, where he died two or three years later. W. B. A. Ramsey was licensed to practice in 1826. While not a brilliant man he possessed excellent judgment, and had he applied himself to his profession he could, undoubtedly, have attained distinction as a jurist. During the greater part of his life, however, he was engaged in filling some official position. In 1832 he was appointed clerk and master of the chancery court and continued in that position until elected Secretary of State in 1847. George W. Churchwell, who died at the beginning of the civil war, was a member of the Knoxville bar for more than thirty years. He was an advocate of fair ability and a man of commanding presence, but was somewhat rough and eccentric in his manners. He was at one time a member of the Legislature, and in 1836 was a strong supporter of Hugh L. White. During the events previous to the war he espoused the cause of the South. His son, William M. Churchwell, was a young man of some brilliancy and was twice elected to Congress. He became a colonel in the Confederate Army, and died during the war.

William G. McAdoo, who served as attorney-general for nearly ten years preceding 1860, began the practice of law in 1849. In 1851 he was elected attorney-general by the Legislature, and after the change in the Constitution was re-elected by the people. He was an excellent prosecutor, one of the best ever on the circuit. He is still living in Knoxville, and a more extended notice appears in another chapter. William Swan received a license to practice about 1838. He had previously been clerk of the circuit court and was then somewhat advanced in life. He obtained a good practice, but was not sufficiently well read to achieve much distinction. He died about 1860.

Ebenezer Alexander, who succeeded Judge Scott upon the bench of the circuit court in 1844, was admitted to practice about 1830. In his youth he received a good literary education in the East Tennessee University, which was then under the presidency of Dr. Coffin. He served for a time as attorney-general and was twice elected to the bench of the circuit court, once by the Legislature and once by the people. He died in 1857 while serving his second term as circuit judge. He was of an amiable disposition and was very popular with the mass of the people. While, perhaps, not as profound a jurist as some of his colleagues, as a judicial officer he gave general satisfaction. He was honest, industrious and impartial. Judge Alexander was succeeded upon the bench by James M. Welcker, who died the following year. He had been admitted to the bar about 1841, and after practicing a few years had abandoned his profession and engaged in farming. At the death of Judge Alexander he was induced by his friends to accept a position upon the bench. During his career as an advocate he was associated with a younger brother, A. G. Welcker, who afterward removed to Chattanooga. The vacancy occasioned by the death of Judge Welcker was filled by George Brown, of Madisonville. He continued upon the bench until the suspension of the courts during the civil war, when he joined the Federal Army. In 1864 Elijah T. Hall was commissioned judge of this circuit by Gov. Brownlow. He continued in that position, by election and re-election, until 1878, when he was succeeded by Samuel A. Rodgers, of Loudon. Upon the establishment of a criminal court at Knoxville in 1870 his brother, M. L. Hall, was chosen to preside over it, and acted in that capacity until 1886. In September of that year he was succeeded by S. T. Logan, who, in accordance with an act of the General Assembly of 1885, also presides over the circuit court. Judge M. L. Hall received his professional instruction in the offices of Robert M. Anderson and Samuel R. Rodgers. He was licensed to practice in 1841. In 1852 he was elected clerk of the circuit court, and from that time until September, 1886, was constantly in office. He continued as clerk of the circuit court until 1864, when he was appointed clerk of the Federal court by Judge Trigg.

The successor of Judge Williams as chancellor was Seth J. W. Lucky, of Jonesboro, who continued in that position until the close of the war. He had previously been upon the circuit court for many years and was highly esteemed, both as a man and a judge. He died in April, 1869. His successor was Samuel R. Rodgers, who continued upon the bench but one year. In 1866 A. O. P. Temple was elected chancellor, and satisfactorily discharged the duties of that office until 1878. He had been a resident of Knoxville for several years before the war, and during the war was a stanch Unionist. He is still living, and since his retirement from the bench has served a term as postmaster. He was succeeded as chancellor by W. B. Staley, of Kingston, who filled the office for one term and is now a resident of Knoxville. The present incumbent is H. R. Gibson. Several other prominent members of the profession, among whom are Thomas L. Lyons, Horace Maynard and W. H. Sneed, have been residents of Knoxville, but they have received sufficient mention in another chapter. The present bar of Knoxville is one of conspicuous ability and among its members are some of the ablest men of the State.

The military achievements of Tennessee have been remarkably brilliant, and Knox County is entitled to no small part of the honor of making and sustaining the reputation of the "Volunteer State." In all the troublous times under the territorial government Knoxville was the rendezvous for volunteers and the headquarters for operations against the Indians, and under their leader, the gallant Gen. White, the citizens of the county were ever ready to endure the hardships and brave the perils of savage warfare for the protection of their homes and country. But as an account of their expeditions and adventures is presented in another chapter, it will not be repeated here. In the Creek war of 1812 and 1813 Knox County and vicinity bore a conspicuous part. In the early part of the war Col. John Williams led out a regiment of militia which marched into the Creek County. The term of enlistment was short, and the men returned without having accomplished anything of moment. In the fall of 1813 Gen. James White, in command of a brigade of three months' militia, joined Gen. Cocke's forces, and it was his brigade, acting under orders from Gen. Cocke, that captured and burned the Hillibee towns.*

Early in 1813 Col. John Williams received a commission to recruit and organize the Thirty-ninth Regiment of United States Volunteers. On June 18, 1813, he had recruited a force of 600 men and they were mustered into the service. The lieutenant-colonel of the regiment was Thomas H. Benton; the major, Lemuel P. Montgomery. The companies were commanded by Samuel Bunch, James Davis, John Jones, John B. Long, John Phagan, Thomas Stuart and William Walker. Bunch afterward became colonel of one of the regiments of militia in White's brigade. Among those who served as first lieutenants were David Lauderdale, David McMillen, Nathaniel Smith, Guy Smith (who also served as quartermaster), A. Stanfield and J. O. Tate. Andrew Greer, N. Dortch,

*See page 466.

M. W. McClellan, M. C. Molton, Simpson Payne, R. Quarles and J. K. Snapp were second lieutenants; and Dicks Alexander, A. G. Cowan, Joseph Denison, R. B. Harvey, Joseph S. Jackson, Ellis Thomas and T. B. Tunstall were third lieutenants. One of the ensigns was Sam Houston. Thus the regiment contained three men who were afterward to become United States Senators.

Col. Williams had expected to go to New Orleans, and was awaiting orders to move, when Judge H. L. White visited Gen. Jackson, and, learning of his urgent need of reinforcements, hastened home and urged Col. Williams to march at once to his assistance. This Col. Williams finally decided to do, and, waiting only long enough to communicate his intentions to the war department, he set out. He reached Gen. Jackson about the 1st of March, and on the 27th of that month participated in the battle of the Horseshoe. His regiment acted with especial gallantry. Maj. Montgomery was the first man to leap upon the works of the enemy, but was instantly killed. Ensign Houston received an arrow in the thigh, inflicting a wound from which he never fully recovered. The regiment continued in the Creek country until after the treaty of peace was signed, when they returned home and were mustered out on June 15, 1815.

The news of the signing of the treaty of peace with Great Britain was received in Knoxville with the greatest rejoicing. The First Presbyterian Church then just erected was illuminated, and a thanksgiving service was held there. Afterward a grand ball in honor of the event was given.

In 1836 a company of two months' militia was raised for service in the Seminole war. Dr. James Morrow was captain, Samuel B. Kennedy, first lieutenant, and Thomas C. Lyons second lieutenant. The troops for East Tennessee rendezvoused at Athens, where R. G. Dunlap was chosen to command the brigade. The regiment to which Capt. Morris' company was assigned was engaged during its term of service in assisting to remove the Cherokees west of the Mississippi, and Lieut. Lyons was promoted to a position upon Gen. Wool's staff. In the Mexican war Knox County took no considerable part. Under the first call for twelve months' men a company was organized at Knoxville on June 10, 1846, with William R. Caswell as captain; Samuel Bell, first lieutenant; Calvin Gossett, second lieutenant, and James Anderson, third lieutenant. The company known as the "Knoxville Dragoons" then went to Memphis where the regiment was organized as the Second Tennessee Volunteer Cavalry, with J. E. Thomas as colonel, R. D. Allison, lieutenant-colonel, and Richard Waterhouse, major.* At the end of their terms of service the

---

*For the movements of these regiments see pages 475 and 476.

members of the company returned to their homes, but a call was soon issued for two regiments to serve for three years, or during the war, and several men re-enlisted. In September, 1847, Jordan T. Council organized a company of infantry, of which he became captain. Tazewell Newman, first lieutenant; Joseph H. Crockett, second lieutenant; Thomas McAffry, third lieutenant, and James Henderson, orderly sergeant. The company was ordered to Memphis where it was assigned the position of Company D, Fourth Tennessee Infantry, with Richard Waterhouse as colonel, J. D. Swan, lieutenant-colonel and McD J. Bunch, major.

During the civil war Knoxville, as the metropolis of this division of the State, was a position of considerable importance, and was early made the headquarters of the Army of East Tennessee by the Confederate military authorities. Knox County, however, was strongly Union in sentiment. At the election held in February, 1861, to determine the question of calling a convention, out of 3,561 votes cast, only 394 were in favor of that measure, and at the election in June "no separation" received a majority of nearly three to one. This sentiment somewhat delayed the organization of troops, and some of the young men, impatient to join the army and fearful lest the war should end before they had an opportunity to do so, hastened to Georgia soon after the fall of Fort Sumter and joined the first regiment of volunteers from that State. But the necessity of collecting a force to suppress the Unionists, who threatened to cut off communication between Virginia and the southwest, soon became apparent. The old fair grounds two miles west of Knoxville was made a rendezvous for the companies organized in East Tennessee, and there, on May 29, the Third (Confederate) Tennessee Regiment was organized from troops mainly from Monroe County, which was strongly secession. Soon after the Fourth and Nineteenth Regiments were organized. On July 26, Gen. Zollicoffer arrived and assumed command of the forces in East Tennessee. He remained in Knoxville until September, when he went to Cumberland Gap, leaving Col. H. B. Wood in command of the post. On November 25 the latter was succeeded by Gen. W. H. Carroll, while at the same time Gen. G. B. Crittenden, the division commander, also had his headquarters at Knoxville.

On the 11th of October the Thirty-seventh Regiment of Infantry was organized with Moses White as colonel, H. P. Moffett, lieutenant-colonel, and W. M. Hunt, major. Considerable difficulty was experienced in providing the regiment with the proper arms. On December 9 it was reported that of the 771 men in the command only 200 were armed, and these with a miscellaneous assortment of rifles, shotguns and muskets, many of which were totally unfit for use. On the next day Gen. Carroll was ordered to join Gen. Zollicoffer, with his brigade, but owing to its insufficient equipment, he was unable to move until toward the close of the month. Maj. G. H. Monserrat was then left in command of the post at Knoxville, and from that time forth no considerable Confederate force was maintained at this point. In March, 1862, E. Kirby Smith assumed command of the Department of East Tennessee, and he, for a time, made his headquarters at Knoxville. Later, during the autumn of 1862 and the following winter, the post was under the command of Gen. J. P. McCown, Gen. Sam. Jones and Gen. Maury, successively. During this time strenuous efforts were made to enforce the conscript act but with only partial success. On April 27, 1863, Gen. S. B. Buckner was assigned to the command of East Tennessee, and Knoxville was his headquarters until the evacuation in September.

From its position the town was difficult of access by the Federal forces, and it was undisturbed by them until June, 1863, when Gen. Sanders with a few hundred men made a raid around it. On the evening of September 4, following, the advance of Gen. Burnside entered the town, but it was not until the next day that he arrived in person and took up his headquarters in a dwelling formerly the residence of John H. Crozier but now occupied by the *Journal*. The remainder of this month and the greater part of October was spent in securing Cumberland Gap and other important points in upper East Tennessee. On October 22 news was received that Longstreet with his corps was on the march up the valley, and Burnside at once ordered the greater portion of his force to Loudon to meet him. The report, however, proved premature as Gen. Longstreet did not leave Chattanooga until the 4th of November, but Burnside, confident that the movement would be made, awaited his enemy's arrival. His army consisted of the Ninth Corps, commanded by Gen. Potter, and composed of two divisions under Gens. Hartranft and Ferrero respectively; the Twenty-third Corps composed of White's and Hascall's divisions, and the cavalry under Gen. J. M. Shackleford, numbering altogether about 10,000 men. The disposition of these forces upon Longstreet's appearance was about as follows: The Ninth Corps at Lenoir's, where a pontoon bridge had been thrown across the river; White's division of the Twenty-third Corps at Loudon, on the north side of the river; a portion of the Twenty-third Corps at Knoxville, under command of Chief-of-staff Gen. John G. Parke; a division of cavalry and mounted infantry under Gen. Sanders, south of the river not far from Rockford, and detachments at Kingston, Maryville and other points. Longstreet's army consisted of the divisions of Gens. Hood,

McLaws and Wheeler, and two battalions of artillery commanded by Cols. Alexander and Leyden, respectively, numbering in the aggregate about 20,000 men. On the 13th of November Gen. Wheeler with three brigades of cavalry detached himself from the main army, marched to Maryville, captured the detachment there, and attempted to capture and occupy the heights south of the river at Knoxville. After a vigorous attack upon the force under Gen. Sanders, however, he was compelled to withdraw, and marched down the river to join the main army which had thrown a bridge across the river at Hough's Ferry. On the 12th of November Assistant Secretary of War Dana and Col. Wilson of Grant's Staff visited Gen. Burnside, and upon conference it was decided to hold Knoxville at all hazards, and Kingston if possible. On the next morning Gen. Burnside accompanied his guests as far as Lenoir's, and at once began making preparations for the withdrawal of his forces to Knoxville. He ordered Gens. Potter and White to Hough's Ferry to delay the passage of Longstreet's army, while at the same time he started his wagon trains for Knoxville. Soon after daylight on the 15th he had his whole command on the road moving toward Lenoir's, which place was not reached until nearly night. There two days' rations were issued, and the army went into camp.

At Campbell's Station about ten miles above Lenoir's the Loudon road enters the Kingston pike extending from Kingston to Knoxville. This was therefore an important point, and before daylight Hartranft's division, accompanied by Biddle's cavalry, was started in advance to seize and hold it. Meanwhile McLaws' division was hastening up on the Kingston road for the same purpose. The roads were in bad condition from heavy rains, and the progress of both were slow, but Hartranft's division gained the position, and by 11 o'clock Burnside's main army had passed the forks of the road and formed in line of battle. Ferrero's division was posted on the right to the north of the wood, Hartranft's division on the left, with White's division in the center. Five batteries of six guns each were placed in commanding positions to the rear of the first line of troops. About 12 o'clock, after some severe skirmishing by McLaws' division, Longstreet brought his command into position with Hood's division, under Gen. Jenkins, on the right, the artillery in the center, at the junction of the roads, and McLaws' on the left. Gallant and well sustained charges were made, first by McLaws' division on Burnside's right, and second by Hood's division on the extreme left, but both were repulsed. It had been the intention to make these assaults simultaneously, but owing to some misunderstanding of orders this was not done. Meanwhile the wagon trains had obtained a start toward Knoxville, and Gen. Burnside now retired his army under a heavy fire to a hill about three-fourths of a mile in the rear. This position was obtained in good order about 4 o'clock, and in a few minutes McLaws renewed the attack upon the Union right, but Burnside, anticipating the movement, had massed his artillery to meet it, and after an hour's hard fighting Longstreet withdrew his forces beyond the range of the Union batteries. The Union loss in this battle was reported at 26 killed, 166 wounded and 57 missing, while the Confederate loss was probably much greater.

The spot where this battle was fought had already become historic. It was the site of one of the oldest forts or stations in Knox County, and near by were the birthplaces of Com. Farragut and Bell Boyd, the celebrated spy.

After the withdrawal of Longstreet's army Gen. Burnside gave orders to retreat to Knoxville. The night was very dark and the roads heavy but by daylight the next morning the army reached its destination. The lines of fortification had already been selected by Chief Engineer O. M. Poe, and the work of intrenching was immediately begun. Ferrero's division was posted on the west, extending from the river to where the railroad crosses Second Creek; Hartranft's division on the north, extending from First to Second Creek along Vine Street, and White's and a portion of Hascall's division on the east, from Second Creek to a point on the river where the old glass-works were located. Artillery was placed on all the hills on and within these lines. A bridge had been thrown across the river, and a portion of the artillery, supported by Cameron's brigade of the Twenty-third Corps, was stationed on the heights to the south.

Meanwhile Gen. Longstreet had pushed in, and to delay his approach the cavalry under Gen. Sanders was dismounted, and on the morning of the 17th sent out four or five miles on the Kingston pike to delay and harrass Longstreet's advance consisting of McLaws' division. The whole of that day was spent in skirmishing, Sanders slowly falling back and McLaws advancing until night, when the former made a stand about 500 yards above the house of R. H. Armstrong where a line of defense consisting of rails, rifle pits, etc., was constructed, extending from the river to the railroad. McLaws occupied a parallel line just in front of Armstrong's house where his artillery was stationed.

Vigorous attempts were made by McLaws during the next day to drive in the Union line, but this was stubbornly resisted as it was imperatively necessary that the position be held as long as possible to give time for the strengthening of the works around the city. Chief Engineer Poe says in his report that every hour was worth a thousand men. About three o'clock in the afternoon the line was so hard pressed that it was impossible longer to maintain it, and Gen. Sanders rode forward from his headquarters to direct the retreat. He had reached a point about the center of his line, and just in its rear, when he received a mortal wound and was carried into the city. Gen. Wolford, however, succeeded in withdrawing his forces in good time, and Gen. Longstreet made the fatal mistake of not pressing the attack. Gen. Sanders was carried to the Lamar House where he died in a few hours after having been baptized by Rev. J. A. Hyden of the Methodist Church. The next night, in the presence of Gen. Burnside and the other officers, he was buried in the yard of the Second Presbyterian Church, Rev. Dr. Thomas W. Humes conducting the exercises. On the 18th of November Longstreet's entire command had come up and were placed in position. As has been stated McLaws' division occupied the space between the river and the railroad; Hood's division extended from the railroad to the Clinton road, while Hart's cavalry brigade completed the investment on the east, from the Tazewell Pike to the river. As the siege progressed, Longstreet received reinforcements from Gens. Sam Jones, "Mudwall" Jackson and "Cerro Gordo" Williams, and the divisions of Hood and McLaws were moved up so that the former's left rested on the Tazewell pike, and the latter's left extended to the Clinton road.

From the 18th to the 24th nothing of great importance occurred, although some skirmishes were kept up, and two or three sallies were made from the Union line, for the purpose of destroying houses which gave shelter to the sharpshooters of Longstreets' army, under direction of Capt. Poe the work of strengthening the fortifications went steadily on, nor had it ceased when the siege was raised. First Creek was dammed at the Mabry Street crossing, and Second Creek at the railroad crossing, thus flooding the low ground along the railroad. Fort Sanders was rendered almost impregnable by a deep ditch in front, and beyond that a net work of wire, and *Cheveux de Frise*.

On the night of the 24th Longstreet sent about 1,100 men under Gen. McLaws across the river near the Armstrong House, and on the next day an attempt was made to carry the heights south of the river. This was unsuccessful, except as to one hill below the university which was taken and a battery placed upon it. This battery, however, proved of little service. From this time until the attack on Fort Sanders the siege presents few points of interest, with the exception of an occasional sortie for the possession of the rifle pits in front of the fort.

It had been the purpose of Gen. Longstreet to starve the Federals into surrender, and he would undoubtedly have succeeded very quickly had he cut them off from all outside sources of supplies. It is stated by Capt. Poe in his report that at the commencement of the siege the army had provision sufficient for but a single day, yet at its close a quantity sufficient to last ten days had been collected. The Holston and French Broad Rivers above Knoxville were not carefully guarded, and large quantities of provisions and provender were floated down in flat-boats under cover of darkness and dense fogs. These supplies were freely furnished by loyal citizens, and were sent down under direction of Capt. Doughty and his company, who remained on the French Broad during the entire siege.

On the 28th of November Gen. Longstreet, learning of the approach of Gen. Sherman with a force of 25,000 men, resolved to attempt to carry the Federal works by assault. Upon consultation with his officers it was at last decided to attack Fort Sanders. This point was determined upon, it is said, through the advice of the engineer, Gen. Leadbetter, who from observation had decided that there was no ditch in front the fort. He was led into this error by seeing a dog pass out of the fort without disappearing from sight as he would have done had he entered a ditch. This was afterward explained by the fact that the animal had crossed over the ditch on a plank.

The attack upon the fort was begun early in the morning of the 29th by three brigades of McLaws' division composed of Mississippi, Georgia and South Carolina Regiments respectively. The engagement lasted about twenty minutes, and was attended with severe loss on the part of the Confederates. The obstacles in front of the fort threw their lines into confusion, and the ditch proved almost impassable. Heavy rains had made the ground very slippery, and no scaling ladders had been provided. Only a few succeeded in scaling the parapet, and these were either captured or killed. The assault was gallantly made and sustained, but the odds were too great for human endurance. The shattered columns were withdrawn, and soon after Longstreet began a retreat up the valley to Morristown. On the 12th of December Gen. Burnside turned over his command to Gen. Foster and left Knoxville. Upon his arrival there in September Gen. S. P. Carter had been appointed provost-marshal of East Tennessee, continuing in that position until the close of the hostilities, discharging the duties of the office with skill and justice.

In the summer of 1864 most of the troops having been withdrawn from Knoxville a regiment of militia was organized for the defense of the town. F. F. Flint was made colonel; F. A. Reeve, lieutenant-colonel; D. G. Thornburg, major; W. R. Patterson, adjutant, and W. J. Perkins, quartermaster. The companies were commanded as follows: Company A, John Baxter; Company B, W. G. Brownlow; Company C, John Netherland; Company D, E. C. Trigg; Company E, Perez Dickinson; Company F, A. A. Kyle; Company G, John M. Fleming and Company H. Capt. Montgomery, the aggregate number of men being 846.

During the continuance of hostilities in East Tennessee the suffering among the poorer people became intense, and in the fall of 1863, Col. N. G. Taylor visited the North and East to procure money and supplies for these unfortunates. He delivered addresses in all the large cities, and succeeded in arousing the sympathies of the people. Large contributions were made, and in order that the supplies might be properly and systematically distributed it became necessary to form an organization in East Tennessee which was effected at Knoxville on February 8, 1864. Thomas W. Humes was made president; M. M. Miller, treasurer and J. M. Fleming, secretary. The society was known as the East Tennessee Relief Association, and during the three years of its existence received and distributed large quantities of supplies to the needy inhabitants.

The first company recruited in Knox County for service in the Confederate Army was Company E, of the Nineteenth Tennessee Infantry, which was organized in May, 1861, with Dr. John Paxton as captain; John Miller, first lieutenant; George Boyce, second lieutenant; L. B. Graham, third lieutenant, and Samuel Hamilton, orderly sergeant. At the reorganization, one year later, W. W. Lackey became captain; S. Abernathy, first lieutenant; H. A. Waller, second lieutenant, and J. L. Waller, third lieutenant. At the battle of Chickamauga, on September 19, 1863, Capt. Lackey was killed and was succeeded by H. A. Waller. This was the only company in the Nineteenth Regiment raised in Knox County. At the organization it numbered 101 members, but twelve only remained at the close of the war. The regiment was organized at the fair grounds near Knoxville on June 10, 1862, at which time the following officers were chosen: D. H. Cummings, colonel; F. M. Walker, lieutenant-colonel; A. Fulkerson, major; V. Q. Johnson, adjutant; J. D. Taylor, quartermaster; H. M. Doak, sergeant-major; J. E. Dulaney, surgeon; Rev. D. Sullins, chaplain, and W. J. Worsham and Rufus Lamb, chief musicians. A considerable number from this county also joined the Fourth Infantry, under Col. W. M. Churchwell, and also the Thirty-first, under the command of Col. William Bradford. Lieut.-Col. James W. Humes and Sergt.-Maj. James White, of this regiment, were from Knoxville.

Company D, of the Sixty-third Tennessee Infantry, was also partially recruited at Knoxville by Capt. A. A. Blair, in May, 1862. The remainder of the company was from Washington and Hawkins Counties. The officers were A. A. Blair, captain; J. R. McCollum, first lieutenant; J. W. Carter, second lieutenant; J. L. Wilson, third lieutenant, and R. N. Collum, orderly sergeant.

Of the First and Second Regiments of Tennessee Confederate Cavalry, a considerable number were from Knox County. The First Regiment was originally organized as Brazleton's battalion, at Knoxville, in August, 1861. It was composed of seven companies under the command of Lieut.-Col. William Brazleton, with William Bradford as major, and operated in East Tennessee and Kentucky. At the reorganization in the spring of 1862 James E. Carter succeeded Brazleton, and Alonzo Bean became major. At Murfreesboro three more companies were added and the organization completed with James E. Carter as colonel; Alonzo Bean, lieutenant-colonel; Alexander Goforth, major, and J. D. Carter, adjutant. The companies composing the regiment were as follows: Company A, from Rhea County, Capt. Keys; Company B, Hamilton County, Capt. J. B. King; Company C, McMinn and Monroe Counties, Capt. Richard Vandyke; Company D, Rhea and Roane Counties, Capt. Greer; Company E, Knox County, Capt. John Jarnagin; Company F, Claiborne County, Capt. Frank Fulkerson; Company G, Blount County, Capt. Wiggs; Company H, Jefferson County, Capt. Neff; Company I, Blount County, Capt. William Wallace; Company K, Jefferson County, Capt. Richard Swearinger. Later two other companies were added: Company L, from Claiborne County, Capt. Blackburn, and Company M, Washington County, Capt. Ed. Gammon. The regiment was assigned to Pegram's brigade. On the first day of the battle of Murfreesboro it participated in the movement around Rosecrans' army, and on the third day was actively engaged. After the battle it was transferred to East Tennessee, and was at Cumberland Gap when that place was surrendered by Gen. Frazier. Later it participated in several engagements in upper East Tennessee, among which was the battle of Blue Springs; was present at the siege of Knoxville, and remained with Gen. Longstreet during his stay in East Tennessee. In May, 1864, the regiment was dismounted and sent to the valley of Virginia under Gen. William E. Jones to meet the Federal forces under Gen. Hunter. In the battle which took place at Piedmont a severe defeat was sustained, and the regiment lost 150 out of 315 men in killed, wounded and captured. After participating in Early's campaign down the valley to Washington it was again mounted in the fall of 1864, and from that time until after the surrender of Gen. Lee, operated in southwestern Virginia and East Tennessee.

The Second Tennessee Cavalry was organized at Woodson's Gap in the spring of 1862 by the consolidation of Branner's and McClellan's battalions. The companies forming these battalions previous to that time had acted somewhat independently of each other, and had been engaged in scouting through East Tennessee. They were commanded as follows: Company A, John Kuhn; Company B, John Rogers; Company C, William Ford; Company D, Capt. Owens; Company E, William E. Smith; Company F, Capt. Stone; Company G, Capt. Clark; Company H, ———— ————; Company I, N. C. Langford; Company K, Capt. Gillespie. The regimental officers were H. M. Ashby, colonel; H. C. Gillespie, lieutenant-colonel; P. A. Cobb, major; R. M. Bearden, adjutant, and Charles Coffin, sergeant-major. The regiment was at first placed in Alston's brigade, but during the following fall was transferred to Gen. Pegram's command. Later it was under Col. Scotts and Gen. W. T. C. Humes successively, and finally toward the close of the war Col. Ashby was promoted to the command of the brigade. The regiment from that time was commanded by Capt. Kuhn, acting lieutenant-colonel, with Capt. William E. Smith, acting major. This was one of the most gallant regiments in the army and received many complimentary orders from its commanders. It participated in the battles of Fishing Creek, Shiloh (a detachment), Perryville, Murfreesboro, Chickamauga and the Atlanta campaigns. It was with Wheeler on his raid into Tennessee during that campaign. Afterward it opposed Sherman on his march through Georgia and the Carolinas, and finally surrendered near Greensboro, N. C. The greater portion of the troops from Knox County in this regiment were in Company I. W. W. Gibbs, who served as third lieutenant in Ashby's company of Branner's battalion, afterward, in the spring of 1863, organized a company of scouts which saw much hard service in East Tennessee.

Four batteries of light artillery were raised for the Confederate service in Knox County. In the spring of 1861 H. L. W. McClung organized a company of 120 men, of which E. S. McClung was senior first lieutenant; A. Allison, junior first lieutenant; William Lewis, senior second lieutenant, and David G. Jackson, junior second lieutenant. The battery consisted of six pieces—four smooth-bore six-pounders, and two twelve pound howitzers. The company was ordered into Kentucky where it participated in the battle of Fishing Creek, after which it joined A. S. Johnston's army and was present at the battle of Shiloh. As a part of Breckinridge's division it was at Vicksburg during the first bombardment. It then accompanied the division to East Tennessee, where it spent several months guarding the bridge at Loudon and at Carter's Station. Later it did guard duty at Saltville, Va. A detail of two guns from this battery and two from another under the command of Lieut. Allison were present with Morgan when he was killed at Greenville, on September 4, 1864, and under Vaughn the battery participated in the fight at Morristown, where Capt McClung and Lieut. Allison were both captured. The remainder of the company took part in the battle at Bull Run, Tenn., and finally surrendered under Gen. Johnston at Bentonville, N. C.

The Rhett Artillery, or Burrough's battery, was organized in June, 1861, by W. H. Burroughs and James C. Luttrell, who were elected captain and senior first lieutenant respectively. The other officers were G. A. Huwald, junior first lieutenant; J. E. Blackwell, senior second lieutenant, and J. J. Burroughs, junior second lieutenant. The battery was first stationed at Cumberland Gap, but upon Kirby Smith's raid into Kentucky it joined his command, and was present at the battles of Richmond and Perryville. After their return to Knoxville, a disagreement arose between Capt. Burroughs and Lieut. Luttrell, the former wishing to resume guard duty, and the latter to continue in active service. Finally, Capt. Burroughs, with the battery, was ordered to Cumberland Gap, and was continued in that vicinity until the close of the war. Lieut. Luttrell was given a detail from the Brigade battery, and, until the surrender at Greensboro, N. C., was engaged in active service under Gens. Pegram, Wheeler and Forrest, successively.

Kain's battery was organized in March, 1862, with W. C. Kain as captain; Thomas O'Conner, senior first lieutenant; Hugh L. White, junior first lieutenant; James Newman, senior second lieutenant; W. C. Danner, junior second lieutenant; and about 125 noncommissioned officers and privates. They proceeded to Chattanooga, where they received their guns and equipment, after which they marched to Bridgeport, and there participated in their first battle. They then engaged in a raid to Winchester, returning across the Cumberland Mountains to Loudon, where they did guard duty for a short time. Late in 1862 one section of two guns was detached under Lieut. White and sent to Murfreesboro, where it participated in the battle. It soon after rejoined the battery at Knoxville, which, under the command of Lieut. O'Conner, marched to Cumberland Gap, where the entire company (with the exception of nine men) were surrendered on September 9, 1863, and sent to Camp Douglass, from which only thirty-two returned alive at the end of the war.

Huwald's battery was organized with G. A. Huwald, captain; G. B. Ramsey, first lieutenant; William Martin, second lieutenant, and Charles McClung, third lieutenant, and numbered about ninety men. It operated in East Tennessee with Pegram's brigade until after the evacuation, when it went to Chattanooga and participated in the battle of Chickamauga. It afterward, at Dalton, Ga., was consolidated with Scott's battery, from Louisiana, after which the officers were G. A. Huwald, captain; G. B. Ramsey, senior first lieutenant; John Turner, junior first lieutenant; — Leftwich, senior second lieutenant; Robert Vestal, junior second lieutenant. It participated actively in the Atlanta campaign, and lost one section by capture at Beaver Creek. The remainder of the company continued on through Georgia, and at the time of the surrender were at Aiken, S. C. There they sold the horses, guns, etc., at auction; divided the money among themselves, and returned home. While on the Atlanta campaign, Lieuts. Ramsey and Turner fought a duel in which the latter received a mortal wound. Afterward Huwald was suspended for playing cards with his private soldiers, and Ramsey then assumed command.

As nearly all of the Union regiments from East Tennessee were organized in Kentucky from bands of refugees very few full companies were made up of men from any one county. It is impossible, therefore, to classify them by counties with any degree of accuracy. Of the First Tennessee Cavalry, Company C was composed chiefly of men from Knox County. This regiment was organized at Camp Garber, Ky., March 1, 1862, as the Fourth Infantry, and so continued until November 1 of that year, when it was transferred to the cavalry service. The first regimental officers were Robert Johnson, colonel; James P. Brownlow, lieutenant-colonel; James O. Berry, major and John Hall adjutant. Afterward, in the cavalry service, M. T. Burkhart and William R. Tracy became majors, but in the summer of 1863 were succeeded by Russell Thornburgh and Calvin M. Dyer, both of whom subsequently became lieutenant-colonels. Henry G. Flagg and Birton Smith were also promoted to the rank of major. The former in August, 1863, and the latter in July, 1864.

Company C was organized by James P. Brownlow, who, upon being chosen lieutenant-colonel, was succeeded by M. T. Burkhart. The latter in a few months was raised to the rank of major, and the command devolved upon Elbert J. Cannon. The final captain of the company was Jacob K. Lones, who was commissioned in December, 1863. John Roberts and James H. Smith both successively held the rank of second and first lieutenants. The whole number of men who enlisted in this company was 122, of whom 41 were killed or died of wounds or disease. The Second, Third, Fourth, and Ninth Cavalries also contained a considerable number of Knox County men.

Of the infantry regiments the Third and Sixth were most largely composed of men from Knox County, although it was well represented in the

First, Second and Eighth. The companies in the Third, organized in whole or in part from Knox County men, were D, F, H, and I. Company D was organized February 10, 1862, with John O'Keefe, captain; W. C. Robinson, first lieutenant; S. L. King, second lieutenant and W. C. Brandon, orderly sergeant. The officers of Company F were J. L. Ledgerwood, captain; James Clapp, first lieutenant; C. Rutherford, second lieutenant and C. Zachary, orderly sergeant. Company H, J. W. Adkinson, captain; J. G. Roberts, first lieutenant, and W. W. Adkinson, second lieutenant. Soon after the organization, J. G. Roberts became captain, and E. C. Roberts, first lieutenant. Company I was organized with E. D. Willis as captain; W. L. Ledgerwood, first lieutenant; J. H. Ellis, second lieutenant, and R. Bince, orderly sergeant; later, by promotion, W. L. Ledgerwood became captain; J. H. Ellis, first lieutenant and J. C. Bayless, second lieutenant.

Of the Sixth Tennessee Infantry, all but two companies, E and F, were recruited mainly from Knox County men. Company A was organized with A. M. Gamble, captain; Thomas D. Edington, first lieutenant, and V. F. Gossett, second lieutenant. In August, 1862, Capt. Gamble was raised to the rank of major, and the remaining officers were regularly promoted; W. W. Dunn becoming second lieutenant. Company B was organized by Spencer Deaton, with James M. Armstrong, first lieutenant; Thomas A. Smith, second lieutenant, and William D. Atchley, orderly sergeant. In May, 1864, Lieut. Armstrong was promoted to the command of the company. The officers of Company C at the organization were Rufus M. Bennett, captain; John P. Baryar, first lieutenant; William L. Lea, second lieutenant, and Joseph A. E. Blang, orderly sergeant. March, 1863, Lieut. Lea became captain, but on the 6th of August, 1864, was killed, and was succeeded by Adam T. Cottrell. At about the same time G. L. Maloney was made first lieutentant and John M. Berry, second lieutenant. Company D was organized by M. D. Bearden with S. L. Gilson, first lieutenant; Thomas Parham, second lieutenant, and William N. Price, orderly sergeant. In January, 1863, James H. Coleman became first lieutenant. He was succeeded in July, 1864, by J. L. Turner. F. B. Nicholl also served as second lieutenant. Company E was from Claiborne County, and was commanded by William Ausmus. Archibald Meyers was captain of Company F, which was from Campbell County. The organization of Company G was as follows: Francis H. Bounds, captain; A. E. Murphy, first lieutenant; A. M. Cate second lieutenant and Ignaz Fanz, orderly sergeant. Only eight companies were organized. The regimental officers upon organization were Joseph A. Cooper, colonel; Edward Maynard, lieutenant-colonel; William C. Pickens, major;

H. W. Parks, adjutant; William Rule, commissary sergeant, and T. T. Thornburgh, sergeant-major. In August, 1862, William C. Pickens was succeeded by A. M. Gamble, and in December, 1863, William Rule became adjutant. Thornburgh was also succeeded by Thomas L. Trewhitt.

One company of the Seventh Regiment of Mounted Infantry was recruited in Knox County. The officers were Charles W. Cross, captain; T. L. B. Huddleston, first lieutenant; S. D. Whitton, second lieutenant, and E. E. Longmire, orderly sergeant.

As has been stated, James White removed from his first location in the fork in 1786, and with James Conner began a settlement in the vicinity of what has since become the city of Knoxville. The first ground cleared by them is said to have been the lot upon which the First Presbyterian Church now stands, but this was not the site of their cabin, which was on the west side of First Creek, just north of where Union Street now is. The strength of the settlement thus begun had so far increased in 1791 as to induce Gov. Blount to fix upon it as the seat of the Territorial government. Early in that year he removed from the fork of the Holston and Watauga Rivers, where he had been located since assuming his official position, and took up his residence on a knoll between the hill upon which the university stands and the river. A few small buildings for the reception of government stores were erected near the mouth of First Creek, and it was in that vicinity that the treaty of Holston was held on the 2d day of the following July.

Although the town was not laid off until in February, 1792, the first number of the Knoxville *Gazette*, issued November 5, 1791, contains a notice of an agreement entered into on October 3 of that year, by James White, the proprietor of the town, and John Adair, Paul Cunningham and George McNutt, commissioners on the part of subscribers for lots, by the terms of which subscribers were to pay a uniform price, and after all the lots had been taken, they were to be assigned by lottery. It is probable, however, that this scheme was never carried out, as no other mention of it could be found. The following account of the founding of the town, written by Hugh Dunlap, is probably accurate: " At the treaty of Holston, in 1791, there were no houses except shanties put up for the occasion to hold government stores. Gen. James White lived in the neighborhood, and had a blockhouse to guard his family. At the treaty they used river water entirely, until Trooper Armstrong (James Armstrong) discovered the spring to the right of the street leading from the courthouse to what is now (1842) called "Hardscrabble." He at the time requested Gen. White, as a great favor, to let him have a lot including the spring when the town was laid off. The General granted his request, and after the town was surveyed made him a deed to the lot. These facts were told me by Gen. White himself, for I was not present at the treaty. I left Philadelphia with my goods in December, 1791, and did not reach Knoxville until about the 1st of February, 1792. I deposited my goods, and kept store in a house used by the Government at the treaty. At the time of my arrival in the town Samuel and Nathaniel Cowan had goods there. John Chisolm kept a house of entertainment, and a man by the name of McLemee was living there. These men with their families constituted the inhabitants of Knoxville at that time. Gov. Blount lived on Barbara Hill, a knoll between College Hill and the river. It was then approached from the town by a path following the meanders of the river. The land upon which Knoxville is built belonged to Gen. White. In February, 1792, Col. Charles McClung surveyed the lots, and laid off the town. I do not remember on what day of the month, it excited no particular interest at the time. The whole town was then a thicket of brushwood and grapevine, except a small portion in front of the river where all the business was done. There never was any regular public sale of lots. Gen. White sold anybody a lot for eight dollars who would settle upon it and improve it."

The new town was called Knoxville in honor of Gen. Henry Knox, then Secretary of War. As the county had not been laid off, no county buildings were at first erected, but lots for a courthouse and jail were reserved by Gen. White. He also set apart a lot for the erection of a house of worship, and two years later donated an entire square for the use of Blount College. This was the square bounded by Gay, Church, Clinch and State Streets.

In 1793 a detachment of United States troops, under command of Capt. Carr, arrived and erected a barrack upon the lot now occupied by the new courthouse. This was a somewhat extensive structure built of logs notched closely together, and extending from Main Street toward the river. The second story projected two feet on every side beyond the walls of the first. In both stories, and in the floor of the second, port holes were left at suitable distances. The square around was cleared of everything that might give protection to an assailant.

Nearly all of the merchants were at first located on State Street. Nathaniel and Samuel Cowan's store stood at the corner of State and Front Streets, opposite Chisolm's tavern. After a year or two the partnership between them was dissolved, and Nathaniel removed to the country. At about the same time a third brother, James Cowan, opened a store near State Street above Main. During the latter part of 1792 Titus Ogden, a merchant and a paymaster of troops and of Indian annuities, arrived and established a store on State Street. He died about a year later and was buried on College Hill.

The commercial importance of the town increased quite rapidly, and during the next two or three years stores were opened by James and Samuel Miller, James Ore, John Sommerville & Co., Charles McClung, Alexander Carmichael and Stephen Duncan, several of whom, however, remained in business but a short time. The last named a few years later was convicted of murder, and with an accomplice was executed at Knoxville.

Next in importance to the merchant was the tavern keeper. John Chisolm as the pioneer landlord soon had several competitors, and in order to maintain the rates he adopted the modern plan and formed a combination. In the *Gazette* of December 17, 1792, John Chisolm, Alexander Carmichael, John Wood and Peter McNamee inform the public that they have opened houses of entertainment in Knoxville upon the following terms: "breakfast and supper, one shilling each; dinner, one shilling and sixpence; constant boarders, $2 per week; whisky, six pence per one half pint."

In 1794 the Territorial Assembly convened in Knoxville. The council held its sessions in the barrack, and the House sometimes in another room of the barrack, but occasionally at Carmichael's tavern at the corner of Cumberland and State Streets. The joint conferences were held in the courthouse. As the seat of government, Knoxville attained an importance not common to frontier villages of a few years' growth. Its society, too, possessed an air of unusual refinement. This was due in a great measure to the influence of Gov. Blount and his wife, Mary Grainger—more to that of the latter perhaps, than of the former. Soon after the town was surveyed the Governor erected a house at the corner of State and Hill Streets, where he dispensed to all an elegant hospitality. Mrs. Blount was an accomplished lady of noble mind and gentle disposition, and from her presence eminated a certain grace and dignity which did much to soften and refine the manners of the pioneer inhabitants. She became a universal favorite, and to show the high esteem in which she was held a fort, a town and a county, were successively named in her honor.

The constitutional convention of 1796 assembled in the office of David Henley, an agent of the war department, a small building in the outskirts of the town. The population of Knoxville at this time had increased somewhat, but as is well known, there were not to exceed forty houses in the place, and these without exception were built of logs. The merchants then in business were Col. McClellan, John Nicholls, James and Samuel Cowan and John Crozier. That the place was one of considerable resort is evident from the fact that it supported five taverns. The largest of these stood on the present site of Schubert's Hotel, and was owned by John Stone.

The town continued to improve slowly, both in wealth and population. In 1810 there was a population of about 400, and a few brick houses had been built. Among the merchants who located in the town during the first decade of the present century were Thomas Humes, James Dardis, James and William Park and Calvin G. and R. Morgan, all of whom became substantial and influential citizens. Mr. Humes came to Knoxville from Mossy Creek, and opened a store at the northeast corner of Gay and Main Streets. Just before his death, which occurred in 1816, he erected what was known as the City Hotel, now a part of the Lamar House. James and William Park occupied the site of Stone's tavern at the corner of Cumberland and Gay Streets, where they continued for many years. James Dardis was located on Cumberland Street, west of the City Hotel. The Morgans, whose store was at the corner of Cumberland and Crozier Streets, did the largest business. They also owned a large tract of land north of Clinch Street.

Other merchants previous to 1820 were Haynie & Jackson, Z. Booth, Samuel Roberts, Bowen & Davis, J. H. Cowan & Co., Charles McClung, & Son, David Nelson, King & Whitson and Anthony & Conway.

On October 20, 1811, the Bank of Tennessee was incorporated, and one year later it went into operation with Hugh L. White as president, and Luke Lea as cashier. The board of directors was composed of John Crozier, James Park, David Campbell, Calvin Morgan, John Hillsman, Robert King and James Dardis. The bank building stood on the northwest corner of Main and Gay Streets. The bank continued in operation until 1828, when it began to close up its affairs. In 1820 a State bank was established at Nashville, with a branch at Knoxville. This institution was located at the corner of Crozier and Cumberland Streets. The cashier was James Campbell, "Scotch Jimmy." It never did a very extensive business, and was closed out in 1833.

In 1809 the Knoxville Water Company was incorporated by the Legislature. The members of the company were John Crozier, Josiah Nicholl, James and William Park, Richard Bearden, George W. Campbell, Thomas Humes, Nathaniel Cowan, John Williams, Pleasant M. Miller, James Dardis, Thomas Dardis, John N. Gamble, James Trimble, Edward Scott, Robert Craighead, Charles McClung and three or four others. Wooden pipes, or rather logs bored through the center, from end to end, were laid to bring the water from what is known as McCampbell's Spring, situated about two miles north of town. The pipes not being strong enough to sustain the pressure, this plan did not prove a success, and it was soon abandoned. In 1814 John Craighead obtained permission from the county court to make a cistern or reservoir in the courthouse yard. Pipes were to be laid to a point on First Creek near its mouth, and by means of a water wheel water was to be forced into the reservoir, and thence distributed over the town. This system, however, was never put into operation.

In 1830 Knoxville contained a population of about 1,500. The merchants at that time were James and William Park, M. and H. McClung, Hon. A. M. White, James H. Cowan, S. T. Jacobs, Calvin Morgan & Son, D. P. Armstrong, Robert King & Son, A. McMillan, E. Williams, John Crozier, Zach. Booth, Samuel Roberts & Son, William Lindsey and William Bowen. At this time but little wholesale business was done. Goods were mostly bought in Baltimore and Philadelphia, and hauled in large wagons the entire distance, at a cost of from $5 to $6 per 100 pounds. The wagons carried from two to three tons, and on the outgoing trips were loaded with ginseng, feathers and other produce. About 1835 a canal was completed to Lynchburg, Va., and that became a shipping point for Knoxville. At nearly the same time steamboats began plying regularly between Knoxville and Decatur, Ala., and the heavier goods were received in that way. They reached Decatur by rail from Tuscumbia, the head of navigation in the Tennessee River below the shoals. It was at this time that the jobbing trade of Knoxville began to assume importance. The pioneers in that business were McClung, Wallace & Co., Cowan & Dickinson, G. M. Hazen & Co. and Robert King & Son, in dry goods, and James King, McClung & French and Bearden & White in groceries. The town soon became the distributing point for all of East Tennessee, western North Carolina, southwestern Virginia and a part of Kentucky. No traveling salesmen were employed, but merchants from the country and surrounding towns came to Knoxville twice a year to replenish their stocks. Dry goods were usually sold on six month's credit, with the privilege of six months more with interest; groceries were sold on shorter time. The steamboat trade increased rapidly, and at one time there were no less than eighteen boats plying between Knoxville and other points on the river. The leading firms engaged in the business were James and William Williams, McClung and French, Bearden & White and James King & Co.

Among the retail dealers of this period were M. M. Gaines, A. G. Jackson, Crozier & Deaderick, McMullan & McElrath.

In 1833 a branch of the Union Bank of Nashville was opened in a building which stood in Cumberland Street, about where the office of

Schuberts Hotel now is; Andrew McMillan was the cashier. In 1837 the building on Main Street was erected, and the bank continued in operation there until the war. The successors of McMillan were Hugh A. M. White and J. J. Craig.

In 1838 Knoxville suffered severely from a fever, somewhat resembling yellow fever in its effect, which became epidemic. Some parts of the town had experienced an unusual amount of sickness during the two previous years, but it did not excite much alarm. The summer of 1838, which was unusually hot and dry, fully developed the disease. It appeared in June, reached its height in September, and disappeared upon the approach of cold weather. It pervaded the whole town, and over one hundred persons fell victims to the scourge. The disease was not well understood by physicians, but it was supposed to have been caused by the miasma arising from the large deposits of decomposing matter which had accumulated in the mill ponds surrounding the town, and which, during the drought, had become exposed to the sun. To prevent a recurrence of the disease the ponds were declared nuisances, and the dams were removed.

In 1854 the city was visited by cholera, which became epidemic in nearly all the towns of the State. In 1838 Knoxville had escaped an attack, but this year it suffered severely. The first victim was Col. John McClellan, a brother of Gen. Geo. B. McClellan, who died on the 30th of August. He belonged to the United State's Army, and was stationed at this point in charge of some Government work on the river. A number of other cases quickly followed, and nearly all proved fatal. It did not spread over all the town, however, but was confined principally to Main Street and the part nearest to the river.

The celebration of the semi-centennial anniversary of the settlement of Knoxville, which occurred on the 10th of February, 1842, forms a memorable event in the history of the town. Almost the entire population of the town and surrounding country were present. The officers of the occasion were Matthew McClung, president; James Park, Robert King, M. D. Bearden, W. B. A. Ramsey, David Campbell, I. B. Havely, Calvin Morgan, Samuel Bell, H. A. M. White, Moses Lindsey, J. E. S. Blackwell and J. H. Cowan, vice-presidents, and D. P. Armstrong, Marshal. Thomas W. Humes, the orator of the day, delivered an eloquent address reviewing the early history of Knoxville, after which a large company of ladies and gentlemen repaired to the City Hotel, where a sumptuous dinner was in readiness. After dinner the chairman of the committee of arrangements, Maj. E. Alexander, read the following regular toasts.

KNOX.

The Day we have Assembled to Commemorate—"Hallowed by recollections of the dangers and privations of a past generation, may it be a festival in all time to come."

The Early Settlers of Knoxville—"Honored be their memories, and gratified our recollections of their perseverance, their courage, and their fortitude."

The Historical and Antiquarian Society of East Tennessee—"Formed for the purpose of collecting and preserving facts connected with the settlement and early history of Tennnessee, may its success be commensurate with the object."

A large number of volunteer toasts and responses followed. The celebration was conducted upon strictly temperance principles, and no wine was served. Rev. William Mack offered the following toast—The Town Spring of Knoxville—"Grateful, sparkling and free, cold water, pure water, bright water for me."

Among those who participated in the exercises were Thomas A. R. Nelson, Dr. J. G. M. Ramsey and Horace Maynard.

The celebration closed with a ball at the Mansion House.

The decade from 1850 to 1860 was characterized by greater activity and growth than any similar period in the history of the town previous to that time. This was due mainly to the opening of the East Tennessee & Virginia and the East Tennessee & Georgia Railroads, which led to the establishment of some extensive manufactories, and considerably augmented the volume of trade. The wholesale business at this time was carried on principally by Cowan & Dickinson, McClung, Wallace & Co., and Walker, O'Keef & Co., dealers in dry goods and general merchandise, and Wallace & McPherson, Harvey Ault, and C. Powell & Co., grocers.

A short time previous to the war the first two named firms united under the name of Cowan, McClung & Co. They also did the largest retail business in the town. Other retail dealers were A. G. Jackson & Co., Plumlee Bros. and Boyd & Piper, dry goods; T. G. Rollins and James C. Moses & Bro., hardware; Dixon & Whitaker and T. J. Powell, insurance; Ed. Armistead, hats and caps; John S. Van Gilder, boots and shoes, Rayl & Vanuxem, books and stationery; Ricardi Bros., confectionery; Byrne & Elliott and Strong & Stevenson, drugs.

This period was also remarkable for the large number of banking institutions established.

Cowan & Dickinson obtained a charter for the Bank of East Tennessee, which they soon after sold to a Mr. Fiske, of New Orleans. About 1852 William M. Churchwell became president, and under his management a system of wild speculation and over-issue was inaugurated, which resulted in its downfall in 1856. The cashier was Samuel Morrow, who afterward, in company with John Baxter, established the Exchange and Deposit Bank.

In 1852 the Miners & Manufacturers Bank was founded by Joseph L. King and William Goodrich. It occupied the old State Bank building at the corner of Gay and Main Streets.

In 1859 the Branners (John R., William A., George M., Joseph and Benjamin) purchased the charter of the Ocoee Bank, of Cleveland, Tenn., and removed it to Knoxville, where it was opened in the building now occupied by the People's Bank. Of this institution John R. Branner was president and Joseph R. Mitchell, cashier. In 1854 the Bank of Knoxville was organized by John L. Moses, Joseph H. Walker and A. L. Maxwell. The following year it was sold to Hugh A. M. White and George M. White. The Farmers Bank was established by Hugh L. McClung in about 1854. He sold it to Shepherd & Wheless, of Nashville, who continued it for two or three years, after which it was consolidated with the Ocoee Bank.

About 1857 a branch of the State Bank was opened in the building now occupied by the Mechanics National Bank, with John H. Crozier as president, and M. B. McMahan, cashier. Mr. Crozier was soon after succeeded by Dr. J. G. M. Ramsey. Notwithstanding the number of other banking institutions this bank, with the Union Bank, did the greater part of the business.

In the preceding pages no mention has been made of the many minor industrial enterprises established in Knoxville during her earlier history, which, of small importance in themselves, were necessary to the welfare of the town, and deserve notice in this chapter. Among the earliest settlers in the town was the firm of Lord & McCoy, who sank a tanyard on Second Creek in 1793, and in 1795 a saddler's shop was opened by John and Robert Hunter. The next year a second shop was established by John Lavender. Grist-mills were early erected throughout the county, and soon scarcely a stream was without one or more upon its banks. During the first eighteen months after organization of the county the county court granted no less than twelve permits for the building of grist and saw mills. Although all the manufacturing industries were conducted on an extremely small scale, their number and variety were much greater than at the present time. Excepting some of the finer dress materials, nearly every article worn or used was supplied by domestic manufacture. The hatter, the shoemaker and the tailor furnished the clothing, while the cabinet-maker and the blacksmith supplied the household utensils. In enumerating the industries of Knoxville in 1830 the *Tennessee Gazetteer* names two spinning factories, ten carding machines, four grist-mills, three saw mills, one brass foundry, six blacksmith shops, two cabinet-makers, three hatters, six saddlers, eight shoemakers, one tinner, five tanners, two coach-makers and two wagon-makers. The foundry mentioned in the above list was established on Second Creek, near Churchwell Street, by William Morse, who also operated a spinning factory and blacksmith shop. After running a few years the entire plant was destroyed by fire. The other spinning factory was built by Nathaniel Bosworth on the same creek, a little higher up, and was somewhat extensive, employing from fifteen to twenty hands. This continued until 1838. In 1833 William Oldham built a cotton spinning factory on First Creek, between Church and Cumberland. The machinery for this mill he hauled in wagons from Lexington, Ky., across the Cumberland Mountains. It was a small establishment, containing only about 300 spindles, and was run entirely by water power. He was preparing to increase its capacity in 1838, when the destruction of the mill dams rendered it useless. He then removed his machinery to Blount County, and established what is now known as the Rockford Mills.

For several years after the settlement of the county cotton was one of the staple productions of Knox County. About 1820, however, its cultivation began to decline, and by the end of that decade it had practically ceased. Probably the first cotton-gin ever erected in Knoxville was built by Calvin Morgan, and stood on Gay Street, near where the Insurance Building now is. A second one was built and operated on Second Creek by a Mr. McCulloch. Wool-carding machines were common throughout the county. The earliest one in the vicinity of Knoxville was put in operation in 1816, by James Scott on First Creek, about two miles above its mouth. This continued in use up to the war. Another was set up and run for a time near where Bosworth's factory stood.

Of the five tanyards in 1830 one was owned by William Morrow, and was situated on First Creek, at the crossing of Cumberland Street. John Webb had one nearly on the opposite side of the street. A third, owned by Robert Lindsey, was located at the east end of Clinch Street, while Rutherford & White operated one on Second Creek, where Caswell's furniture factory now stands. In 1850 F. A. R. Scott built a small oil mill on Second Creek, and the following year opened a tannery in connection with it. In 1853 he sold the mill and tannery to M. B. McMahan, who continued to operate the latter until 1860, when he was succeeded by an incorporated company. During the war John S. Van

Gilder, who was then extensively engaged in the manufacture of boots and shoes, obtained control of it, and in 1865 he was joined by Mr. Scott. These two gentlemen have since continued the business under the name of the Knoxville Leather Company. The cabinet shops were run by Lones & McCroskey and Terence McAffry. The former was situated on the lot where C. W. Park now lives, and the latter on Cumberland Street, between Henley and High. Some time about 1820 a chair factory was erected on Gay Street, about where Ogden Bros.' store now is. It was established by a company of chair-makers from the north, and for a few years furnished a large section of country with chairs. The building stood unoccupied for many years afterward, and served as a target for the small boys, who affected to believe that it was haunted. The first mill in the vicinity of Knoxville was a "tub mill," erected by Gen. James White soon after his settlement. Afterward his son, Moses White, operated a mill on First Creek, near the crossing of Mabry Street, for several years. A second mill was built by John Craighead at the crossing of Main Street, and about 1820 Rufus Morgan built a more extensive one on the same creek. In 1830 the three grist-mills, together with two saw mills on First Creek, were all owned and operated by James and William Kennedy. James Scott also ran a grist-mill in connection with his fulling and carding mill, about two miles farther up the creek.

Previous to 1838 the town was almost entirely surrounded by water and the creeks furnished abundant water power. The depression on the north, now occupied by the depot, was covered with water several feet deep, and was known as the Flag Pond, while on First Creek there were three mill ponds within the space of half a mile. The upper one, known as White's mill pond, extended north and northeast for more than a mile. On Second Creek there were two large ponds. The cutting down of the dams in 1838 drained the ponds, and while they have been partially restored, the water power has never been equal to what it was before that time.

About 1855 a large steam flouring-mill was built upon the site of the Knoxville Rolling Mill, by M. W. Williams, but it was soon after destroyed by fire. It was succeeded by the Knoxville City Mills, on Broad Street, which were recently abandoned. In 1859 F. A. R. Scott and J. C. Deaderick erected what is known as the Trio Mill, on First Creek, which has since been in constant operation.

In 1838 Gideon M. Hazen and M. D. Bearden erected a paper-mill at Middle Brook, three and one-half miles from the city, which was continued until 1886, when the breaking of the dam caused its suspension. It was run about seven months in the year by water power, and the remainder of the time by steam and water power combined. For the past ten years it has been owned and operated by J. A. Rayl and Samuel McKinney, and it will probably be repaired and set in operation again.

The first maufacturing enterprise, upon anything like a modern scale, was established by A. L. Maxwell, who came from New York in 1852, and erected a large machine shop at the corner of Broad Street and the railroad. Mr. Maxwell, who was the senior member of the firm of Maxwell, Briggs & Co., was very extensively engaged in bridge building throughout the South, and designed this shop to supply the iron work for the Howe truss bridges which he was erecting. The building was completed, and the concern went into operation in June, 1853, employing from 200 to 250 hands. Two years later, finding that the bridge material could be furnished more advantageously from Richmond, Va., an interest in the establishment was sold to some Vermont parties, and the Knoxville Manufacturing Company was formed for the purpose of building engines, boilers, etc. This business was continued until just before the war, when the shops were closed, and Mr. Maxwell again took possession of the property.

In 1852 Williams, Moffett & Co. erected a foundry and stove factory on Second Creek, near the present site of the Knoxville Leather Company's works. They employed considerable capital, and for the time did quite an extensive business. In 1856 the establishment was transferred to the firm of Shepard, Leeds & Hoyt, who two years before had built a foundry and car works on the ground now occupied by the railroad shops. They invested a capital of about $20,000, and employed from twenty to thirty hands in the manufacture of cars, car wheels, agricultural implements and plows. In this business Mr. Maxwell successively purchased the interest of Messrs. Leeds, Hoyt and Shepard, until in 1861 he became the sole proprietor. During the siege in 1863, the entire plant along the railroad was destroyed by fire, entailing a loss upon the proprietor of some $250,000.

The advent of the civil war marks the beginning of a new era in the history of Knoxville. At that time she contained a population of about 3,000 souls, representing a growth of nearly seventy years. As a commercial center she had attained no little importance, and two or three manufacturing establishments of respectable proportions had been put into operation. Two railroads had also been recently opened, connecting her with the East and West. Yet, if one may judge from the gazeteers and other publications of the time, she was little known outside of Tennessee, other than as the seat of a university and the former capital of the State. Her population had remained remarkably stationary, receiving only now and then a recruit from the East, in the person of some young professor or teacher. Her citizens, eminently respectable, intelligent, and cultivated, and proud of their splendid traditions and honorable ancestry, had lived to themselves, marrying and giving in marriage until, it is said, nearly every person in the town was related to every other person. Yet it is not to be inferred that these people were devoid of enterprise. Every project looking to the development of the resources of the country was liberally supported. When the Southern Commercial Convention was to be held in Knoxville, the citizens promptly raised $1,000 to provide for the proper reception and entertainment of the guests. Subscriptions to railroads and other internal improvements were in every case supported by large majorities, and that no greater progress had been made, was due rather to environment, than to the character of the people.

During the progress of the civil war Knoxville reaped her full portion of suffering and loss. Property was destroyed, industry paralyzed and trade scattered. In one respect her position during that struggle was without a parallel among the cities of the South. Her population on the great question of disunion was almost equally divided, and the animosities and feuds engendered were bitter in the extreme. In the early part of the war the disunion element being in the ascendancy, and acting in the heat and excitement of war, oppressed and harassed those who remained loyal to the Union; and when during the last two years the positions of the parties were reversed, acts of retaliation were frequently indulged in. But from the revolution wrought by the war Knoxville has also reaped her full measure of prosperity. During those four years thousands of troops gathered from all parts of the country, visited her historic site, and, like the pioneers who beheld it for the first time three-quarters of a century before, were charmed with the fertility of the soil, the salubrity of the climate and the magnificence of the scenery. The valley of East Tennessee, with all the wealth that nature had lavished upon it, was at last discovered to the world, and when peace was restored many of these veterans returned to make it their home, while former residents entered with spirit upon the work of reconstruction and development. Since that time the growth of Knoxville, in both population and wealth, has been remarkably rapid. In 1870 the population had increased to about 9,000; during the next decade it was nearly doubled, and now, on January 1, 1887, it falls little short of 30,000. At the beginning of 1865 less than $20,000 of manufacturing capital remained; now not less than $2,500,000 are invested in the various industrial enterprises of the city.

In commercial operations the growth has been even more rapid. The following carefully prepared statement of the trade of Knoxville was made in 1886: Iron and nail, $500,000; stoves and tinware, $25,000; woolen goods, $140,000; cotton goods, $125,000; dry goods, $1,500,000; clothing, $600,000; boots, shoes and hats, $1,000,000; groceries, $2,000,000; queensware, $200,000; books and stationery, $100,000; drugs and paints, $400,000; candy, $50,000; leather, $100,000; harness and saddlery, $300,000; furniture, $125,000; agricultural implements, $300,000; timber and lumber, $800,000; sash, doors and blinds, $100,000; ax and hammer handles, $50,000; wagons and buggies, $25,000; engines and boilers, $200,000; cars and car-wheels, $400,000; foundry and machine works, $50,000; marble and coal, $1,000,000; zinc spelter, $100,000; a total of $11,285,000.

It is universally conceded that no other city of equal size in America has so large a wholesale trade as Knoxville. The area tributary to this city embraces, in whole or in part, the States of Tennessee, Kentucky, Virginia, North and South Carolina, Georgia and Alabama, while in some lines it includes the entire South. Nearly all the firms are backed by abundant capital, and are controlled by competent, progressive and practical men.

Among the wholesale houses of the present time that of Cowan, McClung & Co., which has previously been mentioned, is the largest as well as the oldest. Formerly they carried a general stock, embracing almost every article sold by the country dealer, but during the last few years, they have confined themselves to dry goods, notions, boots and shoes, in which they have a trade of many hundred thousand dollars annually. Their present, large, four-story, business block was erected in 1870, and they now carry, probably, the largest stock of goods in the country. The individuals comprising the firm are P. Dickinson, F. H. McClung, Matt McClung, C. J. McClung, J. D. Cowan, R. M. Rhea and J. L. Thomas.

The house of Briscoes, Swepson & Co. was founded by George & Briscoe in 1882. The present firm is composed of Daniel Briscoe, P. J. Briscoe, R. R. Swepson, M. D. Arnold, S. C. Roney. They employ seven traveling salesmen, and do a business approximating $1,000,000 annually. Their stock, embracing dry goods, notions, boots and shoes, is very large and complete, and their salesrooms are among the finest in the city.

McNulty & Borches carry a stock similar to the above firms with the addition of carpets and groceries and do both a wholesale and retail business. They occupy a four-story building, 85x100 feet, and give employment to thirty-two people. Their trade reaches half a million dollars annually. The individuals composing the firm are F. McNulty and J. W. Borches.

Since June, 1886, Knoxville has had two wholesale firms dealing exclusively in hats and caps. They are S. H. George & Co. and Davis & Walker, both of which were formed upon the dissolution of the firm of George & Davis. The former consisted of S. H. George, John McMillan and S. C. Dismukes, and the latter, J. R. Davis and M. H. Walker. Both carry large stocks of goods, and do a flourishing business.

Two firms also deal exclusively in boots and shoes. Haynes, Henson & Co. began business in 1878, and until recently handled hats and caps, They occupy a large, three-story building, and carry a complete stock of goods, embracing all grades from the heaviest to the finest.

McMillan, Hazen & Co. began business in 1884 as the successors of R. S. Payne & Co., a firm established in 1870. The individual members are E. E. McMillan, Asa Hazen, M. S. McClellan and Lytton Thomas. Five men are constantly on the road selling their goods, and their annual transactions amount to several hundred thousand dollars.

The firm of McTeers, Payne, Burger & Hood, is one of the most extensive wholesale clothing and gents' furnishing goods houses in the South. They have a trade throughout Kentucky, Virginia, Tennessee, Georgia, Alabama, the Carolinas and Mississippi, amounting to over half a million dollars annually. The business was established by J. T. McTeer in 1876. The present firm is composed of J. T. and C. E. McTeer, R. S. Payne, C. Burger and W. H. Hood.

Sample, Andes & Co. is the style of a firm that recently engaged in the wholesale notion business. They occupy one of the finest houses in the city, and carry as complete a stock as can be found in any similiar establishment in the country. The members of the firm are J. C. Sample, George S. Andes, I. E. Dooley and R. Annan.

The wholesale grocery trade is greater than that of any other line. One of the oldest houses in this business is that of Cone, Shields & Co., which was established in 1867 by Coffin, Martin & Co. The individual members of the present firm are C. and M. A. Cone, J. S. Shields and J. T. Shields, Jr. They carry a large and complete stock of staple and fancy groceries, and have extended their trade throughout a radius of 200 miles from Knoxville.

H. B. Carhart & Co. do an annual business approximating half a million dollars, and give employment to fifteen men, of whom six are traveling salesmen. The business was founded in 1877 by Lewis & Carhart, who were succeeded in January, 1884 by the present firm, consisting of H. B., W. B. and W. E. Carhart. They also conduct a similar business in New York City, under the style of Carhart & Bro.

The house now conducted by Condon Bros. was established in 1870 by Williams & Zimmerman, who were succeeded by the present firm, consisting of Michael J., Stephen P. and Martin J. Condon, in 1880. All are men of practical experience and business ability, and they have built up a large trade throughout East Tennessee and contiguous territory.

The firm of W. B. Lockett & Co. was formed in October, 1883, and consists of W. B. Lockett, Sr., W. B. Lockett, Jr., R. S. Hazen and J. O. Lotspeich. They employ six traveling salesmen, and their annual transactions amount to nearly half a million dollars.

The house of M. L. Ross & Co. was established in 1870 by Carpenter, Ross & Co., who conducted the business successfully until 1879, when they were succeeded by M. L. Ross and W. B. Lockett. In 1883 W. B. Lockett was succeeded by S. B. Dow. They do a very large grocery business, employing five traveling salesmen, and also run a candy factory, which enjoys a good trade.

Knaffl & Locke do an extensive wholesale business. The enterprise in which they are engaged was founded in 1876 by Anderson & McNulty, who were succeeded by the present firm, composed of Rudolph Knaffl and E. C. Locke, in 1881.

Knoxville contains two mammoth wholesale drug houses which would be a credit to any city. The oldest is that of Sanford, Chamberlin & Albers, which was established by E. J. Sanford & Co. in 1864. From a small beginning they have constantly extended their trade, until now they employ four traveling salesmen, and do a business amounting to $300,000 annually. They are also extensively engaged in the preparation of proprietary medicines. The present firm, consisting of E. J. Sanford, W. P. Chamberlin and R. J. Albers, was formed in 1870.

The other firm is that of Chapman, White, Lyons & Co., which was organized in January, 1882. They carry a full line of drugs and druggists' sundries, and have a large trade in proprietary medicines which they manufacture. The individual members of the firm are J. E. Chapman, W. O. White, W. L. Lyons and D. K. Young.

Knoxville also contains the largest queensware house in America. It was established by its present proprietors, Curtis, Cullen and C. S. Newman, in 1872. They have a trade in about every town in the South, and their sales amount to many hundred thousand dollars annually. Besides their main office and warerooms in Knoxville, they have branches in New York and Cincinnati, from which they ship direct to their customers.

Of the wholesale dealers in hardware the firm of W. W. Woodruff & Co., does the most extensive business. They employ about twenty-five men, four of whom are traveling salesmen, and have an annual trade of from $300,000 to $400,000. The house was founded by Mr. Woodruff in 1865, and from a modest beginning, through able management, has reached its present proportions. The other members of the present firm, which was formed in 1882, are William E. Gibbons and C. L. Carpenter.

The next oldest house is that of George Brown, which was established in 1869. Mr. Brown was formerly a prominent lawyer, and served one term as circuit judge. He employs several traveling salesmen, and has a large trade in Tennessee, Kentucky, North Carolina, Virginia and Georgia. He carries a general stock of hardware, agricultural implements, and mill machinery.

The firm of S. B. Luttrell & Co., consisting of S. B. and James C. Luttrell, was formed in 1871, and is recognized as one of the most substantial and reliable firms in the city. As an evidence of their high standing throughout the territory tributary to Knoxville they employ no traveling salesman and yet are able to hold their trade against all competition. Their sales to regular customers aggregate $225,000 per annum, in addition to which, during the past few years, they have furnished an immense amount of supplies to railroad contractors.

In 1880 the firm of McClung, Powell & Co., consisting of C. M. McClung, C. Powell, W. J. McNutt and A. Gredig, succeeded in the hardware line the firm of Cowan, McClung & Co. They increased the stock, added agricultural implements, and continued the business until 1884, when they were succeeded by C. M. McClung, W. P. Smith and W. B. Keener, under the firm name of C. M. McClung & Co. They occupy one of the finest business houses in the city, and carry a large stock of hardware, machinery, and implements of every description. Their annual sales amount to nearly a quarter of a million of dollars annually.

In addition to their jobbing trade nearly all of the above firms sell more or less goods at retail. The wholesale trade in stoves, tinware, etc., is extensive. One of the oldest dealers in this line is J. R. Butt, who began business in 1871, as a member of the firm of Hawkins, Butt & Co. In 1875 the firm was changed to Butt, De Pue & Co., and so continued until 1884 when the partnership was dissolved. Since that time C. W. De Pue and John Cruze have conducted the business at the old location, while J. R. Butt, with J. P. Young and E. L. Jordan, have established an extensive business under the name of J. R. Butt & Co. Both are enterprising firms, and sell large amounts of goods throughout the Southern States, east of the Mississippi.

The firm of Rolen, Seay & Co. was established in 1877 as Harvey, Rolen & Co., and its members have since changed somewhat, several times. They now are T. M. Rolen, T. S. Seay, C. C. Hill, and J. J. Loyd. They carry a large stock of stoves and house furnishing goods, and have a good trade at both wholesale and retail.

J. M. Greer & Co. are extensive dealers in agricultural implements, machinery, buggies, etc. The business was established in Maryville, Blount County, in 1865, and removed to Knoxville about two years ago.

The firm of H. G. Mead & Co. is also engaged in this line of business. The house was established in 1865 by H. G. Mead, who subsequently formed a copartnership with C. R. Love. Although Mr. Mead died in 1882, the old style of the firm has been preserved, and Mrs. Mead retains an interest in the business.

Three firms are engaged in the wholesale liquor business: J. F. Horne & Co. began business in 1870, and now have a trade throughout the country tributary to Knoxville; they employ two travelling salesmen, and do a $50,000 annual business. The house now conducted by W. C. Perry was established in 1870 by W. A. B. Hall, who continued the business until 1877; he carries a large stock of liquors of all kinds and does a good business. Betterton & Co., began business in 1879, but the house was originally established in 1868; they occupy three entire floors in the McGhee Block on Gay Street, and carry a complete line of the best liquors. The individuals composing the firm are J. N. Betterton and J. H. Whitlow.

The retail trade of Knoxville will compare favorably with that of any other city of its size, both as to the number of the firms and the extent of their business. Of the many enterprising houses, only a few of the best known can be mentioned in these pages. They are H. J. Owens, Young, Williams & Co., Thornburgh & Daniels, Meek & Biddle, McMillan & Treadwell, Mitchell & Payne, J. S. Hall, S. W. Flenniken, P. Hannifin, and A. L. Young, dry goods; J. B. Minnis & Co., C. Rutherford, T. P. McDaniel & Co., S. P. Condon, J. Lichtenwanger, Caldwell & Selden, Caldwell & Thornburgh, James Anderson, Gammon & Larue, S. W. Hall & Co., J. L. Hudiburgh, Jett, Gammon & Co., D. R. Mayo, W. B. Scarborough, J. C. & W. A. Schneider, H. A. Kelly, H. E. Kelly, Bearden & Co., Blaufield and Bro., W. M. Miller, groceries; McCrum & Yeager, Gooding & Shughrue, J. W. Slocum, G. W. Albers, Tompkins Bros., J. A. McCampbell, C. J. Moore & Co., Spence & Co., W. M. Weber, W. J. Worsham, J. D. West and D. H. Zbinden, drugs; Brandau, Kennedy & Co., Huddleston, Smith, Powers & Co., Berwanger Bros., M. Nelson & Co., S. & A. Seaskind, A. Lobenstein and F. Hart, clothiers; Anderson, Cooley & Co., Brown Bros. & Co., Cruze Bros. and J. T. Rowntree & Co.,* hardware; G. W. Adney & Co. and G. R.

---

*While many of these firms sell more or less goods at wholesale, they have been classed in the department in which they are the most prominently identified.

Williams and Bro., stoves and tinware; J. C. Cullen, glass and queensware; Brown, Carter & Huddleston, Epps, McMillan & Co., H. W. Hall & Co., Haynes & McCoy, J. E. Lutz & Co. and Atkins & Brownlee boots and shoes, hats and caps; Ogden Bros. & Co., Ramage & Co. and William & W. E. Williams, books and stationery; H. W. Curtis, Hope Bros. & Co., Moses Greer, Jr., & Co., J. & L. Wenning, jewelry, watches etc.; Steen & Marshall and John A. Gilbert, music and musical instruments; G. W. Akin, Mrs. A. N. Hodge, Mrs. C. F. Rollings, millinery; F. J. Callan, N. Cuquel, G. W. Hand, D. Moore and W. H. Button, merchant tailoring; S. P. Angel, W. Jenkins & Co., C. F. Maskall and W. G. Ware, sewing machines; P. Ritter, J. Blaufield and C. Kohlhase, cigars and tobacco; P. Kern, Bell Bros., I. E. Barry & Co. and M. Taylor, fruits and confections; V. Burger & Son, A. David & Co., J. W. Gaut & Son, Smith & Bondurant, J. Allen Smith & Co., L. C. Matthews and R. Sammon, produce and commission merchants; S. & E. S. Barker, Brooks & Goodall, Cruze Bros., James George, Trent & Toms, T. J. Youmans & Co. and T. Johns, coal; Shepard, Mann & Johnson and S. Newman, undertaking; E. W. Eckardt, A. G. Rhodes, Boyd, Allen & Co. and S. T, Atkin & Co., furniture.

Knoxville is well supplied with first-class hotels, which are liberally patronized. The principal ones are the Hattie House, John C. Flanders, proprietor; Schubert's Hotel, H. Schubert, proprietor; Atkin House, I. N. Scott, manager; and the Lamar House, H. P. Truman & Co., proprietors.

The leading livery men are W. M. Bell & Co., Peyton Carter, J. M. Shetterly & Co., Daniel Cawood, P. A. & T. J. Roberts, Bird & Staub, P. B. Brown and J. H. Atkin.

It is not the purpose of this chapter to enter into an elaborate discussion of the advantages of Knoxville as a manufacturing center. The close proximity of large deposits of valuable iron ore, and the best coal, combined with a central location, render it one of the most desirable sites in the United States for the manufacture and manipulation of iron in all its forms, while an abundance of all kinds of timber adds another most important factor in many branches of industrial enterprise. But an incontestable proof of the advantages of this city for the investment of capital in manufactories is the uniform success of those already established.

The first attempt to manufacture iron and rolling mill products in Knoxville was made by the Confederate authorities during the war. Some machinery which had been confiscated at Loudon, Tenn., was moved to Knoxville and set up, but, owing to the absence of skilled workmen, its operation was not a success. After the Federal occupation of the town another attempt to operate the mill was made by H. S. Chamberlain, a quartermaster in the army, but it, too, was a partial failure. At the close of hostilities, John H. Jones, one of the former owners of the machinery, came to Knoxville, and a company composed of S. T. Atkin, L. C. Shepard, H. S. Chamberlain and John H. Jones was formed to put the mill into operation. At about that time, in April 1866, D. and J. Richards and D. Thomas, experienced iron men from Pennsylvania, purchased the interest of Messrs. Atkin and Shepard. Soon after, Mr. Jones sold out to W. J. Richards and T. D. Lewis, also men of extensive experience in the iron business. The company was then reorganized under the name of Chamberlain, Richards & Co. They at first labored under many disadvantages, as raw material was obtained with considerable difficulty. In the winter season coal was brought by boat from Emory Gap, but during the summer it was hauled by wagons from Winter's gap at a cost of 50 cents per bushel. In 1867, under the direction of D. Thomas, a mine at Coal Creek was opened, and in the fall of that year the first car-load of coal was shipped over the Knoxville & Ohio Railroad. Soon a foundry was added to the rolling mill, and other improvements made. At this time the present president of the company was a bookkeeper for the firm. In 1869 the company was incorporated under the name of the Knoxville Iron Company, with a capital stock of $300,000, and the capacity of its works was greatly increased. The plant now covers an area of about three acres, and consists of three mills; an eighteen-inch nail-mill, a ten-inch bar-mill and an eight-inch guide-mill, containing altogether nine single puddling furnaces, three heating furnaces, forty nail machines and four trains of rolls. The product consists of merchant bar, nails, railroad, car and miscellaneous forgings, and light T and street rails, the annual capacity being 12,000 tons, with a value of about $500,000. To run the works, thirteen engines, with an aggregate of 800 horse-power, are required, and constant employment is given to about 300 men, to whom about $10,000 is paid monthly. The company are also largely engaged in the mining of coal, and have extensive mines at Coal Creek on the Knoxville & Ohio Railroad, about thirty miles north of the city. They have a capacity of 500 tons of coal daily, and besides supplying the rolling mills, furnish large quantities to railroads and gas companies in Tennessee and adjoining States.

The officers of the company are W. R. Tuttle, president; W. S. Mead, secretary and treasurer, and George L. Reis, general manager.

In 1867 Clark, Quaife & Co. erected a small foundry for the manufacture of stoves, hollow ware, etc. Later they began making car wheels, and this branch of the business proving a success, an incorporated company, with a capital stock of $47,000, was formed in 1872, with A. L. Maxwell as president, and Harvey Clark, secretary. Thirty thousand acres of iron land in Carter County was purchased, upon which a cold blast charcoal furnace was erected for the purpose of supplying the shops with iron. The brown hematite ore found on this land is among the best in the country, and a furnace which is still standing was erected there very early in this century. Under the management of Mr. Maxwell, which continued until 1881, the business steadily increased, and the Knoxville Car Wheel Company became known throughout the South for the excellence of its products. In 1881 the company was reorganized with a capital stock of $107,000, and since that time the works have been considerably enlarged. A well equipped machine shop, boiler shop, and a foundry for making all kinds of soft castings have been added. Fifty hands are employed in the shops, and as many more at the furnace. The capacity of the car shops is 125 wheels and of the furnace ten tons daily. The present officers of the company are C. H. Brown, president, and D. A. Carpenter, secretary and treasurer.

Another successful and important manufacturing establishment of Knoxville is operated by the Southern Car Company, which was organized June 1, 1881, with a capital stock of $80,000. Their line of operations consists of the manufacture of freight and mining cars of all descriptions. They employ from 125 to 150 men, and turn out from six to eight cars per day. The works are located just west of the city limits on the E. T. V. & G. R. R., and cover an area of about ten acres.

The Knoxville Foundry and Machine Shops were established in 1865 by J. W. North & Co., who continued the business until 1870, when it was transferred to the firm of Rogan & Co., composed of L. H. Rogan, William McAfferty and William De Groat. In 1874 J. B. Kelly became a partner, and during the ensuing years the business was conducted under the name of Rogan, Kelly & Co. In 1878 a stock company with a capital of $25,000 was organized, with Peter Staub as president, J. B. Kelly, secretary, and L. H. Rogan, manager. The shops were then transferred from Broad Street to their present location, where new buildings were erected. Since that time the business has steadily increased, until now it represents an invested capital of $100,000. The present officers of the company are Peter Staub, president; J. B. Kelley, general manager and secretary, and Charles Fouche, treasurer.

The Clark Foundry and Machine Company was organized in 1881, with H. W. Clark, president, and Simpson Cornick, secretary and treasurer. The enterprise has been highly successful, and has been increased each year, until now over thirty workmen are constantly employed. They make a specialty of mill machinery, but manufacture all kinds of castings and machines.

The Knoxville Brass and Iron Foundry, owned and operated by Stamps & Mehaffy; the wrought iron fence manufactory of H. O. Nelson, and the machine shop of Dempster & Co. are also establishments of some importance, employing from three to ten men each.

The milling interests of Knoxville have recently been greatly extended by the erection of a mammoth mill, with a capacity of 150 barrels of flour per day. It is owned by the Knoxville City Mills Company, and was completed in January, 1885. It is equipped with the latest improved machinery for the manufacture of the finest grade of flour, and its products find a ready market in all parts of Alabama, Georgia, Tennessee and North Carolina. An elevator with a capacity of 50,000 bushels was erected with the mill, but was destroyed by fire in June, 1886. It will soon be replaced by another with a capacity of 75,000 bushels. The company was incorporated in 1884 with a capital stock of $30,000, which has since been increased to $50,000. The officers are J. Allen Smith, president, and Charlton Karnes, secretary and treasurer.

Another excellent flouring-mill has been built on First Creek, a short distance below the site of Scott's old mill. It is owned and operated by Peters, Jones & Co. The Trio mills owned by Scott, Dempster & Co. are also still in operation. The mill at the crossing of Main Street on First Creek after undergoing several transformations, and passing through the hands of many successive owners, is now operated by the Champion Manufacturing Company who use it to grind meal and mill feed. Recently mills of this character have been erected by the Knoxville Cooked Feed Company, and T. P. McDaniels & Co.

The manufacture of furniture forms one of the most important industries of Knoxville, but it is still in its infancy. It is doubtful if any city in America affords greater advantages to this branch of industrial enterprise, and the capital now employed could be multiplied many times without reaching the limit of profitable investment. Of the firms now engaged in this business, that of Boyd & Caswell is one of the oldest. The enterprise was established in 1873 by Howe Bros., who continued it for about three years, when they were succeeded by William Caswell & Co. In 1880 S. B. Boyd, the proprietor of a carpet store, consolidated his business with that of the company, and an extensive retail house furnishing store was established in connection with the factory. In August, 1886, the partnership was dissolved, Mr. Caswell retaining the manufactory, and Mr. Boyd the sales department. The latter has associated with himself John M. Allen, R. J. Stevenson and S. B. Boyd, Jr., under the firm name of Boyd, Allen & Co..

Mr. Caswell employs about forty men, and makes a specialty of fine furniture, parlor suits, and bedroom sets. S. T. Atkins & Co. began business in 1876, and now employ about thirty-five men in the manufacture of all grades of furniture. They sell their goods almost exclusively at retail and to the city trade. They also operate a saw mill with a capacity of 10,000 feet per day, and cut all of their own lumber.

In 1882 the Knoxville Furniture Company was organized with a capital stock of $50,000. The officers are T. R. Price, president; H. S. Mizner, treasurer, and A. J. Price, superintendent. They obtain their material from mills on the Clinch River, and manufacture a medium grade of furniture which they sell at wholesale in all of the States east of the Mississippi and south of the Ohio. Schaad & Rotach is the style of a firm which began business in June 1885, they make a specialty of the finer grades of furniture. They buy their lumber from mills in the vicinity of Knoxville, but the marble which they use is obtained from their own quarry, situated about five miles west of the city, on the Clinton pike.

Of the other wood-working establishments, that of the Standard Handle Company is one of the most extensive. The company was incorporated in 1881 with a capital stock of $60,000. The officers are Edward Nicoll, president; F. J. Leland, vice-president, and C. M. Woodbury, secretary and treasurer. They use only hickory timber, and manufacture all kinds of handles.

The Barker Manufacturing Company are extensively engaged in the manufacture of wooden-ware and handles. The business was established in June, 1883, by J. H. and F. Barker. The officers of the present company are F. Barker, president; H. N. Saxton, Jr., secretray, and J. H. Barker, treasurer. The Knoxville Box and Keg Company was established in 1872 by D. R. Samuel, who, in 1880, admitted his son, W. B. Samuel, into partnership. Their line of manufacture embraces packing boxes of all kinds, kegs, wagon felloes and wood specialties and novelties.

In the manufacture of saddlery and harness Knoxville rivals any other city of its size in the country. The firm of Oates, White & Co., consisting of E. T. Oates, J. C. White and Samuel W. Graves, was established in 1877. They have a large capital invested in the business, and use only the most improved machinery and appliances. They employ about forty workmen in the various departments, and manufacture harness, saddlery and collars. Their products, together with a full line of saddlery hardware, they sell at wholesale throughout the Southern States.

In 1867 Maj. Thomas O'Conner and James O'Conner established the business now conducted by James O'Conner & Co. It was on a very small scale at first, but it has grown steadily until it has reached its present large proportion. They now employ about sixty-five men in the manufactory, and distribute their goods throughout the Southern States, east of the Mississippi.

Other firms and individuals engaged in this line of manufacture, but with somewhat limited capital, are S. Van Gilder & Co., D. M. Haynes & Bro., J. M. McAffrey and H. L. Karnes.

The lumber business of Knoxville and Knox County is increasing more rapidly than any other branch of industry, but its development is by no means complete. Large tracts of the finest timber line the banks of the Holston and French Broad and their tributaries, and these streams with the Tennessee River, during six months in the year, afford every facility for the rafting of logs. One of the largest mills now in operation is owned by D. M. Rose & Co. who began business in Sevier County in 1876. In 1880 they removed to Knoxville, and erected a small mill on the south side of the river. Since that time their business has constantly increased, and they now have a capacity of 50,000 feet of lumber per day.

The Scottish Carolina Timber & Land Company, with a capital stock of $1,000,000, has recently completed a mill with a capacity of 50,000 feet per day. It is located on the river, a short distance below the Knoxville & Augusta Railroad bridge, where they contemplate building a boom at a cost of $40,000. They own large tracts of timber land in upper East Tennessee.

Mills with a capacity of 5,000 to 10,000 feet per day are also operated by S. T. Atkin & Co., L. E. Craig and Burr & Terry, while many small mills are distributed throughout the county. It has been estimated that during 1886 there were cut in Knox County 5,000,000 feet of lumber, and that in 1887 this amount will be fully doubled.

Of the planing mills and sash and door factories, the most extensive is that of Burr & Terry. It was established in 1867 by Richardson & Burr who were succeeded in 1869 by the firm of Richardson, Burr & Terry. Mr. Richardson died the following year and the business has since been conducted by the present firm. They have a large capital invested, and employ about twenty-five men.

The firm of Stephenson & Getaz began business in 1882. Their mill is equipped with all the latest improvements in machinery and appliances, and about thirty men are employed in the manufacture of all kinds of building material.

L. E. Craig engaged in this line of manufacture in 1879 at the mouth of First Creek, where he has since continued. He employs twelve men, and does an extensive business. His mill is operated by water power.

The manufacture of carriages, buggies and other vehicles, is becoming an important branch of industry in Knoxville. The firm most extensively engaged in this business is that of Post, Simmons & Co., composed of S. T. Post, C. N. Simmons and F. H. Post. The enterprise was established in 1870 by S. T. Post & Son, who conducted it with signal success until 1882, when the present firm was formed. They employ about twenty men and make a specialty of heavy wagons. They are now erecting a new factory with the intention of doubling their capacity.

The Knoxville Buggy Works were established in March, 1885 by C. Geiger under the management of James A. Nisonger. They manufacture carriages, buggies and light wagons, for the local trade. An extension of the shops is now being made and when completed about twenty-five men will be employed. The present proprietors are T. T. Goodall & Co.

The shops now owned and operated by T. C. Eldridge, was established in 1872 upon a comparatively small scale, but during the past eight years under the present management, the facilities have been greatly increased. From ten to fifteen workmen are constantly employed, turning out about 100 vehicles annually, Sheridan & Quincy, former employes of Post, Simmons & Co., have recently engaged in this line of manufacture.

After the disappearance of the primitive mills no attempt was made to manufacture cotton or woolen goods until within the past ten years. In 1877 the Knoxville Woolen Mills Company was organized with a capital stock of $180,000, and commenced the operations of a mill at Sanfordville, in McMinn County. From the first the undertaking proved a success, and in 1884 the company determined to increase their facilities by erecting new buildings. With this object in view they increased the capital stock to $200,000, purchased thirteen acres of land adjoining the city limits, and erected one of the most convenient and best appointed woolen-mills in the country. The new mill was completed and put into operation in 1885. It is a substantial brick structure, 50x400 feet, and three stories high, and is equipped with seven sets of cards and 193 looms. It employs about 150 hands. The product consists exclusively of all wool jeans. The officers of the company are E. J. Sanford, president, and R. P. Gettys, secretary, treasurer and general manager.

In November, 1885, an incorporated company with a capital stock of $150,000 completed the erection of a large cotton-mill 78x210 feet, two stories high, and in March, 1886, between 5,000 and 6,000 spindles and 176 looms were put into operation. The mill is fitted up with the best machinery made, and in the spinning department a new process not in use in any other mill is employed, by means of which a great saving in time, power and labor is effected. The product of this mill consists entirely of brown sheetings of grade suited to both the domestic and foreign trades. At present about twenty-five bales of cotton are used per week, but only one-half of the mill is occupied, and the doubling of its capacity is now under contemplation. The mill is under the management of Mr. C. J. Sweet, a man of long experience in the manufacture of cotton, having acted for many years as superintendent and agent of some of the largest mills in New England. He is assisted by his sons, also experienced cotton manufacturers.

The Knoxville Ice Company is an enterprise of great importance to the city. The business was inaugurated in 1876 by J. C. Mustard, on a small scale as an experiment, and such was the success of the venture that in 1881 the present company was formed with a capital stock of $40,000. Extensive improvements were at once made, new buildings erected and the most improved machinery supplied. The water used for the manufacture of ice is obtained from a large spring, and is distilled before freezing. The works now have a capacity of thirty tons per day, and the trade of the company extends throughout East Tennessee. The officers of the corporation are Peter Kern, president; Ignas Fanz, secretary and treasurer, and T. D. Lewis, manager.

The quarrying and manipulation of marble has become one of the most important industries of Knoxville and Knox County, but it is of such recent origin that it may be said to be in a transition state, and to give a satisfactory account of the many companies which have been organized for the prosecution of the business is impossible. Worked systematically by men of experience and sufficient capital quarries within easy reach of transportation yield rich returns, but in the hands of inexperienced persons with small capital, the business affords many opportunities for failure.

One of the most successful firms engaged in quarrying marble is that of J. J. Craig & Co. Their business was established in 1880 by Col. J. J. Craig, who has been very largely instrumental in developing the resources of the county in this especial department of industry. They now operate four quarries, five miles northwest of Knoxville, furnishing employment to about fifty hands. Recently the members of this firm organized the Great Southern Marble Company with the following officers; John J. Craig, president; John J. Craig, Jr., secretary and treasurer; W. B. McMullen, general manager, and J. M. Edington, superintendent of quarries.

The Knoxville Marble Company is the oldest company now in the business, having been organized on July 11, 1873. The members of the company at that time were William Patrick, president; George W. Ross, secretary and treasurer; James Patrick, and John H. Holman. They purchased the old government quarry at the forks of the French Broad and Holston, and have since continued to operate it. The marble obtained from their quarries is conceded to be the soundest in East Tennessee, and for building purposes it is unsurpassed. When polished it presents a handsome appearance, and it is used largely for mantels and decorating purposes. They work from fifty to seventy-five hands, run four steam-drills and two saw mills with two gangs of saws each, and turn out products to the value of over $100,000 yearly. They own sixty-five acres of land, and operate three quarries. They ship to all the large cities in this country, and are now engaged in filling an order for a European market. Since January, 1886, the officers of the company and sole proprietors of the business have been John M. Ross, president, and George W. Ross, secretary and treasurer.

The Phœnix Marble Company was incorporated in 1885 with a capital stock of $20,000. They operate quarries in Hawkins County, and have a mill with three gangs of saws in Knoxville. The officers of the company are John P. Beach, president, and Charles Pitman, secretary and treasurer. Mr. Beach is also the senior member of the firm of Beach & Co., who began business in 1880. They work a quarry two and one-half miles east of Knoxville, where they employ about twelve hands. They also operate a mill, in which fifteen hands are employed in cutting and polishing marble for furniture, and inside decoration. The largest mill of this kind in Tennessee was erected in 1886 by W..H. Evans & Son, who are extensively engaged in the business in Baltimore, and who built a small mill and opened a quarry in Hawkins County in 1881. Their mill in Knoxville contains twelve gangs of saws, and has a capacity of 1,800 feet of finished marble per day, furnishing employment to 160 men. During 1887 the capacity of the mill will be more than doubled.

The coal business in so far as Knoxville is concerned has been developed during the past twenty years, although a company was organized for the purpose of dealing in coal as early as 1855. It was known as the Knoxville Coal Company, and the members were John S. Moffett, John Shields, M. W. Williams and A. L. Maxwell. A small steamboat called the "Holston" was purchased, and coal was brought from points on the river below, but the demand for it was so limited that the company soon suspended operations.

In May, 1858, the Cumberland Mountain Coal & Land Company was organized with a capital stock of $1,200,000. The officers and members were G. B. Lamar, president; Thomas H. Calloway, treasurer, and — Jackson, secretary; Campbell Wallace, Thomas C. Lyons, C. M. McGhee, Robert Morrow, Euclid Waterhouse, A. L. Maxwell, M. B. Prichard and Samuel Congdon. In 1867 the company was reorganized as the East Tennessee Iron & Coal Company, with Charles M. McGhee, president. A large tract of land in Campbell, Scott and Anderson Counties, had been previously purchased, but owing to the manner in which grants had been issued by the Government, where conflict of title existed, and several years have been spent in settling these claims. The company, now own 50,000 acres of the finest, and most accessible coal land in East Tennessee, extending along the line of the Knoxville & Ohio Railroad, for thirteen miles, and the work of developing mines will be begun during 1887. Since 1882 A. L. Maxwell has been the president of the company.

In 1868 the Coal Creek Mining & Manufacturing Company was organized, with Henry S. Wiley as president, and Charles H. Berkley, secretary. The capital stock is $2,500,000, of which about three-fourths is held in New York. They own one of the finest bodies of mining lands in the world. The tract is thirty miles in extent, and embraces 240,000 acres. They also own a large interest in about 70,000 acres more. They operate no mines themselves but lease to other companies. The following are the present officers: E. J. Sanford, president; E. R. Chapman, of New York, secretary and assistant treasurer; and W. P. Chamberlin, treasurer and assistant secretary. The Poplar Creek Coal & Iron Company with a capital stock of $1,000,000, also owns a large tract of land which they lease to other companies. The officers are E. R. Chapman, president, and T. H. Heald, secretary and treasurer. The Wheeler Coal & Iron Company, with a capital stock of $375,000, has the same officers. It was organized about 1870, and owns 4,400 acres of land, on the Knoxville & Ohio Railroad, about thirty-five miles from Knoxville. A third company, with the same officers, is known as the Wyley Coal Company. It has a capital stock of $40,000

The Coal Creek Mining Company was organized in 1880, with a capital stock of $150,000. They operate four mines having an aggregate annual out-put of 120,000 tons, and employing 400 men. The officers are T. H. Heald, president, and E. F. Wyley, secretary and treasurer.

The Coal Creek Coal Company was organized in 1868, by M. C. and

C. C. Wilcox, E. A. Reed, P. A. Maniner, S. S. Tuttle and E. C. Camp. They own land on Coal Creek, and operate a mine having an out-put of about 75,000 tons yearly. The officers now are E. C. Camp, president, and Henry Camp, manager.

The Standard Coal Company, organized in 1882 with capital stock of $100,000, operates a mine at Newcomb, from which is shipped annually about 60,000 tons. The officers of the company are W. W. Woodruff, president, and E. E. McCroskey, secretary and treasurer.

The East Tennessee Coal Company was incorporated in 1876 and began operations at Coal Creek. They now own 900 acres of land at Jellico upon which their mines are located. They have a capacity of 400 tons per day, and ship large quantities to Alabama, North and South Carolina, Georgia, Kentucky and throughout Tennessee. The officers are E. J. Davis, president, and B. A. Jenkins, secretary and treasurer.

After coal, iron and marble, zinc is the next most abundant and valuable mineral found in East Tennessee. The first works for the manufacture of zinc oxide were erected at Mossy Creek in 1872. Four years later mines were opened and operations begun on an extensive scale in Union County, and in 1881 spelter works were completed at Clinton. In 1883 these works were purchased by the Edes, Mixter & Heald Zinc Company, who have since continued to operate them. The ore is obtained from mines on Straight Creek, and from Mossy Creek. The company has a capital stock of $100,000 and ships annually about 1,250,000 pounds of spelter. The secretary and manager is Maj. T. H. Heald, of Knoxville. The other members of the firm reside at Plymouth, Mass.

Of the present banking institutions of Knoxville the People's Bank is the oldest. It was established in 1865 by C. M. McGhee, John R. Branner, Thomas H. Calloway and J. R. Mitchell under the firm name of J. R. Mitchell & Co. In May, 1866, it was incorporated under its present name with a capital stock of $35,000, C. M. McGhee becoming president and J. R. Mitchell, cashier. This bank, controlled as it has been by some of the wealthiest and most prominent business men of the city, has always enjoyed the confidence of commercial circles. The present officers are J. R. Mitchell, president, and F. A. Moses, cashier.

In 1873 the East Tennessee National Bank was organized as the successor of the First National Bank, of Knoxville, established soon after the war. The capital stock is $100,000, while the surplus and individual profits amount to nearly $90,000. The annual discounts exceed $500,000, and the deposits average over $600,000. Its directors are R. C. Jackson, C. M. McGhee, R. S. Payne, W. W. Woodroff, E. J. Sanford, S. B. Boyd, C. M. McClung, Daniel Briscoe and James M. Meek,

The president is R. S. Payne; vice-president, E. J. Sanford, and cashier, F. L. Fisher.

The Mechanics National Bank, organized in March, 1882, also has a capital stock of $100,000. It is under able management and has been remarkably successful. Its surplus now amounts to $51,000 and its deposits average over $400,000, while its exchange account with its bank in New York in 1886 amounted to $2,500,000. The directors are W. P. Washburn, S. T. Harris, M. L. Ross, H. H. Ingersoll, S. B. Luttrell, S. P. Evans, J. W. Borches, J. C. Luttrell and J. T. McTeer. S. B. Luttrell is president; M. L. Ross, vice-president and Sam House, cashier.

The Merchants Bank is a private institution of high standing, owned by John S. Van Gilder, who has been engaged in the business for over twenty years.

Probably no city of its size is better represented in the line of fire insurance companies than Knoxville. The oldest is known as the Knoxville Fire Insurance Company; it was organized in 1879 with a capital stock of $100,000. It is under able management and has been successful from the beginning. On January 1, 1886, the reserve fund amounted to $26,674.98, and the net surplus to $26,993.10, a gain in the net surplus, during 1885, of $5,798.80. The company does a general fire insurance business throughout the State, and has reliable agents in the leading commercial centers. The directors of the company are as substantial a body of men as could be selected from the successful business men of the city. They are D. A. Carpenter, S. B. Luttrell, C. M. McGhee, Joseph T. McTeer, F. W. Taylor, Sr., R. C. Jackson, W. P. Washburn, W. W. Woodruff, James M. Meek, C. M. McClung and M. L. Ross. The president of the company is D. A. Carpenter; vice-president, W. W. Woodruff, and secretary and treasurer, W. H. Simmonds.

A new company, known as the Protection Fire Insurance Company, was incorporated under the same management in 1885, and now has assets amounting to $108,093.84.

The East Tennessee Insurance Company began business on May 1, 1885, with a capital stock of $150,000, and already has a surplus fund amounting to about $35,000. The company is ably and conservatively managed, and commands the entire confidence of the public. The members of the company are C. J. McClung, president; B. R. Strong, vice-president; C. Powell, secretary; P. Dickinson, F. L. Fisher and C. E. Luckey.

The Island Home Insurance Company was recently organized, with the same officers and directors, and incorporated with a capital stock of $200,000.

At what time the first Masonic lodge in Knoxville was organized could not be ascertained, as all old records pertaining to it had been destroyed. It was known as Mount Labanus Lodge, and was established at a very early period in the history of the town. Of the lodges now in existence, the oldest is Master's Lodge, No. 244, the records of which have also been destroyed.

Maxwell Lodge, No. 433, was organized in November, 1871, with L. H. Rogan as W. M. It has since been fairly prosperous and now has a membership of about forty.

Oriental Lodge, No. 453, was organized under a dispensation granted November 10, 1873, with N. S. Woodward as W. M., J. V. Fulkerson, S. W. and A. Caldwell, J. W. It contains some of the best members of the fraternity in the State, and is in a highly prosperous condition.

Pearl Chapter, No. 24, R. A. M., was organized in 1841, with the Most Eminent James W. Paxton, as H. P. It has worked continuously to the present time with the exception of a few months during the civil war. The present H. P. is Arch. Ferguson. The present membership is fifty-six.

Couer de Leon Commandery, No. 9, K. T., was organized on May 5, 1868, under a dispensation granted by R. E. Sir John Frizzell, Grand Commander of Tennessee, with the following officers: John W. Paxton, E. C.; William Morrow, G.; A. N. Maxwell, C. G.; W. H. Lillard, P.; H. M. Aiken, S. W.; S. B. Dow, J. W.; Spencer Munson, Rec.; J. A. Mabry, Treas.; U. A. Rouser, Standard Bearer; William Rule, Sword Bearer; H. C. Hawkins, W. and John W. Cruze, S. At the burning of the Masonic Hall, the Commandry lost about $2,000 worth of property. It now has a membership of seventy, with S. B. Dow as E. C.

Knoxville Consistory, No. 10, S. P. R. S., under the Peckham Cerneau jurisdiction, was instituted on July 7, 1884, with H. H. Ingersoll, Thirty-third degree, as C. C. Among the other officers are A. J. Albers, Thirty-second degree; R. H. Sansom, Thirty-second degree; A. Gredig, Thirty-second degree; J. H. Keeling, Thirty-second degree; J. L. Curtis, Thirty-second degree; G. W. Albers, Thirty-third degree; W. A. Galbraith, Thirty-second degree; E. E. McCroskey, Thirty-second degree; John E. Clyman, Thirty-second degree; S. G. Bowman, Thirty-second degree; J. H. Doughty, Thirty-second degree, and J. W. Cruze, Thirty-second degree.

Tennessee Lodge, No. 4, I. O. O. F., was organized on March 20, 1848, with the following charter members: A. A. Barnes, A. R. Crozier, P. M. McClung, William M. Churchwell, and James Rodgers. The lodge has since been successfully maintained and now has a membership of sixty-three with J. R. McBath as Noble Grand.

Knoxville Lodge, No. 138, was organized on November 23, 1869. The charter members were James M. McAffry, L. C. Shepard, E. G. McClanahan, J. D. J. Lewis, W. H. Parker and J. C. Ristine. The present membership is twenty-three. J. L. Culverhouse is Noble Grand.

Golden Rule Lodge, No. 177, was instituted on July 2, 1874, with R. Y. Hayes, G. B. Burlson, J. B. Campbell, J. E. Newman, W. R. Stephenson, W. C. Putnam, George W. Roth, P. F. Jenkins and E. B. Mann as charter members. The present membership is fifty-three.

Knoxville Encampment, No. 11, was organized soon after the institution of Tennessee Lodge, with the following members: James A. Deery, A. A. Barnes, W. M. Churchwell, William Hunt, Daniel Lyons, William Lyons and M. D. Bearden.

Teutonia Lodge, No. 141, K. of H., was organized August 20, 1875, with about eighteen members. It is now in a prosperous condition, and has a membership of 149, with J. W. Benziger as Dictator. L. A. Gratz, a member of this lodge is the present Supreme Dictator.

Relief Lodge was organized in 1876, and now has but a small membership.

Fidelity Lodge, No. 9, A. O. U. W., was organized in August, 1876, with John Burks as Past Master Workman, and Fred Esperandieu, Master Workman. Soon after the organization of this lodge Phœnix Lodge, No. 14, was instituted with a membership of about fifty-three. A few months later Peabody Lodge, No. 44, was established. These two lodges existed as separate bodies until December, 1886, when they were united under the name of the former.

Pioneer Council, No. 34, A. L. of H., was organized September 10, 1879, with a small membership which rapidly increased, and has since averaged about one hundred and twenty-five.

Knoxville Council, No. 110, R. A., was instituted in June, 1878, with L. A. Gratz as Past Regent, A. L. Maxwell, Regent, and Julius Ochs, secretary. Its original membership of twenty-five has increased to sixty-eight.

Peace Commandery, No. 1, U. O. of G. C., was organized on July 11, 1876,* a short time after the incorporation of the Supreme Commandery. Hope Commandery, No 2 was instituted August 16, 1876, but did not receive its charter until the following November, at which time the members numbered forty-one.

Ed. Maynard Post, No. 14, G. A. R., was organized December 23, 1883, with the following members: A. S. Prosser, L. A. Gratz, W. R. Carter, W. J. Ramage, W. W. Dunn, W. C. Brandon, Ignaz Fanz, C. H. Brown,

---
*See page 308.

W. R. Tuttle, P. D. Roady, S. J. Todd, B. Goodhart, and George L. Maloney. The first Commander was A. S. Prosser who was succeeded by L. A. Gratz. The present officers are W. J. Ramage, C.; W. W. Dunn, S. V. C.; Ignaz Fanz, J. V. C.; L. Harvey, Adjt.; W. A. Gage, O. D.; J. R. Galyon, O. G.; Thomas D. Lewis, Chaplain; J. W. Stewart, Surgeon; L. W. Schirman, Q. M.

Felix K. Zollicoffer Camp, Confederate Veterans, was organized December 10, 1885, with one hundred and thirty-five members, and for the following admirable purposes; "The object shall be to perpetuate the memories of our fallen comrades, and to minister so far as practicable to the wants of those who were permanently disabled in the service, to preserve and maintain that sentiment of fraternity born of the hardships and dangers shared in the march, the bivouac and the battle ground. It is proposed not to prolong the animosities engendered by the war, but to extend to our late adversaries on every fitting occasion, courtesies which, in our case, a common citizenship demands at our hands. We propose to avoid everything which partakes of partisanship in religion and politics, but at the same time we will lend our aid to the maintenance of law and the preservation of order." The present membership of the camp is about one hundred and sixty-five. Alexander Allison is Commander and P. B. Shepherd, First Lieutenant Commander.

The medical profession has always been ably represented in Knoxville. In the *Gazette* of April 20, 1794, Dr. Thomas McCombs informs the public that he intends to remove and locate in Knoxville about May 15, where he proposes to enter upon the practice of medicine. He hopes his long studies and experience under the most eminent physicians in the Atlantic States, and his attention to his profession will insure him the patronage of the public. During the same year Dr. Robert Johnson, also advertises that he has located in Knoxville. Of those now remembered Dr. Joseph C. Strong was the earliest. He was finely educated, and was an excellent physician. He continued to practice until his death, which occured about 1844. Dr. James King, who died in 1838, was a contemporary of Dr. Strong. Dr. Donald McIntosh began practice at a little later date. Others who were prominent previous to the war were Francis A. Ramsey, William J. and Leonidas Baker, Joseph W. and John Paxton, R. O. Currey, P. Fatio, J. Woodward, James Rodgers and John M. Boyd, the last two of whom are still living. Dr. J. G. M. Ramsey, who had been a pupil of Dr. Strong, opened an office in Knoxville in 1820, but two years later removed to the Forks, where he continued until the war. On May 7, 1845, a number of medical practitioners met in convention at Knoxville, and organized the Medical Society of East Tennessee. Only six counties were represented at this time, but the society increased, annual meetings were held, and branches were organized in several counties. The Knox County society was incorporated in 1856 with the following members: William J. Baker, James Rodgers, William Rodgers, J. Morman, Joseph W. Paxton, John Paxton, Richard O. Currey, C. W. Crozier, James Sawyers and others. This section has been maintained up to the present time, although the East Tennessee society was recently disbanded. In April, 1852, the first members of a quarterly, called the "East Tennessee Record of Medicine and Surgery," edited by Frank A. Ramsey, appeared. It was continued but one year. In January, 1855, "The Southern Journal of the Medical and Physical Sciences," a monthly edited by R. O. Currey, was removed from Nashville to Knoxville, and for a time was published by Kinsloe & Rice. It was subsequently returned to Nashville.

The history of the press in Knoxville previous to the civil war is given in another chapter. The two leading dailies of the present time, the *Tribune* and *Journal* are the lineal descendants of the *Knoxville Register* and *Knoxville Whig*, respectively. At the close of the war the *Register* was revived under the name of the *Messenger of Peace*, by M. J. Hughes, and was the first Democratic newspaper published in East Tennessee, after the close of hostilities. On June 29, 1867, the initial number of the *Knoxville Daily Free Press*, a six-column morning paper, was issued by John M. Fleming & Co. Four months later, Ramage & Co. founded the *Knoxville Daily Herald*, also a morning paper, the same size as the *Free Press*. Ramage & Co. then purchased the *Messenger of Peace*, and published it under the name of the *Knoxville Messenger*, as the weekly edition of the *Herald*. January 7, 1868, the *Daily Free Press* and *Herald* were consolidated as the *Daily Press and Herald*, and the weekly *Free Press* and the *Messenger* as the *Press and Messenger*. These papers were then published by Ramage & Co., and edited by John M. Fleming. On March 18, 1876, Mr. Fleming having severed his connection with the *Press and Herald*, formed a partnership with Samuel McKinney, and established the *Knoxville Daily Tribune*, of which the former became editor-in-chief. One week later they purchased the *Press and Herald* and merged it into the *Tribune*, while at the same time the *Weekly Tribune* took the place of the *Press and Messenger*. On March 14, 1877, the *Tribune* was sold to the Tribune Publishing Company, composed of Nashville and Knoxville capitalists. At about the same time the *Evening Age*, which had been established a short time before by C. W. Charlton, was purchased, and on the 31st of March the paper opened as the *Tribune and Age*. Soon after the old name of the *Tribune* was resumed, and John M. Fleming again became the editor. On February 2, 1878, the paper was purchased by F. M. Paul, who continued its publication until October 13, 1879, when he sold it to Moses White and Frank A. Moses, the former being the editor and the latter business manager. On August 27, 1880, it was purchased by Bean, Summers & Wallace. James W. Wallace and Alexander Summers became the editors and Joseph H. Bean, business manager. In February, 1886, Wallace received a government appointment, and since that time Summers has had entire editorial control. When the present proprietors purchased the *Tribune*, it was a seven-column folio, and the office was poorly equipped. They at once began to improve it, and it is said to have been the first newspaper in Tennessee to banish advertisements from its first page. They then purchased the *Evening Dispatch*, and enlarged the Sunday edition of the *Tribune* to thirty-two columns. The next improvement was to enlarge the regular daily edition to the same size. In 1884 a costly new press was bought, and the weekly *Tribune* enlarged to an eight-page, fifty-six column paper. In 1886 additional printing machinery and appliances were purchased, and the Sunday edition was enlarged to the same size as the weekly. The *Tribune* is under the management of enterprising and progressive men, and is ably edited. The weekly edition is probably the most widely circulated and influential newspaper in East Tennessee.

In November, 1863, W. G. Brownlow resumed the publication of the *Knoxville Whig*, adding to its title *and Rebel Ventilator*. It represented the extreme faction of the Republican party of Tennessee as it existed for the first few years after the war. Although Gov. Brownlow's immediate supervision of the paper ceased upon his election to office, he continued to direct its policy. In 1870 the *Chronicle*, daily and weekly, was established by William Rule and H. C. Tarwater, and in 1875 the *Whig* and the weekly *Chronicle* were consolidated under the name of the *Whig and Chronicle*. In 1879 L. C. Houk and H. R. Gibson founded the *Weekly Republican*, which continued until 1882, when an incorporated company purchased the *Chronicle* and the *Republican*, changing the name of the weekly edition to the *Republican Chronicle*.

In 1885 William Rule and ——— Marfield established the *Journal*, daily and weekly, and in 1886 they purchased the *Chronicle*, and merged it into the *Journal*. This paper represents the best and most liberal element of the Republican party, and Mr. Rule, the editor, is recognized as one of the ablest journalists in the South.

In December, 1886, the *Sentinel*, an evening daily, was established by the Sentinel Publishing Company. It is Democratic in politics, and has a large and increasing circulation. This completes the list of daily papers. In 1885 J. H. Atkins began the publication of a Sunday paper, a lively Republican sheet called the *Topic*, which has since been changed to the *Times*.

Knoxville was incorporated by an act of the Legislature passed October 27, 1815, and the first meeting of the board of aldermen was held at the courthouse on the 13th of the following January. The members were Thomas McCorry, Rufus Morgan, James Park, Thomas Humes, James Dardis and John McCullen. Anderson Hutchinson was appointed recorder, David Nelson, high constable, and John McCullen, treasurer. Thomas Emmerson was the mayor. A tax of 25 cents on $100, $1 on each poll, and $5 on merchants was levied for corporation purposes. At the next meeting Thomas Humes, Rufus Morgan and John McCullen were appointed to build a market-house on Market Square, between Prince and Crooked Streets. In June, 1817, $340 was appropriated for the improvement of the streets, $120 to be expended on Cumberland, $80 on State, and $60 on Water Streets. In February, 1822, a fire company was organized with Calvin Morgan as captain and John Boyd, Carey Thatcher, David Campbell and William Park, lieutenants. An ordinance passed at the same time required every owner of a dwelling, store or office to provide a leather bucket. At the next meeting Thomas Aiken and James Hickey were appointed night watchmen, whose duty it was to patrol the streets and to call the hour and the state of the weather at the end of each hour. In January, 1826, the town was divided into three wards, the First Ward to embrace all east of State Street, the Second all between State and Prince Streets, and the Third all west of Prince Street.

Nothing occurred of any especial interest in the transactions of the board until in April, 1852, when it was decided to submit to a vote of the people a proposition to subscribe $50,000 to the East Tennessee & Virginia Railroad. The proposition was carried by a vote of fifty-nine to twenty-six, but, on account of the conditions upon which the subscription was tendered, the railroad company refused to accept it. On the 26th of March, 1853, a proposition to subscribe $50,000 to the Knoxville & Lexington Railroad (now the Knoxville & Ohio) was carried by a vote of ninety-two to one, and on October 4, 1856, it was voted to increase the amount to $100,000. In 1853 the market-house was erected, and in 1867 the city hall was added. In 1856 the Knoxville Gas Light Company was organized and chartered for a period of forty years. R. R. Simpson is the present president, and R. C. Jackson, secretary and treasurer. The corporate limits of the town have been enlarged several times. In 1856 they were extended to include the depot, and in 1868 East Knoxville, which had previously existed as a separate corporation, was added. On January 1, 1883, Mechanicsville, now known as the Ninth Ward, was admitted.

The first street railroad company was incorporated January 5, 1876, with a capital stock of $40,000. It is known as the Knoxville Street Railway Company.

The Market Square Street Railway Company was incorporated in August, 1882, with a capital stock of $20,000. The officers are Dr. A. B. Tadlock, president, and W. H. Simmonds, secretary and treasurer. The Mabry, Bell Avenue & Hardie Street Railway was incorporated in 1885 with a capital stock of $20,000. The officers are R. N. Hood, president; R. H. Edington, vice-president, and B. L. Smith, secretary and treasurer. The combined length of the three lines is about six miles.

In January, 1882, the Knoxville Water Company was incorporated with a capital of $250,000. A reservoir was constructed on the highest hill in the city, and a system of mains and pipes was laid. The water is obtained from the river just above the city. R. N. Hood is president of the company, and J. M. Brooks, secretary.

In January, 1886, the old charter of Knoxville, after having been amended several times, was superseded by a new one. Under its provisions the city government is vested in a mayor and nine aldermen, who constitute the legislative branch, and a board of public works of three members, who constitute the executive branch of the municipal government. The mayor and aldermen are elected for a term of two years, and the chairman of the board of public works for four years. The last named officer and the mayor are chosen by the qualified voters of the city, and the aldermen by the voters of their respective wards. The associate members of the board of public works are nominated by the mayor and confirmed by six votes of the board of aldermen.

The following is a list of the mayors of Knoxville, with the date of election: Thomas Emmerson, 1816; James Park, 1818; W. C. Mynatt, 1822; James Park, 1824; W. C. Mynatt, 1827; Joseph C. Strong, 1828; Donald McIntosh, 1832; S. D. Jacobs, 1834; W. C. Mynatt, 1835; James King, 1837; W. B. A. Ramsey, 1838; Samuel Bell, 1840; G. M. Hazen, 1842; M. M. Gaines, 1843; Samuel Bell, 1844; Joseph L. King, 1846; Samuel B. Boyd, 1847; George M. White, 1852; James C. Luttrell, 1859; William G. Swan, 1855; James H. Cowan, 1856; Samuel A. White, 1856; Thos. J. Powell, 1857; James White, 1858; Joseph Jacques, 1858; A. M. Piper, 1858; J. C. Luttrell, 1859; M. D. Bearden, 1868; John S. Van Gilder, 1870; William Rule, 1873; Peter Staub,

1874; D. A. Carpenter, 1876; Joseph Jacques, 1878; S. B. Luttrell, 1878; H. B. Branner, 1880; Peter Staub, 1881; R. S. Payne, 1882; W. C. Fulcher, 1883, and James C. Luttrell, 1885.

In 1869 the erection of a United States building was begun at Knoxville under the superintendency of J. H. Holman, with A. B. Mullet as supervising architect, and George W. Ross, disbursing agent. The building is constructed entirely of marble, and is one of the most substantial structures in the country. It was completed in 1873 at a cost of $392,000. It is three stories high. The lower floor is occupied by the postoffice; the second floor by the office of the pension agent, revenue collector, district attorney and the clerks of the district and circuit court, and the third floor by the courtroom and rooms for juries, judges and the United States signal office.

The subject of education early engaged the attention of the citizens of Knoxville, as is evidenced by the establishment of Blount College in 1794, but as a history of this institution, together with that of East Tennessee College and the succeeding university, is given in another chapter of this work, no mention will be made of them here.* Under the act of 1806, providing for county academies, Hampden Sidney Academy was incorporated with the following trustees: Nathaniel Cowan, John Crozier, Thomas Humes, John Adair and George McNott, to whom were added the next year Isaac Anderson, Samuel G. Ramsey, Robert Houston, Francis H. Ramsey and John Sawyers. The number was still further increased by an act of 1811, appointing Thomas McCorry, George Wilson, James Park, Thomas Emmerson, Hon. L. White and John Hillsman. No organization was effected until April 4, 1812, when Hon. L. White was chosen president, George Wilson, secretary, and Thomas Emmerson, treasurer. At this meeting it was decided to put the academy into operation, and steps were taken to procure suitable teachers. William Park, who was about to go to Philadelphia, was requested to select a principal and an assistant teacher. The following description was furnished to aid him in making a selection: "A president of the academy is wanted, who must be a good scholar, capable of teaching the Latin and Greek languages, and the sciences. He must, moreover, be a man of genteel deportment and unexceptional moral character. A minister of talent and a considerable show of eloquence would be greatly preferred, and especially one who has heretofore taught with success. To an able teacher the trustees propose to give a salary of $800 per annum." The assistant, it was asserted, "must be a man of good moral character, capable of teaching reading, writing, English

---

*See pages 416 and 447.

grammar and arithmetic. One who understands surveying and bookkeeping, also, would be preferred. To such a man the trustees will engage to pay a salary of $500 per annum." To this it was added: "The salubrity of the climate and the cheapness of living render the proposed salaries here equal to much larger ones in most places to the eastward."

Notwithstanding these preliminaries the academy was not opened, and no further attempt was made until four years later, when David A. Sherman, a graduate of Yale College, was employed as principal. Under his direction the academy was opened on January 1, 1817, in the building formerly occupied by the East Tennessee College, which had suspended in 1809. Among the original subscribers to the support of the institution, the largest contributors were John Crozier, Thomas Humes, Hon. L. White, Joseph C. Strong, Pleasant M. Miller and Calvin Morgan, each of whom gave $100.

In October, 1820, the trustees of East Tennessee College decided to put that institution into operation again, and an agreement was entered into whereby the college and academy were united, D. A. Sherman, the principal of the academy, becoming president of the college. From that time until 1830 the academy had no separate existence. In October of that year the trustees held a meeting, and reorganized under a new charter, granted by the preceding Legislature. Dr. Joseph Strong was chosen president, H. Brown, secretary, and James H. Cowan, treasurer. The services of Perez Dickinson, a young man recently arrived from Massachusetts, were secured as teacher, and the academy was once more opened in the old college building. Mr. Dickinson continued in charge of the academy until the spring of 1832, when, to the regret of the trustees, he resigned. During the following summer a frame building, two stories high, was erected for the use of the institution upon a lot purchased from Hugh L. McClung, situated on Locust Street. For some reason, however, the academy did not prosper, and after several changes of teachers it was suspended in 1834. By an act of the General Assembly, passed in 1838, $18,000 was appropriated annually for the use of county academies, and the trustees determined to reopen Hampden Sidney Academy. The building was repaired, and the school put into operation in November, 1839, under the care of Rev. N. A. Penland. He continued for nearly two years, when he was succeeded by William D. Carnes, who resigned in October, 1842. During the next four years W. S. Williams, J. H. Lawrence and M. Rowley were successively employed as teachers. In May, 1846, the academy was consolidated with a public school which had been established in Knoxville, but this arrangement did not prove satisfactory, and at the end of one year it was terminated. In October, 1847, Rev. Mr. Elwell was installed as teacher, and so continued until March, 1850, when he resigned, and was succeeded by John B. Mitchell. In 1850 a new charter was obtained, and the board of trustees was reorganized, with William Swan as president, Joseph L. King, secretary, and James H. Cowan, treasurer. In 1852 Mr. Mitchell accepted a position as teacher in the East Tennessee University, and from that time until the beginning of the war the academy was in session but a few months. At the close of the war Prof. J. K. Payne opened a school in the building, but he soon after transferred his services to the university. On March 22, 1866, three or four of the old trustees met and reorganized by electing William Heiskell president, and James Roberts secretary and treasurer. On September 3, following, M. C. Wilcox opened the academy, and continued in charge until January, 1868. Soon after the property was leased to the university, to be used for a preparatory department, but after one year this lease was terminated. About two years later the building and lot were sold, and a new lot, at the corner of State and Reservoir Streets, was purchased at a cost of $2,500. In 1876 the erection of the present excellent three-story brick building was begun, and completed the following year. It was then leased to the corporation at a nominal rent for the use of the public schools.

In 1827 the Knoxville Female Academy was established. On April 26, of that year, a number of enterprising citizens met in the office of Robert King and effected an organization by electing Joseph C. Strong, chairman, and F. S. Heiskell, secretary. Committees were then appointed to secure teachers and procure a suitable building. These preliminaries having been duly arranged the school went into operation the September following, with John Davis as principal, and Mrs. Davis, Miss Morse and Miss Littleford, as assistants.

At the meeting of the Legislature in October, the academy was incorporated with the following board of trustees: F. S. Heiskell, William C. Mynatt, William S. Howell, S. D. Jacobs, A. McMillan, Dr. Joseph C. Strong, Hugh L. White, Robert King, Robert Houston, Matthew McClung, Calvin Morgan, William B. Reese, M. Nelson, James King, James McNutt, James Park and Donald McIntosh. Steps were at once taken toward the erection of a building. Two lots adjoining each other on Main Street were donated as a site by Dr. Strong and Matthew McClung. The new building was completed in January, 1829, at a cost of nearly $3,000. The largest contributors were John Crozier and Charles McClung, each of whom gave $200. Several others gave $100 or more. John Davis did not prove a satisfactory principal, and he was soon called upon to resign. His successor was Joseph Estabrook, a graduate of Dartmouth College, and an excellent teacher, and under his management the academy was more prosperous than for many years after his resignation. In 1834 he was elected to the presidency of East Tennessee College, and was succeeded by Henry Herrick, who continued in charge of the academy until 1838. The next year Rev. J. B. Townsend was installed as principal.

In September, 1841, a meeting of the trustees was held to consider a proposition from the Holston Conference of the Methodist Church, to give their patronage to the institution, provided they could share in its control. It was proposed to increase the number of trustees to thirteen, and to permit the conference to appoint a board of nine visitors, the two bodies to constitute a joint board for the election of teachers, etc. It was further stipulated that four of the trustees should be appointed by the conference. This proposition was agreed to, and the academy was thus, in effect, transferred to the conference. Rev. J. E. Douglass, of Alabama, was elected principal, and the institution, under the new management, was reopened September 1, 1842. At the end of one year Mr. Douglass resigned, and was succeeded by Rev. D. R. McAnally, under whose administration the academy was placed in a flourishing condition. In 1846 the charter was amended to permit the conferring of degrees, and the name was changed to the East Tennessee Female Institute. The transfer of the academy to the control of the Holston Conference had not been satisfactory to many of the original subscribers, and in 1847 a movement was inaugurated to sever its connection with that body. It was asserted that the members of the conference had not fulfilled their promise to support the school, and that the trustees had transcended their authority in consenting to the change in management. This opposition finally prevailed, and the old board of trustees again assumed exclusive control. The first graduates from the institute were Margaret H. White and Isabella M. White, Theodosia A. Findley and Harriet A. Parker, who in 1850 received the degree of mistress of polite literature. The next year Mr. McAnally resigned the principalship, and the trustees experienced considerable difficulty in securing a satisfactory successor. At last J. R. Dean was elected, and continued for three or four years. In 1856 he was succeeded by R. L. Kirkpatrick, who remained until the beginning of the war, when the building was taken for a hospital. In January, 1865, three trustees, Thomas W. Humes, Horace Maynard and George M. White met and accepted a proposition from John F. Spence, to open a school, provided the provost-marshal would restore the building. This he did, and during the following spring Mr. Spence opened the school. He continued about two years. From that time until 1881 many attempts were made to establish a school, but all proved unsuccessful. In September, 1881, the building was leased by the board of education for a girls' high school, for which purpose it was used until 1885. Since that time it has been occupied by Mrs. Lizzie C. French, who is conducting a very flourishing female seminary.

The system of public schools in operation in Knoxville had its origin in the board of mayor and aldermen, by whom, on December 16, 1870, a committee, consisting of W. A. Henderson, J. A. Rayl and J. R. Mitchell, was appointed "to take into consideration the propriety of establishing a system of free schools." The committee, at the next meeting, presented a favorable report, and on the 21st of January, 1871, the matter was submitted to the decision of the people, and carried by a vote of 433 to 162. Accordingly, a tax of one mill on the dollar was levied for the support of schools, and a board, consisting of J. A. Rayl, chairman, W. A. Henderson and Dr. John M. Boyd, was appointed to inaugurate the new system. These gentlemen, although much pressed by the duties attendant upon their business and professions, gave the subject thorough study, and met in frequent consultation. They were assisted in their work by John K. Payne, professor of mathematics in East Tenneseee University, a teacher of large experience, who freely offered his services in the interest of education. Through the influence of Rev. Dr. Thomas W. Humes, the committee procured aid from the Peabody Fund to the amount of $2,000, which was of great assistance in the prosecution of the work only just begun. As few suitable buildings could be obtained, the committee rented the basements of churches and such other rooms as they could, and on September 4, 1871, the schools were opened in nine houses situated in various parts of the city, with about 1,000 children in attendance.

It was the desire of the committee to have a system of graded schools, but owing to the nature of the buildings, as well as to many other difficulties to be encountered in establishing such schools where they have never before existed, could be only imperfectly effected the first year. However, what was possible under the circumstances was done, and the schools were continued ten months, employing fifteen teachers. In the summer of 1872 the school committee advised the city council to purchase for a schoolhouse the building known as the Bell House, originally erected and used as a hotel. The advice of the committee was favorably considered, and the building was secured at a cost of $5,500. The needed repairs and alterations having been made, the school opened in September with greatly improved facilities for grading, which rendered necessary the employment of more teachers. Accordingly twenty teachers were employed, several of whom had taught in the schools in 1871, and all entered upon their duties with an earnest desire for the prosperity and ultimate success of the schools. Until December, 1873, the schools were under the management of a committee appointed by the mayor, consisting of members of the city council holding their office but one year. On the 12th of December the city council passed an ordinance creating a board of education, consisting of five persons, to be elected by the city council, for a term of five years, one member retiring each year. The first board consisted of J. A. Rayl, chairman; C. D. McGoffey, secretary; J. W. Gaut, treasurer; F. A. Reeve and W. W. Woodruff.

In 1874 a new house was erected on Morgan Street at a cost of $6,000, and a school known as the Peabody School was established. In 1877 the trustees of Hampden Sidney Academy erected a new building on State Street, and tendered it to the board of education for the use of the public schools. The offer was accepted, and the next year a school for girls was opened in it. In 1881 the schools had again become crowded, and through the courtesy of the trustees of that property the Female Institute on Main Street was obtained for the use of a girls' high school. This building was occupied until 1885, when the school was transferred to the Barton Block at the corner of Church and Gay Streets. In 1886, at a cost of $35,000, one of the finest public school buildings in the South was erected for the accommodation of girls from the third to the tenth grades, inclusive. It is a three-story brick, and is fitted up and furnished with all the modern conveniences.

On January 1, 1883, that portion of Knoxville known as the Ninth Ward was admitted into the corporation, and in February following graded schools were organized in a building which had been previously erected, and which has since come into the possession of the city.

From the first, colored schools have been maintained upon an equal footing with the white schools. Since 1881 these schools have been in charge of colored teachers exclusively, and have been admirably well managed by them.

In 1864, before the close of the war, the United Presbyterian Board of Freedmen's Missions opened a school in Knoxville for the colored children, and continued it until the opening of the public school. One of the teachers in this school, Miss Emily L. Austin, of Philadelphia, afterward erected a small house in the Third Ward, and there taught a small private school for several years. In 1880, the accommodations for the colored pupils of the public school having become insufficient, a new building known as the Austin School was rented. For this purpose the city furnished a lot and $2,000, and Miss Austin procured the remaining $8,000 required to complete the work, from voluntary subscription, in the Northern cities. In the new building, one room was reserved for an industrial school, which was established, and opened under the direction of Miss Austin. Work was begun with a sewing school and kitchen garden school for girls, and later a carpenter shop was built for the boys, although many difficulties were met with the new feature proved a success, and larger rooms and better facilities soon became a necessity.

In 1885 the Slater Training School for the manual training of colored children was incorporated with the following board of trustees: Rev. Dr. Thomas W. Humes, president; E. E. McCroskey, vice-president; Miss Isa E. Gray, of Boston, treasurer; Miss E. L. Austin, secretary; W. S. Mead, C. Seymour, A. S. Jones (of Washington, D. C.) and R. B. Hayes (of Fremont, Ohio), and the work of raising funds for the erection of a new building was begun. By the citizens of Knoxville $1,000 was contributed, and nearly $5,000 was obtained from friends of the cause in the North. In 1886 a house three stories high, with a brick basement, was erected, and furnished with all modern improvements. In September the school was opened with an attendance of over 200. Three grades of the city schools are taught in the building, and these pupils are required to take a course in the industrial department. For the boys a carpenter shop and a printing office have been fitted up, and each placed in the hands of a competent teacher. The girls receive instruction in sewing, cooking and housekeeping. In connection with the school a Young Men's Christian Association and a Shakespeare Club, composed of the teachers of the colored school, are maintained, and nothing that tends to the elevation of the colored race, morally, intellectually and physically, is neglected.

The following is a list of the superintendents of the Knoxville city schools since their establishment: Alexander Baird, Jr., 1872-75; Rev. H. T. Horton, 1875-78; R. D'S. Robertson, 1878-81; Albert Ruth, 1881.

COMPARATIVE STATISTICS.

Year.	Number of Pupils Enrolled.	Average Attendance.	Number of Teachers Employed.	Cost per Pupil Enrolled.	Expenditures.	Scholastic Population.
1874	1,102	780	20	$11 24	$ 7,522 11	1,829
1875	840	609	20	13 81	11,600 00	1,992
1876	1,500	849	20	11 84	12,916 76	1,992
†1877	.....	...	20	.....	12,178 21	.....
†1878	.....	...	23	8 12	12,420 22	.....
1879	1,509	980	24	9 05	13,659 83	2,100
1880	1,759	1,253	..	8 48	14,913 44	*2,748
1881	1,984	1,512	26	7 91	15,690 05	3,044
1882	2,137	1,558	30	7 55	16,086 20	3,044
1883	2,265	1,519	34	8 18	19,920 69	3,196
1884	2,787	1,955	44	8 92	24,421 30	4,315
1885	2,781	2,142	50	9 98	27,753 97	4,817

* Before 1880 the scholastic population included only those between the ages of six and eighteen.
† No report made.

Intimately connected with the colored public schools is the Knoxville College, a normal and training school for colored teachers. It is controlled and supported by the United Presbyterian Board of Missions, but receives the colored students appointed to cadetships in the University of Tennessee, and also a portion of those receiving State normal scholarship. The work was begun in September, 1875, when a normal school was opened in East Knoxville, under the superintendency of Rev. J. P. Wright, and a new building was begun on an eminence northwest of the city. This building was completed in 1876. It is a brick, 64x84 feet, four stories high, and contains seven large class rooms, and a chapel capable of seating 400 students, besides several rooms for teachers.

In 1877 two small buildings were erected for the use of pupils who wished to board themselves, and the following year a cottage was built for the use of the president and his family. In 1881 a large dormitory and boarding house 45x110 feet, four stories high, was added to the main building.

The school opened in 1875 with three instructors. The next year there were four, and since that time the number has increased to twelve. The students in attendance have increased in the same proportion, and the capacity of the institution is now taxed to the utmost. In addition to instruction in all the branches of education, the girls are given lessons in sewing and cooking. All of the work connected with the institution is performed by students, and thus expenses are reduced to a minimum. The present president of the college is Rev. Dr. J. S. McCulloch.

Outside of Knoxville, the only town in the county of any considerable importance is Concord, situated on the East Tennessee, Virginia & Georgia

Railroad, and also on the Tennessee River about —— miles below the city. It was laid off in 1854 upon land owned by James M. Rodgers. The first store was opened by George Gilbert, and the first dwelling was erected by S. Calloway. Among the other merchants before the war were Pate & Russell, William Boggle and William King. Those of the present time are Cox & McNutt, Russell & Boyd and Pepper & Galbraith, dry goods and groceries; C. B. Newhouse, groceries and provisions, and Joseph Doak, drugs. Within the past five years Concord has become the center of a large marble business. It is surrounded by quarries producing the finest varieties of marble in East Tennessee, and is the shipping point for them. In 1881 forty-one carloads were shipped, in 1882, 113, in 1883, 238. Since that time the increase has been even more rapid. The following quarrying companies are situated in the territory tributary to Concord: Lima & East Tennessee, organized in 1882; Stamps, Wood & Co., 1884; Buckeye, Gem, Concord, Bond, Kincaid and Great Bend, organized in 1884; Steinert, organized in 1885, and the Republic organized in 1886.

In 1883 a mill for the sawing and polishing of marble was erected at Concord by the Juanito Company, and run by them until January, 1886, when it was purchased by the Enterprise Marble Company. They at once made extensive improvements, and are now doing a large business. As they purchase all their marble they are enabled to obtain stone to suit their customers, and as they keep a large stock of slabs on hand, they can always fill orders upon short notice.

Besides Concord, the stations upon the East Tennessee, Virginia & Georgia Railroad in Knox County are Lenoirs, Bearden, Ebenezer, Caswell and McMillan. Those on the Knoxville & Ohio Railroad are Powell Station and Bull Run.

To assign to any one of the three denominations—Presbyterians, Methodists or Baptists—the honor of priority in the work of bringing the gospel into the frontier settlement of Knox County, is impossible. It is certain, however, that one did not precede another more than a few months. Brave and hardy ministers of each denomination kept pace with the vanguard of civilization, and as soon as a few settlers had established themselves in a neighborhood, those "ambassadors of the Lord" sought them out and their coming was always hailed with delight. The simple announcement that there would be preaching at a station on a certain day was sufficient to bring together the entire population for miles around. Nor did it matter to what denomination the minister belonged. To these pioneers, destitute of all those means of entertainment common to older communities, a meeting served to satisfy the inherent desire for some kind of social excitement. Besides as a class they were eminently a godly people, and no opportunity of renewing their spiritual strength was neglected.

The denominations mentioned, however, were at that time more widely different in their doctrines and methods than at the present day, and it was not long until religious controversies sprang up. The Presbyterians and Baptists were both Calvinists of the strictest sect, yet in almost every other respect they were antagonistic. The Methodists, being Armenians in belief, were in opposition to both. The Presbyterians included in their membership the more cultivated portion of the community, and, having an educated ministry, they naturally established and controlled nearly all the schools, especially those of a higher grade. The strength of the Baptists lay among the poorer, and, as a rule, the uneducated people. The Methodists occupied a middle ground. In the following pages the growth of each denomination will be traced separately, beginning with the Methodists.

In the fall of 1787 the elder of the Nollichucky Circuit received letters from persons low down on the Holston and French Broad Rivers, informing him of their destitute condition. It was decided, after consultation, that Thomas Ware, one of the ministers of that circuit, should visit them and attempt to form a circuit. He went in the autumn of 1788, and after a winter of toil and exposure succeeded in forming the French Broad Circuit. But little is known of this circuit, except that it was probably south and west of the French Broad River, and included what is now Cocke, a part of Jefferson, Sevier, Blount and Knox Counties. The next year Daniel Asbury was assigned to this circuit, but as it does not again appear upon the records of the general conference until after the cessation of the Indian wars, it is probable that Asbury failed of success, and a portion of the circuit was attached to Holston.

It is scarcely probable that either of these men organized societies in Knox County, but if they did they were south of the Holston and French Broad. One of the oldest societies in the county was organized in the southeast part on the French Broad River, near the Seven Islands, among the Cunnynghams, Huffakers and Greens. Two of the early pioneer Methodist preachers went out from that region, Jesse Cunnyngham and Jesse Green. James Green, a brother of the latter, was for many years a local preacher.

Another society was organized at about the same time near where Logan's Chapel and camp-ground were afterward built, and perhaps one was established in the neighborhood of the Frenches, Rules and Goddards, six or seven miles south of Knoxville. The first church organized north of the river was at Macedonia, four miles east of Knoxville, where the Aults, Wagoners, Haynies and Luttrells lived. This became a great rallying point for the Methodists early in the present century, and was one of the first places at which camp-meetings were held.

But little is definitely known of the early work in Knox County. On November 1, 1800, Bishop Asbury, while on his way from the Cumberland settlements to North Carolina, accompanied by Bishop Whatcoat and William McKendree, visited Knoxville, and were entertained by Joseph Greer, an old friend of Asbury's. The Bishop preached in the "State House" to a congregation of about 700 people, only a portion of whom could gain entrance to the house. Asbury, in speaking of this day in his journal, says, "We came off in haste, intending to make twenty miles that evening, but Francis A. Ramsey pursued us to the ferry, ferried us over, and took us to his excellent mansion." In the autumn of 1802 Bishop Asbury visited Knoxville twice, and on both occasions was entertained by Col. Ramsey and Mr. Greer. At neither time, however, did he hold religious services in the town. November 25 he preached at the home of Justus Huffaker, a local preacher, living near Seven Islands in the French Broad. This year had been one of great prosperity to the church in the Holston country, and two new circuits were formed. The French Broad, the one containing Knox County, extended westward from the west line of Greene County, on both sides of the French Broad and Holston Rivers. To this circuit during the next ten years the following assignments were made: In 1802, Luther Taylor; 1803, John Johnson; 1804, E. W. Bowman and Joshua Oglesby; 1805, Ralph Lotspeich; 1806, James Axely; 1807, Benjamin Edge; 1808, Nathan Barnes and Isaac Lindsey; 1809, James Trower; 1810, William Pattison; 1811, George Elkin and Josiah Crawford.

In November, 1812, Bishop Asbury, accompanied by William McKendree, made his last visit to Knoxville. This time he was the guest of Father Wagoner, "one of Otterbine's men," whose son afterward became a local preacher. There had been great interest manifested in religion during the previous year, which is remembered for the large number of accessions to the church, and the conference from which Bishop Asbury was returning had established a Knoxville Circuit, to which Samuel H. Thompson was assigned. He was succeeded the following year by Richard Richards, a man of strong mind and of great popularity. He afterward became addicted to strong drink, and was expelled from the church. Later he reformed, and was again received into membership. In 1814 James Dixon was assigned to the Knoxville Circuit. He was a man of remarkably strong intellect, and defended the doctrines of his church with signal ability. He carried on a protracted controversy in the papers with Dr. Isaac Anderson, the founder of Maryville College, and acquitted himself to the satisfaction of his church. In 1819 he was again sent to Knoxville, and the following year had the care of the church at Greenville, in addition to his Knoxville charge. During that time he became afflicted with epilepsy, and suffered in a most remarkable manner. He was helpless and almost unconscious for several weeks, and when his consciousness did return he had forgotten everything he had before known. He could not read, and was compelled to learn his letters a second time.

In 1815 John Henninger was assigned to the Knoxville Circuit. He was succeeded by Nicholas Norwood in 1816, Josiah B. Daughtry in 1817, and George Atkin in 1818. The next year Knoxville was made a station, and Knox Circuit, to which Robert Hooper was assigned, was formed. Meanwhile several new churches had been organized in Knox County. One of these was a few miles west of Knoxville, when a building known as Manifee's Meeting-house was erected. Another church and camp-ground was established three miles northwest from the town, and was called Lonas' Camp-ground. About 1833 the camp-ground was removed to Fountain Head Springs, six miles north of Knoxville, where a log church was built at a very early day. A church and camp-ground were also early established at Hopewell, thirteen miles east of Knoxville, and another at Mount Pleasant, seventeen miles northeast. April 7, 1810, John Manifee made a deed to two acres of land lying north of Beaver Creek to John Childress, Solomon McCampbell, Jeremiah Tindall, George Lucas, Daniel Yarnell, Michael Yarnell and Thomas Wilson trustees, for the purpose of building a meeting-house and camp-ground to be free to all denominations. This was known as Bell's Camp-ground, and was frequently used by the Methodists.

At precisely what time a Methodist congregation was organized at Knoxville is not known, but it occurred about 1816 or 1817. The principal mover in its organization was Rev. John Haynie, who had united with the church at Wagoner's in 1809, and who had now removed to Knoxville to labor for the cause of Methodism. He at once began preparations for building a house of worship, and through his friend, a Mr. Nelson, he obtained as a site a lot on the hill, in East Knoxville, from Hugh L. White. A small frame structure was erected, and on account of the liberal donation received from Judge White it was named in his honor. Among the most prominent of the early members of this church were John Haney, Frederick Ault, Henry Graves, J. Roberts, William Seay, Mr. Hudiburgh, Mr. Formwalt and Joseph Bell. A Sunday-school was organized previous to 1822, and was probably the first in the county. Henry Graves was the first superintendent.

In 1824 the Holston Conference was organized in a small red house on the south side of Main Street, not far from the church.

From 1820 to 1840 Knoxville constituted a station only a portion of the time. For short periods it was at two or three different times included in Knox Circuit to which were then assigned two ministers. In 1836 a brick church was erected upon a lot on Church Street, donated by Dr. James King. It cost about $5,000 and was first occupied by the Southern Commercial Convention. The old church on Methodist Hill was then given to the colored members, who continued to occupy it until the beginning of the war. Previous to that time the colored members, of whom there was a considerable number, had worshiped in the same house with the white members. Later, a minister was assigned to East Knoxville, who gave one-half his time to the colored congregation, and the other half to a white congregation which assembled at Temperance Hall. During the war the house on Methodist Hill was destroyed by the Federal troops, who also occupied the brick church.

At the close of hostilities the Methodist Episcopal Church South began the work of collecting its scattered members and reorganizing congregations. In Knoxville they found themselves extremely weak. Only one of the old board of trustees, Samuel T. Atkin, remained, and their property was in the hands of the Methodist Episcopal Church. Not discouraged, however, they obtained a lot, erected upon it a new church, and brought suit to recover their former property. Meanwhile they held services in the First Presbyterian Church. After considerable litigation, a favorable decision of the courts was obtained, and the Methodist Episcopal Church was ordered to restore the property to the trustees of the Methodist Episcopal Church South.

In 1877 the erection of the present excellent brick building standing upon the site of the old church was begun, and on February 3, 1878, it was dedicated by Bishop Wightman. The members of this church now number over 600. In 1870 a congregation was organized in North Knoxville with about sixty members. A plain and unpretentious frame building was erected on Broad Street and dedicated on June 25, 1871. The congregation and membership grew very rapidly, and soon became one of the most popular churches of the city. Nine years ago, under the ministry of Rev. W. W. Bays, it became necessary to enlarge the house and render it more commodious. The pastors who have served this church are George D. French, B. O. Davis, J. L. M. French, W. W. Bays, J. H. Keith, J. T. Frazier, R. H. Parker and H. W. Bays, who is serving his third year. The church has very recently erected an elegant brick building on the corner of Broad Street and Fifth Avenue, which, when completed will be one of the most imposing church edifices in the State. It will cost about $20,000. During the past two years the membership has increased 255 and now numbers about 500. In some respects this church has no equal in the Holston Conference. The official board is aggressive, plucky and determined, while the ladies of the communion are one of the chief sources of power.

In 1885 a second church in North Knoxville was built by the co-operation of the two older congregations, and is known as Centenary Church. It has a membership of 114.

In 1886 a neat frame house was erected on the old site on Methodist Hill, and a congregation now worships there under the ministration of Rev. W. H. Bates.

Among the other congregations in the county belonging to the Methodist Episcopal Church South are Concord, Geitzentanner, Lyon's Bend, Erin, Ebenezer, Pleasant Hill, Asbury, Cedar Grove, Riverdale, Brookside, Macedonia, Bethlehem, Wood's Springs, Stony Point and Hopewell..

At two or three different times a periodical, under the auspices of the Holston Conference, has been published at Knoxville. The first was the *Holston Messenger*, established in 1824 by Rev. Thomas Stringfield. It had formerly been published at Huntsville, Ala., as the *Western Armenian* and *Christian Instructor*. It was continued at Knoxville but a short time. On May 5, 1846, the first number of a weekly paper, the *Methodist Episcopalian*, appeared, and continued as such about four years, when it was changed to the *Holston Christian Advocate*, which was also published about four years. In December, 1862, a religious weekly called the *Holston Journal* was established under the management of C. W. Charlton, but upon the evacuation of Knoxville, the following September, it suspended. Since 1884 the *Holston Methodist*, originally established in Bristol, was removed to Knoxville, where it is now issued by the Holston Publishing Company, of which W. H. Valentine is business manager. The editor is Rev. R. N. Price. The *Methodist* is a large eight-column folio weekly, and is one of the best church papers in the country.

On May 27, 1864, a call for a convention of members and preachers of the Holston Conference, loyal to the United States Government, to be held in Knoxville on the first Thursday in July, was issued by William G. Brownlow, J. A. Hyden, E. E. Gillenwater, William T. Dowell, James Cumming, Thomas Russell, William H. Rogers and

David Fleming. At the appointed time fifty-four delegates assembled in the Episcopal Church, and organized by electing E. E. Gillenwater chairman, and Robert G. Blackburn secretary. The most important action of this assemblage was the adoption of the report of a general committee favoring a return to the Methodist Episcopal Church, subject to the approval of its general conference. This action was ratified by that body at its next meeting, and under its authority the Holston Conference of the Methodist Episcopal Church was organized at Athens on June 1, 1865. During this year the First Methodist Episcopal Church at Knoxville was established under the pastorate of Rev. Dr. John F. Spence. The officers elected were W. G. Brownlow, R. D. Jaurolman, E. N. Parham and C. W. De Pue, trustees, and S. P. Angel, William Rule, H. C. Tarwater, F. M. Wheeler and J. F. Ambrose, stewards. For three years services were held in the courthouse and the First Baptist Church. In 1867 the erection of the present church on Clinch Street was begun, and completed in 1869. It is a large and commodious brick structure, having a seating capacity of 600. The congregation is a large and growing one, numbering at present over 300 members. A Sunday-school is also maintained with a membership of over 200. In 1872 a second church was organized by Thomas H. Russell with about thirty members, and soon after a house of worship was erected in Asylum Street. It is a brick structure and cost about $4,000. The members now number about 120. A Sunday-school, of which Charles McGlothen is superintendent, is maintained with a membership of over 200. There are now in Knox County thirty-five congregations under the care of the Holston Conference of the Methodist Episcopal Church, with an aggregate membership of 1,931 in full connection, and 207 probationers. The circuits and congregations are as follows: Knoxville, Clinch Street, I. A. Pierce, pastor; Asylum Street, J. W. Holden, pastor; Knox Circuit, W. C. Daily, pastor; Rocky Dale, Antioch, Fountain Head, Corinth, Clapp's Chapel, Copper Ridge and Macedonia; New Salem Circuit, M. A. Rule, pastor; Jones' Chapel, New Salem, Oak Grove, Hendron's Chapel; Little River Circuit, P. H. Henry, pastor; Logan's Chapel, Cox's, Bethlehem and Walker's; Thorn Grove Circuit, R. O. Ayres, pastor; Pleasant Hill, Thorn Grove, Cedar Ridge, Oak Grove, Underwood, Huckleberry Springs, Asbury, Union and Sunny View; Loveville Circuit, J. M. Durham, pastor; Ebenezer, Scott's Chapel, Beaver Ridge, Bell's, Palestine, Boyd's Chapel, Pleasant Hill, Grigsby's Chapel and Valley Grove.

To the Presbyterians is due the honor of having established the first regularly organized congregation of which there is any record. The following account of the first religious service, and subsequent organization of a church, is condensed from a manuscript prepared by the late Dr. J. G. M. Ramsey in 1875. "Tradition says that in the early autumn of 1789 or 1790 a surveying party composed of land explorers, adventurers, hunters and farmers had met at the junction of the French Broad and Holston, and that while thus assembled, they were approached by a clerical looking individual on horseback, who informed them that he was on his way to Houston's Station beyond Little River, where some of his old acquaintances from Virginia had settled, and that his mission was to organize the Presbyterians of this region into congregations. In the party whom he addressed were many who had belonged to Presbyterian congregations in their native States, and he was eagerly besought to make an appointment to preach upon his return, at Gilliam's Station. To this he consented, and upon the appointed day an immense crowd assembled, including nearly all the settlers for miles around. They came from Baker's Creek, Pistol Creek, Little River, Elijah Creek, Stock Creek, all the country south of the French Broad, and in the north from House Mountain to Grassy Valley. The place chosen for the meeting was a large Indian mound, which, until recently, stood at the fork of the French Broad and Holston, immediately back of where afterward was erected the house of the late Dr. Ramsey. From this mound the canebrake was removed and seats were arranged upon it. The text, chosen by the speaker was 2 Corinthians v, 20, from which he preached an eloquent sermon. At its conclusion he announced that any parents who wished to offer their children in holy baptism to the Lord, would be allowed that privilege. Many embraced the opportunity, and some of nearly adult age, who had been born in the wilderness, were admitted to the ordinance. While these services were going on another minister came upon the ground, and having been introduced, was invited to preach a second sermon. He stated that he had been circulating among the forts and stations, and that, hearing of the appointment, he had come to the meeting. He commended the sermon which he had heard, but said that the subject had not been exhausted, and proceeded to preach from the same text. He was Rev. Hezekiah Balch, and the first speaker Rev. Samuel Carrick. It was arranged that there should be a second service at an early date, which was accordingly held, and resulted in the organization of a Presbyterian Church near Gilliam's Station. It was named "Lebanon-in-the-Fork," afterward abbreviated to Lebanon. Among the first members of this church were the families of James White, James Cozby, John Adair, James Armstrong, Deveraux Gilliam, Archibald Rhea, Sr., Archibald Rhea, Jr., James and Alexander Campbell, Jeremiah Jack, George McNutt, Col. Francis A. Ramsey, Thomas Gillespie, Robert

Craighead, Robert Brooks, Joseph Love, Jacob Patton and Robert Houston. Rev. Samuel Carrick was installed as minister, and located with his family near what has since been known as Carrick's or Boyd's Ford on the Holston. Mr. Carrick was very popular, and Lebanon soon became the center of a very large congregation. A church about eighteen feet square without windows or floor was erected. It was not large enough to contain the worshipers, and in good weather and always on communion days the services were held in a grove of cedars near by. In 1793 it became necessary to build a house on a larger scale and of a more imposing appearance. Col. Ramsey donated nine acres as a site, and upon an eminence in the center of a grove of cedars, a house 40x60 feet, of logs, straight and well hewed, was erected. The ground around had long been used as a cemetery by trappers, traders, and later by the soldiery and settlers within reach, and was consequently the first burial ground in this region. Among the first Christian interments was that of Mr. Carrick's wife. It occurred on the day of the expected Indian attack upon Knoxville in 1793, when all the male inhabitants had gone out for the protection of the town. The burial of Mrs. Carrick's body, therefore, devolved upon the women, and by them alone, it was brought in a canoe, and deposited in the churchyard. About 1803 Mr. Carrick was succeeded by Rev. Isaac Anderson, who divided his time between Lebanon and the Washington congregation which had been organized on Roseberry Creek. He continued in charge of these churches until 1813, when he removed to Maryville. During his pastorate in 1810, a new church of stone was erected upon the site of the old church at Lebanon. This was used until some time in the forties, when the present frame house was erected.

Almost from its organization the Lebanon congregation maintained a school in connection with the church. The first school was taught in 1791, in a shanty standing near the church. It had been a hunter's lodge for years before. The teacher's name was Thompson, an Englishman, who continued to enlighten the youth of the neighborhood for many years. A new house was soon built on the Dandridge road. It was somewhat more comfortable than the first but still rude in the extreme. It had neither floor nor windows, and the seats were made from rough puncheons, supported upon round pins driven into them. The teacher was a strict disciplinarian, and brought with him the old English customs of using the dunce block and fool's cap. The former was improvised from the stump of a small sapling which had been left standing about two feet high in the middle of the room. The fool's cap was made from an old copy-book twisted into the proper shape. The chief text book was

Dilworth's spelling book. The Bible and the catechism were also taught, and the deacons of the church were regular in their visits to the school to see that the latter subjects were not neglected.

Other houses and teachers followed, and about 1828 a building was erected on the line between the farms of Dr. Ramsey and James Jack. This became quite a high school, in which the classics were taught. In 1835 an association was formed for the purpose of establishing an academy. The trustees were Maj. Aaron Armstrong, Dr. J. G. M. Ramsey, James Jack, John Naill and Isaac Patton. A building, 18x36 feet was erected, and Noble A. Penland, then pastor of the Lebanon church was installed as teacher. This institution was known as Mecklenburg Academy.

Meanwhile other congregations had been organized and other schools established. The church at Knoxville was organized by Mr. Carrick, soon after he became pastor of the Lebanon Church, but nearly all of its members had previously been enrolled with the latter congregation. Its first ruling elders were James White, George McNutt, John Adair, Archibald Rhea, Sr., Dr. James Cozby and Thomas Gillespie, the first three making the original bench. In September, 1794, the Territorial Legislature incorporated Blount College, with Mr. Carrick as president,* and he was continued in that capacity and also as pastor of the church until his death in 1809. The church was then without a regular pastor until 1812, when Rev. Thomas H. Nelson was installed. Up to this time no house of worship had been erected, religious services having been held in the courthouse and at the barracks. During the year previous, however, under the inspiration of a sermon preached by Rev. Samuel G. Ramsey, three commissioners: John Crozier, Joseph C. Strong and James Park, had been appointed to contract for the building of a house. This duty they accordingly performed, and late in the autumn of 1812 the work upon the brick meeting-house had sufficiently advanced to allow of its occupancy, although it was not entirely completed and furnished until 1816.

At this time there was a debt of $529.17, which was assumed by the three commissioners mentioned above. The sight consisting of one acre was donated by James White.

Soon after the completion of this house, a portion of the members became disaffected, and in 1818 sent up a petition to Union Presbytery for permission to organize a new congregation, alleging as a reason, the insufficient accommodation of the old church. This was considered, however, by the other members as but the pretext of the "Hopkinsian"

---
*See page 416.

James Rodgers M.D.
KNOX CO.

party for withdrawing from the old organization, and when the petition, having been refused by the presbytery, went upon appeal to the synod of Tennessee, a remonstrance was sent up. The synod nevertheless disregarded the remonstrance, overruled the decision of the presbytery, and ordered the petitioners to organize the Second Presbyterian Church of Knoxville.*

An appeal was then taken by the session of the First Church to the General Assembly of 1820, but the decision was allowed to stand.

Mr. Nelson continued in charge of the church until his death in September, 1838, and under his pastorate 204 names were added to the communion roll. During this time also the following elders had been elected: Thomas Humes, James Campbell, John Craighead, Moses White, Robert Lindsey, James Craig, Dr. Joseph C. Strong, James Park and William Park.

After the death of Mr. Nelson, the pulpit of the First Church was supplied successively by Samuel Y. Wyley, Joseph I. Foot, Charles D. Pigeon and Rev. Reese Happersett, none of whom continued more than a few months. In 1841 Robert B. McMullen, then a professor in the East Tennessee University, was installed as pastor, and continued as such until the latter part of 1858, when he became president of Stewart College at Clarksville. The following year W. A. Gallatin was elected pastor. He continued until February, 1864, when he was sent South by the Federal military authorities. In March, 1855, a new house of worship, which had been begun in 1852 upon the sight of the old house, was dedicated. This building, from November, 1863 to May 1, 1866, was used by the United States authorities, first as a hospital, then as barracks, afterward as quarters for refugees from upper East Tennessee, and finally was turned over to the Freedman's Bureau, and was used by them as a colored schoolhouse.

In February, 1866, Rev. James Park, who had recently returned to Knoxville from Georgia, was requested by several members to preach. Having no house he, upon his own responsibility, rented the Baptist Church, which was then vacant, and there continued to hold services until the following May, when the First Church was restored to the congregation. At this time there were but thirty-nine members, of whom David A. Deaderick, William S. Kennedy and George M. White were the elders. Under the care of Dr. Park the church prospered, and many accessions were received. In 1869 the church building was repaired and refurnished, and the lot improved at a cost of more than $5,000. On May 21, 1876, Dr. Park was again elected pastor, and has since con-

---
*Historical Discourse by James Park, D. D.

tinued in charge of the church. During his pastorate, a period of a little more than twenty years, about 600 members have been added to the church which now has a membership of about 300.

At a *pro re nata* meeting of the Presbytery of Knoxville, held at Sweetwater, December, 18, 1873, the petition of several members of the First Church, and a few other persons to be organized as the Third Presbyterian Church of Knoxville, was granted, and a committee, of whom Dr. Park was chairman, was appointed to attend at Knoxville on the Friday night before the third Sabbath in January, 1874, hold a meeting to embrace the Sabbath, and organize the new congregation. This duty was discharged, and in January, 1874, the church was constituted embracing twenty-nine communicants, four ruling elders and four deacons. Until a house of worship could be erected, services were held in the Caldwell Schoolhouse. In 1876 the present fine brick structure, situated on Fifth Avenue, was dedicated.

For the first eighteen months this church was served with efficiency by Rev. J. P. Gammon, during which time the number of communicants was about tripled. Mr. Gammon was succeeded by Rev. Dr. W. A. Harrison, who has since had pastoral charge of the church, and under his care the membership has increased to nearly 500. The present elders are Dr. Benjamin Frazier, Dr. J. D. Carter, W. H. Simmonds, Dr. John M. Kennedy, James L. Cooley, Lewis Roth, A. McDonald, Joseph A. Porter and Samuel A. Caldwell. The deacons are F. A. R. Scott, Thomas E. Oldham, J. C. J. Williams, Joseph L. Bauman, James P. McMullen and George McCully.

Near the close of the last century, and at about the time of the organization of the First Presbyterian Church at Knoxville, two other Presbyterian Churches were established in Knox County by Rev. Samuel G. Ramsey, a brother of Col. Francis A. Ramsey. They were Pleasant Forest, situated about two miles north from Concord Station, and Ebenezer, situated upon the site of the present Ebenezer Station, near the latter place. Mr. Ramsey established a sort of preparatory school for young men, which was known as Ebenezer Academy, and for a few years this was the leading educational institution in the county. Here attended Dr. J. G. M. Ramsey, W. B. A. Ramsey, Richard G. Dunlap, and his brothers Hugh G. and William C., John and Robert Singleton, Joshua Armstrong, William Moore, Charles McClung, also Matthew and James McClung, and the sons of Gov. Blount. Mr. Ramsey had for an assistant a portion of the time a young man, John Bain, who had been educated under Rev. Samuel Doak, and who was preparing for the ministry.

While Mr. Ramsey was thus educating the young men, Mrs. Ramsey conducted a school for girls, and so excellent was the instruction given that she received several pupils from Knoxville. For some time before his death Mr. Ramsey became enfeebled by disease, and was finally compelled to resign his pastoral charges. He was succeeded by Richard King. Mr. King was a man of fine intellect, and an excellent speaker. Physically he was very large and corpulent, so much so that in his later years he sat in a chair while preaching. About 1825 Mr. King was succeeded by William Higgleton, who continued until 1830, when William A. McCampbell was chosen pastor.

Until 1833 the two churches, Ebenezer and Pleasant Forest, were united in one congregation known as the Grassy Valley congregation. In that year the members in the vicinity of Pleasant Forest formed a separate organization with seventy-three members, and installed Samuel H. Doak as pastor, while McCampbell continued at Ebenezer. Mr. Doak was succeeded in 1838 by Samuel G. Willis, and he in turn the next year by A. A. Mathes. In 1848 Rev. Dr. James Park became pastor of both churches, and so continued until 1853. After the completion of the railroad Pleasant Forest was reorganized as Concord and erected a church at that station, while the congregation at Ebenezer removed two miles north of its old location and organized as Cedar Springs Church. In 1859 Dr. Park again became their pastor, and so continued with a short interval during the war until 1866. He also supplied their pulpit on Sunday afternoons for two years longer.

These churches have always been old school, and now form a part of the presbytery of Knoxville, the origin of which is as follows: In April, 1839, the general assembly of the Presbyterian Church, by its famous "excision act," having cut off the presbytery of Union, the few members including only about eight ministers still adhering to the old school doctrines, met near Greenville, Tenn., and organized Holston Presbytery. In October, 1846, this presbytery was divided by a right line running from Cumberland Gap to the southeast corner of Blount County, and the portion to the west of that line was erected into the presbytery of Knoxville.

Two periodicals have at different times been published at Knoxville in the interests of the Presbyterian Church. The first was the *Western Monitor*, established about 1819, and the other the *Presbyterian Witness*, established some time in the forties and published by Kinsloe & Rice.

Contemporaneously with the founding of Ebenezer and Mount Pleasant Forest by Mr. Ramsey, Washington Church situated on Rosebury Creek, was organized by Rev. Dr. Isaac Anderson, one of the ablest men who ever occupied the pulpit in East Tennessee. He also established there a school known as Union Academy. In 1803 Mr. Carrick resigned his charge of Lebanon Church, and from that time until 1813 Dr. Anderson divided his time and attention between Washington and Lebanon. He had adopted the peculiar doctrine known as "Hopkinsianism," and under his teaching, many not only among his own congregation but among members of neighboring churches had been converted to his belief. After he removed to Maryville his old admirers did not forget him, and in 1818 he was invited by some of the members of the First Presbyterian Church at Knoxville, to return and preach to them. This he did, and the result was the organization of the Second Presbyterian Church of Knoxville, which took place on October 24, 1818. The elders chosen at this time were Archibald Rhea, John McCampbell, Thomas Craighead, Joseph Brown and John Taylor. An acre lot was purchased from Gideon Morgan, and the work of erecting a house of worship was immediately begun. By April, 1820, this work had so far advanced, that the building was dedicated by Dr. Anderson. It was not entirely completed, however, and for nearly ten years the walls remained unplastered.

Dr. Anderson continued to preach in the church until 1829, during which time 153 members were added. The next regular pastor was Rev. Jefferson E. Montgomery, who began his labors in 1831, and remained until 1838. In October, 1840, he was succeeded by Rev. William Mack, who resigned three years later. Under the ministry of these two men, 225 names were added to the communion roll. In February, 1845, John W. Cunningham was installed as pastor, but was succeeded in about a year by Rev. J. H. Meyers, who continued until April, 1857. The sixth minister was J. H. Martin, who served the congregation from July, 1857, to October, 1863. During his pastorate the present church building was erected, at a cost of $14,236.84. It was begun in the fall of 1859, and dedicated November 11, 1860. During the latter year, a chapel for Sunday-school, prayer meetings, etc., was built from the materials of the old church, at a cost of $2,219.

For two years during the war the church was without a pastor, after which Rev. R. P. Wells preached for a few months. In October Rev. Nathan Bachman began his labors, which continued for several years. He was succeeded by F. E. Sturgis. The present pastor is T. S. Scott, who was called from Rockford, Ill., in 1885. The present membership of the church is nearly 500. A Sunday-school has been successfully maintained since, some time prior to 1832, and its pupils now number over 500. Among those who have served as superintendents may be mentioned Hugh A. M. White, J. H. Cowan, Campbell Wallace, John R. Henry and W. P. Washburne.

On April 24, 1886, a new congregation was organized in North Knoxville, and known as the Fourth Presbyterian Church; Rev. E. A. Elmore is the pastor.

The churches mentioned, together with Spring Place, six miles east of Knoxville, organized several years before the war, and New Prospect in the Fourteenth District, organized in 1871, constitute what was once the new school element, and now belong to a Union Presbytery of the Presbyterian Church. Shannon Dale, a church recently organized on the Tazewell Pike, is also a member of this body.

This Presbytery in common with the others in the synod withdrew from the general assembly of the Presbyterian Church in 1858, but at a meeting held at New Market in 1863, a resolution not to license or receive a member who sympatized with the Southern Confederacy, was adopted, and at the next meeting which was held at Spring Place Church on September 2, 1864, a resolution was adopted favoring a return to the general assembly of the Presbyterian Church.

On August 23, 1866, the members of Knoxville Presbytery who had remained loyal to the United States, met at Baker Creek Church in Blount County and organized Holston Presbytery. This continued as a separate body until the union of the old and new school presbytery was formed, when it was consolidated with other presbyteries in the synod of Tennesssee. The only congregation organized in Knox County under the Holston Presbytery was Pleasant Forest, now in Kingston Presbytery.

The first Cumberland Presbyterian Church in Knox County was organized in the year 1824, near the place known as Low's ferry, the residence of the late Gen. S. D. W. Low, about two miles from the present village of Concord, which took its name from this church. Andrew Russell, William Rodgers, William Gounds, J. W. Craig, Thomas Boyd and S. D. W. Low were among the first ruling elders and deacons. James Guthrie, George Russell, George Donnell, James Blair, Samuel B. West, Hiram Douglass and A. Templeton were early ministers. A camp-ground was also established at this church, where for many years meetings were held annually in July or August. The congregation, numbering about eighty members, is now worshiping in its fifth house, which is located in the village of Concord. The present pastor is Rev. J. S. Porter.

A second church, known as Marietta, was organized soon after Concord at the mouth of Hickory Creek in the Ninth Civil Distict, and a third, Beaver Creek, was established in the Eighth District, near the present site of Powell's Station. Union Church in the Tenth District, two miles west of Campbell's Station, was organized about 1863, and West Emory, two miles southwest of Ebenezer, in 1879.

In the spring of 1883 a commission, composed of Rev. E. J. McCroskey, J. R. Butt and T. W. Kellar, was appointed by the presbytery to take steps for the establishment of a church in Knoxville. Mr. McCroskey entered upon the work of soliciting subscriptions, and as soon as a sufficient amount had been obtained a lot was purchased, and the erection of a house begun. In the spring of 1885 the work had progressed sufficiently to allow of the occupancy of the building, but it is not yet entirely completed. In March, 1885, the congregation was organized with J. R. Butt and T. W. Kellar, elders; J. B. Malcolm and T. W. Carter, deacons. W. H. Baugh was installed as pastor, and so continued until June, 1886, when he was succeeded by J. V. Stephens. The present membership of this church is 110, and of the entire county about 600.

Previous to 1837 the churches in Knox County belonged to Knoxville Presbytery, but on March 15 of that year, by authority of the synod, Hiwassee Presbytery was organized at Lebanon Meeting-house, in Monroe County. It embraces all of East Tennessee from the upper line of Knox County to the Hiwassee River. The first moderator was John Tate, and the first stated clerk, Floyd McGonegal.

The Baptists began preaching and organizing churches in Knox County about 1790. It may have been a year or so earlier than that, as a church was organized at the mouth of Richland Creek, in Grainger County, in 1788. The oldest church in the county, still in existence, is Little Flat Creek, which was organized in 1796. Among the earliest ministers may be mentioned William Johnson, Isaac Barton, Richard Wood, Elijah Rogers, Thomas Hudiburgh, Duke Kimbrough, Robert Fristoe, Thomas Hall, Richard Newport and West Walker. Nearly all were men of limited education, and received no pay for their services, but they possessed a rude and fervid eloquence, well suited to the mass of their hearers, and their congregations grew. It was not long until the Baptists had outnumbered both the Presbyterians and Methodists, and they have ever since maintained that position. As the history of the denomination in Knox County is largely the history of the Tennessee Association, it will be traced in connection with that body.

On the 25th of December, 1802, delegates from nineteen Baptist Churches, formerly belonging to the Holston Association, assembled at Beaver Creek Meeting-house, in Knox County, and organized the Tennessee Association. William Johnson was chosen moderator and Francis Hamilton, clerk. A plan of association and statement of religious principles was adopted, embracing, with some slight alterations, an extract from "Asplund's Register."

Of the nineteen churches represented at this meeting five were located in Knox County. They were Beaver Ridge, represented by Aquila Low, Thomas Hudiburgh and Jesse Councill; Hickory Creek, represented by William Helms and John Finley; Fork of Holston and French Broad, represented by Alexander Bleakley; Little Flat Creek, represented by Richard Newport, Eli Scaggs and George Halmark, and Beaver Creek, represented by Francis Hamilton, John and Hezekiah Boyles. These churches, as reported the following year, embraced an aggregate membership of 172.

The first annual session of the association was held at Big Spring Church, in Grainger County, with the same officers as at the preceding meeting. Elder Richard Wood preached the introductory sermon from Acts xx, 28. Letters from twenty-three churches were received, showing a total membership in the association of 1,615. In 1806 Stock Creek Church with twenty-four members was organized, and its delegates, Aaron Smith and Abraham Reid, were admitted to seats in the association. During the next two or three years the association did not prosper, and the membership in 1809 aggregated only 1,466. Accordingly, November 4, of this year, was appointed a day of fasting and prayer for the revival of religion. In 1815 the subject of foreign missions was first introduced to the association. At the next session Luther Rice, the agent of the Baptist Board of Foreign Missions, was present, and a constitution for a local missionary society was adopted, with the reservation, however, that the churches were not to be bound by the action of their delegates. In 1817 twelve churches, situated in the counties north and northwest of Knox County, withdrew and formed Powell Valley Association, leaving seventeen congregations in the Tennessee Association. At the next session the churches in Knox County were represented as follows: Hickory Creek, John Courtney, Henry Loward, Arnold Moss, Sterling Kemp, John Freeman and Rowland Childs; Stock Creek, Joseph Johnson, James Trice and James Childers; Little Flat Creek, Peter Graves; Forks of French Broad and Holston, Randall Davenport; Beaver Ridge, Thomas Hudiburgh, Obed Patty and Eli Cleveland, and Beaver Creek, Willis Hammons. The last named church had not been represented for ten years previous. At this session a meeting of the missionary society was appointed to be held at Robert Tunnell's, in Knox County in May, 1820. At the session in 1822 the number of churches in the association had increased to twenty-eight, and it was agreed to divide it by a line running from Chilhowee Mountain with the Little Tennessee River, to the Holston; thence northwest so as to include the east fork of Poplar Creek and Hickory Creek in the upper end. A committee was then appointed to meet at Pisgah on the fourth Saturday in

May, 1823, to form a constitution for the lower association which was known thereafter as the Hiwassee Association. This left eighteen churches in the Tennessee Association, but other congregations were soon after formed and admitted. In 1830 the number had increased to twenty-six, and in 1835 to thirty. In 1836 Beaver Creek Church changed its name to Beaver Dam Creek. It afterward became simply Beaver Dam.

In 1829 a congregation was organized at Union Meeting-house, and its delegate, Thomas Hunt, was admitted to the association. From this time until 1843, however, it was not again represented. At that session J. S. Waters and Z. Reeder were its delegates. In 1830 a church known as Third Creek was organized in Knox County, and in 1833 its delegates, J. Hillsman and Samuel Love, were admitted to the association. In 1835 Hickory Creek Church withdrew. At about this time the schism in the church between the mission and anti-mission factions began to threaten serious damage to the cause. Queries from individual churches with reference to tests of fellowship, were received each year by the association, but the danger of expressing a decided opinion was apparent, and it was avoided as long as possible. In 1837, however, the query was received from Zion Church—"Is it right to fellowship the Baptist State Convention or home missionary and temperance societies?" The reply was, "We advise our churches not to make the joining or not joining of institutions any test of fellowship." This resulted in the withdrawal of two churches and serious divisions in others. The anti-mission party, however, were very largely in the minority, and the Tennessee Association stood unshaken. In an address issued by the association in 1843 to the Baptists of the State, urging the importance of a general association, is the following: "We rejoice that so much union seems to exist on the subject, and cannot help looking back to the origin of this convention, when it was followed by an opposition fierce and clamorous; we rejoice that whilst the anti-mission spirit has been prowling around our association and convention, we have been so far preserved from its withering and destructive influence, and instead of being annihilated by its insults and torpedo touch, our churches, under the blessings of the God of missions, have been greatly increased and built up in their strength."

During these troublous times new churches continued to be established. Those in Knox County were Mount of Olives, in 1837; New Hopewell, 1840, and Knoxville, 1843.

As has been stated in the early history of the Baptist churches in East Tennessee its greatest numerical strength lay in the country and remote from towns, therefore it is not strange that the organization of a church at Knoxville occurred at so late a date, and that when it did occur the membership was so small, numbering as it did only twenty-six white persons, and twenty colored. It is remarkable, however, that its organization was suggested by a man not a member of any church, and was effected chiefly through his instrumentality. That man was James C. Moses, who, with his brother John L. Moses, had then recently arrived at Knoxville. He afterward was the first person baptized into the fellowship of this church, was its first clerk, a member of its first board of deacons and trustees and the first superintendent of its Sabbath-school.

On the 15th of January, 1843, a sort of mass meeting, composed mainly of Baptists from the surrounding country, met in the upper room of the courthouse, at which time arrangements were made for completing the organization of a congregation on the following Sabbath. The ministers present upon this occassion were Rev. Messrs. Kennon, Kimbrough, Milliken, Bellue, Coram and Ray. During the next few months the church grew rapidly, and by August the enrollment reached eighty-five. Thirty having been added by experience and seventeen by letter, while seven had been dismissed and one excommunicated. This large increase was due to two revivals, which were held during the spring and summer. The first was conducted in the First Presbyterian Church by Rev. Dr. Baker, of Texas, and the other by Rev. Israel Robards, a man of great power, who drew large crowds to hear him. He continued for several successive days and nights, and awakened a deep interest.

The first pastor of the church was Rev. Joseph A. Bullard, who remained but one year. Prominent among his successors may be mentioned G. W. Griffin, L. B. Woolfolk, J. L. Lloyd, J. F. B. Mays, George B. Eager, C. H. Strickland, and the present pastor, E. A. Taylor.

In 1844 the erection of a church on Gay Street was begun, and completed about two years later. This served the congregation as a place of worship until 1886, when one of the finest churches in the South was erected upon the site of the old church. It will cost when completed $30,000. Of this sum, one member, Capt. W. W. Woodruff, contributed one-half.

This church now has a membership of 640, and maintains a Sunday-school with over 500 scholars.

In November, 1873, a second congregation was organized in Knoxville, and a house of worship was erected on McGhee Street. The location was found to be unsuitable, however, and in November, 1880, the congregation was disbanded. A short time after a mission was established in the northern portion of the city, and there in November, 1885, Calvary Church was organized with Rev. O. L. Hailey as pastor, and L. Huddleston, W. C. McCoy, W. A. J. Moore, G. W. Peters, J. J. Martin, J. R. Dew and J. A. Galyon as trustees. It has since been highly prosperous, and in one year the membership has increased from 53 to 115. But to return to the association.

In 1844 the "New Hampshire Confession of Faith" was adopted. The radical difference between these articles and those adopted at the first session in 1802 is conclusive evidence of the great revolution which had taken place in the church. From this time until the beginning of the civil war, the association continued to prosper. In 1862 there were within its bounds thirty-nine churches, having an aggregate membership of 4,119, of whom 125 were colored. Six new churches have been established in Knox County. They were, Adair Creek, 1845; Brick Chapel, Lyon Creek, Mount Pisgah and Mars' Hill, now Gallaher's View, 1855, and Sinking Creek, 1859.

During the war nearly all the churches suffered more or less from loss of both members and property, and some were entirely destroyed. But the work of reviving old churches and establishing new ones was entered upon with zeal and energy, and in 1870 there were forty-five churches and 4,705 members within the bounds of the association. Of this number fifteen churches and 1,755 members were included in Knox County.

In 1873 Little River Association was formed, and the following year, seven churches, including all of those in Knox County south of the Tennessee River, except Stock Creek, withdrew from the Tennessee Association to join Little River, now Chilhowee Association.

Since January, 1870, new churches have been constituted in Knox County as follows: Stock Creek, 1870; Sharon, 1871; Pleasant Gap, 1874; Meridian, 1874; Pleasant Hill, 1875; Mount Harmony, 1875; Fair View, 1877; Guesses Creek, 1877; Hill's Chapel, 1879, and Calvary, 1885. There are now in the county twenty churches belonging to the Tennessee Association, having a combined membership of 2,434, and four belonging to the Chilhowee Association, with an aggregate membership of 642, making a total of twenty-four churches, and 3,076 members.

At three different times periodicals have been published at Knoxville, under the auspices of the Tennessee Association. The first was established in 1855, and was known as the *Baptist Watchman*, a weekly, edited by M. Hillsman. It continued only a few years. In 1868 D. M. Braeker began the publication of the *East Tennessee Baptist*, which in 1870 was consolidated with the *Christian Herald*. In 1880 the *Beacon* was established by Rev. J. B. Jones. After about two years it was consolidated with the *Reflector*, of Nashville, and has since been published in Chattanooga as the *Baptist Reflector*.

Until 1844, ten years after the first bishop of the diocese of Tennessee was consecrated to his office, no Episcopal Church had been organized in East Tennessee. Several attempts had been made to establish a church at Knoxville, but each had resulted in a discouraging failure. In March, 1844, Thomas W. Humes, who was a candidate for the ministry, began to serve as a lay reader on the morning of each Lord's day, but, owing to the deep prejudice existing in the community against the Episcopal Church, the movement met with strong disfavor, and the congregations were small. On the 9th of June, Rev. Charles Tomes, of New York, by appointment of the bishop, took charge of the parish, and entered upon his work with energy and zeal. The services were at first conducted at a dwelling-house, but were soon transferred to a small building at the northeast corner of Gay and Church Streets, which was donated for that purpose by Andrew R. Humes. This building was neatly fitted up as a chapel, and was occupied for over two years. On July 22, 1845, the corner-stone of St. John's Church was laid with appropriate exercises by the bishop of the diocese. At about this time T. W. Humes, having been ordained a deacon at Columbia the preceding March, became an assistant to the rector. On September 21, of the following year, Mr. Tomes resigned the rectorship, and was succeeded by Rev. Mr. Humes, who continued in that position, with the exception of about two years in the early part of the war, until 1869, when he also resigned. During the two years previous to September, 1863, the rectorship was occupied by Rev. William Vaux, of Loudon.

In the year 1844 the communicants of St. John's Church numbered twenty-one. Upon the resignation of Mr. Tomes in September, 1846, they had increased to forty-one. During the next fifteen years of Mr. Humes' first incumbency about 154 were added, and about 132 were lost by death and removal, leaving in September, 1861, a membership of sixty-two. During the next two years this number was diminished so that, upon Mr. Humes resuming the rectorship in September, 1863, he found only thirty-six communicants; they were increased during the next five years to ninety. Rev. William Graham succeeded to the rectorship in January, 1869, and served until the autumn of 1870. He was followed by Rev. John H. Smith, who resigned at the end of nearly four years, and was succeeded by Rev. Thomas Duncan. Mr. Duncan ministered to the congregation very satisfactorily for nearly six years.

In 1867 Dr. Humes, the rector of St. John's Church, and his assistant, William Mowbray, laid the foundation of the church of the Epiphany in North Knoxville. The first services were held in the cemetery. The next Sunday the basement of a steam mill was procured, and this was used for a time. Through the instrumentality of Charles McGhee a lot was soon after obtained, and during the next year the present church, located on Broad Street, was completed. Mr. Mowbray served the church as rector for about two years, when, after an interval, he was succeeded by Rev. Everard Meade, who continued in charge of the church for several years. The next rector was A. A. McDonaugh, who also remained about ten years. The present rector is Rev. A. Buchanan. The church now numbers over 100 communicants, and is in a highly prosperous condition.

The Church of Christ, or Disciple's Church as it is some times denominated, had its beginning in 1870; a few of that faith meeting in hired rooms and from house to house for prayer and Bible study. Gradually growing stronger they, on the first Lord's day of September, 1874, under the direction of L. H. Stine, a young minister, then just from school at Bethany, W. Va., united in a covenant to worship God according to the Holy Scripture, and became a regularly organized congregation with A. C. Bruce as elder and N. R. Hall and George T. Rhoades as deacons. Their number at this time was eighteen, all poor. They have gradually increased until now they count seventy-six on the roll of membership. The present officers are N. R. Hall and Lewis Tillman, elders; T. P. McDaniel, George T. Rhoades and M. O. Cooley, deacons. During the more than twelve years elapsing since their organization they have had only about two years of preaching. The other while the elders have conducted the worship, and but few Lord's days have passed without the meeting of the Sunday-school and the congregation in their regular service. The ministers who served the congregation at different times are E. F. Taylor, A. S. Johnson and N. G. Jacks. For a number of years the congregation met at the corner of Depot and Broad Streets, then at their church house on McGhee Street. Recently they have built a house of worship on Park Street, a very neat frame with round tower and cathedral windows in front, and having a seating capacity of 500, and there they now regularly meet on Lord's day. The church is now without a pastor, but efforts are being made to have the pulpit filled for the coming year.

The Church of the Immaculate Conception, Roman Catholic, was established at Knoxville in 1851, and from that time until 1855 was under the care of Rev. Father H. V. Brown. The first church building was erected soon after the organization, on Walnut Street near Vine. It was used until 1886, when the present fine brick was completed. The congregation now numbers over 1,000 members, and a Sunday-school is maintained with an attendance of about 300. The successors of Father

Brown have been J. L. Biemans, March, 1855, to October 24, 1857; J. Bergrath, October, 1857 to May, 1865; A. J. Ryan, May, 1865 to June, 1867; Joseph S. Keane for one year from June, 1867, and M. J. Finnegan from June, 1867 to July, 1872; since the latter date the church has been under the care of Rev. Francis Thomas Marron.

The first Evangelical Lutheran congregation organized in Knox County was Zion, established on May 18, 1823, seven and one-half miles south of Knoxville on the "Picken's Gap Road," by Rev. George Easterly. The original members were George Houser, Peter Long and Henry Long, together with their wives, to whom were added upon the day of organization by confirmation: Jacob and Frank Long, Sarah and Lydia Houser, Joseph Sane, and William Baker and wife, the latter of whom is still living.

The first building erected was a log structure, which was occupied until 1859, when the present frame was completed at a cost of $1,200. The pastors of this church have been George Easterly, Jacob M. Schaffer, J. K. Hancher, J. C. Bart, J. Cloninger and George H. Cox.

A second congregation was organized about seven miles northeast of Knoxville, about 1829, by Rev. Adam Miller, who became its first pastor. Since his incumbency, this church has been supplied by the same pastors as Zion Church. In August, 1873, a congregation, known as Bethel, was organized about four miles southwest of Knoxville on the Maryville road, by Rev. George H. Cox, who has since continued as its pastor. The original members were L. E. Williams and wife, A. A. Rudder and wife, Alexander Henson and wife, Mrs. S. Maxey and N. B. Williams.

In 1869, at the request of Dr. Passavant, a benevolent gentleman of Philadelphia, Rev. John Heckle came to Knoxville and organized an Evangelical Lutheran Church, among the incorporators of which were Peter Kern, C. Sturn and John Aurin. A frame house, 31x50 feet, was soon after erected and dedicated. At that time there was a debt outstanding and held by members amounting to $2,700. This was promptly and generously canceled by the creditors. Mr. Heckle continued in charge of the church over four years, and after an interval of about eighteen months was succeeded by the present pastor, J. George Schaidt, a graduate of the Philadelphia Theological Seminary. Under his pastorate the church has greatly prospered, and now has a membership of about 180.

The Welsh Congregational Church, of Knoxville, was the first church of the kind organized in the county. Many Welsh people came to the city from Pennsylvania in April, 1866, and were the leading managers and workmen in the rolling mill. Many of them were pious and faithful

Christians, and for about three years united themselves with the Second Presbyterian Church, assembling for Divine worship in their lecture room, but in June they resolved to organize a congregation of their own, and to build a church edifice on Atkin Street, in Mechanicsville, now the Ninth Ward. Accordingly, a neat frame house, capable of seating about 250 persons, was erected at a cost of $3,000, to which $1,000 for improvements and repairs have since been added. These amounts were paid by the free contributions of the Welsh people, assisted by the liberal donations of the citizens of Knoxville and other places. The first trustees and deacons were Joseph Richards, John Jones and Thomas Davis. On February 12, 1870, Rev. Thomas Thomas was installed as pastor, and continued until the close of 1871. In September, 1872, Rev. Robert D. Thomas (Lorthryn Gwynedd) commenced his ministry, and labored successfully for three years. In July, 1877, he returned, and continued, as pastor until June, 1882, when he resigned, and in November, 1883, was succeeded by Rev. D. D. Davis. The latter remained until December, 1885, since which time Mr. Thomas has served the congregation. A good Sabbath-school, a Band of Hope and a temperance society are also maintained. The present officers are Robert D. Thomas, pastor; David Richards and David C. Richards, deacons; E. J. Davis, treasurer; David J. Richards, secretary, and E. J. Davis, superintendent of the Sabbath-school.

A preliminary organization of the Pilgrim Congregational Church was made in June, 1886, by Supt. C. C. Creeg. In September following E. Lyman Hood was called to the pastorate, and on December 19 the organization was completed with twenty-three members. No house of worship has yet been erected, but services are held in the Young Men's Christian Association rooms.

Previous to the war the colored members of all denominations in most instances worshiped with the white congregations, but since that time they have maintained separate organizations.

The First Baptist Church known as Mount Zion was organized in March, 1866, by Rev. Talton Emory with thirteen members. A house which has since been remodeled and enlarged was erected in 1869, and is now valued at $6,000. The present membership is nearly 1,000. Two other Baptist Churches have since been organized.

The African Methodist Episcopal Zion Church was organized about 1866, and worshiped for a time in a house on Clinch Street. They are now occupying their third house, an excellent frame building erected in 1883. The membership of this church is very large.

The African Methodist Episcopal Church was organized in 1884 by

J. W. Grigsby, and in 1886 they erected a neat frame house on Crozier Street.

Shiloh Presbyterian Church was organized about 1869, and is now a member of Union Presbytery. Its house of worship is situated on Clinch near Henley. The membership is about 135.

The Second Congregational Church was organized April 21, 1883, by S. P. Smith, the present pastor, with eighteen members. Under the auspices of the American Missionary Association, the Methodist Church on Mabry Street was purchased, and has since been organized. The congregation numbering about sixty members includes some of the best colored citizens of the city.

Attempts to establish common schools in Knox County were made as early as 1830, but, as in other sections of the State, little of value was accomplished. Under the system inaugurated in 1839, somewhat more benefit was derived from them, but the funds for their support were inadequate and the instruction afforded by them was of very inferior character. Under the law of 1867 an attempt was made to put a system of public schools in operation, and for a brief period considerable progress was made in that direction. The first school was opened in the Thirteenth Civil District on May 14, 1865, and on September 13, 1869, the one hundred and twenty-sixth school was opened. Of this number twenty-three were for colored children. The lack of sufficient funds and the irregularity of their payment, the absence of suitable hours and a not inconsiderable hostility on the part of the public, conspired to render the system unsuccessful. No tax was levied by the county court, and although a tax of three mills on the dollar was voted by the citizens of Knoxville, no levy was made by the board of aldermen. With the funds received from the State, amounting to $2,225.47, a few schools were opened in the city, but these ceased, as did those in the country, upon the repeal of the law in December, 1869. Under the law of July, 1870, the county court levied a tax sufficient to run the schools for four or five months in the year, but as no county superintendent was elected, there was a general lack of discipline and thoroughness. The county board of education, composed of district commissioners, was too unwieldy and consequently inefficient for almost all practical purposes. In 1873 the present school law went into effect, and in April of that year Mr. T. C. Karns was elected county superintendent. In August the boards of directors were chosen, and soon after schools were organized in every district. For 1873 the rates of county tax for school purposes were 10 cents on each $100 worth of property, $1 on each poll and ten per cent of the privilege tax. The same rates were maintained in 1874 and 1875. The total amount of money received during the latter year from both State and county tax was $23,698.31, while the aggregate expenditures was $37,877.72. The total scholastic population was 9,689, of whom 5,603 were enrolled in the schools. The number of schools opened was 100 white and twenty-one colored,

Since that time there has been a steady improvement in the schools of the county. Better houses have been erected, numerous institutes have been held, thereby increasing the efficiency of the teachers, the schools have been better graded, and the length of the session has been increased. The county superintendent in his report for 1886 says: "Our schools in Knox County were in a very prosperous condition during the past year. The increase in scholastic population, enrollment average, daily attendance and uniform grading show that we have made greater progress than in any previous year. There were in operation 127 schools, the most of which continued five months. There were erected during the year five handsome school buildings, furnished with neat desks and comfortable seats, at a total cost of $3,700. The amount of funds received from the State and county amounted to $34,544,39. The expenditures aggregated $35,769,94. The scholastic population excluding Knoxville was 11,149, and the enrollment 8,749."

The following named persons have held the office of county superintendent: M. C. Wilcox, T. C. Karns, H. M. Brother, H. C. Hamstead, W. C. Gibbs, Frank M. Smith, J. R. Shipe and John W. Saylor.

BIOGRAPHICAL APPENDIX.

KNOX COUNTY.

H. M. Aiken, president and sole owner of the Tennessee & Ohio Railroad, was born in Morgan County, Ohio, March 4, 1844, and in early boyhood was taken to Virginia. He graduated at Washington and Jefferson College in 1863, and in the law department of the University of Pennsylvania. A year later he came to Knoxville, and was admitted to the bar in 1865. He practiced his profession five years, then became clerk of the United States Courts eight years, since which time he has devoted his attention to railroading and steamboating. The Tennessee & Ohio Railroad connects Rogersville with the East Tennessee, Virginia & Georgia Railroad, and is sixteen miles in length; the bridge over the Holston River is said to be the highest in the State. This road was constructed in 1858, and purchased by Mr. Aiken in 1879. He also owns a line of steamers, which ply the St. John's River, Florida. In 1867 he married Mary, daughter of Gov. Brownlow, to whom six children have been born, all now living. William A., the father, was born at Hamburg, Penn.; was a minister in the Presbyterian Church, and filled one charge in Virginia twenty-five years. In 1866 he came to Knoxville, and resided here until his death, May, 1886. The mother, Martha Osborn, is a native of Ohio, and now resides in Knoxville. Our subject is one of a family of five children, two of whom are deceased.

Capt. Samuel P. Angel, now a prominent and influential citizen and merchant of Knoxville, Tenn., is a son of Samuel and Martha G. (Burrow) Angel. He was born in Carter County, Tenn., in 1840. His father was born in 1807 and died in 1872. His mother was born in 1813 and died in 1864. Capt. Angel was reared in Elizabethton, Tenn., by parents who were strict Methodists in faith and practice, and acquired an excellent education at Duffield Academy of that town. In 1863 he enlisted in the Federal Army, joining Company G, Thirteenth Regiment Tennessee Cavalry, as a private, but was soon promoted to orderly sergeant of that company, to sergeant-major of the regiment in 1864, to adjutant of the regiment, in 1865, and to captain of Company H in the same year. At the battle of Saulsbury, N. C., he was wounded in the right hand, and had a horse shot from under him. At the close of the war the brigade to which Capt. Angel's company belonged, having been ordered South in pursuit of Jefferson Davis, the fleeing ex-President of the Southern Confederacy, he passed through Lexington, Ga., and was the first Federal soldier to enter the residence of Hon. Alexander H. Stephens in a rather social call, and received the kind hospitalities of that distinguished gentleman. Mr. Stephens received them most cordially, and entertained them elegantly at "tea," and said he supposed that they had come to arrest him. To his great ease and comfort he was informed that they had neither instructions nor authority to do so. After peace was declared and the armies were disbanded, Capt. Angel located in Knoxville, Tenn., and engaged in his present business in October, 1865, leading dealer in guns, sporting goods, sewing machines, etc. In the same year he married Miss Julia E. Piper, then a member of a family of social prominence in Rogersville, Tenn. She was the daughter of William and Lucinda (Beal) Piper, the former a native of Virginia, and the latter of Tennessee, and was born in 1848. There were born unto them five children, three of whom are living as follows: Blanch, Samuel P., Jr., and William P. Capt. Angel joined the Edward Maynard Post, No. 14, G. A. R., of Knoxville, the same year of its organization, and is still an honored member of the same. In religion Capt. Angel is a Methodist, and is an active, zealous and efficient member of the Methodist Episcopal Church. In 1884 he was elected by the annual session of the Holston Conference a lay delegate to the general conference of that church, held in Philadelphia, Penn., and attended its sessions. For a number of years he has been prominently identified with the Sunday-school work of his church, and the union work of the county, and is at present not only president of the Knox County Sunday-school Convention for the second time, but is president of the East Tennessee Sunday-school Convention for the present year. Capt. Angel has an honorable record of patriotic and useful labor, and is a valuable citizen of the community in which he lives.

D. F. De Armond, an old and prominent farmer, was born in Knox County July 17, 1807. He is the son of Richard I. and Rhoda (Hinch) De Armond, natives of North Carolina and Virginia. The father was one of the early settlers of East Tennessee. Our subject was educated in the subscription schools of his native county, and has never attended a free school. His education was very limited, but, notwithstanding this, he has acquired, by study and observation, sufficient knowledge to enable him to transact all ordinary business. In 1831 he married Miss Sarah Hines, a native of Knox County, Tenn., born December 28, 1812, and died September 13, 1883. She was the daughter of Robert Hines. To our subject and wife were born twelve children—ten sons and two daughters. Five of these children are deceased—four sons and a daughter. The daughter died when but five years of age. Of the four sons deceased two lost their lives in the Federal Army and one in the Confederate Army. The fourth was a Federal soldier, and died of lung disease a few years after the close of the war. The children now living are Columbus, James, Dowe, David, Marian and William. Our subject was justice of the peace for a number of years, and was postmaster at Gap Creek for thirty years. He is the owner of more than 800 acres of Knox County land, and is a Democrat in politics.

Moses A. M. Armstrong, register of Knox County, Tenn., was born in the year 1861, and is the son of Thomas N. and Ann Eliza (Love) Armstrong, both natives of Knox County, Tenn. The father is a successful farmer, and is now engaged in agricultural pursuits in this county. Our subject, five brothers and one sister are the surviving members of a family of eight children born to the union of their parents. Moses Armstrong grew to manhood on the farm, and secured a good education at Asbury, this county. He is a charter member of the land improvement company, of Knoxville, which was organized in December, 1886, and he was elected to his present office August 5, 1886. He is a young man of energy and push, and the future is bright before him.

J. K. Ault, a farmer, and a native of Knox County, Tenn., was born December 4, 1834. He is the son of Michael and Mary (Brown) Ault, both natives of Tennessee, and of German and Scotch lineage respectively. The subject of this sketch was reared on a farm, and educated in the common schools. In 1858 he chose for his companion in life Miss Margaret Karns, a native of Tennessee, who bore him six children, two of whom are deceased. Those living are Charles L., William G. and James W. Charles L. was born September 18, 1859, and is a contracting carpenter. He married Miss Rachel Rutherford in 1879, and their children are Lizzie and Margaret. The next is James W., a grocer, at 192 Mabry Street, Knoxville, who was born July 26, 1865, and who married Miss Cyntha J. Bounds in 1883. Two children, Bettie Lee and Lena May, have blessed this union. Our subject owns a farm of seventy-five acres of land in the Second District of Knox County, and 300 acres in Loudon County. In 1874 his wife died, and in 1875 he married Miss Martha Rutherford, who bore him four sons and three daughters, one son and one daughter being deceased. Those living are Albert H., Henry A., Margaret D., Cyntha C. and Robert B. Mr. Ault and his sons are members of the Methodist Episcopal Church South, and are Democrats.

R. D. Badgett, farmer, was born July 13, 1820, within a mile of where he now resides. He is the sixth of eight children born to Burwell F. and Lucy (Faulkner) Badgett. (For further particulars of parents see sketch of B. F. Badgett.) Our subject attended school several years at the East Tennessee University, and taught school during the year 1851. At the age of twenty-four he engaged in business for himself and was in only moderate circumstances. Besides $40,000 which was destroyed and stolen during the late war, he owned a fine farm of 166 acres under a splendid state of cultivation, and located on the Tennessee River nine miles southwest of Knoxville. In March, 1855, previous to the war, he married Miss Eliza Jane Reeder, a native of Blount County, born in 1833 and the daughter of Maj. Reeder. Mr. and Mrs. Maj. Reeder were born and reared in Virginia. He immigrated to Tennessee, a poor man, at quite an early day, but by industry has accumulated quite a fortune. To our subject and wife were born these children: Susie R., Barckley Majors (deceased), Susan Reeder, Charles, Nannie V., Cassandria E. (Mrs. C. N. Martin), Elizabeth Wallace, Rebecca J. and Roberta C. Mr. Badgett is a Democrat in politics, casting his first presidential vote for James K. Polk, and he and his family are members of the Methodist Episcopal Church. He is a Master Mason, and served his district as school commissioner two years.

B. F. Badgett, a successful agriculturist of the Eleventh District, was born May 4, 1833, near the mouth of Little River. He is one of nine children born to B. F. and Lucy (Faulkner) Badgett, natives of Buncombe County, N. C., where they were reared and married. About 1813 they immigrated to Tennessee, settling near Stock Creek in Knox County. B. F. Badgett, Sr., took quite an interest in the political affairs of his county and State and was a very successful farmer. He and his wife were of purely Irish descent. Our subject had excellent educational advantages, and lacked only six months of graduating in the classical course at the East Tennessee University. When twenty-two years of age he married Miss Clementine Gillespie, a daughter of Cowin Gillespie, of Blount County, Tenn. The result of this marriage was the birth of six children: William C., Lucy A. (deceased), Eglentine (Mrs. S. L. Tillery), Mary (deceased), Ransome N. and Florence C. Mrs. Badgett died August 16, 1874, and October 23, 1877, Mr. Badgett married Miss Josephine M. Cottrell, a native of Knox County, and the daughter of Samuel and Louisa T. (Sommers) Cottrell. To Mr. and Mrs. Badgett was born one child named Rebecca. Mr. Badgett is a Democrat in politics and cast his first presidential vote for James Buchanan. He is a member of the Methodist Episcopal Church and his wife is a member of the Missionary Baptist Church. He is a Master Mason and a prominent citizen of the county. He has been quite successful as a farm manager and had accumulated considerable property before the war but lost a great deal of it during that event. He now owns 418 acres of land, nine miles southwest of Knoxville. He has some rich deposits of very valuable marble and ore on his farm.

S. E. Badgett, a successful tiller of the soil, was born February 7, 1834, on a farm, where he has since resided. He is the third of nine children born to Ransome and Sophira (Hunter) Badgett. Ransome Badgett was born and reared in Surry County, N. C., on the Yadkin River. He came to Tennessee in 1812, settling on the farm where his son now resides. He organized a company for the war of 1812, and equipped it at his own expense. He was a very enthusiastic and successful farmer, and accumulated considerable property. He was one of the men who ran the State line between Georgia and Tennessee. He died in 1862, aged about ninety years. He was a very prominent civil engineer, and assisted considerably in establishing the boundary lines of the different counties of his part of the State, and also made quite an extensive study of medicine, his books being purchased in England by his father. His father, James Badgett, was born and reared in North Carolina, where he died. Ransome Badgett's wife died in 1865, aged about seventy-one years. Our subject was educated in the common schools of Knox County, and after reaching his majority was united in marriage to Miss Drucilla Sharp, a native of Union County, a member of the Missionary Baptist Church, and the daughter of Andrew and Sinai (Zackery) Sharp. Mr. Badgett inherited some property from his father, but by his success as a farmer, manager and practical business man, has added considerable to what he then received. He owns 125 acres of splendid land well improved and well cultivated, situated nine miles southwest of Knoxville. He is a Democrat in politics, and cast his first presidential vote for the Whig candidate of 1856.

J. H. Ballard, dairyman, was born in Albemarle County, Va., August 17, 1838. He received a common-school education, and grew to manhood on the farm. He began for himself by collecting for people in Charlottsville, Va. In 1861 he joined the Confederate Army as a private in Company K, Second Virginia Calvary. This corps, before it was known as Company K, was called "Albemarle Light Horse." He reached the rank of captain, and was in many of the principal battles and skirmishes. He served fourteen years of his life as deputy collector, deputy marshal and United States Gauger in Virginia. In 1863 he married Miss Sallie A. Whitehead, of Nelson County, Va., who is the daughter of Floyd L.

Whitehead, of Virginia. To this union were born eight sons and one daughter, two of the sons being deceased. Mr. Ballard came to Knoxville, Tenn., in 1886, purchased a tract of ninety acres of land situated near Knoxville and in the Second District. On this tract he is farming and dairying. He is not a political schemer, but is a faithful Republican. He is the son of Thomas and Lucy B. (Duke) Ballard.

A. A. Barnes, a retired lawyer, at present engaged in farming, was born in Chelsea, Vt., in 1821, and is the second of four children born to Henry and Hannah (Rolfe) Barnes, both born and reared in Massachusetts. His grandfathers were both soldiers in the Revolutionary war. Our subject graduated at the University of Vermont in 1845, and studied law at Knoxville under Horace Maynard. He was admitted to the bar in 1849, and then practiced law with Mr. Maynard, afterward with Maj. Thomas C. Lyon. He married Miss Louisa T. Lyon, the daughter of William and Mary Payne (Clark) Lyon, natives of Maryland and Virginia respectively. Mr. Lyon came to Tennessee when eighteen years old, and shortly after his marriage moved to Knox County, where he remained until his death. He was appointed marshal of East Tennessee by Gen. Jackson in 1828. Mrs. Barnes is the youngest of eight children. Her brother, Maj. Lyon, was an aid-de-camp under Gen. Wool in removing the Indians from Tennessee to Indian Territory, was quite a prominent and successful lawyer at Knoxville, and was appointed supreme judge of Tennessee to fill the unexpired term of the judge deceased. Capt. William Lyon, great grandfather of Mrs. A. A. Barnes, donated the land and built the first Presbyterian Church in Baltimore, Md. Mrs. Barnes has a gold watch which was brought to America by Capt. William Lyon, Sr., and is about one hundred and fifty years old, a relic of a past age. To our subject and wife were born three children: Susan Wallace (deceased), Mary Rolfe and Lou Lyon (now Mrs. Rev. F. E. Sturgis, D. D.). Mr. Barnes was formerly a Whig, but now votes with the Democratic party. He and wife and family are members of the Second Presbyterian Church in Knoxville. During the late war he was general ticket and freight agent on the East Tennessee, Virginia & Georgia Railroad. After the war he was appointed general ticket and freight agent on the Memphis & Charleston Railroad for seven years. He originated and signed the first bill of lading of cotton from Memphis to Liverpool. He is a prominent member of the I. O. O. F., and is Past Grand Master of Tennessee, and is also Past Grand Representative of the Grand Lodge of the United States. He is a ruling elder of his church, and was twice appointed commissioner to the general assembly of the Presbyterian Church.

J. F. Baumann, senior member of the firm of Baumann Bros., and the leading architect of Knoxville, Tenn., was born in Monroe County, Tenn., January 16, 1844, and is a son of William and Catherine (Snyder) Baumann, both natives of Germany. They came to America when young, and were married in New York. Later they found their way to Monroe County, Tenn. The father was an architect and builder. In 1854 they moved to Knoxville where the mother is still living. Our subject was educated in that city, and in early life learned the carpenter's trade, as he progressed he also commenced taking contracts. Since 1876 he has devoted his energies to architecture. Among the prominent buildings for which he has furnished plans are the First Baptist Church, Broadstreet Methodist Episcopal Church, Catholic Church, Third Presbyterian Church, Staubs' Theatre, the Girls High School building and nearly all of the ward school buildings in the city. Besides he has planned some of the finest residences and business blocks in the city. In 1878 he married Miss Ella K. McCafferty of Alexandria, Va., and they have now three children—one son and two daughters. Mr. Baumann is a member of the Third Presbyterian Church, having been deacon for several years. He is also a member of the Masonic fraternity; a member of the Western Association of Architects, and he is also vice-president of the State association of architects. He is thoroughly identified with the progress and advancement of the city, and enjoys the respect and confidence of the entire community. Mrs. Baumann is a member of the Baptist Church.

William M. Baxter, general solicitor for the East Tennessee Railroad system, was born August 30, 1850, in Alexander, N. C. He is the eldest son of Hon. John Baxter, who appears in the State department of this work. William was brought to Knoxville when six years of age, and here received his primary education. He finished his education at Earlham College, Richmond, Ind.; at Kenyon College, Gambier, Ohio, and at Hobart College, Geneva, N. Y., graduating from the last named institution in 1870 as fourth in a large class. He then began reading law under his father, and two years later was admitted to the bar, becoming a partner of his father. In 1875 he moved to Chattanooga in order to practice his profession, but three years later, his father having been appointed United States circuit judge, he returned to Knoxville and took up the large practice of his father. In 1880 he married Mary, daughter of John Kirkman, of Nashville, and to them were born two children: John K. and William M. In 1882 Mr. Baxter was chosen to his present position and in 1886 he was nominated Republican candidate for supreme judge of the State, and though defeated he had the satisfaction of running over 1,000 votes ahead of his ticket. Mr. Baxter, like his father, has shown himself to be a very able man before a jury. Both he and wife are members of the Episcopal Church.

Herman G. Bayless, M. D., a successful practioner of Knoxville, Tenn., was born in Covington, Ky., March, 25, 1854, and is the son of John C. and Rosa (Lewis) Bayless. The father was born in Louisville, Ky., and was a prominent minister of the Presbyterian Church. Previous to his death, which occurred in 1875, he was minister in charge of the First Presbyterian Church, of Covington and Ashland Ky. The mother was a native of South Carolina, born in 1826 and died in 1858. Our subject was reared in Covington and Ashland Ky., and acquired his literary education at Center College, situated at Danville, Ky. In 1873 he entered the Ohio Medical College, at Cincinnati, Ohio, where he graduated in 1878. He then passed a year at the Good Samaritan Hospital of Cincinnati, after which he began the practice of medicine at Augusta, Ky., where he remained until 1883. He then went to Europe, and spent two years in the hospitals of Vienna, Austria, and London, England. He returned to America, and in January, 1886, located in Knoxville, where he has since resided practicing his profession. June 25, 1879, he married Miss Mary Armstrong, of Augusta, Ky., who is the daughter of Hon. A. C. Armstrong (deceased). To them has been born one child, Herman A. Dr. Bayless is a member of the Masonic, A. L. of H., and other benovelent associations of Knoxville. He and wife are members of the Second Presbyterian Church.

Capt. F. C. Beaman is a native of Malone, N. Y., born Dec. 25, 1836. He received a collegiate education at Middleberry College, Vt., and upon him was conferred the honorary degree of A. M., but his joining the United States Army precluded his receiving the degree of A. B. He enlisted as a private in Company G, Ninety-eighth New York Volunteers, and was promoted through the successive ranks of his company until he became captain. He received the last promotion for gallantry displayed at the battle of Cold Harbor. After the war he located in Knox County, Tenn., and in 1866 engaged in teaching school. In 1868 he married Miss Mary J. Sherrod, daughter of Jonathan Sherrod. She was born in Tennessee, June 13, 1850, and to her marriage were born four sons and three daughters: Orin C., Ruth, Blanche, Clarence, Maggie, Ernest Andrew and James Garfield. After teaching in the graded schools of Knox and Sevier Counties for ten years Mr. Beaman received the chair of ancient languages in the Grant Memorial University at Athens, Tenn., where he remained for four years, and then resigned on account of ill health. He removed to Knox County and began farming, having purchased land near Knoxville, on which he has carried on farming and dairying until recently. He is now engaged in building and arranging a pleasure park, which consists of forty-five acres, in which is a lake containing ten acres and a school of springs which are noted for their medicinal properties. He has selected a healthful and beautiful spot, which promises to be a favorite resort for pleasure and health. The park is situated two and a half miles from the center of the city, and one mile beyond the terminus of the Bell Avenue and Mabry Street Railroad line. Mr. Beaman is a Republican in politics, and he, wife and eldest three children are members of the Methodist Episcopal Church. He is an excellent citizen, and is well liked by all who know him. He is the son of Timothy and Rebecca (Allen) Beaman. The father was a native of Vermont and was elected representative to the New York Legislature. He was the brother of F. C. Beaman, of Adrain, Mich., who served twelve years in the United States Congress. The mother was a native of New York, and was related to the Allens of Revolutionary fame.

J. N. Betterton, of the firm of Betterton & Co., wholesale liquor dealers of Knoxville, Tenn., is a native of Campbell County, Va., born August 22, 1843, and the son of Thomas and Charlotte (Callaway) Betterton, both natives of Virginia. The father was born in 1807, was a merchant farmer and died in 1861. The mother was born in 1811 and died in 1872. Our subject was reared in the county of his birth, and educated at Bristol, Tenn. In August, 1861, he enlisted in the Confederate Army, joining Staunton Hill Artillery, with which he served throughout the war. He removed to Tennessee in 1868, and located at Knoxville, where he engaged in the wholesale liquor business as a member of the firm of W. J. Betterton & Bros. In 1870 he was united in marriage to Mrs. Zephana Steptoe, of Virginia, who was born in 1843, and who is the daughter of J. H. Whitlow, a member of the firm of Betterton & Co. She is a member of the Methodist Episcopal Church. In 1880 our subject became a member of the present firm. He is a member of the Felix K., Zollicoffer Camp, No. 3, Confederate Veterans, and also of the Chilhowee Club, of Knoxville.

Adam B. Blake, farmer and one of the oldest living citizens of Knox County, Tenn., was born in South Carolina September 4, 1800, and is the son of John Blake, a native of Ireland, who was born April 14, 1766, and died April 3, 1850. The mother was a native of Ireland, born December 15, 1773, and died November 13, 1837. Her father was a native of Ireland, born December 2, 1768, and completed his education in Glasgow, Scotland; came to Pennsylvania, and here married Miss Mary Smith; came to Tennessee and settled in Knox County, rearing ten children; was a beloved pastor of the Presbyterian Church, and died August 30, 1826. His wife was born in Pennsylvania April 10, 1777, and died October 11, 1853. Our subject received a very limited education in the common schools, and in 1824 came to Tennessee, settled in the Seventeenth District of Knox County, where in the same year he wedded Miss Jane M. I. Kennedy, daughter of Rev. James Kennedy. She was born in Knox County February 14, 1806, and from her girlhood has been a member of the Presbyterian Church. Mr. Blake has also been a member of the same church from early youth. Nine children were the result of our subject's marriage, one, James K., died when forty-two years of age, he was the eldest of the family. The remainder of the family who are married and living in Knox County, are Mary Jane, John T., Emily W., William H., Nancy E., Eliza A., Adam B. and Samuel M. Our subject is a successful, enterprising farmer, and has accumulated considerable wealth. He is the owner of 600 acres of land in Knox County, which are well improved. He has not been much of a politician, but inclines toward the Democratic party.

John T. Blake, farmer, was born in Knox County, Tenn., January 23, 1833. He is the son of Adam B. and Jane M. I. (Kennedy) Blake, natives of South Carolina and Tennessee respectively. Our subject was educated in the common schools of his native county, and early in life turned his attention to farming, which occupation he has followed successfully ever since. In 1861 he was united in marriage to Miss Martha E. Cobb, a native of Knox County, born March 5, 1845. Two sons and four daughters have blessed this union. One son, Samuel A., and one daughter Martha J., are married. The son, a farmer, married Miss Mary Hodges, and the daughter married Robert Kennedy, a farmer. Our subject is the owner of 412 acres of fine land in the Sixteenth, Seventeenth and Twenty-third Districts of Knox County, and is considered one of the wide-a-wake, thorough-going farmers of the county. He is a Democrat in politics, and for more than thirty years has been a zealous member of the Presbyterian Church.

William H. Blake, farmer, was born in Knox County, Tenn., January 23, 1838. He is the son of Adam B. and Jane M. J. (Kennedy) Blake, natives of North Carolina and Tennessee, born in 1800 and 1806 respectively. Our subject secured his primary education in the common country schools, and later attended Holston College in Blount County. After leaving the latter institution he was united in marriage to Miss Mary A. Cobb, who presented him with five children: Margaret J., born February 13, 1866; James K., born December 25, 1866; Alice E., born December 27, 1872; Robert B., born February 26, 1877, and Anna Porter, born

May 14, 1879. Mr. Blake owns over 250 acres of land in the Sixteenth District and 160 acres in the Twenty-third District of Knox County, Tenn. This land is well improved, and our subject has a comfortable home. He takes a great interest in farming and stock raising, in which he is quite successful. He is a stanch Democrat in politics, and he and wife are members of the Presbyterian Church.

George Bond, farmer, was born October 21, 1796, in Virginia, and with his father moved to Knox County, Tenn., December 25, 1802, settling in the neighborhood where Mr. George Bond has since resided. He is the eldest of thirteen children born to Isaac and Sarah (Fryar) Bond. Isaac Bond was a very successful farmer and highly respected citizen. Mrs. Bond was born and reared in Ireland. Her father, William Fryar, immigrated to America about the time of the Revolutionary war, settling in Knox County within three miles of where Mr. Bond now resides. George Bond, grandfather of the subject of this sketch, was born and reared in England as was also his wife, Elizabeth Bond. The latter was disinherited on account of her marriage, and she and her husband immigrated to Virginia, where they reared a family of seven children of which number Isaac Bond, father of subject, was the third child. Our subject received his education after he was twenty-one years of age, while on a trip down the river on a flatboat in Alabama. He remained three months to dispose of his boat load of produce, and while there attended school. When twenty-five years of age he married Miss Eliza Swan, daughter of James and Catherine Swan. Nine children were the result of our subject's marriage: James A., a prominent physician for many years; Sarah L. (Mrs. J. N. Seaton); Hugh M. (deceased); Isaac H., a successful merchant in McMinn County, Tenn.; Catherine J. (Mrs. H. Tedford, deceased); Isabella C. (Mrs. H. Tedford); Stephen F., a prominent farmer of Limestone County, Texas; Mary Eliza, and Martha (deceased). Mrs. Bond died in 1868, and Mr. Bond took for his second wife June 11, 1872, Mrs. Mary Rhea formerly Miss Mary Rockhold. Mr. and Mrs. Bond are members of the Southern General Assembly of the Presbyterian Church. Mr. Bond has been a member of the church sixty-three years, and has been a ruling elder in the same for sixty years, He has resided in the locality where he now lives eighty-four years, and has reared a family of eight children, who are among the most intelligent and respected citizens of the different localities where they live. Mr. Bond has left the impress of his most excellent influence, not only upon his children but upon all with whom he comes in contact. In politics Mr. Bond is Democratic, casting his first presidential vote for the Whig candidate of 1820. He has been a remarkably, energetic and successful farmer. He owns 500 acres of excellent land twelve miles west of Knoxville, 225 of which are well improved and well cultivated. On this farm are very rich deposits of marble, the finest to be found in Tennessee. Mrs. Bond was a daughter of William and Harriet (Netherland) Rockhold, natives of Maryland and Virginia, and were of English and German descent respectively. Mr. Rockhold was magistrate of his district for about twenty-five years. Mr. John Netherland, uncle of Mrs. Bond, was for many years a prominent attorney at Rogersville, and was a candidate for governor against Isam G. Harris.

James W. Bowman, farmer and hunter, was born in Knox County, Tenn., July 10, 1823, and is the son of Samuel and Elizabeth (Green) Bowman. The father was born in Virginia, June 8, 1783, was a successful farmer, and was brevetted captain in the war of 1812. He died at his home in 1874, having lived eighty-nine years within five miles of that place. Our subject received a fair education, and soon began cultivating the soil. In 1845 he married Miss Mary Goddard, a native of Knox County, Tenn., born January 14, 1827, and the daughter of John and Ann Goddard. To this union were born eight children of whom four sons and one daughter are now living. These are Dr. S. G.; Joseph S., a farmer; Isabella (Mrs. J. D. Winkle), and W. P. and John C. who are farming with their father. Our subject is the owner of 1,000 acres of land, all in one body, situated on the French Broad River. The land is well improved and contains fine marble. Mr. Bowman is an energetic farmer and is quite comfortably situated. He frequents the Cumberland and Smoky Mountains, and often has the good fortune to bring down deer or other game. For the last few years he has been going to the Smoky Mountains to spend the fall of the year, and with his fine pack of hounds, killed thirteen deer at one time. Mr. Bowman is a strong Democrat, and has served as justice of the peace and also as deputy sheriff. He is at present taking much interest in the raising of live stock, especially Shorthorn cattle.

Samuel B. Boyd, of the firm of Boyd & Caswell furniture dealers, was born in Virginia in 1828, and received his education in his native State. In 1851 he came to Knoxville, and in 1853 married Isabella R. Boyd, a native of Knoxville, Tenn.; the fruits of this union were eight children, seven now living. In 1857 Mr. Boyd embarked in the dry goods trade, in the firm of Piper & Boyd, which firm existed only about one year, after which our subject continued the business alone until 1861, when he entered the Confederate service, serving in the ordnance department until captured at Bristol and taken to Camp Chase, where he was held prisoner until the close of the war. He then returned to Knoxville and became a member of the dry goods firm of Rayl & Boyd, where he remained until 1871, after which he handled carpets and house furnishing goods alone until 1880; the present firm was formed in August, 1880. He is a director in the East Tennessee Insurance Company, also director of Gray Cemetery for the last twenty-eight years. He has been treasurer of the State Deaf and Dumb Asylum for twelve years, and trustee of the same for twenty-eight years. For fifteen years he was secretary of the board of East Tennessee National Bank and has been director ever since its organization. He was a member of the executive committee for eighteen years. He was the second of a family of five children (two now living) born to James S. and Elizabeth (King) Boyd, natives of Martinsburg, Va., where the mother died in 1833. The father then moved to Illinois four years later, and engaged in merchandising for many years in Carmi, White County. His death occurred in 1883.

Samuel B. Boyd, M. D., junior member of the well known firm of physicians, J. M. and S. B. Boyd, of Knoxville, Tenn., was born in that city March 24, 1853, and is the son of Samuel B. and Susan H. (Mason) Boyd, natives of Virginia. The father was a prominent member of the Knoxville bar, and occupied a position on the chancery court bench; he died in 1855. The mother died in 1885. Our subject was reared in Knoxville, and finished his literary education at the University of Tennessee, entering the preparatory department of that institution in 1866, and graduating in 1873. He at once began the study of medicine with his brother, Dr. John M. Boyd, in Knoxville, and during the years 1873-75, attended the University of Pennsylvania, at Philadelphia, where he graduated in 1875. He then returned to Knoxville, and at once began practicing his profession which he has continued up to the present with evident success. He is a member of the Knox County Medical Society, of which he has served as president, secretary and treasurer, and is the present secretary of the city board of health. In 1876 he married Miss Maggie A. Baker, a native of Tennessee, born at Sinking Creek in 1857, and the daughter of Dr. Harvey Baker. Two children were the fruits of this union, one, D. W. Boyd, is living. Both Mr. and Mrs. Boyd are members of the Methodist Episcopal Church South.

John Wilson Boyd, agent of the Eastern Tennessee, Virginia & Georgia Railroad Company at Concord, Tenn., was born March 7, 1833, in Knox County, and within four miles of where he now resides. He is one of seven children (two now living) born to Thomas and Anna (Wilson) Boyd. The father was born January 8, 1781, in Knox County, and died in 1876. He was well educated, and was nominated for representative of Knox County, but declined the nomination, although urged strongly by his friends to accept. He was greatly interested in the advancement of all religious and educational enterprises, and was also very active in effecting the construction and building of the East Tennessee & Georgia Railroad. He was an elder in the church to which he belonged for many years. Mrs. Boyd was born in Anderson County, Tenn., in 1799, and died in 1853. She was a devoted Christian worker, and an excellent woman. J. W. Boyd received his education principally at Cumberland University, where he graduated in 1856, the first literary graduate who attended that institution from East Tennessee. He ranked with the best students in mathematics, and was a good student in the other branches. After graduating he taught school, and shortly afterward was offered, and accepted, the presidency of Ewing and Jefferson College, in Blount County, which position he held until the close of the war. He then moved to his farm near Concord, and taught school and farmed for the following two years. In 1866 he was offered (unsolicited by Mr. Boyd), and accepted, the position he now occupies. He is a member of the Cumberland Presbyterian Church, having been elder and clerk of the session for many years. He is a member of the Masonic fraternity, of which he was Worshipful Master for several years. Previous to the war he was a Whig in politics, but later voted the Democratic ticket, and at present votes with the Prohibition party, and takes a great interest in the advancement of the temperance interests. He has been solicited by his friends many times to accept the nomination of representative from Knox County. In 1856 he married Miss Mahulda J. Lester, who was born in 1835, and who is the daughter of Henry D. and Malinda Lester, of Lebanon, Tenn. Mr. Lester was high sheriff of Wilson County for many years, and was a prominent citizen of that county. Ten children were the result of our subject's marriage: Alice E., John L. (now clerk in the East Tennessee National Bank, Knoxville, Tenn., and was train dispatcher for some time), Henry D. (a merchant of Concord, Tenn.), Thomas A. (Western Union Telegraph operator at Nashville), William J. (telegraph operator at Concord), Minnie A., Lavinia J. (deceased), Edwin T., Mamie F. and Freddie M. (deceased). Mrs. Boyd was reared in the Baptist Church, but after her marriage attached herself to the church of her husband's choice, and with him has ever since been a devoted member.

H. L. Bradley, dealer in wall paper and shades, was born in Knox County April 27, 1827. He was reared on a farm and educated in the common schools. He came to Knoxville in 1848, and here learned the carpenter's trade, at which he worked until 1855, and then went in the car shops, being boss of the wood work of the East Tennessee, Virginia

& Georgia Railroad. He continued at this business until 1864, when he began merchandising in a general way, continuing until 1876, when he changed his line of business to the present. In 1852 he married Miss Margaret C. York, of Knox County, Tenn., and the fruits of this union were eight children, five living—one son and four daughters. He is a Republican in politics, and for twenty-three years has been in business in Knoxville. By his own efforts and industry he has accumulated considerable property, and is now in comfortable circumstances. He was one of seven children, six now living, born to John and Malinda (Dowell) Bradley, both natives of Virginia. The father was born about 1772. He was a soldier in the war of 1812, and a farmer by occupation. The mother came with her parents to Tennessee at an early day.

T. J. Bradley, a miller of the firm of Peters & Bradley, was born January 1, 1834, in Knox County. He is one of the eleven children born to Archlers and Nancy (Bradley) Bradley, natives of Virginia. They came to Knox County, Tenn., and here passed the remainder of their days. Our subject received a good common-school education, and was thrown upon his own resources when twenty-one years of age. He first engaged in farming, and at the age of twenty-two chose for his companion during life Miss Evaline Ledgerwood, a daughter of William and Ailcy Ledgerwood. This union resulted in the birth of six children: Charlton W., Ailcy (widow of John Thompson), George, Maynard, Marshall (deceased) and Clarence. After following agricultural pursuits for about twenty years he then engaged in merchandising with his son, the style of the firm being Bradley & Son. At the end of six years he became a member of the firm of Peters & Marston, the style of the firm being Peters, Marston & Co. This partnership continued six months, when Mr. Marston died and the firm name then became Peters & Bradley. From a small beginning they have increased their business to its very prosperous and extensive condition. Although commencing life with very little capital, Mr. Bradley, by great industry and careful financiering, has become quite comfortably fixed. Mr. and Mrs. Bradley are members of the Methodist Episcopal Church. Mr. Bradley is a Republican in politics.

Daniel Briscoe, of the wholesale dry goods firm of Briscoe, Sweepson & Co., is a native of Mississippi, and was reared and educated at Oxford, Miss. He graduated there in 1861 and soon after enlisted in the Eighteenth Mississippi Infantry, but was afterward assigned to the quartermaster department, and located at Knoxville, Greeneville and Bristol, Tenn., until the close of the war, after which he embarked in the dry goods trade at Morristown, Tenn., until 1882. In March, 1864, he led to the hymenial altar Miss Kate C. Ernest, a native of Greene County,

Tenn., and to them were born eight children, six now living. The mother of these children died in December, 1883. In 1886 Mr. Briscoe came to Knoxville and established the firm of which he is a member. He is one of the directors of the East Tennessee National Bank, and a stockholder in the East Tennessee and Island Home Insurance Companies. P. J. and Martha (Allen) Briscoe, parents of our subject, were natives of Mississippi and East Tennessee, and died at Canton, Miss., in 1869 and 1871 respectively. Our subject is a member of the Masonic fraternity.

Lewis F. Brooks, farmer, was born June 7, 1821, in Rockbridge County, Va., where he was partly reared. He is the eldest of five children born to Lawson S. and Catherine (Myer) Brooks. The father was born and reared in Albemarle County, Va., and was a soldier in the war of 1812 under Gen. Scott. He was wounded at the battle of Lundy's Lane. His father, Lawson Brooks, was a lieutenant under Gen. Green in the Revolutionary war, and was killed at the battle of Camden, S. C. In May, 1845, our subject married Miss Minerva J. Wesson, a daughter of Isaac and Tobitha Wesson, and this marriage resulted in the birth of nine children: C. A., Gertrude (Mrs. A. W. Trout), Frances I. (Mrs. Ira J. Weeks), Harriet O. (Mrs. C. R. Summers), Paulina T. (Mrs. James A. Walkinshaw), Lelia W., Isaac J. (a physician and a graduate of the Ohio Medical College of Cincinnati, Ohio), Lawson L. and Robert N. Mrs. Brooks died August 18, 1873, and Mr. Brooks took for his second wife Mrs. Elizabeth Spencer, formerly Miss Wilson, a daughter of James P. and Elizabeth (Peed) Wilson. Mr. and Mrs. Brooks are members of the Methodist Episcopal Church South. He is a Democrat in politics, and cast his first presidential vote for James K. Polk. He moved to Mason County, Ky., in 1868, and lived there until 1884, when he moved to his present location where he has since resided. Mr. Brooks owns ninety-three and a half acres on the Kingston Pike about three miles west of Knoxville. He is of Scotch descent, his grandmother being a native of Perthshire, Scotland.

J. L. Brown, a practical engineer and farmer of the Seventh District, was born in Knox County, Tenn., December 13, 1828, and is the fourth of eight children born to Joshua and Frances (Blakeley) Brown. The father was born and reared in Knox County, Tenn., and served two campaigns as a soldier in the Creek Indian war under Gen. Jackson. He followed the occupation of a farmer, in which he was very successful; died December 31, 1841, and was buried January 1, 1842, being forty-nine years of age. Mrs. Brown was a native of North Carolina, and when only a girl came to Knox County. She died in March, 1883, aged eighty-five years. Our subject received unfavorable advantages for an education, but made the best of those advantages. December 18, 1850, he married Miss Martha J. Hall, a daughter of William and Nancy (Nelson) Hall. She bore him one child, Pink Lawson, who is now a music teacher. From 1851 Mr. Brown taught school, more or less, each year for ten years, and for fifteen years after he had abandoned teaching was engaged in surveying. In connection with this he has superintended the management of his farm. He owns 210 acres of land well cultivated and well improved, situated ten miles north of Knoxville. Mrs. Brown and daughter are members of the Missionary Baptist Church. Mr. Brown is conservative in politics, voting for principle, not for party. He cast his first presidential vote for Gen. Winfield Scott.

Alfred Buffat, farmer and miller, was born in Switzerland December 8, 1840, son of P. F. and Sylvia (Tauxe) Buffat, both natives of Switzerland. They came from that country to the United States in 1849. Their mode of travel, illustrative of the means of that day, was from Aigle (Switzerland) to Paris (France) by stage, from Paris to Havre by rail, from that city to New York by sail (being more than forty days at sea), from New York to Charleston, S. C., by steamer, from the last named city to Dalton, Ga., by rail, thence to Chattanooga by stage, and from that city to Knoxville by steamer. They remained in the vicinity of that city a few months, after which they purchased a farm of 300 acres in the Second District of Knox County. Here the father followed farming. He built a flouring-mill in 1860, and formed a partnership with his son, Alfred, in 1865, for milling. He was born November 7, 1809, and died on his farm in 1874, aged nearly sixty-five years. The mother was born in 1819, and is now sixty-seven years of age. She succeeded her husband in the business partnership with her son. Alfred Buffat, the eldest of nine children, received only a limited education when young. A few years in a primary school in Switzerland, then a few months of attendance to school in a slab-seated old log schoolhouse in this country, constituted the school advantages that he enjoyed; but he made amends for this lack of opportunities, by applying himself closely to study during all his spare moments. On September 14, 1865, he married Miss Eliza Bolli, who was born in Paris (France) on the 18th of May, 1842. Her father, Edward Bolli, was a native of France, and her mother, Eliza (Porta) Bolli, was a native of Switzerland. She removed with her parents to Brazil, her father being Swiss consul at Pernambuco for several years. On account of ill health he removed to the United States, and settled in Knox County, where he died in 1854. To our subject and wife were born six sons and two daughters: Edward F., Charles A.,

Ernest (deceased), William E., Flora F., Samuel T., Elise B. and Walter D. Mr. Buffat was elected school director for his district in 1882. After one year's experience in that capacity, he became convinced that the interests of the schools of his district required the establishment of a system for their management and of rules for their government. After a proper study of the matter, in the autumn of 1883, he proposed to the board of his district a plan for grading the schools of the district and rules for the government of these schools. This was met with approval by the board who appointed a committee to select text books and to fix the limits of the different grades. The plan was put in operation in the Second District at once. County Superintendent J. R. Shipe approving the plan, urged the directors of other districts to adopt it also. Through his efforts and those of his successor, J. W. Saylor, this system and rules were adopted throughout Knox County. Mr. Buffat is also the author of a set of grammar charts, and takes a great interest in educational matters. He took no active part in the late war, and is not a politician. He is a member of the Christian Church.

George H. Burr, one of the firm of manufacturers of doors, sash, blinds, etc., and general lumber dealers of Knoxville, Tenn., is a native of Connecticut, born in 1829, and a direct descendant of Aaron Burr, the great American politician and Vice-President of the United States, he having been elected by Congress as such with President Thomas Jefferson in 1800. He is the son of Moses and Harriet B. (Banks) Burr, both natives of Connecticut. The father was born in Greenfield, Fairfield Co., Conn., in 1806. The mother was born in 1809. She was the daughter of Thomas and Abigail (Murwin) Banks, both natives of Connecticut. He was a member of the Presbyterian Church. Our subject was reared in Weston, Conn., and acquired his education at the public schools of that place. He began life as a coachmaker, but that business was too slow for a man of his energy and ambition. At the close of the civil war he saw great opportunities in the new South, and came to Tennessee in 1867, locating in Knoxville, and engaged in saw milling and general lumber business. He was married, October 19, 1854, to Amelia Andrews, who was born in Connecticut in November, 1830, and is the daughter of Jonathan and Abigail (Murwin) Andrews, both natives of Connecticut. The father was born in April, 1802, was a farmer, and died in 1849. The mother was born in 1804, and died in 1854. Both our subject and wife are members of St. John's Episcopal Church.

J. R. Butt is a son of J. R. Butt, Sr., and Leanah T. (Coffman) Butt, both natives of Virginia. The father was a farmer by occupation, and both he and the mother are now deceased. Our subject was a native Virginian, born February 26, 1845. He lived on the farm until fourteen years of age, and while growing up received a very limited education. But notwithstanding this he has by reading and observation acquired a good practical education. In 1859 he came to Tennessee, and at the age of sixteen learned the tinner's trade. During most of the late war he made supplies for the Confederate Government. In 1865 he chose for his companion Miss Laura Vickars, of St. Albans, W. Va., and two children: Will L. and Frank M., were the fruits of this union. Mr. Butt is a Democrat in politics, and he and Mrs. Butt are members of the Cumberland Presbyterian Church. He took an active part in making up the stock for the Scates Warm Air Furnace Company, of which he is a director. He has also held the position of alderman of the city.

Rev. Henry E. Byerley, pastor of Little Flat Creek, Graveston, Beaver Dam and Sharon Baptist Churches, of Knox County, Tenn., was born in Grainger County, Tenn., August 29, 1849, and is the son of James and Elizabeth (Skaggs) Byerley. The father was born in Knox County June 12, 1807, was a farmer and died July 13, 1881. Though of limited education he was a most successful man, and was highly respected by all who knew him. The mother was born in Knox County (now Union) October 15, 1805, and died January 18, 1877. Both parents were members of the Baptist Church. Our subject came with his parents from Grainger to Knox County, when about a year and a half old, and has lived in the latter county ever since. He attended the common district schools in youth, and finished his education at Walnut Grove Academy, and the University of Tennessee. He then engaged in farming, which occupation he has followed successfully. He professed religion at Murphey's Chapel (Methodist Episcopal) in August, 1865, and was baptized the second Sabbath in November following. June 7, 1879, he was ordained a minister of the Baptist Church by Revs. H. C. Hamsted, P. A. Morton and J. A. Robinson. He has filled the pulpit almost all the time since his ordination, and is considered one of the most successful ministers of the county, his qualifications and work in the Church being highly appreciated. He was married, January 30, 1873, to Martha A. Luttrell, of Knox County, who was born February 27, 1853, and who is the daughter of Joseph W. and L. E. (Carter) Luttrell, both of Knox County. To this union seven children have been born, only three now living, viz.: a son (unnamed) born January 10, 1874, died at birth; son (unnamed) born February 4, 1875, died at birth; Luo L., born March 1, 1879; Charles S., born September 29, 1881; son (unnamed) born October 3, 1883, died at birth; James W., born

July 26, 1884, and died September 3, 1885, and Mattie Pearl, born May 29, 1886. Mrs. Byerley is also a member of the Baptist Church. By a previous marriage James Byerley, father of subject, became the father of five sons, one of whom died. The other four enlisted in the Federal Army during the late war. One was wounded at Resaca and died later at Knoxville. The other three are now living in Grainger County. The mother of our subject was also married previous to her union to James Byerley and had one son, who also enlisted in the Federal Army, was captured, and died in a Confederate prison. The five sons were members of the same company. Our subject was one of two children born to the union of his parents and the only survivor of that marriage.

T. R. C. Campbell, the subject of this sketch, was born August 18, 1833, in that section of country lying on the north bank of French Broad River, known as Riverdale. It was here that Knox County was first settled, and among the early settlers of this region was William A. Campbell, who came from Virginia about 1790 and settled on the present homestead of our subject. Here the father of our subject, James Campbell, was born. He served under Gen. Jackson in the campaign against the Creek Indians. Our subject received a finished education at Maryville College, Blount County. In 1865 he married Miss Anna E. Davis, of Sevier County, a graduate of a Moravian school at Salem, N. C. This union resulted in the birth of five children: James R., who is a graduate of the State University, Thomas B., M. Linda, John and Lucy. Mr. and Mrs. Campbell are deeply interested in all subjects pertaining to educational advancements, and their children are reaping the benefit of this interest. Mr. Campbell owns a very productive farm of 500 acres, called "the Riverdale Farm," and on this, besides his own commodious dwelling, is situated Riverdale schoolhouse and also a mill for flouring and lumbering. Formerly Riverdale postoffice was kept here. Mr. Campbell is an excellent citizen and neighbor as his many friends can testify.

D. A. Carpenter, president of the Knoxville Fire Insurance Company, and secretary and treasurer of the Knoxville Car Wheel Company, of Knoxville, Tenn., is a native of Rock Castle, Ky., and was born March 24, 1837. He is the son of William S. and Malinda E. (Merryman) Carpenter, both natives of Kentucky. The father was born in 1818; was a machinist by occupation, and died in 1886. The mother was born in 1819, and died in 1847. Both were members of the Baptist Church. Our subject was reared in the town of his birth, and came to Tennessee in 1857, locating and engaging in merchandising in Anderson County, where he remained until the breaking out of the Rebellion. In July,

1861, he went to Kentucky, going to that State at the suggestion of prominent Union Tennesseans to meet Col. James Carter, and ascertain when the Union Tennessee Volunteers would be supplied with arms, Col. Carter having previously gone to Washington City in company with Andrew Johnson. Consequently our subject was the first man to refugee from East Tennessee to Kentucky. The trip was made on horseback, and was fraught with danger and hardships, the whole country being overrun with and in the possession of the Confederates. Securing the desired information he returned to Clinton, Tenn., and reported the same. In the latter part of July he returned to Kentucky, and August 10, 1861, enlisted in the Federal Army, joining Company C, Second Regiment of Union Tennessee Volunteer Infantry, the name of which was subsequently changed to that of Tennessee Mounted Infantry. He was mustered in as a private, and upon organization of the company was elected first lieutenant, and at the organization of the regiment was made adjutant of the same. In August, 1862, he was promoted over ten captains to a majorship of the Second Regiment, Tennessee Union Mounted Infantry. A large portion of the regiment, also including himself, was captured at Rogersville, Tenn., and imprisoned, first at Libby prison for six months, then one month at Macon, Ga., and then two months at Charleston, S. C. While in prison our subject was commissioned colonel by Gov. Johnson. He was mustered out of service at Knoxville October 8, 1864, and went at once to Clinton, Anderson Co., Tenn., and engaged in merchandising. Previous to this he was married, June 23, 1863, to Sophia A. Berry, a native of Kentucky, who was born in 1842. To them have been born six children. Our subject and wife are members of the Broad Street Southern Methodist Episcopal Church. In March, 1865, he was elected sheriff of Anderson County, and August 17, 1865, was appointed by President Johnson assessor of internal revenue for the Second District. In 1869 he removed to Beaver Creek, Knox County, and engaged in farming, and two years later removed to Knoxville, where he engaged in the wholesale grocery business, being a member first of the firm of Carpenter & Ross, next of Carpenter, Ross & Co., next of Carpenter, Ross & Lockett, and last of Carpenter, Ross & Co., remaining in business until 1878. In 1876-77 he was elected mayor of Knoxville. He organized the Knoxville Fire Insurance Company in 1878, of which he is president, and has been since its organization, and in 1881-82 was elected president of the Knoxville Car Wheel Company, of which he is at present secretary and treasurer. He has also served as vice-president and general manager of both the Oak Dale Iron, Coal & Transportation Company and Walden Ridge Railway Company.

John H. Carriger, M. D., was born in Carter County, Tenn., August 18, 1825, and is the son of John and Margaret (Elliott) Carriger. The father was born in Pennsylvania in 1776, and immigrated to Tennessee about 1779, located in Carter County, where he farmed until his death, which occurred in 1848. Two of his elder brothers were soldiers in the Revolutionary war and participated in the battle of King's Mountain. They were both killed at St. Clair's defeat in the Indian war in 1791 in the Miami country. The mother was a native of Ireland, born in 1786, and came to America when three years of age. Her parents located near Jonesboro, Washington Co., Tenn. She died in 1854. Both parents were members of the Baptist Church, although Mrs. Carriger was baptized in the Episcopal Church. Our subject was reared in Carter County, and attended school first in the immediate neighborhood, next at Elizabethton, then at Jonesboro, and finally at Washington College in Washington County. April 3, 1846, he began the study of medicine under Dr. Michael Carriger at Tazewell, Tenn. In 1848 he attended lectures at Transylvania University at Lexington, Ky., and later graduated from Jefferson Medical College at Philadelphia in the class of 1850 and 1851. He then began the practice of medicine at Tazewell, Tenn., where he remained until the fall of 1852, when he removed to Columbus, Ga., remaining at the latter place until 1874. He next spent several months visiting in New York City, and in December, 1874, located in Knoxville, where he has practiced medicine up to the present. He is a member of the Knox County Medical Society and the State Medical Association. In October, 1853, Dr. Carriger married Musidora Cocke, a native of Hawkins County, born August 10, 1826. She died March 30, 1883, leaving one child, Dr. J. Sterling Carriger, who is now associated with his father in the practice of medicine. J. Sterling Carriger began the study of medicine in 1882, with his father, and during 1883–86 attended medical lectures at Bellevue Hospital Medical College, New York. After graduating he returned to Knoxville and began the practice of his profession. Our subject was married a second time, October 22, 1883, to Vandalee Durham, a native of Knox County, and one child was the result of this union, named Arthur Lee. The Doctor is a member of the K. T. Commandery of Knoxville.

William W. Carson, professor of mathematics in the University of Tennessee, was born in Adams County, Miss., June 2, 1845. His father's parents were Col. Joseph Carson, a lawyer of St. Stephens, Ala. (then a part of Mississippi Territory), who commanded the regiment of Mississippi Volunteers in the Creek war, and Caroline C. Green, of Adams County, Miss. His mother's parents were William S. Waller (cashier of the old Bank of Kentucky from 1809 to 1835, located at Frankfort, and from 1835 to 1852 of the Lexington branch of the present Bank of Kentucky) and Catherine S. Breckinridge, natives of Kentucky. His parents, James Green Carson and Catharine Waller, married when quite young, and had four sons and one daughter. They lived (he being a cotton planter) for ten years on the plantation inherited from his mother in Adams County, Miss., and then moved to the richer alluvial lands of North Louisiana, spending most of their summers until the war, however, with her family in Kentucky. The father died in 1863 at the age of forty-eight. The mother, now seventy-two years old, makes her home with her son, the subject of this sketch. Prof. Carson was the second son. In 1863 he enlisted as a private in Company B, Fourth Louisiana Cavalry, Confederate Army, and served with that regiment until the close of the war, having been promoted a few months before the end to sergeant-major. He was instructed by tutors at home until 1863. In 1866 he entered Washington College (now Washington and Lee University), Va., as a student. Two years later he received the civil engineer's diploma, and won the prize medal awarded for the best examinations in practical mathematics, natural philosophy and chemistry. Continuing at Washington College another year he served as instructor in engineering and at its close received the mining engineer's diploma. In 1873–74 he took a further course in chemistry at the school of mines in New York City. Before and after this last he was engaged as a civil engineer in different kinds of city and railroad work and hydrographic surveys. In 1877 he was elected to the chair of mathematics in Davidson College, N. C., which he filled for six years. Wishing then for more lucrative employment he resigned and engaged in mercantile life in Memphis. This proving unsuccessful, he returned to teaching, and in 1885 was elected to his present position. In 1880 he married Miss Rachel Finnie, of Memphis, who was born, however, in Caseyville, Ky. They have three children: Katie W., James F. and Emma F. Both Professor and wife are members of the Presbyterian Church.

M. B. Carter, an influential farmer of Knox County, Tenn., was born in that county November 10, 1840, son of James M. and Rebecca (Johnson) Carter. The father was a native of Knox County, born August 17, 1812, and died July 5, 1885. The mother was a native of North Carolina, and died in her thirty-fifth year. Our subject received a fair education, and in boyhood assisted his father on the farm. After his marriage to Miss Elizabeth Leeper, in 1866, he began farming for himself. Mrs. Carter was born in Bradley County, Tenn., September 29, 1847, is the daughter of James M. and N. E. (Prater) Leeper, and to her marriage have been born two sons and nine daughters, all living but one daughter, Nannie, who died when quite young. The children living are, Mary Alice, Julia, Elizabeth, James Madison, Margaret Ann, Aurelia A., Jennie Minnie, Gertrude, Robert Lee and Jodie Cleveland. Our subject began life with nothing but a pair of willing hands. He is now the owner of 450 acres of good land in the Eighteenth District of Knox County, Tenn., and on this land are quantities of zinc which are being taken out in abundance. There is also pink marble on the farm, and as the soil is fertile the farm ranks among the best of the county. Mr. Carter is an ardent Democrat, and he and wife are both members of the Methodist Episcopal Church South.

W. R. Carter, of the firm of Goodheart & Carter, bookbinders and stationers of Knoxville, Tenn., is a native of Knox County, of that State, born November 14, 1844, and is a son of W. H. and Mary (Chandler) Carter, natives of Tennessee. The father was born in March, 1814, was a farmer by occupation, and died July 16, 1882. The mother was born in 1822, and is now a resident of Knox County. She is a member of the Methodist Episcopal Church, of which her husband was also a member. Our subject was reared on a farm, and acquired his early education in the common schools, but subsequently attended Walnut Grove Academy in Knox County. April 1, 1862, he enlisted in the Federal Army, joining Company C, First Regiment of Tennessee Cavalry, was elected corporal of the company at its organization, and was afterward promoted to sergeant, which position he held until the close of the war. his regiment passing through some of the hardest battles of the war. After that event he returned to his home in Knox County, and, at the end of two years spent in school, learned the carpenter's trade, which he followed for twelve years. During this time he had removed to Knoxville, where he continued his occupation. October 29, 1868, he wedded Miss S. J. Harris, a native of Knox County, born January 12, 1847, and the daughter of J. J. Harris, a native of the above county. By this union our subject became the father of two boys: E. E. and E. R. In 1882 our subject was elected recorder of deeds for Knox County by a majority of 1,300, and served in this capacity for four years, making one of the best recorders the county ever had, as his work will show. He systematized the recorder's office thoroughly, for which he received the hearty and warm endorsement of the bar, as well as the citizens of his county. "A place for everything and everything in its place" was and is his motto. After leaving that office he formed a copartnership with Briscoe Goodheart, and engaged in the manufacture of blank books, blanks and bookbinding, and also dealing in stationery, which business he is engaged in at present. He is a member of Ed Maynard Post, No. 14, G. A. R., of Knoxville, of which organization he is a charter member, and has served as Officer of the Guard, Adjutant, and is at present a member of the Department Council of Administration and Aid to the Commander-in-Chief, and now Junior Vice-Commander of his post. He and wife are members of the Fourth Presbyterian Church of Knoxville. He is a man of sober and steady habits, sticking to whatever he undertakes, has a host of warm personal friends, and is well posted on most all leading questions of the day. Nothing he delights in more than relating war stories and hair-breadth escapes.

Peyton Carter, a liveryman and farmer of Knox County, Tenn., was born in that county March 13, 1845, and is the son of Peyton (Sr.) and Lucinda Carter, both natives of Virginia. They came to Tennessee about 1827 and settled in Knox County. Our subject received a common-school education, and in 1868 married Miss Martha M. Shipe, daughter of Alexander Shipe, a farmer and tanner. She was born in Knox County, Tenn., October 11, 1847, and by her marriage became the mother of two children: Walter H. and Charles B. The former was born August 5, 1869, and the latter February 18, 1873. Mr. Carter is the owner of 325 acres of well improved land in District No. 16, Knox County, and is also the owner of the largest livery and feed stables in Knoxville. They are situated at 282 Crozier Street, 16 and 18 Hardee Street, and 13 and 15 Sullivan Street. He is the sole proprietor of the stable, and in it he has a capacity for 100 wagons and 200 horses. It covers 20,350 feet of ground, and is provided with rooms for gentlemen and families. He has connected with it free scales for the use of farmers. Mr. Carter is a Republican in politics, and a stirring, energetic business man.

W. P. Chamberlain, of the firm of Sanford, Chamberlain & Albers, was born in Cuyahoga County, Ohio, December 2, 1840, and is the son of Leander and Susannah (Willey) Chamberlain. The father was born in Connecticut, and when young went to New York, where he met and married Miss Willey. In 1840 they moved to Cuyahoga County, Ohio, and there passed the remainder of their days on the farm. He died in 1884, being in his eightieth year, and she in 1887, being in her eighty-fourth year. Both were zealous workers in the Christian Church. Our subject was reared on a farm, and educated in the common schools and at Hiram Institute. In 1861 he volunteered in Company A, Twenty-third Ohio Infantry, Federal Army, being among the first to offer his services. Having served as a private a short time he was promoted to second lieutenant, and later to first lieutenant. In 1864, his term of enlistment having expired, he came to Knoxville and took charge of the government corrall and workshop. The following year he engaged in the drug business, and has carried it on successfully ever since. In 1873 he married Miss Kate E. Harper, of Hamilton, Ohio, and to them were born three sons and a daughter. Harper L. and Frederick W. are the only ones now living, one son and the daughter having died in infancy. Mr. and Mrs. Chamberlain are members of the Second Presbyterian Church. For about two years he was president of the Knoxville Street Railroad Company; is president of Mozart Club and a member of the Loyal Legion. He is of English descent on both the paternal and maternal sides.

Charles B. Christian, farmer of the Ninth District, was born January 31, 1838, near where he has since resided. He is the third of six children born to Walter L. and Jane (Hope) Christian. Walter L. Christian was born March 22, 1806, in Amherst County, Va., and immigrated to North Carolina after he was grown. After living there a few years he came to Tennessee where he remained until the close of the late war, when he went to Dalton, Ga., for a short time. He then moved to Knox County, from there to the old home place, and finally went to Rush County, Kas. He died October 19, 1883. His first wife was born in 1800, and died July 12, 1852. May 30, 1855, he married his second wife, Lorinda Galbreath, who bore him two children. She was born January 25, 1821, and died December 3, 1879. Walter L. Christian was an elder in the Cumberland Presbyterian Church for forty years, and was a highly respected citizen. His father, Henry Christian, was a soldier in the war of 1812, and his father was a soldier in the Revolutionary war. Our subject, Charles B. Christian, received his education in the common schools of Knox County, and at the age of twenty-one enlisted in Company B, Sixty-third Tennessee Infantry, August 8, 1861, and served until the close of the war. He was captured in April, 1865, and carried to Fort Delaware from which he was released June 10, 1865. September 25, 1870, he married Miss Ann E. Hardin, who was born September 20, 1846, and who is the daughter of John G. and Sallie R. (Gallaher) Hardin. John G. Hardin was major of the State militia, and took a great interest in the affairs of the county. He was a practical business man and accumulated a vast amount of property. To Mr. and Mrs. Christian were born six children: William T., John W., Carrie V., Frank H. (deceased), Katie and Mary H. Mrs. Christian is a member of the Cumberland Presbyterian Church, and Mr. Christian, although not a member of any church, supports all churches as well as all other worthy enterprises. He is a Democrat and a Master Mason.

Nicholas Clapp, farmer, was born in Knox County, Tenn., July 22, 1816, son of Solomon and Pherba (Smith) Clapp, both natives of North Carolina. Our subject received meager advantages for an education, but by observation and study has become a well read man. He was reared on a farm and has followed agricultural pursuits all his life. He started in life with little or no capital and is now the owner of 250 acres of land in the Fifth District of Knox County, and is considered one of the promnent and enterprising citizens of Knox County. He was married when twenty-four years of age, to Miss Lucinda Gibbs, daughter of Daniel Gibbs, and a native of Knox County, born December 25, 1812. To this union were born two sons and six daughters. The two sons and three of the daughters are deceased, viz.: Rachael Minerva, died when six years of age; Martha Elizabeth, died August 13, 1855, aged fourteen; Rufus Solomon, died at the age of five; William R., died aged thirty-one, and Sarah Jane (wife of William Miller), died aged forty. The names of the daughters now living are Alvira Cornelia (Mrs. A. P. Farmer), Orlena M. (Mrs. R. J. Gibbs) and Pherba E. (Mrs. W. R. Kerns). The mother of these children died November 28, 1871, and the father married Miss Mary A. Gibbs in 1872. She is a native of Knox County, born June 16,.1836. Mr. Clapp has been a member of the Methodist Episcopal Church from early boyhood; he was a Whig in politics before the war, a strong Union man during the war, and since that event has been a stanch Republican. He is a member of the Masonic fraternity.

Henderson Clapp, farmer, was born in Knox County, Tenn., June 1, 1820. He is the son of Solomon and Pherba (Smith) Clapp, natives of North Carolina and of Dutch and English extraction respectively. Our subject received poor educational advantages, but, by his own exertions, has obtained sufficient knowledge to enable him to transact all ordinary business. He was reared on a farm, and although he learned blacksmithing and worked at the trade much of the time until he was twenty-four years of age, he has, since that time, devoted most of his life to the independent occupation of farming. In 1845 he married Miss R. Shell, daughter of William Shell. She was born August 16, 1824, and died October 19, 1885. To this union were born seven sons and two daughters—two of the sons, Richard R. and R. LaFayette, are deceased. The names of the living children are Lurina E., James S., Linwill Foyd, William Joseph, Mary E., H. M. Brownlow and Solomon Conrad. Mr. Clapp has been one of the largest real estate owners of Knox County, but he has distributed land among his children and at present owns seventy-five acres of land in the Fourth District. He is also one of the real estate owners of Knoxville. He has served as justice of the peace for a number of years, and although he has never been a strong politician he has voted the Republican ticket on all State and National questions.

Walter M. Cocke, attorney at law, is a native of Knoxville, where he was reared. He graduated at the University of Tennessee in 1879, after which he read law with Judge H. H. Ingersoll, and was admitted to the bar in 1881. He then associated himself with his preceptor in the practice of his profession until June, 1886, since which time he has practiced alone. The Cocke family has figured prominently in the early history of Tennessee. We find by referring to other portions of the work that the great-great-grandfather of our subject, William Cocke, was one of the representatives from Sullivan County, who met with representatives from Washington and Greene Counties at Jonesboro, August 23, 1783, for the purpose of forming an independent association, the plan of which was drawn by Messrs. Cocke and Hardin. At the convention, which met at Greeneville November 14, 1784, he was chosen brigadier-general of the militia for the new State of Franklin, and also counsel of State. He was a member of the House of Representatives, which met at Knoxville August 25, 1794, and of the convention which met at the above place January 11, 1796. He was also on the committee to draft the consolidation for the State of Tennessee. He and William Blount were elected the first United States senators from Tennessee. Gen. John E. Cocke, the son of William Cocke, was a member of the House of Representatives which met at Knoxville March 28, 1797, and afterward distinguished himself in the war of 1812. The grandfather of our subject, William E. Cocke, was born in Grainger County. and practiced law and medicine there until his death. Our subject's father was a native of Grainger County, and came to Knox County in 1852. He graduated at Cumberland University, and was of the law firm of Cocke & Henderson at the time of his death.

M. B. Collier, a successful agriculturist of the Eighth District, was born March 21, 1847, in Knox County, and is the son of Thomas and Jane (Brown) Collier. Thomas Collier was born and reared in Washington County, and came to Knox County with his mother when eighteen years old, his father having died some time before. He was born in 1821, and has been clerk and elder in the Cumberland Presbyterian Church over forty years, and was the leader in organizing the first Masonic lodge in Beaver Creek Valley. In his younger days he was quite an able and promising singing school teacher. He is now living with his third wife. His children are prominent and prosperous citizens of the different localities in which they reside. Our subject received his education in the common schools of Knox County, and at the academy of Oak Grove. He assisted his father on the farm until twenty-four years of age, when he married Miss Alice McBath, who was born July 26, 1852, and who is the daughter of Robert and Sallie McBath. The result of this union was the birth of four children: Robert Hoyal, Ivy McBath, Thomas Carl (deceased) and Clio Brown. Mr. Collier is a Republican in politics, casting his first presidential vote for Horatio Seymour. He is a member of the Cumberland Presbyterian Church, and is a Master Mason. He owns 125 acres of land one mile northeast of Powell's Station. Mr. Robert McBath was born in Scotland, and was brought to America when only six years old. Here he married Mrs. McBath, who was also a native of Scotland. One of their daughters, Caroline, was a graduate of the Female Institute at Knoxville. Two of his sons were majors in the Federal Army, and all are prominent citizens. William McBath was elected circuit court clerk immediately after the close of the war, and served three terms. He also represented Knox and Sevier Counties in the Legislature one term. He was quite a frequent correspondent for several papers, notably the *Nashville Union* and *Cincinnati Enquirer*.

Sampson D. Cole (deceased), one of the leading farmers during his life of the Third Civil District, of Knox County, Tenn., was born in Anderson County, Tenn., May 11, 1817, and was the son of Alexander Cole, a native of Tennessee, born of Virginia parents. The father died when our subject was but ten years of age. He made his home with an uncle, at New Market, Tenn., after his father's death, and learned the saddler's trade. Later in life he removed to Jacksboro, Tenn., where he worked at his trade. He next removed to the Third District of Knox County, where he followed farming and worked at his trade until his death, which occurred April 20, 1874. He served as justice of the peace, at Jacksboro, and also of the Third District of Knox County. He was an elder of Washington Presbyterian Church, and was universally respected and esteemed by all who knew him, he being an industrious, energetic and enterprising citizen. He was married August 8, 1839, to Eliza Anderson, who died, October 20, 1850. To this union three children were born, one of whom is living. He was married the second time to Martha J. Crawford, March 23, 1852, who died August 12, 1860. To this union five children were born, three of whom are living. He married Nancy J. Crawford, May, 2, 1861, who is a native of Tennessee, and was born November 2, 1831, and is the daughter of Anderson and Sarah (Meek) Crawford, both natives of Tennessee. To this union five children were born, as follows: Samuel, March 7, 1863; James, November 5, 1864; Thomas, November 19, 1866; Laura, August 13, 1868;

Eva, August 7, 1870. The mother is a member of the Washington Presbyterian Church.

Martin J. Condon, a member of the board of education of Knoxville, is a son of John and Bridget (Gray) Condon, both natives of Ireland, where they grew up and were married. After living for some time in the old country they came to America, and soon found their way to Tennessee. The father was a railroad conductor by occupation. The immediate subject of this sketch was born October 29, 1857, in Hawkins County. His early education was obtained in the country schools, and his subsequent education at Georgetown College. Soon after he engaged as porter in a wholesale grocery house, and by industry and close attention to business, gradually rose to one of the highest positions. In 1880 he and his brothers, Mike J. and S. P., bought out his employers, Williams & Zimmerman, and have carried on a successful and extensive business since. In 1885 our subject was elected to his present position, and the same year he was united in marriage to Miss Margaret M. McMillan, by whom he has two sons: Martin J. and Paul A. Mr. Condon is a good business man, and an active member of the Catholic Church.

Mike J. Condon, senior member of the firm of Condon Bros., wholesale grocers, of Knoxville, Tenn., is a native of Massachusetts, born in Springfield, September 29, 1846, and the son of John and Bridget (Grey) Condon, natives of County Clare, Ireland. The father was born October 24, 1824. The mother was born September 8, 1818. They were married in July, 1844, and immigrated to America in June, 1846, locating in Springfield, Mass. They subsequently removed to Hartford and New Haven, Conn., residing in the latter place until 1856, when the father was employed on the construction of the Virginia Midland Railway, and in 1857 removed to Rogersville, Tenn., and was employed in building the masonry of the bridge on the Rogersville & Jefferson Railway. In 1861 he entered the Third Regiment of Confederate Engineer Troops, and in the fall of the same year, while blockading Big Creek Gap with a detachment of men, was wounded and captured. He was in prison at Camp Chase, Ohio, ten months, and then exchanged. He served in the army until the surrender in 1865. He walked from Virginia, where they surrendered, below Lynchburg, to Rogersville, and in 1865 removed to Knoxville, where he died in April, 1885. The mother still lives and is now a resident of Knoxville. Our subject was reared principally in Hawkins County, Tenn., and acquired only a limited education, at Arnott's schoolhouse, in that county. He commenced working on the railroad at the age of thirteen. Until 1861 he worked on a farm; then till 1864 he went with his father in the Confederate

Army. After the war he served an apprenticeship at stone cutting with his father, until 1868, when he became associated with his father in contracting. In 1869 he married Miss Kate E. Moore, a native of Martins, Va., of Irish parentage, born in 1849, and who was educated in a convent at Washington, D. C. This marriage resulted in the birth of ten children. Both Mr. and Mrs. Condon are members of the Catholic Church, and he is a member of the Catholic Knights of America, and of the Irish Catholic Benevolent Union of America. Mr. Condon was connected with the building of twenty-five miles of the Cincinnati Southern Railway; the East Tennessee, Virginia & Georgia, from Atlanta to Macon; the Red Clay Cut Off; the Knoxville & Ohio; the extension of the Knoxville branch of the Louisville & Nashville Railway, and is now engaged on a contract for the building of forty-four miles of the Memphis & Birmingham Railway, in Alabama and Mississippi. In 1876 he established the wholesale grocery house, of which he is senior partner. In politics Mr. Condon is a Republican; served as alderman in the city council of Knoxville two terms, and was a candidate for railroad commissioner, on the Republican ticket, in 1884, being elected by nearly 9,000 majority.

Martin J. Condon, member of the board of education of Knoxville, is the son of John and Bridget (Gray) Condon, both natives of the "Evergreen Isle," where they grew up and were married. After living some time in the old country they came to America, and found their way to Tennessee. The father was a railroad contractor by occupation. The immediate subject of this sketch was born October 29, 1857, in Hawkins County. He received his primary education in the common schools, and subsequently attended Georgetown College, where he completed his education. Soon after he engaged as porter in a wholesale grocery house. By industry and close attention to business he gradually arose to one of the highest positions in the house. In 1880, he and his brothers, Mike J. and S. P., bought out his employers Williams & Zimmerman, and have carried on a successful and extensive business since. In 1885 Mr. Condon was elected to his present position. The same year he married Miss Margaret M. McMillan, by whom two children, Martin J. and Paul A. were born. Mr. Condon is a good citizen, and a member of the Catholic Church.

S. Y. Conner,—one of the successful and enterprising farmers of the Sixth District, was born December 2, 1822, in Knox County, Tenn., and is the tenth of twelve children born to William and Sallie (Cox) Conner, both native Virginians, and both of whom were reared in their native State. They came to Tennessee at a very early day. William Conner was a soldier in the Creek Indian war. He was lieutenant of his company, to which position he was promoted owing to the signal bravery he displayed, and his efficiency as a soldier. Both he and wife were of German-Irish descent. When our subject was twenty-three years of age, he married Miss Mary Tindell, a daughter of Charles and Mary (McLain) Tindell, prominent and highly respected citizens of their locality. Mr. Tindell was elected to the office of constable, which position he filled successfully one term. To Mr. and Mrs. Conner were born eleven children: John Tate, Mary S. (Mrs. Webber), George W., James, Joseph, Sarah A., Louisa (Mrs. Williams), Susan, Almeda N., William P. (deceased), and one who died in infancy. Mr. Conner is a Democrat in politics, casting his first presidential vote for Henry Clay, and he and Mrs. Conner are members of the Missionary Baptist Church. Mr. Conner owns 300 acres of land all nicely improved, and located on Bull Creek, twelve miles northwest of Knoxville.

W. A. A. Conner, a prominent farmer of the Second District, was born in Knox County November 4, 1823, and remained under the parental roof until twenty-six years of age. He then married Emily A., daughter of John Smith (one of the pioneers of the county), and located at his present home place. He began life with very limited means, but by industry and frugality has gained a very comfortable home. He resided seventeen years in a log cabin, after which he built his present commodious residence. November 2, 1862, he was conscripted by Confederate officers, but escaped the same night, and made his way to Kentucky, where he remained until the Federal troops occupied Knoxville, after which he returned to his home. He served as justice of the peace, from 1864 to 1884, and was chairman of the county court from 1875 to 1877. At the organization of the Knoxville, Tazewell & Jacksboro Pike Company he became a stockholder, and soon after filled the various offices of director, secretary and treasurer. To his marriage referred to in the beginning of this sketch, ten children have been born—four deceased. He and his family are members of the Baptist Church, and he has filled two terms of one year each, as moderator for the State of Tennessee. He and nine sisters constitute a family, of which but two survive. The parents, Thomas and Margaret (Alldredge) Conner, were natives of Virginia and North Carolina respectively, and came to this county in early childhood. The former was born in 1794 and died in 1875, and the latter's death occurred about 1877.

John W. Conner, county court clerk, of Knox County, Tenn., is a native of that county. He was born September 2, 1862, and educated in the common schools of the county. At the age of seventeen (1879) he received an appointment through the influence of Congressman L. C. Houk, under John Sherman, then Secretary of the Treasury as messenger at Washington, from which he was promoted through a competitive examination to a $1,200 clerkship in the same office which he resigned in 1883 to accept a clerkship under Col. Henry R. Gibson in the pension office at Knoxville. This position he held until relieved by President Cleveland in 1885. In August, 1886, he was elected to his present office as a Republican, defeating J. F. J. Lewis, a Democrat, by 700 votes, and who had held the office for twelve years. Though the youngest county official in the State, he fills the office with credit and efficiency. He was married May 6, 1884, to Miss Katie R. Nichols, of Washington, D. C., to whom one son has been born. His parents, Joseph Wesley and Zerada E. Conner, were both natives of Knox County, Tenn. The father followed agricultural persuits until the commencement of the civil war, when he enlisted in the Sixth Tennessee Infantry, Union Volunteers, and served as a private until his death at the battle of Resaca, Ga. The mother is still living, and is a resident of Knox County. The parents were both of Irish descent.

J. L. Cooley, contractor and builder, is a native of Rogersville, Tenn., born in February, 1845. He was reared and educated at Rogersville, and during the war served in the Third Regiment of Confederate Engineer Troops. After the war, in January, 1867, he married Miss Laura A. Johnson, a native of Carroll County, Va., to whom eight children have been born, one deceased. Mr. Cooley engaged in general merchandising in Grayson County, Va., until August, 1869, when he located at Morristown, Tenn., and followed contracting and house building until May, 1871. He then came to Knoxville, and has since continued the contracting business in partnership with his brother, F. B. Cooley (whose sketch appears below. Among the many fine residences of Knoxville erected by them may be mentioned those of James Cowan, Capt. Chamberlain, Judge Meek, F. H. McClung, etc. Their annual amount of business ranges from $50,000 to $75,000.

Fleming B. Cooley, one of the stirring business men of Knoxville, is the son of Andrew J. and Lucy (Evans) Cooley. The father was a native of Virginia, and when young went to Abingdon, that State, to learn the carpenter's trade. Soon after he moved to Rogersville, Tenn., a good portion of which he built. While there he married Miss Evans, and to them were born ten children—three sons and three daughters now living. During the war he moved to Virginia to escape the persecutions of political enemies, but after the war returned to Tennessee and located in Knoxville, where he followed his trade. He was an energetic, industrious man, and in his business employed many workmen. When his sons were but five or six years of age he provided them with little benches and put a skillful workman over them. Fleming, the subject of this sketch, was born in Hawkins County, Tenn., January 8, 1848. Owing to the interruption caused by the late war his education was limited to the common schools. In 1869 he came to Knoxville and worked at the bench about two years, when he and his brother, J. L., commenced contracting on a small scale. Since then they have gradually increased their business until now they are ranked among the first contractors of the city. In addition they run a sash and blind factory, and are partners in a hardware store. In 1872 our subject married Miss Elizabeth Tarr, of Grainger County, Tenn., and a member of the Presbyterian Church. After her death he wedded Miss Bettie Carmichael, of Alabama. By the first marriage he has one daughter, and by the second, three sons and two daughters. Mr. Cooley is a Democrat in politics and he and wife are members of the Presbyterian Church. The Cooley Bros. have built some of the best buildings of the city.

W. R. Cooper, Supreme Keeper of Records of the Supreme Commandery U. O. G. C., and vice-president of the Central Guarantee Life Association of Knoxville, Tenn., a native of Campbell County, Tenn., was born near Jacksboro, February 13, 1847, and is the eldest son of Gen. Joseph A. Cooper, who was known among his troops (Union) during the war of the Rebellion as "Fighting Joe." During the war he visited his father several times while in the field, and at one time clandestinely left home to enlist in the Union Army, but was caught by his uncle and brought back, after a tramp of one day and night. During the last two years of the war he attended school in Cincinnati, Ohio. He came to Knoxville in 1866. On the 22d of June, 1869, he entered the internal revenue service, as a deputy collector, under his father, holding that position until July 10, 1879. This period of service was largely confined to the planning, ordering and leading raids against illicit distilleries in the mountains of East Tennessee. He was one of the charter members of the U. O. G. C., and was appointed to his present position in the order by the late Dr. John H. Morgan, the "founder," and at that time its Supreme Commander.

John J. Craig, Jr., secretary and treasurer of the Tennessee Marble Association and the Great Southern Marble Company, is of the firm of John J. Craig & Co., of this city. He was born in Knox County, Tenn., September 20, 1860, and after attending the State University, graduated at the Queen City commercial college in 1879. He then accepted a position with the Canton Banking & Insurance Company of Canton, Miss., until December 9, 1880, and then with the banking house of John S. Hornor & Son of Helena, Ark., as bookkeeper until June, 1886, at which date he came to Knoxville and has since been actively engaged in the marble trade. In 1883 he married Miss Lucy Cage, a native of Canton, Miss., and to them was born one child. John J. (father of our subject) was born in Lauderdale County, Ala., in 1820, came to Knoxville in 1839, and clerked for McClung, Wallace & Co. until 1844, after which he returned to Alabama, and in 1847 married a Miss Lyon, of Knox County. He remained at his home in Alabama until 1852, when he was elected cashier of the Knoxville branch of the Union Bank, which position he filled until the bank was closed by the war. He then resided with his family in Cincinnati, Ohio, two years, after which he engaged in the banking business in New York City until 1869. He then returned to Knox County, and resided on the old homestead until the same was sold to the State for the location of the present insane asylum five miles below Knoxville. Mr. Craig is a pioneer in the East Tennessee marble trade and the introducer of the fine variegated varieties.

Samuel B. Crawford, M. A., chairman of the faculty, professor of military science and commandant of cadets of the University of Tennessee, was born in Knox County, Tenn., November 13, 1850. His father, Barnes Crawford, was born in the State of New Jersey, and when young came to Knoxville, being among the early settlers. He was a manufacturer of carriages. The mother, Amanda Lones, was born in Knoxville. Their family consisted of five children, four now living. The only son, our subject, had to depend principally upon his own exertions for an education. After attending the public schools of this city he entered the University of Tennesee, from which he graduated in 1873. The same year he married Miss Mattie Eckle, a native of Knoxville, by whom he had four children, two now living: Jean B. and Saxton. The two deceased were named Bessie and Lennis. Soon after marriage Prof. Crawford was chosen commandant of cadets, holding that position two years. For about three years he taught in the preparatory department, but soon after was made professor of military science and tactics and commandant of cadets, also adjutant professor of mathematics. In June, 1886, he was elected chairman of the faculty. Prof. Crawford is one of Knox County's boys who began life's work under adverse circumstances, but by persistent effort has accomplished much toward making life a success. He and wife are members of the Methodist Episcopal Church South.

Capt. John H. Cross, a farmer of the Tenth District, was born November 3, 1843 in Anderson County, Tenn., where he grew to manhood. He came to Knox County in 1865 and settled near his present residence. He is the second of seven children born to William and Jane (Black) Cross, both natives of Anderson County, Tenn. William Cross is a very prominent citizen of the county where he lives. He represented Anderson County in the State Legislature three terms, and is the only Democrat who has ever represented Anderson County in the Legislature since the war. Although seventy-five years old he is hale and active for that age. His father, Britton Cross, came from Virginia and settled in Middle Tennessee. He afterward located in Anderson County, where he continued to reside until his death. Mrs. William Cross, mother of our subject, was born in Anderson County, where she spent her whole life. She died April 2, 1885. Our subject received his education in the common schools of Anderson County. August 13, 1861 he enlisted in Company H, First Tennessee Infantry, and after eight months' service was transferred to Company C, Third Tennessee Infantry, was commissioned first lieutenant and afterward promoted to the captaincy of his company. He served three years and eight months, and was mustered out of service in March, 1865, at Nashville, Tenn. He participated in the battles of Resaca, Kenesaw Mountain, Atlanta, Nashville, Jonesboro, Fishing Creek, Chickamauga and in numerous other lesser battles and severe skirmishes. On one occasion he was given 100 men and sent nine miles northeast of Mossy Creek, Jefferson Co., Tenn., where he was attacked by three regiments of rebel cavalry, was surrounded once or twice and cut his way through each time. He fought the three regiments over the nine miles back to camp, and forty-four of his men were captured, killed and wounded. But his men killed twenty-seven men of the enemy. He was a brave soldier, an efficient officer, and enjoyed the highest esteem and confidence of his superior officers, by whom he was placed in positions of great trust. May 28, 1868, he married Miss Ann A. Pate, daughter of John F. and Margaret (Marley) Pate, both natives of Knox County. The latter died about 1856. To Mr. and Mrs. Cross were born three children: Mary (deceased), William (deceased) add Frank. Mr. and Mrs. Cross are members of the Presbyterian Church of which he is deacon. He is a Democrat in politics, and cast his first presidential vote for George B. McClellan. He is also a Master Mason. He owns a fine farm of 256 acres, and is in excellent circumstances.

W. W. Cruse, one of the stirring, enterprising farmers of Knox County, Tenn., and a native of that county, was born August 22, 1839. He is the son of A. B. and Margaret (Brown) Cruse, both natives of Tennessee. Our subject received his education in the common district schools, and began tilling the soil while still quite young. In 1862 he chose for his companion through life Miss Charlotta E. Payne, who bore him three children—two sons and one daughter. The sons' names are Jacob A. and John M., and the daughter's name is Lucy Jane. The mother's death occurred March 10, 1874, and in September of the same year he was united in marriage to Miss Nancy E. Hines, and by this union became the father of two sons and two daughters, viz.: Arthur Temple, Chester Ellis, Margaret E. and Sarah Evaline. Mr. Cruse owns three different tracts of land, containing respectively 150, 110 and 50 acres. He is a Republican in politics, and is at present superintendent of the workhouse in Knox County.

J. W. Cruze, Sr., one of the deacons of the First Baptist Church, of Knoxville, Tenn., is a native of Blount County, Tenn., born December 19, 1824, and is the son of James and Lennes (Childress) Cruze, both natives of Virginia. The father was born in Prince Edward County in 1797, and immigrated to Tennessee about 1808, settling in Knox County, where he farmed until his death in 1852. He was a soldier in the war of 1812. The mother was born in Buckingham County in 1807, and died in 1863. Both were members of the Baptist Church. James Cruze, grandfather of our subject, served seven years as a soldier in the Revolutionary war. Our subject was reared in Blount and Knox Counties, and attended the common schools. In 1849 he married Margaret Sherrell, a native of Blount County, born in 1826, and the daughter of John and Annie Brakeville, both natives of Tennessee. To this union have been born nine children, five of whom are living: James H., Rachel M., Elizabeth, John W., Jr., and C. C. Our subject followed agricultural pursuits until 1852, after which he engaged in merchandising, and this continued until the panic of 1873, when he met with reverses and retired from business. He retained his property, however, and at present is in comfortable circumstances. In 1847 he enlisted in the war between the United States and Mexico, joining the Thirteenth Regiment of Alabama Infantry, United States, under Capt. Egbert Jones. He became a member of the First Baptist Church, of Knoxville, in 1849, and is now and has been a deacon in the same since 1860. His wife is also a member of the same church.

J. H. Cruze, member of the board of education of Knoxville, and son of J. W., Sr., and Margaret (Sherrell) Cruze, was born in Knoxville March 6, 1852, and after passing through the public schools completed his education at the University of Tennessee. At the age of nineteen he began his business career as a salesman for the firm of Woodruff & Co. In 1875 he engaged in the hardware business in partnership with a Mr. Gredig. Soon after he purchased his partner's interest and has continued alone until July 1, 1887, when he entered into partnership with Mr. E. Buffat under the firm name of Cruze & Buffat. In connection with that he is a member of the firm of Cruze Bros., dealers in coal and coke, and has been dealing quite successfully in real estate. In 1876 he married Miss Lucy Knaffl, daughter of Dr. Knaffl, of Nashville, by whom he has two children: Clifford and Edna. Both Mr. and Mrs. Cruze are members of the First Baptist Church. Politically Mr. Cruze is a Democrat, and he was for several years a member of the board of mayor and aldermen, and as such gained the reputation of fearlessly expressing and voting his convictions. He has been very successful, and now takes rank among the first business men of Knoxville.

J. W. Cruze, Jr., junior member of the firm of Cruze Bros., dealers in coal and coke, and son of J. W., Sr., and Margaret (Sherrell) Cruze, was born March 18, 1864, in the city of Knoxville. His educational advantages were confined to the public schools of the city. Upon reaching his majority he did business for a coal firm until 1886 when he and his brother J. H. Cruze opened their yard at 55 Hardee Street. Since that time he has done an extensive business, handling about 16,000 tons yearly. In 1886 Mr. Cruze married Miss Esther, daughter of Joseph Post, of Knoxville. Mr. Cruze is a member of the First Baptist Church, and in politics is a Democrat. Although young as a business man he is rapidly coming to the front.

John Cruze, one of the substantial merchants of Knoxville, is a son of James and Catherine (Brakebill) Cruze, both natives of East Tennessee. The father's people came from Virginia and the mother's from Pennsylvania, being among the early settlers of this part of the State. The father was a farmer by occupation. Of their family of nine children seven are now living. Our subject was born in Knox County October 27, 1838. He was reared on the farm, and at the age of seventeen came to Knoxville to learn the tinner's trade. Having worked as journeyman until after the war he began business for himself on a small scale, and has been increasing the same ever since. He has been associated with several different firms, and is now a member of the firm of DePue, Cruze & Co., having one of the largest stove and tinware establishments in the city. In 1860 he was united in marriage to Miss Isabella Henry, of Knoxville, and the fruits of this union were six children, four now living —one son and three daughters. Mr. Cruze is a Mason, and he and wife are members of the First Baptist Church. He has been intimately connected with the business interests of Knoxville for thirty-four years.

Albert Davis, farmer, was born November 21, 1825, in Grainger County, Tenn. In 1853 he moved to Knox County, where he has since resided. He is the third of twelve children born to the union of James and Lavicy (Cockrum) Davis, both natives of South Carolina, and both were brought to Tennessee by their parents when children. James Davis was a minister of the gospel in the Baptist Church. He died in 1872, aged seventy-one years. Mr. and Mrs. Davis were of German and English descent and Mr. Davis' great-grandfather was a native of Ireland. Our subject acquired his education mostly at home and by his own exertions. When twenty-one years of age he began life for himself and has made the principal part of what he now owns by his own exertions. In 1848 he married Miss Deborah Ann Cate, a daughter of Charles and Elizabeth (Lloyd) Cate, natives of North Carolina, where they were reared and educated. They came to Tennessee in 1816 and settled in Grainger County. To them were born eight children: Marian (deceased), Jasper, Taylor (deceased), Elizabeth (deceased) and four who died in infancy. Mr. Davis is a Democrat in politics, casting his first presidential vote for Z. Taylor. He was a stanch Union man during the late war. He and wife have been members of the Missionary Baptist Church for forty years and he has been deacon in the same for thirty years. He was also for many years clerk of the church. Mr. Davis has a fine farm of 200 acres and is a successful and enterprising farmer.

C. Deaderick, M. D., one of the most prominent physicians of Knoxville, Tenn., was born in that city August 22, 1847, and is the son of David and Elizabeth J. (Crozier) Deaderick, both natives of Tennessee. The father was born in the year 1797 and filled various public positions, the last of which was that of clerk and master of the chancery court at Knoxville. His death occurred in 1873. The mother was born in the year 1804 and died April 14, 1887, aged eighty-three years. She was a member of the Third Presbyterian Church, of which her husband was also a member. Our subject was reared in the city of his birth, and attended the University of East Tennessee, finishing his education at the Washington and Lee University at Lexington, Va. He entered that institution in his seventeenth year and graduated in 1869. He began the study of medicine in that year under Dr. John M. Boyd at Knoxville, and in the fall of the same year entered the University of Pennsylvania at Philadelphia, graduating in 1871. He at once returned to his native city and began the practice of medicine, which he has continued up to the present, having established one of the largest practices in the city. He is a member of the Knox County and the State Medical Societies and a member of the American Medical Association. He was recently appointed examining surgeon of the United States Pension Office at Knoxville. Dr. Deaderick was married in 1875 to Rebecca Williams, a native of Warren County, N. C., born in 1852, and the daughter of John T. and Mary (Somerville) Williams, natives of North Carolina. Mrs. Deaderick is a member of the Episcopal Church.

Hon. James A. Doughty was born in Knox County, Tenn., July 1, 1823, in what was then called Lyon's Bend, on a farm now owned by Robert Badget, seven miles from the city, and is the son of Benjamin and Mary W. (Camp) Doughty, natives of Tennessee and Virginia respectively. Our subject was reared in Knox County, and educated at Maryville College, Blount County, Tenn. Previous to coming to college he had learned the saddler's trade in Knoxville, and this occupation, together with teaching, assisted him in working his way through college. In May, 1849, he wedded Miss Sarah A. Martin, a native of Blount County, Tenn., born in 1821, and to this union three children were born— one son and two daughters. Mrs. Doughty died in 1855, and in 1857 Mr. Doughty married Elizabeth Taylor, of Anderson County, Tenn., who bore him one child, a daughter. In 1877 he married Adelia Murphy, daughter of the late Maj. James A. Murphy, of Knox County. After his first marriage our subject engaged in farming and merchandising in Anderson and Blount Counties, and studied law up to the breaking out of the late war. At that time he allied himself with the Union people of East Tennessee, and in August, 1861, he, with about 300 other Tennessee Unionists, went to Kentucky, and was mustered into the First Regiment of Union Tennessee Infantry, at Camp Dick Robinson, Ky., he having been elected captain of Company K before reaching that point. In December, 1862, he was commissioned by Andrew Johnson, military governor of Tennessee, to raise a regiment of cavalry, and after spending $1,000 of his own private funds, and after losing his companies for want of supplies before October, 1863, succeeded in raising about 500 men, who were designated the Seventeenth Tennessee Cavalry by Gen. A. E. Burnside. This regiment participated in the siege of Knoxville, and was instrumental in saving the Federal Army from starvation or surrender, a fact noticed in the official report by Gen. Burnside. In January, 1864, this regiment was consolidated with the Twelfth Regiment, and became the Thirteenth Regiment, of which his cousin, George W. Doughty, was made major. After the consolidation of the regiment our subject was commissioned to raise artillery batteries, of which he was promised the lieutenant-colonelcy, but was denied the promised reward to make way for the advancement of individuals who stood more in favor with those in authority. He served throughout the war, and returned home greatly damaged and injured in health, but was not long idle at home until he was called to serve his State in another capacity. In

1865 he was elected to the House of Representatives of Tennessee, to represent Anderson and Campbell Counties. He was re-elected in 1867, and served four years with honor and distinction. He was sometimes called the leader, and sometimes the father of the Radical party, and so he was on some subjects, especially in reference to the status of the negro. He was the first man to vote on the constitutional amendment which gave the negro the privilege of testifying in court, and the right of suffrage. He attended the border State convention at Philadelphia, in 1866, as a delegate, and took a deep interest in the resolution to give the negro the right of suffrage. The report of the committee having the resolution in hand was adverse to its passage on the grounds of inexpediency. There was but the majority report, which was received by the convention. Seeing how matters stood, and that the question was about to be solved, our subject gathered a few prominent friends of the measure together, among whom were United States Senators Fowler, of Tennessee; Hamilton, of Texas, and Moss, of Missouri, who constituted themselves a committee, and prevailed on the convention to permit them to make a minority report for the sake of argument. So well did the friends of the measure improve their time and opportunity that the resolution was adopted, and to our subject is largely due the honor and credit of its passage at that time. During his legislative career Col. Doughty was one of the leaders of all important movements, and earnestly worked for the advancement of the vital interests of the State. He was ever the champion of the negro, the railroads and educational interests, and was the author of the present school law of Tennessee, which has since been amended. He was chairman of the committee on agricultural funds, and aided as such in securing the congressional appropriation to be deposited in the University of Knoxville for the use of the people of the State. In 1867 he began the practice of law at Clinton, Tenn., and continued the same until 1873, when he removed to Sneedville, Tenn., and here practiced until 1883, after which he removed to Knoxville. He is a member of Ed Maynard Post, No. 14, G. A. R., and an excellent citizen.

Dr. Charles M. Drake, physician of Knoxville, Tenn., was born in Greene County of that State, December 20, 1854, and is the son of Dr. W. W. and Amanda (Evans) Drake. The father was born in Rockbridge County, Va., in 1818, and attended Tusculum Literary College in Greene County and graduated from Jefferson Medical College at Philadelphia, Penn. At his death, which occurred February 10, 1871, he was considered one of the most prominent physicians of East Tennessee. The mother was born near Russellville, Tenn., in 1824, and was the daughter of Walter Evans, one of the pioneers and large land owners of Jefferson County, Tenn. Our subject was reared in Greene County and attended school at Tusculum College. In 1872 he began the study of medicine, and the same year entered Jefferson Medical College at Philadelphia, where he graduated in 1875. He was elected assistant surgeon of the Philadelphia Charity Hospital, which position he resigned to come to Knoxville, where he practiced medicine two years. He then returned to Philadelphia and became assistant to Profs. Joseph and William H. Pancoast. Six years were spent in the above position, during which time he visited Europe and the various city hospitals. From 1877 to 1880 he was assistant demonstrator of anatomy at Jefferson Medical College. In 1882 he married at St. Paul, Minn., Miss Nellie Averill, a native of Minnesota, born in 1856, and the daughter of Gen. John T. Averill. Dr. Drake removed to Knoxville in 1883, on account of his wife's health, but her death occurred there in April, 1887. Dr. Drake is a member of the Knox County and State Medical Societies, and has contributed a number of articles to medical journals.

J. C. Duncan, manager of the Western Union Telegraph Company, and also manager of the East Tennessee Telephone Company of Knoxville, was born in Cumberland County, Va., in 1840. When eighteen years of age he began to learn telegraphy. During the war he was with the Army of Tennessee as an operator. In the year 1866 he came to Knoxville and took charge of the Western Union Telegraph office, which position he has held ever since. He has been a student and experimenter of electrical and phonetic science, and since 1880 Mr. Duncan has been manager for the East Tennessee Telephone Company at Knoxville. For a companion through life he chose Miss Fannie J., daughter of Gen. Joseph A. Brooks, and this union was blessed by the birth of two sons. Mr. Duncan is an honest, straightforward business man, and as such is appreciated by his many friends. He has been in the telegraph service twenty-nine years.

East Tennessee Coal Company. Among the largest enterprises in the mining of coal in this State is the above named company, which was organized in 1871 and incorporated July 24, 1883, with a paid up capital of $40,000; since then it has increased its stock to $50,000. This firm is the owner of over 3,000 acres of the celebrated Jellico coal fields. While only capitalized at $50,000 the cost value of their property is $115,000; $65,000 being carried as a surplus. The mines are located at Jellico, Tenn., at the junction of the Louisville & Nashville Railroad and East Tennessee, Virginia & Georgia Railroad. The location is superior to any in East Tennessee, giving shipping facilities north to the Ohio River and south in all the Southern States as far as the Gulf of Mexico. The following gentlemen constitute the board of directors, viz.: S. B. Luttrell (president Mechanics National Bank), D. C. Richards (president Enterprise Machine Company), J. B. Hoxsie (general manager Crystal Ice Company), D. D. Nicholas (president Gem Marble Company), W. T. Lewis, E. J. Davis and B. A. Jenkins. The signal success of this industrial enterprise is due to the ability and thorough knowledge of its officers, E. J. Davis, president and general manager, and B. A. Jenkins, secretary and treasurer. Mr. Davis is a native of Wales, and immigrated to America in 1867, locating at Knoxville, Tenn. He is a slater and stone cutter by trade, but embarked with a small purse, with several others, into the coal business in 1871, and has since been engaged in the upbuilding of this now recognized as one of the largest enterprises of the kind in the State. Mr. Jenkins is a native of Pennsylvania, and is a graduate of a Pennsylvania academy and of Eastman's Business College. He first connected himself as bookkeeper, and afterward was elected secretary and treasurer of the company. Much of the success of this organization is due to the energies of this young man, who is now one of its largest stockholders. No company is deserving of higher recognition than this organization, for its widespread popularity is due to its prompt, liberal and reliable transactions in the prosecution of its business.

East Tennessee National Bank was organized at Knoxville, July 26, 1872, with a capital stock of $100,000, and the following list of directors, viz.: Joseph R. Anderson, R. Love, James H. Ernest, Franklin W. Taylor, Sr., William Brazelton, Joseph Jaques, Richard C. Jackson, Jesse A. Rayl, Samuel McKinney, Franklin H. McClung, Jasper W. Lillard, Samuel E. Boyd and J. E. Raht. Richard C. Jackson was elected president, Franklin H. McClung, vice-president, and W. B. French, cashier. The present directors are R. S. Payne, E. J. Sanford, S. B. Boyd, W. W. Wordworth, Daniel Briscoe, C. M. McClung, J. M. Meek, R. C. Jackson and C. M. McGhee. R. S. Payne is president, E. J. Sanford, vice-president, and F. L. Fisher, cashier. The following is the report of the bank, after business, March 4, 1887: *Resources*—Loans and discounts, $501,069.23; overdrafts, $1,557.41; United States bonds to secure circulation, $25,000; United States bonds to secure deposits, $50,000; other stocks, bonds and mortgages, $20,429.12; due from approved reserve agents, $221,322.76; due from other National banks, $27,309.96; due from State banks and bankers, $10,856.85; real estate, furniture and fixtures, $2,700; current expenses and taxes paid, $8,819.95; premiums paid, $18,940.62; checks and other cash items, $10,396.37;

bills of other banks, $35,000; specie, $106,713.81; legal tender notes, $115,000; redemption fund with United States treasurer (5 per cent of circulation), $1,125; due from United States treasurer, other than 5 per cent redemption fund, $40; total, $1,156,281.08. *Liabilities*—Capital stock paid in, $100,000; surplus fund, $20,000; undivided profits, $94,385.29; National bank notes outstanding, $22,500; individual deposits subject to check, $812,422.47; demand certificates of deposits, $10,537.17; United States deposits, $15,119.01; deposits of United States disbursing officers, $31,118.08; due to other National banks, $35,794.77; due to State banks and bankers, $4,404.29; notes and bills rediscounted, $10,000; total, $1,156,281.08.

R. H. Edington, dry goods merchant, and senior member of the firm of R. H. Edington & Co., extensive rock-masonry contractors, of Knoxville, Tenn., is a son of James and Fanny (Johnson) Edington, and was born in McMinn County, Tenn., January 22, 1842. His parents were natives of Tennessee, and his father was a millwright by occupation. He died in 1844. The mother was born in 1809, and died in the year 1876. R. H. Edington was reared in the county of his birth, and acquired a limited education in the country schools of that day. Later in life, however, he added to his education materially by his own exertions, which, with natural ability, fitted him for a successful and active career. He began life at the bottom, and was obliged to borrow money with which to procure his marriage license. Until after his marriage he was not able to write his own name or do the easiest sum in arithmetic. But success followed him, and he is to-day in easy circumstances, paying taxes on about $14,000 worth of real estate. In 1861 he wedded Margaret Henderson, a native of Tennessee, who presented him with seven children, six of whom are living. Mrs. Edington died in 1876, and in June, 1877, our subject married Catherine J. Groner, a native of Tennessee, born in 1846, the daughter of Wilson and Margaret (Brown) Groner. To this union five children have been born. Mr. Edington became a member of New Hopewell Baptist Church at the age of fourteen, and has continued a member of that denomination up to the present. He and his wife are members of the First Baptist Church, of Knoxville, of which he is a trustee.

T. C. Eldridge, proprietor of the Knoxville Carriage Factory, is the son of David Eldridge, a native of Pennsylvania. When young the father moved to Ohio, where he learned carriage-making, and ran a shop many years. While on a trip to Natchez, Miss., he met and married Miss Elizabeth Gauley, a native of England, who came to America when about sixteen years of age. In 1872 they moved to Knoxville, where both spent the balance of their days. Of their family of four children—three sons and one daughter—our subject is the second. He was born March 2, 1852, in Ohio; was educated in the common schools, and while growing up learned the trade of his father. When seventeen years of age he started out for himself. After traveling and working as journeyman for a number of years he found his way to Knoxville, his father having established a factory at that point in 1872. He took charge of it six years later, and has run it successfully ever since. In 1881 he married Miss Sallie Knaffl, daughter of Dr. R. Knaffl, of Nashville, and by her became the father of two daughters: Maudie and Osie. Mr. Eldridge is a Republican in politics. Financially he has met with excellent success, having started with a very small capital, he now runs a good factory, working from seven to twelve hands.

William Epps, senior member of the firm of Epps, McMillan & Co., dealers in boots, shoes, hats, trunks, umbrellas, etc., is a native of Knox County. He was reared on the farm, came to Knoxville in 1877, and filled various clerkships until the firm of which he is now a member was formed in 1881. The other two members of the firm are Alex McMillan and Flem. Hazen, both natives of Knoxville. They employ three assistants, besides the members of the firm. The paternal great-grandfather of our subject came from Holland, and located in Virginia, from which State the grandfather came to Knoxville in the early settlement of this county. He was in the war of 1812. The father of our subject, Richard Epps, was born in this county, and served one year in the Confederate cavalry service. He is at present engaged in agricultural pursuits in Knox County. The mother of our subject, Armenia Epps, is a native also of Knox County, and William is the second of her family of nine children, all of whom are living.

Capt. S. P. Evans, clerk and master, is a native of Roane County, Tenn., where he was reared and educated. He grew to manhood on the farm, and at the time of Grant's first election to the presidency, came to Knoxville as United States marshal, which position he held for twelve years, when he was appointed to his present office. In 1872 he was united in marriage to Miss Emma Godby, by whom he had six children, four still living. Mr. Evans has been a member of the Coal Creek Coal Company since 1883, and was sheriff of Roane County before he came to Knoxville. At the breaking out of hostilities during the late war, he enlisted in the Fifth Tennessee Federal Infantry, and at the organization was elected second lieutenant, from which he was promoted to the rank of captain, serving as such until the close. He is the fourth of a family of ten children, seven now living, born to the union of P. H. and Rebecca

Parks, natives of East Tennessee. The father resided in Cocke County in early life, then in Roane County about forty years, and there died in 1882. The mother's death occurred in the same county about 1880.

Ignaz Fanz, secretary and treasurer of the Knoxville Ice Company, was born in Baden, Germany, August 1, 1842, and educated in the old country. At the age of fifteen he came to America and located at Knoxville, Tenn., where he began learning the machinist's trade, but was obliged to abandon this on account of not understanding the English language. For a time, during the war, he manufactured powder, and then he and a brother engaged in the butcher's trade. In 1862 he went out in Company G, Sixth Tennessee Infantry, Federal Army, and served until the close of the war, being sergeant a short time. After the cessation of hostilities he returned to Knoxville, and soon began manufacturing the celebrated Fanz's East Tennessee pork sausage, which he has made ever since. In 1866 he married Miss Emma J. Cooley, an East Tenneesee lady, and to them were born five children—one son and four daughters. Both Mr. and Mrs. Fanz are members of the Third Presbyterian Church. He is a Republican in politics, and a member of the G. A. R.

F. L. Fisher, cashier of the East Tennessee National Bank, is a native of Union County, Penn., born in 1853, and was reared and educated in that county. He then came to Tennessee with his parents, who located on a farm in Hamblen County. In 1876 he came to Knoxville and accepted a clerkship with a wholesale grocery firm two or three years. He then began in the bank as bookkeeper, from which he was promoted to teller, and from this position to that of his present as cashier in 1883. In February of the same year he was united in marriage to Miss Ella Locke, a daughter of Maj. Locke, of this city. Our subject is the sixth of eight children born to Daniel and Amelia (Loudenslager) Fisher, who are natives of Pennsylvania and of German descent. The father died in Hamblen County at seventy-five years of age. The mother is still living at the old home.

W. H. Fizer, proprietor of the Palace Livery Stable of Knoxville, Tenn., is a native of Mount Sterling, Ky., born in 1860, and is the son of S. L. and Mary (Jones) Fizer, both natives of Kentucky. The father was born in 1833, is a painter by occupation and resides at Mount Sterling. The mother was born in 1844. W. H. Fizer was reared in the town of his birth and attended the public schools. In 1879 he removed to La Grange Iron Furnace, in Stewart County, Tenn., where he entered the furnace store as clerk, and succeeded in working his way up to assistant superintendent of the furnace, a position he held until he removed to Bibb Furnace, Alabama, in 1881. At this place he occupied a similar position for one year, and then the same position at Bass Furnace, Alabama, for two years. He then went to Shelby Iron Works, Alabama, where he secured large ore contracts. While at this place he married, in August, 1885, Tennie Gurley, of Knoxville, who was born in that city in 1860. At the end of two years he removed to Knoxville and opened his present business. His stable building is one of the largest and most complete in the State. It is a two-story brick, fronting 150 feet on Reservoir Street and 200 feet deep, is stocked with fine horses and elegant rigs. Mr. Fizer is a young man of thorough business worth and sterling character, and is one of the representative young business men of Knoxville.

B. P. Flenniken, farmer and mechanic, was born in Knox County, Tenn., October 11, 1830, and while still quite young, began earning his own living. He went to Middle Tennessee, where he learned brick-making and the masonry trade, and has followed this all his life in connection with farming. In March, 1859, Miss Malissa Ann Tipton daughter of William C. Tipton, became his wife. She was born in Knox County, Tenn., October 1, 1837, and two children were born to her marriage, viz.: William B. who lived but a short time and John Howell, a manly little fellow, the pride of his fond parents and the delight of the household, who died after a short stay of three years. Mrs. Flenniken has been an invalid for eight years. Both Mr. and Mrs. Flenniken are worthy and consistent members of the Methodist Episcopal Church South. Mr. Flenniken has a good farm of 170 acres of land in District No. 13, of Knox County. He recently purchased a nice homestead near Knoxville but on the opposite side of the Tennessee River, and here he expects to pass the remainder of his days. He also owns two houses and lots in Knoxville.

E. H. Flenniken, a native of Knox County, Tenn., was born in 1832, and lived on a farm until twenty years of age, after which he learned the brick-mason's trade and followed that until 1861, when he returned to agricultural pursuits. This occupation he followed for three years, after which he resumed his trade in connection with brick manufacturing in Knoxville, and continued this for twenty-seven years. He retired from business in 1881, and has since devoted his time to looking after the interests of his farm and town property. He was formerly president of the Kingston Pike Company, and is at present a stockholder and director in the same. . In 1862 he married Miss Mary Adaline French, also a native of Knox County. His great-grandfather, Wallace Flenniken, located within four miles of the present site of Knoxville, and a house that he built here, and in which he reared part of his family, is still standing near the Maryville dirt road. He resided in the house until his death October 11, 1828. The grandfather of our subject, Wallace Flenniken, was reared here and served in the war of 1812. Samuel Flenniken, father of our subject, was born in Knox County, near the old Flenniken farm mentioned above, and followed the carpenter's trade in connection with farming, until his death in 1877. He married Elizabeth Howell, a native of Knox County, and a family of eight children was reared, four of whom are still living: Our subject, two brothers and a sister. Mr. Flenniken is a Mason, and he and family are members of the Methodist Episcopal Church.

W. B. Ford, circuit court clerk, was born in Knox County in 1851, and is the son of James P. and Susan (Haynes) Ford, natives of Virginia, who came to this county about 1810 and 1825 respectively, and were here married. The mother died in 1876, and the father June 8, 1887. The father was a successful tiller of the soil, and a much respected citizen. Our subject was one of twelve children (nine of whom are living) born to his parents. He received a good education at Mossy Creek College and at the State University, leaving the former institution in 1876. He then followed the teacher's profession until 1879, at which date he went in the United States revenue service as storekeeper and gauger until 1882, after which he was elected to his present position. In 1873 he was united in marriage to Orlena Henderson, a native of Knox County. Mr. Ford is a member of the I. O. O. F., and the Missionary Baptist Church. His grandfather, Joseph Ford, was a native of Virginia, and settled in the Fourteenth District of Knox County. The Ford family are all Republicans, the father and grandfather formerly being Whigs.

J. W. Fowler, a farmer of the Sixth District, was born April 28, 1817, in Knox County, where he has since resided. He is one of twelve children born to John and Elizabeth (Dorsey) Fowler, both of whom were born and reared in Franklin County, N. C. They came to Tennessee in 1816, settled in the district where their son now resides, and here passed the remainder of their days. Samuel Fowler, grandfather of our subject, was a soldier under Gen. Washington, and participated in the battle in which Gen. Braddock was killed. He was reared in Virginia, and his father was a native born Englishman. His wife's maiden name was Fanny Lawson; she had two brothers who were captains in the Revolutionary war, one in the colonial and the other in the British Army, and both were killed. Our subject never attended school six months in his life, but acquired his education by his own efforts while at home. He lived with and provided for his father until the latter's death. When twenty-eight years of age he married Miss Mary Conner, who was born in 1820, and who is a daughter of William and Sarah (Cox) Conner. This union resulted in the birth of eight children: John W., William P., Elbert S., Louisa J. (deceased), Samuel P., Nancy E. (Mrs. Herrell), Sarah E. (Mrs. Yarnell) and James A. Mr. Fowler and family are members of the Methodist Episcopal Church, Mr. Fowler having been a member of the same for forty-five years. He is a Republican in politics, and cast his first presidential vote for William H. Harrison. He was elected justice of the peace in 1860, and has been re-elected each successive election since. Mr. Fowler has reared eight children and one grandson, S. W. Marshall, who are highly respected citizens of the different localities in which they live, and but one of the nine has ever taken a drink of ardent spirits. They are all ardent prohibitionists. Mrs. Fowler's grandfather, Curd Cox, was a soldier in the Revolutionary war, being only a youth at that time. Her father was orderly sergeant under Gen. Jackson in the war of 1812. Mr. Fowler's maternal grandmother's maiden name was Sedgick, and she was a native of Maryland.

W. M. Fox, a successful agriculturist of the Tenth District, was born November 7, 1834, in the Ninth District of Knox County, where he grew to manhood. He came to the locality where he now resides in 1871, and here he has since lived. He is one of the fourteen children born to Austin and Margaret (Walker) Fox, both natives of Burke County, N. C., where they were married in 1820. They came to Knox County in 1829, settling on Beaver Creek. The father died in 1840, and the mother in October, 1864; they were both of Scotch-Irish descent, and both were members of the Methodist Episcopal Church. At the time of his death the father owned 800 acres of well improved land, all well cultivated. Our subject's grandfather, John Fox, was a soldier in the Revolutionary war, and was a practical and successful farm manager. W. M. Fox, married Miss Louisa Ellen Nelson, May 21, 1865. She was a daughter of David and Charlotte (Lanes) Nelson. Mrs. Nelson died January 3, 1880, aged seventy years. Mr. Nelson's father, Suthy Nelson, lived to the remarkably advanced age of one hundred and fifteen years. He was a soldier in both the Revolution and the war of 1812. To our subject and wife seven children were born: David N., Charlotta B., Mollie T., Etta J., William M., Joseph O. and Daisy Adelia. Mr. Fox is a Democrat in politics, although he usually votes for principle instead of party; is a member of the Masonic fraternity, and he and wife and two elder daughters are members of the Missionary Baptist Church. Mr. Fox began life a poor man, and, besides paying over $2,000 security debts, has a fine farm of 400 acres of land located two miles east of Concord.

During the late war Mr. Fox was recruiting officer for the Federal Army, and proved a very efficient officer in that capacity.

J. W. Fox, of the firm of Bird & Fox, liverymen and stock traders, was born in Knox County, Tenn., in 1849, and was reared on a farm at Beaver Creek, securing his education at the country schools, and after reaching manhood began dealing and trading in stock. He soon purchased a farm in the county, continuing stock trading, shipping, etc., in connection with farming. He served as deputy sheriff of Knox County in the years 1874-75 under Mat. Swan. He located in Knoxville in April, 1885, where he continued buying and shipping stock. In November, 1886, he formed a partnership with J. W. Bird in the livery business. They keep about thirty head of horses in the livery trade, and still continue trading and shipping to Southern markets. The father of our subject, J. W. Fox, Sr., was a native of Burke County, N. C., and came to Knox County in childhood, where he followed farming and stock trading until his death in 1881. Ann Galbraith Fox, the mother, was a native of Anderson County, Tenn., and also died in 1881. Our subject is a Free Mason and the eldest of four sons and three daughters, all living.

Henry Frazier (deceased) was born January 22, 1825, in Knox County, and within one mile of the Frazier homestead. He received a common-school education, and having a decided taste for agricultural pursuits always followed that occupation. He devoted much time to the improvement of his farm, and was considered one of the best farmers in his immediate neighborhood. He took a great interest in education, and was the main support of the school of his neighborhood. He was a member of the Methodist Episcopal Church South, and very enthusiastic in the cause of religion, having with the aid of a friend, erected Delphi Academy, near his home, which was after some years used as a church, and he was for some years steward and also superintendent of the Sunday-school. He died in his sixty-second year in the full triumph of a living faith, and was buried in the family graveyard. He was the husband of Margaret Underwood, whose first husband was Jonathan Pickle. The marriage of Mr. Frazier occurred in 1856, and to this union were born seven children: Gustavus, Sarah and Alice (twins), James, Adra, Ida and Angus, three of whom are married. Mr. Frazier gave liberally to support the gospel, and was a good man. Mrs. Frazier is now living at the old home in close proximity to her children.

W. H. French, a farmer, was born in Knox County, Tenn., April 25, 1820, and is the son of George and Elizabeth French, natives of Virginia and Pennsylvania, respectively. Our subject is of Dutch extraction and one of three sons and two daughters born to his parents. Our subject, a brother, and one sister are all who are living. W. H. received a very limited education and early in life turned his attention to farming. He began his life's work with very little capital, but is now the owner of 215 acres of Knox County land, situated in the Twenty-first District, all well improved. He has lately turned his attention to stock raising and excels in this. He is an uncompromising Republican but does not care for office, and although sixty-seven years of age is still strong and healthy.

W. B. French, farmer, and prominent citizen of Knox County, was born in that county March 11, 1850. His father, Jacob French, was of German descent, and a native of Virginia. His mother, Sarah (Kountz) French, was of German descent, and a native of Tennessee. Our subject received a rather limited education in the country schools, and early in life began cultivating the soil. August 5, 1874, he was united in marriage to Miss Susan M. Haynes, daughter of Jordan and Elizabeth Haynes, and the fruits of this union were four sons and two daughters, only two sons and two daughters now living, viz.: Urban Alexander, Jacob Dexter, Lilly and Sarah Opha. Our subject is the owner of 285 acres of well-improved land, and is also interested in raising live stock. He is a justice of the peace in his district, is postmaster at French, is a Republican in politics, and he and his wife are members of the Methodist Episcopal Church.

J. V. Fulkerson, a farmer, miller and dairyman near Ebenezer, was born September 20, 1848, in Rogersville, Hawkins Co., Tenn. He is the youngest of four children born to James L. and Alice G. (Armstrong) Fulkerson. The father was born in Washington County, Va., in 1814, and came to Tennessee about 1835, settling first in Hawkins County. He died in 1849. The mother of our subject was born in Hawkins County, Tenn., and died on the farm where her son is now residing, in 1872, aged eighty-five years. J. V. Fulkerson received the principal part of his education at Abingdon, Va. At the age of twenty-seven he married Miss Lula Oldham, a native of Knoxville, Tenn., and the daughter of Thomas E. and Georgianna (English) Oldham. Seven children were the result of our subject's marriage, viz.: Alice Armstrong, Margaret Virginia, Lula Oldham, Floyd Hurt, Thomas Oldham, Georgianna English and James Lyons. Mr. Fulkerson is a Democrat in politics, and he and Mrs. Fulkerson are members of the Presbyterian Church, of which he has been a ruling elder for one year. He has served his district as school commissioner, and was appointed a member of the live stock sanitary commission in 1884, and is still holding the office. He is a Master Mason and a Knight Templar. Mr. Fulkerson's great-grandfather, George Rogers, a native of Ireland, came to America shortly after the Revolutionary war, and settled in Hawkins County, Tenn., the county seat of which was named in honor of him. He was for some time hotel keeper at Rogersville, and it was at his house that Gen. Jackson compelled a fastidious young man who desired to lodge alone in a room, to sleep in Mr. Roger's corn crib, being forced in by main strength by Gen. Jackson, when he refused to occupy the place prepared for him. Our subject's paternal great-grandfather, James Fulkerson, was a native of Germany, as was also his wife. J. V.'s grandmother's name was Vance, a first cousin of the father of Zebadee Vance, ex-governor of North Carolina, and at present United States senator. Our subject's uncle, Abraham Faulkner, represented the Ninth Congressional District of Virginia, two years in Congress. Another uncle, Samuel V. Faulkerson, was judge of the Ninth Judicial District of Virginia for many years, and after the breaking out of the late war was appointed colonel of the Thirty-seventh Virginia, and was afterward commissioned brigadier-general, but was killed a short time afterward. Our subject began life for himself, when nineteen years of age, in the drug business at Knoxville. This he followed for sixteen years. He then traveled for the wholesale firm of S. D. Mitchell & Co., then with W. C. Ingles & Co., then with Oldham & Hunter, and after being eleven years on the road began working at $8 per month, and when he quit working was drawing a salary of $1,500 per year. In August, 1883, he abandoned the business on account of ill health, and has since followed agricultural pursuits. He owns 500 acres of land, all well cultivated, and located on the East Tennessee, Virginia & Georgia Railroad, near Ebenezer. In 1853 Mr. F. S. Heiskell married Mrs. James L. Fulkerson. He was born in 1787, in Woodstock, Va., where he grew to manhood. He learned type setting under his brother, and he and his brother-in-law established the *Knoxville Register* in 1815, one of the strongest Whig organs in East Tennessee. He was State and National printer, and represented Knox County several times in the Legislature, riding from Knoxville to Nashville several times on horseback. He was a strong Jackson man, although he was an enthusiastic Whig in principle. Mr. Heiskell and Gov. Brownlow carried on a very exciting discussion for some time in the newspapers, and Mr. Heiskell, very ably and successfully defended the principles he advocated. He purchased and moved to the farm, where Mr. J. V. Fulkerson resides, in 1835, where he continued to reside until his death, which occurred in 1883. He was buried at Rogersville. He was a self-made man, acquiring his education by his own exertions.

Charles M. Funck, manager of the marble works of W. H. Evans & Son, Knoxville, was born in Cumberland, Md., January 17, 1854, but while yet quite young removed to Baltimore. While growing up he had the benefit of the public schools until thirteen years of age, when he was left an orphan. His parents, Henry and Rosina (Hausch) Funck, came from Germany when children. The father served in Company K, Second Maryland Infantry, Federal Army, nearly three years, but was discharged on account of ill health. He afterward joined a construction corps, and served until the close of the war. He was a cabinet-maker by trade. The mother died in 1864, and the father in 1867. Of their family of seven children—three sons and four daughters—the three boys were of a mechanical turn of mind. Our subject began his business career as cash boy in a dry goods house. From that he arose to salesman, and continued in that capacity for about nine years. After spending four years in Florida, farming, he returned to Baltimore, and was bookkeeper and cashier for the Baltimore Ice Company. In 1877 he married Miss J. Cora Wilcox, of Baltimore, who bore him five children. One son and two daughters are now living. In 1886 Mr. Funck came to Knoxville to assume the duties of his present office. He has managed this large establishment ably, and justly deserves the esteem in which he is held.

William Gallaher, farmer of the Ninth District, was born May 11, 1812, on the farm where he has since resided. He is the tenth of eleven children born to George and Sarah (Oats) Gallaher. George Gallaher was born and reared in Virginia, and after his marriage came to the place where his son now lives. This was about 1800. He was an active worker in the Cumberland Presbyterian Church, and died in 1837, at the age of seventy-six. Mrs. Gallagher died about 1820. Our subject received his education in the common schools of the Ninth District. At the age of twenty-six he married Miss Mary King, who was born in 1819, five miles south of Knoxville, and who is the daughter of Rev. Jeremiah and Mary (Freeman) King. Her father was reared in North Carolina, and was a prominent and successful minister of the gospel in the Methodist Episcopal Church. He was for many years presiding elder. He died about 1822. To our subject and wife were born ten children: George H., Thomas J., John F., William N. (deceased), William B. (deceased), Lucy A. (deceased), Robert H., Joshua J. (deceased), David C. and Sallie E. (Mrs. Dr. Charles Lee). Mrs. Gallaher, up to the time of her death, was a member of the Cumberland Presbyterian Church, as was also Mr. Gallaher and the children. She died January 3, 1887, about sixty-nine years old. Mr. Gallaher owns a fine farm of 1,100 acres, on Clinch River, twenty-two miles from Knoxville. In politics Mr. Gallaher is a Democrat, casting his first presidential vote for Martin Van Buren.

Robert H. Gallaher, farmer, was born April 16, 1851, on the farm where William Gallaher now resides. He received his education in the subscription schools of the Ninth District, and at Croton College, in Monroe County. He is the seventh of ten children born to William and Mary (King) Gallaher, who were of Irish and Scotch lineage, respectively. (For further particulars of parents, see sketch of William Gallaher.) Robert H. Gallaher, subject of this sketch, married Miss Roxie Crookshank, the daughter of Thomas and Lavenia (Boyd) Crookshank. Mr. Crookshank was born in April, 1831, in Jefferson County, Tenn. After his marriage he moved to Knox County, and settled at Concord. In 1881 he moved to Grayson County, Tex., where he is now living, and is a member of the Presbyterian Church. His wife was born July 17, 1842, in Knox County, Tenn. She died in September, 1869. She was an active worker in the Cumberland Presbyterian Church. To our subject and wife were born six children: Effie J., Willie R., Joshua J., David C., George B. and Carrie Sue. Mr. Gallaher is a Democrat in politics, and he and his wife are members of the Cumberland Presbyterian Church. He owns 225 acres on Clinch River, situated about twenty miles from Knoxville.

George Gallaher, farmer of the Eleventh District, was born April 14, 1836, in Roane County, Tenn., and is the fifth of eight children born to Thomas and Permelia (Williams) Gallaher. Thomas Gallaher was born in 1801 on Clinch River, where he grew to manhood. He took great interest in the politics of the country, and was postmaster for several years. He was of English and Irish descent, and died in 1873. His wife was born and reared in Knox County, and was also of English and Irish descent. She died in 1838, being about thirty-two years of age. Our subject received his education in the common schools of Roane County, and in 1858 married Margaret Fox, daughter of Austin and Margaret (Walker) Fox. To Mr. and Mr. Gallaher were born three children: Thomas (deceased), Sophronia (Mrs. William Rodgers) and Charles. Mrs. Gallaher died August 20, 1868, and Mr. Gallaher took for his second wife, Miss Sarah Walker, June 8, 1871. She is a daughter of Elijah and Sarah Walker. Mr. Gallaher is a Democrat in politics, and he and wife are members of the Missionary Baptist Church, of which he was elected deacon in February, 1887. He owns a fine farm of 320 acres near the Kingston road, nine miles west of Knoxville, and is a successful farmer.

J. M. Gass, M. D., physician of Knoxville, Tenn., a native of Jefferson County, Tenn., was born April 7, 1836, and is the son of Ewing and Parmelia (Scruggs) Gass, both of whom are dead. Our subject was reared on the farm, and acquired his literary education at Greeneville and Lebanon, Tenn. He was married, June 24, 1867, to Nancy Davis, who was born in 1839, and is the daughter of James Davis, of Greene County, Tenn. Both are members of the Cumberland Presbyterian Church. He began the study of medicine under Dr. John R. Boyd, of Greeneville, Tenn.; later graduated from the medical department of the University of Nashville, and then began practicing in Greeneville, from where he removed to Morristown, and in August, 1883, removed to Knoxville, where he has since practiced his profession, having built up a good practice. He is a member of the Knox County Medical Society, and also of Oriental Lodge, F. & A. M., of Knoxville.

J. W. Gaut, general produce, grain and commission merchant, was born in Jefferson County, Tenn., February 26, 1823, and in early boyhood moved with his parents to Monroe County, where he grew to manhood on a farm. He came to to Knoxville in 1853 and embarked in the general produce and commission trade, being the first merchant in East Tennessee to confine himself to a certain line of goods. In 1848, previous to his coming to Knoxville, he married Miss Jane Boldman, a native of Greene County, Tenn., to whom thirteen children have been born, four sons and two daughters still living. From 1855 to 1858 he was in the wholesale grocery, grain and provision trade, after which he sold his interest and moved his family to Savannah, Ga., at which place he continued a general commission business until the commencement of the war. After the war he followed business two years in Atlanta, Ga., after which he came to Knoxville and resumed his former business, which he has since continued with the assistance of his sons. Mr. Gaut is one of the board of trustees for the University of Tennessee, was on the board of education (Knoxville city schools) five years, and for a number of years was president of the Knoxville board of trade which he assisted in organizing in 1871. Mr. Gaut's grandparents, John and Lutitia Gaut, were of German and Irish extraction respectively, but were natives of America. They settled in Jefferson County about 1780 or 1785, and their family consisted of thirteen children, two of whom are still living, and the average age already attained by the family of fifteen, including parents, is seventy-five years. Two of the above family (uncles of our subject) were in the war of 1812. Robert Gaut, father of our subject, was born in Jefferson County in 1801, and followed agricultural pursuits through life. He moved from Tennessee to Illinois in 1863, and died there in 1865. The mother of our subject, Mary (Wood) Gaut, was a native of Jefferson County, and died in 1846. Of her family of six children all are living but one daughter, our subject being the eldest of the family. He and his family are all members of the Methodist Episcopal Church South, holding memberships at Church Street Church, of which Mr. Gaut is and has been for many years an efficient member, and for twenty years past always sent as a lay delegate to the district and annual conference of his church. He also served as lay delegate in the general conference of 1874, 1878 and 1882 respectively.

J. L. George, farmer, was born August 31, 1848, in Blount County, Tenn., where he remained until 1872, when he moved to his present residence. He is the third of seven children born to J. W. and Eliza J. (Badgett) George, both of Irish descent. Mrs. George was born and reared at the mouth of Little River. She died October 22, 1877, aged about fifty-seven. Mr. J. W. George was born and reared in Blount County, where he is still living. The grandfather of our subject, Samuel George, came from Virginia to Tennessee at a very early day. He was justice of the peace of his district for many years and was prominently known as a flatboat builder and produce shipper. He reared a family of eight children, J. W. being the youngest born and the only child now living. J. W. is an energetic, enterprising man, and is one of the most influential and prominent citizens of the locality where he is known. He accumulated a vast amount of property, but much of it was destroyed or stolen during the late war. Mr. George married his second wife, Mrs. Mary Dorton, formerly Miss Hood, a sister of Gen. R. N. Hood, of Knoxville, March 2, 1880. By this union two children were born. Our subject received his education in Ewing and Jefferson College and at Emery and Henry, near Abingdon, Va. At the age of twenty-seven he married Miss Bettie Heiskell, a daughter of Milton Y. and Caroline (Kelso) Heiskell. William Heiskell, father of Milton Heiskell, was born and reared in Virginia, and came to Knox County at a very early day. He represented Knox County in the State Legislature several years, and took quite an active part in legislative affairs and in politics. He also took a prominent part in politics during the late war, and was quite an able supporter of the Union cause. Mr. Milton Heiskill received his education at Emery and Henry College, Virginia, and received his medical education at the medical college at Philadelphia, where he graduated. He is now practicing medicine at Knoxville, and is meeting with excellent success as a physician. To our subject and wife were born six children: Milton Heiskell, Isaac Wright, Joe Leath, Charley Kelso and two who died in infancy. Mrs. George is a member of the Methodist Episcopal Church South. Mr. George is a Democrat in politics, casting his first presidential vote for Horace Greeley, and is a Master Mason. He owns 227 acres of land twelve miles southwest of Knoxville, and is a very successful farmer.

W. F. Gibbs, clerk of the criminal court for the district of Knox, is a native of Knox County, and was educated at Walnut Grove Academy and the University of Tennessee. He grew to manhood on the farm, and was elected constable of the Fifth Civil District in 1874, and re-elected in 1876, serving four years in all. In 1878 he was appointed deputy sheriff of Knox County, under Sheriff Reeder, and in 1880 was reappointed by Sheriff C. B. Gossett. In the year 1882 he was elected to his present office, being the regular nominee of the Republican party, and was re-elected in August, 1886, which term he is now filling. He is the son of John and Sarah W. (Blain) Gibbs, who are natives of Knox and Grainger Counties, Tenn., respectively. The father is a successful farmer, and is now following agricultural pursuits in this county. He was deputy sheriff six years at the close of the war. February 22, 1887, our subject was united in marriage to Miss Mamie Sullivan, a native of Washington, D. C., and the daughter of Dennis Sullivan (deceased), of that city. Mr. Gibbs is a member of the A. O. U. W.

Hon. Henry R. Gibson, chancellor of the Second Chancery Division of Tennessee, is a native of Maryland, born in 1837, and graduated at Hobart College, Geneva, N. Y., in the class of 1862. A year later he married Miss Fanny M. Reed, of Brooklyn, N. Y., and there have been born to them three children: Nellie, Woolman (deceased) and Fanny. His father, Woolman Gibson, farmer and merchant, was born in Queen Anne County, Md., in 1800, and died in Washington, D. C., in 1877. His mother, Catherine (Carter) Gibson, who is also deceased, was a native of Georgetown, D. C. His great-grandfather, Woolman Gibson, served under Washington in Braddock's defeat, and afterward settled near the battleground, now the site of Pittsburgh, Penn. From this branch descended several of the noted Gibsons of Pennsylvania and Ohio. An uncle of Chancellor Gibson's mother, Daniel Wells, was one of two patriots who killed the British commander, Gen. Ross, at the battle of North Point, near Baltimore, in the war of 1812, and the name of this hero stands first on the shaft of the Baltimore Battle Monument. Chancellor Gibson entered the military service of the United States March 17, 1863, on the general staff of the Army of the Potomac. He participated in the second battle of Fredericksburg, in the battles of Chancellorsville and Monocacy and in the preliminary skirmishes of Gettysburg. He was honorably discharged from the service, August 4, 1865. After the war he attended the Albany (N. Y.) Law School, and upon the completion of his studies, and after receiving his license to practice law from the supreme court of New York, came to Knoxville and began the practice of his profession. In 1866 he moved to Campbell County, and in 1869 was chosen a delegate to the State Constitutional Convention from Campbell and Anderson. He was prominent in the convention, but owing to some obnoxious provisions in the constitution, refused to sign it. In 1870 he was elected to the State Senate, was a Grant electoral candidate in 1872, and a Garfield electoral candidate in 1880. In 1875 he represented the counties of Campbell, Union and Scott in the Tennessee House of Representatives. In 1881 he was appointed postoffice inspector, in which position he investigated the Star Route cases in California, Oregon, Idaho, Nevada, Utah and Arizona, and was highly commended by his superiors for his zeal and efficiency. In 1883 he became the editor of the *Knoxville Chronicle*, consolidating with it the *Knoxville Republican*, and making it the leading Republican paper in the South. In June, 1885, he was appointed by President Arthur, United States pension agent for the Southern States. In August, 1886, he was elected to his present office of chancellor by a majority of 13,621. He is a member of the Ed. Maynard Post, G. A. R., of Knoxville, and Senior Vice-Commander of the Department of Tennessee and Georgia G. A. R. Chancellor Gibson is a scholarly and vigorous writer, and as an orator has made a State reputation. His legal acquirements and habits of industry and research, eminently fit him for the responsible duties of Chancellor. Yet in the prime of life and possessed of good bodily vigor, Chancellor Gibson has open to him other and still larger fields of usefulness and fame.

S. L. Gilson, farmer of the Eleventh District, was born in Rush County, Ind., in 1829, and came to Tennessee in 1856, settling first at Knoxville, where he ran the stage from that place to Loudon the following four years. Since 1860 he has been engaged in farming. He is a son of Daniel and Jane (Bruce) Gilson, both of whom were born and reared in Washington County, Va. After their marriage they immigrated to Rush County, Ind., but moved from there to Iowa in 1840. Mr. Gilson died in 1841, and his widow moved her family back to Rush County, Ind., where she died in 1875, aged about eighty-three years. Mr. Gilson was of Irish and his wife of English descent. S. L. Gilson had very limited educational advantages, and after reaching manhood was united in marriage to Miss Catherine J. Lones, who was born in 1836 near where she now resides. Fifteen children were the result of our subject's marriage, viz.: Joseph W., John R., Thomas W., Lenora A. (now Mrs. S. H. Cooper), Nettie G., Horace M., Nancy J. F. (deceased), Sarah Mack, Emma C. (Mrs. A. Rohel), Mary C., Samuel H., Daniel F., Mary M., Jessie C. and one who died in infancy. Mr. Gilson is a Republican in politics, and he and wife are members of the Christian Church. In 1862 he enlisted in Company D, Sixth Tennessee Volunteers, and was first lieutenant of his company. He was discharged at Carthage in 1864 on account of disabilities. Mr. Gilson began life a poor man, and what he now owns are the fruits of his own industry and good management. He has 273 acres of good land, all well improved and under a good state of cultivation, located seven miles west of Knoxville.

John W. Glenn, professor of agriculture, horticulture and botany, of the University of Tennessee, was born near Athens, Ga., September 18, 1832, son of John W. (Sr.) and Mary (Jones) Glenn, both of whom were natives of Virginia. The father was a millwright in early life, but later turned his attention to the ministry. He was in the conference that divided the Methodist Episcopal Church, being one to help organize the Methodist Episcopal Church South. He had a good farm, which was superintended by his wife. She was a good financier and a woman of sound judgment. For thirty-two years Mr. Glenn was presiding elder, and consequently from home nearly all the time. But Mrs. Glenn proved equal to the occasion, and gave her children the best educational advantages to be had. In 1867 he died, being sixty-nine years of age. The mother lived to be about seventy, dying in 1871. In their family of ten children, eight are now living—five sons and three daughters—one of the sons became a lawyer, one a minister, and two became educators. Our subject was reared on the farm, and after attending home schools, graduated from Emory College, Georgia, in 1853. In 1854 he married Mary J. Orr, sister of Hon. G. J. Orr, of Georgia, and to this marriage were born three children: Lula, Frank A. and George W. Both he and wife are members of the Methodist Episcopal Church South. In 1856 he founded Madame La Vert School of Georgia, at the head of which he stood until 1859, when he was called to the chair of mathematics in East Alabama College and remained here until the breaking out of the war, when, as captain, he led a company of students into the Confederate service, holding that position until the final surrender. He then taught in the same college for some time, and then took charge of Martin Institute, near Athens, Ga. In 1882 he was called to his present position. Prof. Glenn has benefitted the agricultural interests, not only of this, but of other States, by public lectures, by articles in the leading agricultural journals and by taking an active part in framing and securing the passage of wholesome laws on this subject.

C. J. Gooding, senior member of the drug firm, Gooding & Shughrue, is a native of England, born in 1849. He graduated at the Pharmaceutical Association of Great Britain in 1866, came to America in 1869 and located in New York City, where he remained until he came to Knoxville in 1874. He filled prescriptions with the leading drug firms of the city until February 17, 1886, after which he embarked in the trade for himself at his present location, at the corner of Gay and Asylum Streets. Messrs. Gooding & Shughrue confine their stock strictly to drugs, and have an extensive prescription business. December 31, 1875, Mr. Gooding was united in marriage to Miss Martha Johnson, a native of Knox County. Our subject, and his brother George, who is now residing in England, are the only children born to George and Charlotta Gooding. The father was born, reared and always resided in England, and at the time of his death, which occurred in 1880, was superintendent of the Abbergavenny Asylum. The mother was also a native of England, and died there in 1870.

L. A. Gratz, attorney at law, is a native of Prussia, Germany, born in 1843, and was reared and educated there. He came to America in 1861 and enlisted, on the Federal side, in the Fifteenth Pennsylvania Infantry, in the three months' service, at the expiration of which time he re-enlisted, this time in the Ninth Pennsylvania Cavalry, of which he became first lieutenant. In 1862 he was transferred to the Sixth Kentucky Cavalry as first major, in which capacity he served throughout the war. December 25, 1863, he was detailed on the staff of Gen. Carter until mustered out at Goldsboro, N. C., in July, 1865. The same year he married Miss Elizabeth Trigg Bearden, a native of Knoxville, who bore him five children. Soon after the war Mr. Gratz located in Knoxville, having at that time great confidence in the future growth and development of that city. He laid out Gratz's addition to the city, and Gratz Street is named in honor of him. The same year of his coming to Knoxville he was admitted to the bar, and has ever since enjoyed a lucrative practice. He has twice served as city attorney of Knoxville. He is now serving a second term as Supreme Dictator of the K. of H., and in 1884 was employed by the order as counsel in the famous case against Judge Breckenridge, defaulting treasurer, which case was finally terminated in favor of the order at Louisville, March 2, 1887. His parents, Sol and Henrietta (Barshall) Gratz, were both natives of Prussia, where they passed their days, dying in 1875 and 1860 respectively.

Capt. J. M. Greer, the leading dealer in agricultural implements of Knoxville, is a son of John and Annis (Hood) Greer, both natives of Blount County, Tenn., where they still live and where the father cultivated the soil. The father is about eighty and the mother about seventy years of age. Our subject was born in Blount County, October 21, 1844, was reared on a farm, and, after attending the district schools, entered the Indiana State University, but the war came on and interrupted his studies. In 1862 he enlisted in Company A, Fifty-fourth Indiana Mounted Infantry, Federal Army. Toward the close of the war he was commissioned captain of Company E, Third Tennessee Mounted Infantry. In 1865 he engaged in general merchandising at Maryville, Blount County, and five years later opened a hardware store in the same town. In 1867 he married Miss Martha E, Courier, a native of Knox County, by whom he had four children—two sons and two daughters. In 1884 Mr. Greer came to Knoxville and built the spacious hall where he now does business. When he first proposed entering mercantile pursuits he asked his father to lend him means, the father refused, thinking it would soon be spent and little or no show for it, but offered to give him a farm if he would follow that pursuit. Not to be turned from his purpose he borrowed the necessary sum from a good neighbor. Success crowned his efforts, and he is now a man of wealth, and has an enviable reputation as a business man. In connection with his other business Mr. Greer is secretary and treasurer of East Tennessee Hedge Company. He has also held the position of postoffice inspector a term, and that of internal revenue assessor of the Second District, four years. He is a Republican, and a member of the I. O. O. F.

Col. Nathan Gregg, internal revenue collector for the Second District of Tennessee, with headquarters at Knoxville, is a native of Tennessee, born in 1834, the son of Maj. Abraham Gregg, also a native of Tennessee, who was born in 1789, and served under Gen. Jackson in the Creek war, acting as courier for that officer, carrying dispatches through Tennessee to Gen. Harrison in Indiana. In the war caused by the removal of the Cherokee Indians he served with the rank of major. His death occurred in 1876. The mother was also a Tennessean, and the daughter of John Davidson, of North Carolina, he being of the family of that name and State who distinguished themselves during the Revolutionary war. She died in 1852. Our subject was reared in Sullivan County, and acquired his education in the common schools of the day. Up to the breaking out of the civil war he was engaged as a contractor, and also followed farming, March 4, 1857, he married Miss Katie Marrell, daughter of Isaac Marrell, of Washington County, Tenn. In April, 1861, Mr. Gregg enlisted in the Confederate service, joining Company B, of the Nineteenth Regiment Tennessee Infantry, of which company he was elected second-lieutenant. He succeeded to the command of the company on the death of First Lieut. Connelly, at the battle of Fishing Creek, Ky., and at the battle of Shiloh again succeeded to the command of the company upon the wounding of Capt. Willet. On the second day of the battle he was shot entirely through the body by a minie-ball. As he was considered mortally wounded, he was discharged from the army. He recovered, however, and in the fall of 1862 assisted in raising the Sixtieth Regiment of Tennessee Infantry, at the organization of which John H. Crawford, of Washington County, was elected colonel, and our subject lieutenant-colonel. Col. Crawford soon afterward resigned, and our subject was commissioned to succeed him as colonel by the secretary of war for "gallantry on the battlefield of Shiloh." He served as colonel of the Sixtieth Regiment until the close of the war, surrendering at Charlotte, N. C., in 1865, he being included in the terms of Gen. Johnston's surrender. He then returned to Sullivan County, and upon the enfranchisement of Confederate soldiers in 1870 was elected sheriff of that county, and was re-elected in 1872, 1874 and 1876. He retired in September, having held the office for six years and five months. The following November he was elected to represent Sullivan County in the State Legislature, being elected as an avowed Isham G. Harris Democrat, and was the only Democrat from East Tennessee who openly and boldly declared before the election as being in favor of Mr. Harris for United States senator. During the session of the Legislature of 1877, he was a low tax Democrat, and supported Frank Wilson for governor on that platform. Col. Gregg was re-elected to the Legislature in 1879, and again in 1882. In April, 1885, he was appointed by President Cleveland to his present position.

Samuel Benton Giffin, a progressive young farmer of Knox County, was born in that county in 1857, and is the son of William and Nancy (King) Giffin, both of whom were natives of Tennessee. Our subject was educated in the country schools, and is a self-made man. He is a zealous member of the Baptist Church, and an ardent Republican in politics. In 1884 he chose for his companion through life an estimable young lady, and is now living on one of the most valuable farms in Knox County, which consists of 104 acres of well improved land. He takes considerable interest in fine stock, and is considered one of the successful and prominent farmers of the county. He also takes a great interest in all public enterprises, and although a young man and just beginning life, the future looks bright before him.

Judge Major Learoy Hall. The ancestors of our subject were among the first settlers of what is now Knox County. The grandparents, Thomas and Nancy (Hays) Hall located here from North Carolina about 1796. Thomas Hall served in the Revolutionary war, and was held prisoner by the British at Charleston about six months. He resided here in what is now the Seventh District of Knox County from 1796 until his death in 1833. His wife died about 1835. Thomas Hall was of English and his wife of Scotch-Irish descent. William Hall, a son of Thomas, and father of our subject, was born in Orange County, N. C., in September, 1788, and came to this county with his parents, residing within the present limits of the Seventh District until his death. He followed farming all his life, and was 'a great friend to education, being school commissioner many years, the only office he would ever hold. He married Nancy Nelson in 1813, and her death occurred in 1837. He followed her in 1868. Judge M. L. Hall, the immediate subject of this sketch, was born in the Seventh District of Knox County August 16, 1814, and was the eldest of eight children, six of whom are still living. He was reared on a farm, and secured such educational advantages as the rural districts at that time afforded. At the age of nineteen he began teaching school, which occupation he followed a short time after his marriage in 1836, and then began the study of law with Judge Robert M. Anderson, continuing with Samuel R. Rodgers until he was admitted to the Knoxville bar in January, 1841, his license being signed by Circuit Judge Edward Scott and Chancellor Thomas L. Williams. Our subject was elected clerk of the circuit court in 1852, which office he held without opposition until the close of the war, being re-elected in March, 1864, but resigned in April of the same year to accept an appointment from Judge Trigg to fill the office of clerk of the United States Circuit and District Courts and United States commissioner, all of which he resigned in August, 1870, to accept the office of judge of the criminal court, which had just been created July, 1870. He filled this office until 1886, when he was defeated for the first time in his life by Judge Logan, and has since resumed the practice of law, and is also engaged in writing a treatise on criminal law. Sarah (McCampbell) Hall, the faithful companion of our subject since 1836, was born near Frankfort, Ky. Their marriage was blessed by the birth of eight daughters and three sons, all now deceased but three daughters. The sons, William, John and Robert were all in the Federal service during the war. The Judge is Swedenborgian in his religious views.

G. G. Hardin, farmer was born April 6, 1836, on the farm where he is now residing. He is the son of John G. and Sarah R. (Gallaher) Hardin. John G. was born and reared in Hardin Valley, and was a very successful farmer, dealing quite extensively in stock. He was a son of Amos Hardin and a grandson of Col. Thomas Hardin, a pioneer settler of Hardin Valley. He was also a prominent man in county affairs, and was colonel of the State militia. Mrs. John G. Hardin was born and reared within three miles of where her son now resides. She died September

5, 1863. Her father, George Gallaher, was very enterprising, a good farmer and was a highly respected citizen of Knox County. Our subject received his education in the common schools of Knox County, and remained with his parents until thirty-two years of age, when he married Miss Matilda C. Smith, a native of Roane County. She died in 1872, leaving two children: Charles L. and Sallie B. Mr. Hardin married his second wife, Tennessee Hardin, in 1881. Mr. and Mrs. Hardin and their children are members of the Cumberland Presbyterian Church. Mr. Hardin is a Democrat in politics, and cast his first presidential vote for John C. Breckenridge. He has a good farm of 250 acres all well cultivated, and is located seven miles from Concord. His children have had good educational advantages, and his daughter is quite a success as a school teacher. His son is attending school in California. His father's ancestors were of Irish descent, and his mother's of English.

J. J. Hardin, school teacher and farmer, was born January 16, 1850, in Hardin Valley. He is the ninth of ten children born to John G. and Sarah R. (Gallaher) Hardin. (For further particulars of parents see sketch of G. G. Hardin.) Our subject secured his education at Hiwassee College, Monroe County, and at Ewing and Jefferson College. In 1870 he went to California and engaged in farming near Hollister. In 1872 he moved back to Hardin Valley, and one year later moved to where he now resides. The same year he married Miss Annie Crookshank, who was born August 5, 1855, and who is the daughter of Thomas and Lorenia (Boyd) Crookshank. Mr. Thomas Crookshank was one of the most extensive mule dealers in this part of the country and was a very prominent member of the Masonic fraternity. To Mr. and Mrs. Hardin were born four children: Lavenia S., Ernest M. (deceased), George B. and Willie M. During the winter of 1873 Mr. Hardin taught school at Hardin Valley. He also taught school at Fairview Academy, at Corner Creek Academy for seven years, and at Greybeal's Academy one year. As an instructor and disciplinarian he gave excellent satisfaction, being considered one of the best educators who has ever taught in the Ninth District. He owns 225 acres of good land on Clinch River, which is well cultivated. Mr. Hardin is a Democrat, and he and wife are members of the Cumberland Presbyterian Church.

James Hardin, farmer, was born November 8, 1813, near his present residence. He is the seventh of ten children born to Amos and Mary (Gallaher) Hardin. Amos Hardin was born February 25, 1780, near Richmond, Va. He was a prominent minister of the gospel in the Baptist Church, was secretary of the board of missions, and in many ways was active in the interests of the church. He was a leading school teacher of Hardin Valley, also a very extensive and successful farmer, and was justice of the peace of his district for forty years, giving universal satisfaction as magistrate. He died in 1840, at the age of sixty-one years. His father, Col. Joseph Hardin, was born near Richmond, Va., in 1734, and commanded a regiment during the Revolutionary war. After that event he immigrated to Greene County, but lived there but a short time when he moved to Knox County. He was a member of the General Assembly fourteen years, and was a candidate for re-election when he died. The mother of our subject was born in Pennsylvania, and died about 1846. Her father, James Gallaher, came from Pennsylvania to Tennessee in 1780. Our subject, James Hardin, received his education in the common schools of Knox County, and began business for himself at the age of twenty-one. He inherited 200 acres of land from his father, and has added enough to this to make 600 acres. He married Miss Sarah Hope, a native of Loudon County, born in 1821, and the daughter of James and B. (Walker) Hope, natives of Burke County, N. C. Mr. Hope was a soldier in the Creek war. He was a farmer, and died September 5, 1840. Mrs. Hope died in 1842. To our subject and wife were born ten children: Mary B. (deceased), Malinda H., Lurinda G. (Mrs. McCallum), Amos G. (deceased), Major W., Sarah J. (deceased), James B. (deceased), Cynthia A. (deceased), Lenora (Mrs. Crozier) and Laura. Mrs. Hardin is a member of the Cumberland Presbyterian Church, while Mr. Hardin is a Baptist in principle. He has been a life-long Democrat, casting his first presidential vote for Martin Van Buren.

 R. W. Hardin, farmer, was born April 6, 1822, in the house where he has since resided. He is the youngest of ten children born to Amos and Mary (Gallaher) Hardin. (For further particulars of parents see sketch of James Hardin.) Our subject received his education in the common schools of Knox County, and was thrown upon his own resources after the death of his father in 1840. In 1843 he married Miss Amanda King, a daughter of Rev. Jeremiah and Mary King, and the fruits of this union were the birth of eight children: Amos (deceased), Mary (Mrs. Gallaher), Tennessee (Mrs. G. G. Hardin), Sarah Jane (deceased), Adelia (Mrs. J. M. Smith), Nancy (deceased), Alice Florence (deceased), and Robert John (deceased). From a farm which his father gave him our subject had acquired considerable property, and owned 750 acres of excellent land, a large lot of fine stock and many valuable negroes. The most of this property was lost during the late war. Mr. Hardin is a Democrat in politics, casting his first presidential vote for James K. Polk, and he and children are members of the Missionary Baptist Church. He was elected magistrate of the Ninth District in 1846, served sixteen years, and was re-elected but refused to serve. In 1875 he was elected again, and is still holding the office. During all the time he has held the office only two of his judicial decisions have been appealed to a higher court, and there they were confirmed. Mr. Hardin strives, under all circumstances, to discharge the duties of his office conscientiously and honestly, and by so doing has given universal satisfaction.

G. M. Harrill, proprietor of the Knoxville Freight Transfer Line, was born in Hawkins County, Tenn., March 14, 1844, and is the son of J. S. and Emaline (Robertson) Harrill, both natives of Hawkins County, Tenn. Misfortunes fell upon the family which led to the separation of the father and mother. The mother afterward married Alex Young, by whom she had two children—a son and a daughter. She died in the year 1875. Our subject was taken to Roane County, and there lived until eleven years of age. He afterward went to Blount County, and there worked until he was eighteen years of age, securing for his services a horse, saddle and bridle. During the war he was in the quartermaster's department, United States Army. In 1866 he came to Knoxville to engage in the transfer business, owning half of his team, and driving it himself. He now runs fourteen good teams, and, besides this, is interested in agricultural pursuits. His marriage to Miss Sophia E. Crawford, of Knox County, in 1872, was blessed by the birth of one daughter. His first wife died in 1876, and two years later he married Miss Mattie McNew, of Campbell County, who bore him three children—two sons and a daughter. Mr. Harrill is a member of the Methodist Episcopal Church South. From 187– to 1875 he was passenger agent for the Nashville, Chattanooga & St. Louis Railroad, and from 1875 to 1879 he was with the St. Louis & Southeastern.

Hon. Joe Harris, legislator, humorous writer and merchant, of Knoxville, Tenn., one of the most widely known men in East Tennessee, is a native of that State, born in 1850, the son of S. K. and R. C. (Sawyer) Harris. The father is a native Virginian, born in 1818, and came to Tennessee in his infancy, locating in Knox County. He is, and has been for a number of years, a member of the Knox County Court. The mother was a native of Massachusetts, born in 1822, and died in 1878. Our subject was reared in Knoxville, educated at the University of Tennessee and the Maryville (Tenn.) College, and finished his education at Princeton (N. J.) College. He also took a course at a business college. He studied law for three years, and, though well qualified for the practice of that profession, took up the business of merchandising instead. He was elected to represent Knox County in the State Legislature in 1886, and served with distinction in that body, being recognized by his colleagues as a man of brilliance and overflowing wit. For a number of years he has been a contributor of humorous articles to such leading newspapers as *The Detroit Free Press* and *Burlington Hawkeye*, also the local press under the *nom de plume* of "Sol Turpin." He is a man of great genius and resources, being adapted to almost any class of business or walk of life, and enjoys the esteem and respect of his acquaintances. He was married June 8, 1879, to Miss Jugie Richardson, of Kentucky, who was born in 1863, and who is the daughter of Hon. J. W. Richardson, of Kentucky.

S. G. Heiskell, of Knoxville, attorney at law, is a native of Monroe County, Tenn., and was born August 7, 1858; came with his parents to Knoxville to live at the age of three years, and graduated at the University of Tennessee in the class of 1877; attended law lectures at the University of Virginia at Charlottesville; was admitted to the bar in Somerville, Ala., and, since his admission, has practiced successfully at Knoxville. In 1882 he was a member of the city council of Knoxville, also city attorney. The same year he was elected chairman of the Knox County Democratic Executive Committee, and president of the Knoxville Public Library, which has since become the Lawson McGhee Memorial Library. In 1884 he was again city attorney for Knoxville, also Cleveland and Hendricks' elector for the Second Congressional District. In 1885 he was again chairman of the Democratic Executive Committee of Knox County. In 1886 he was the Democratic nominee for Congress in the Second Congressional District, and now represents that district on the Democratic State Executive Committee of Tennessee. William Heiskell, father of S. G. Heiskell, was born at Hagerstown, Md., but passed the greater part of his life in the State of Virginia. He was a member of the House of Delegates of Virginia, and afterward moved to Monroe County, Tenn., which he represented in the Tennessee Legislalature. He was a member of the board of trustees of the University of Tennessee for many years. He accumulated a large property, mostly by agricultural pursuits, and died at Knoxville in September, 1871. He was of German descent. Julia J. (Gahagan) Heiskell, wife of William Heiskell, is a native of the State of Georgia, and is still a resident of Knoxville. She is of Irish descent.

M. T. Henson, farmer and stock dealer, was born in January, 1832, in Knox County, where he has since resided. He is the ninth of twelve children born to John and Mary (Cottrell) Henson. John Henson was born in Virginia, and when twelve years old came with his father to

Tennessee. He died in Knox County in 1876, aged eighty-four years. He was a soldier in the war of 1812, was a member of the Missionary Baptist Church for sixty years, and was deacon of the same for forty years. The mother of our subject was born and reared in Knox County, was a consistent Christian woman, and her influence was felt not only by her family, but by all with whom she came in contact. She died on the old home farm August 14, 1855, aged fifty-five years. Mr. William Henson, grandfather of our subject, was born and reared in Withe County, Va. He died about 1863, aged ninety-nine years. At the time of his death he could read the finest print as easily as at any time of his life. He was a respected citizen, a kind neighbor, and was of French and "Tuck-a-Hoo" descent. Our subject received only a common-school education, but has by reading and observation become well informed on all the current topics of the day, and is considered a man of intelligence and sound judgment. He learned the brick mason's trade, but liking farming better, gave it up and engaged in agricultural pursuits, which he has followed ever since. The fruit of his exertion is a fine farm of 238 acres, eight miles southwest of Knoxville. At the age of twenty-two he married Miss D. Compton, who bore him thirteen children: L. W., William L., L. C., Vilanto (Mrs. Stinnett), Matilda B., Sarah M. (Mrs. Jett), Clementine B., D. R., Ida B., John G., Charles C., Mary J. and Nathan H. Mrs. Henson was born in Sevier County, Tenn., in 1831, and is the daughter of William and Charlotta (Cunningham) Compton. Mr. Henson is a Democrat in politics, and he and wife and nine children are members of the Missionary Baptist Church.

Thomas H. Hicks, M. D., physician of Knoxville, Tenn., was born in Columbus, Colorado Co., Tex., November 7, 1856, and is the son of Dr. J. F. and Sallie W. (Harbert) Hicks, both natives of Madison County, Tenn. The father was born in 1830, and graduated from the medical colleges at Memphis, New Orleans and Baltimore. At present he is practicing at Bristol, Tenn. The mother was born in 1837, and is still living. Both are members of the Baptist Church. Our subject resided with his parents in Texas until his thirteenth year, when he removed with them to South America, where they resided for a year and a half. They then returned to the United States and located in Tazewell County, Va., where they remained until 1874, and then removed to Bristol, Tenn. In September, 1874, he entered the University of East Tennessee, at Knoxville, and graduated in June, 1879. In October of the same year he entered the medical department of the University of Tennessee, at Nashville, graduating in February, 1881. He next attended the Eclectic Medical College, at Cincinnati, Ohio, and graduated in June, 1881, and the following fall entered and graduated at the Hahnamann Homœopathic College, in Philadelphia. October 1, 1882, he entered the Homœopathic Hospital at Ward's Island, New York City, where he spent a year as resident physician. He then returned to Bristol, Tenn., and remained until March, 1886, when he came to Knoxville, where he has remained up to the present practicing his profession.

J. Willard Hill, M. D., physician of Knoxville, Tenn., was born in Portland, Me., October 15, 1853, and is the son of Dr. O. F. and Charlotta (Parsons) Hill. The father was a native of New Hampshire, and practiced medicine in Portland, Me., and from 1854 to 1880 was one of the practicing physicians of Knoxville, where he died in June, 1881. The mother was a native of Vermont, and died in 1862. Our subject was reared in Knoxville, but from 1869 to 1879 attended various colleges in Europe, graduating first from the Canton College, of St. Gall, Switzerland, and then entered the academy at Neuchatel, Switzerland. In 1873 he began the study of medicine at Strasburg, Germany, from which school he graduated in 1878. He attended lectures at Paris, France, and then returned to America, and in 1879 began practicing medicine at Knoxville, Tenn. In 1882 he returned to Europe, and attended lectures at Glasgow, Scotland, and Vienna, Austria. He next returned to Knoxville and resumed his practice, continuing up to the present, and has built up a large practice. He is a member of the Knox County Medical Society, of which he was president in 1886, and is the present secretary. Our subject was married in 1873 to Miss Cecile L. Roger, who was born in 1853, of French parents, on the island of Porto Rico, West Indies. To them have been born two children: Charles Willard, born in Strasburg, Germany, August 29, 1875, and Adele, born December 24, 1881. Our subject is a member of the Episcopal and his wife of the Calvinistic Church.

Isaac Hines (deceased) was a farmer and miller, and the son of William Hines, a native of Maryland. He was born September 15, 1795, and died in 1872. He secured a limited education, and early in life engaged in agricultural pursuits. He was a soldier in the war of 1812, and in 1815 he was united in marriage to Miss Mary L. DonCarlos, a daughter of William Carter DonCarlos of Virginia. She was born May 7, 1800, and died in 1863. To this union were born three sons and nine daughters, one son, A. D. C. and six daughters are now living. In 1863 Mr. Hines took for his second wife, Mrs. Rhoda Wilson, whose maiden name was Rhoda Hickey. She was born in Blount County, Tenn., December 11, 1822, and is the daughter of David and Fanny Hickey. This marriage resulted in the birth of one son and one daughter. The son, George Washington, is a farmer, and is living with his mother on the old homestead; the daughter, Nancy C., is also living at home. Our subject was a worthy and consistent member of the Baptist Church, having belonged to that organization for more than forty years, and his death was much regretted.

A. D. C. Hines, a mechanic and farmer, was born in Sevier County, Tenn., March 20, 1825, and is the son of Isaac and Mary L. (DonCarlos) Hines. The father was born in Knox County, Tenn, September 15, 1795, and is the son of William Hines, a native of Maryland. The mother was born May 7, 1800, and was the daughter of Prof. Carter DonCarlos, of Virginia. Our subject received a fair education in the common schools, and when twenty-five years of age went to Illinois, where he remained two years. He then returned to Knox County, and purchased an old farm near his father's homestead. To his marriage to Miss Pressure M. Bowman, in 1855, were born eight children—six sons and two daughters. The youngest son died when five months old. This family of children deserves more than merely a passing notice. The eldest child: Isaac B., is a graduate of the Knoxville University, and is now engaged in the signal service at Block Island, R. I. The second child, John M., is a graduate of the Grant Memorial University, of Tennessee, and is now engaged in agricultural pursuits in California. The third child received a common school education, and is now engaged in the same occupation as his brother, John M. The fourth son, Samuel B., graduated at the Grant Memorial University of Tennessee, and is now engaged in the livery business in California. The fifth child, A. D., left the public schools, and after attending one year at Harrison Seminary, of Sevier County, went to Carson College, where he is now a student. He is also a teacher of penmanship in that college. The two daughters: Millie E. and Mary L., are living at home. Our subject has a well improved farm of 240 acres in the Fifteenth District of Knox County, and besides this he is the owner of about 500 acres of other land. He is a Democrat in politics, and a worthy member of the Baptist Church. Mrs. Hines was born in Anderson County, Tenn., November 7, 1835, and is the daughter of Rev. J. N. Bowman, of the Methodist Episcopal Church.

S. P. Hood., M. D., physician of Knoxville, Tenn., and a native of Newport, Cocke Co., Tenn., was born November 9, 1834, and is the son of Rev. Nathaniel and Isabella W. (Edgar) Hood, both natives of Tennessee. The father was born February 14, 1804, was a minister of the Presbyterian Church, and died in 1874. The mother was born April 28, 1807, died in 1848, and was of Scotch-Irish descent. Both grandfathers were soldiers in the Revolution. Our subject was reared in Jefferson County, Tenn., and attended Maryville College, where he graduated in 1855. He began the study of medicine in 1856, under Dr. Beriah Frazier, of Knoxville, and in 1858 entered the Nashville Medical College, and later graduated from the University of Virginia. This was in 1863-64. He entered the Confederate Army in 1861, and served as assistant surgeon in the hospitals at Knoxville and Bean Station, Tenn. Later he served as surgeon, first of Rucker's Legion and then of Col. James Carter's First Regiment of Tennessee Confederate Cavalry. At the close of the war he located and practiced his profession at Mossy Creek, Jefferson Co., Tenn. In 1885 he came to Knoxville, where he has since resided. He is a member of the Jefferson and Knox Counties medical societies, being at one time corresponding secretary of the former. In 1883 he had charge of all the small-pox cases of Hamblen and Jefferson Counties. He was married in 1857 to Margaret Goodwin, a native of Grainger County, Tenn., born in 1835, and the daughter of Jacob Goodwin, a native of Tennessee. To this union six children were born, all of whom are living. The mother was a member of the Presbyterian Church, and died in 1879. Dr. Hood is also a member of the same church.

John W. Hope, senior member of the well known jewelry firm of Hope Bros. & Co., was born in Knoxville in 1842, and learned the silversmith's trade with his father. At the commencement of the war he enlisted in the First Georgia Regulars, and served until 1863, when he was transferred to the Thirty-second Virginia Mounted Battalion. He was captured and held as a prisoner sixteen months. In 1865 he married Miss Rachel Ebaugh, a native of Knoxville, by whom he had five children, two deceased. Mr. Hope is a Free Mason, and with his family is a member of the Methodist Episcopal Church. His father, Daniel L. Hope, was born in Knox County in 1799, and learned the silversmith's trade at Huntsville, Ala. After which he returned to Knoxville and followed his trade until his death. Mary E. (Welch) Hope, mother of our subject, was reared in Virginia, and died about 1848. Our subject's grandfather, Thomas Hope, was a native of England, and came to Charleston, S. C., where he followed the architect and builder's trade a short time. He then married Elizabeth Large, and came to Knox County in the early settlement of the same. After the death of his father our subject became a member of the firm of Hope & Miller, who were succeeded in 1879 by Hope & Bro., and they in turn were succeeded by the present firm, in January, 1885. D. J. Hope, brother of our subject, and W. D.

Dreher, are the other members of the firm. They carry a stock of about $50,000, consisting of fine foreign and American watches, in gold and silver cases, articles of jewelry for personal adornment, diamonds in modern and unique settings, etc. D. J. Hope was born in Knoxville in 1847, and, like his brother, was brought up to his present trade from youth. In 1875 he married Miss Hattie Owen, a native of Norwalk, Ohio, to whom one daughter was born. This lady died in 1877, and D. J. afterward married Elizabeth Richards, a native of Pennsylvania, but was reared in Knoxville. Mr. Dreher was born in New York City in 1844, and came to Knoxville, in January, 1885, since which he has been connected with our subject in the jewelry trade.

John F. Horne, of the firm of J. F. Horne & Bros., wholesale liquor dealers, of Knoxville, is a native of Knox County, born in 1843, was reared in Knoxville and educated at the University of Tennessee. At the age of fifteen he began life for himself, as a farmer. In April, 1861, he enlisted in Company A, Ninth Tennessee Regiment of Artillery, of which company he was a sergeant. He served until his capture at Cumberland Gap, September 9, 1863, from which time until the close of the war he was held as a prisoner of war, first at Camp Douglas, then at Fort McHenry, Baltimore, Md., and finally at Point Lookout, an island at the mouth of the Potomac River. June 13, 1865, he took the oath of allegiance to the United States and started on his return home, walking the entire distance from Richmond to Knoxville, and that too in a miserable state of health. Between the close of the war and 1870 he engaged as salesman for different firms in Knoxville, New York and Baltimore, and in 1870 he established the wholesale liquor house of J. F. Horne & Bros., of which he is senior member. He became a member of Felix K. Zollicoffer Camp No. 3, Confederate Veterans, at its organization, and is at present an active member. He is the son of Rev. George and Amanda (Luttrell) Horne, natives of Wythe County, Va., and Knox County, Tenn., respectively. The father was born in 1796, and removed to Tennessee about 1800. He was a minister of the Meth-Episcopal Church South, and died in 1867. The mother was born in 1808, and died in 1884. She was the sister of James C. Luttrell, Sr. (deceased), ex-mayor of Knoxville, and aunt of James C. Luttrell, Jr., the present mayor.

W. H. Howell, farmer and stock raiser, was born in Grainger County, Tenn., June 23, 1826. He is the son of James H. and Rebecca (Havens) Howell, natives, respectively, of Virginia and Tennessee. Our subject's educational advantages were rather limited, as he grew to manhood on the farm, and, as he expressed it, "was reared between the plow handles."

In his twentieth year he began working for himself, and in 1852 he chose for his life companion Miss Minerva Smart, daughter of James R. Smart. She was born in September, 1837, and by her marriage to our subject became the mother of six sons and four daughters. One son, named James Benjamin, is deceased. Those living are John Mc., Martha E., Robert S., Azalee T., William H., Donald Henry Luther, Adam Daniel, Louisa Rebecca and Sallie D. M. Our subject is the owner of 1,100 acres of land lying on opposite banks of the Holston River, and on this farm are quantities of fine marble. Mr. Howell is a member of the Presbyterian Church, and an excellent citizen.

J. B. Hoxsie was born in Rhode Island December 17, 1832, and is the son of Reynolds and Lucretia (Cranton) Hoxsie, both natives of Rhode Island. For a livelihood the father followed manufacturing cotton, and he and wife were zealous members of the Baptist Church. The father died many years ago, but the mother is now living in Rhode Island. Our subject was educated at East Greenwich Providence Conference Seminary, from which he graduated in 1850. While growing up he determined to be a machinist, serving an apprenticeship at Taunton, Mass. After graduating he went to Cuba as a machinist in the railroad service, and when he returned, assisted in building the Mobile & Ohio Railroad. In 1856 he came to Knoxville, and engaged with the East Tennessee & Virginia Railroad as engineer on a passenger train, but afterward arose to master mechanic. During the war he remained true to his country, exerting his best efforts for the maintenance of the Union. When the Confederates burned the bridges across Watauga and Holston Rivers they left the railroad crossing them in three sections. Transportation was impossible by railroad, there being neither cars nor engine on the section between the rivers. No one could devise a plan to cross except the building of a bridge which would take too much time. At this juncture Mr. Hoxsie proposed to have the engine and cars across within thirty-six hours if he could have sole control of the working force. The river was rapid and the banks steep and deep. Having cut down the banks a little he made arrow-shaped sinkers, filled them with rocks, ran stringers across, and within the proposed time had an engine and four cars over. In 1863 Gen. Burnside made him general superintendent of all the roads running from Knoxville. For six years after the war he was superintendent of the East Tennessee & Virginia Railroad, and after its consolidation with the Georgia Railroad, he was master of transportation. He is vice-president of the Knoxville Ice company, director in the East Tennessee Coal Company, manager of the Crystal Ice Company, and was previously president of the Knoxville Car Wheel Company.

In 1857 he married Miss Zilpha DePue, of Sussex County, N. J., and to them were born three children, all daughters. Mr. and Mrs. Hoxsie are members of the Methodist Episcopal Church.

Hon. L. Huddleston, of the firm of Huddleston, Smith & Little, wholesale and retail clothiers of Knoxville, is a native of Grainger County, Tenn., born April 8, 1834, and the son of John F. and Mary (Smith) Huddleston, natives of Tennessee. The father was born of English parents, September 24, 1807, and died August 6, 1883. The mother was born June 25, 1814, and is now residing with our subject. He was reared in the counties of Grainger and Union, and acquired his education in the public schools. At the age of twenty he engaged as salesman in a mercantile establishment, and eighteen months later he and his brother, O. W. Huddleston, began merchandising at Graveston, Knox County. They remained here two years and then removed to Maynardville, Union Co., Tenn., where they continued until our subject's removal to Knoxville, in January, 1884. He was first a member of the firm of Brock, Huddleston & Co., which firm was changed at the expiration of about eighteen months, Mr. Brock retiring, and S. T. Powers entering. Nearly two years later Mr. Powers withdrew, and the firm became as at present. In March, 1858, Mr. Huddleston was elected county court clerk of Union County, he being elected by a small majority over the strongest man in the county. He was re-elected in 1862. During the above period he served also as deputy clerk and master of the chancery court of Union County, under his brother, O. W. Huddleston, and after his brother's death filled the unexpired term of clerk and master. In November, 1880, he was elected to represent the counties of Anderson, Grainger, Knox and Union in the State Senate, of which he was an active member though in poor health. In December, 1871, he wedded Miss Mary E. Carr, the daughter of James K. Carr of Claiborne County, Tenn. She was born June 25, 1856, and died February 21, 1878, leaving two sons: Harry L., born November 5, 1872, and John L., born January 11, 1875. Mr. Huddleston is a member of the Calvary Baptist Church of Knoxville, and his wife a member of the Maynardville Baptist Church.

J. C. Hudgings, M. D., a successful practitioner of Knoxville, Tenn., was born in Monroe County of the same State, September 6, 1849, and is the son of Edward and Mary (Carter) Hudgings. The father was born in Virginia in 1823, and is now a farmer of the above named county. The mother was born in Tennessee in 1832, was a member of the Methodist Episcopal Church South, and died in 1886. The father was also a member of the same church. Our subject was reared in the county of his birth, and acquired his education at Hiwassee College, within a mile of his home, from which school he graduated, and then moved on the farm for a few years in order to secure necessary funds with which to fit himself for the medical profession. In 1874 he graduated from Jefferson Medical College at Philadelphia, and then located at Strawberry Plains, Jefferson Co., Tenn., where he practiced his profession. March 3, 1875, he married Hattie C. Clark, a native of Virginia, born in 1858, and the daughter of Edwin and Mary (Sessler) Clark, natives of Virginia. Two children were the fruits of our subject's marriage. In January, 1876, Dr. Hudgings removed to Knoxville, where he remained until the fall of 1878, when he removed to Texas, but returned to Knoxville the following spring, and has remained in that city ever since, practicing medicine with success. In 1881 he was elected city physician and re-elected in 1882 and 1883, going through the smallpox epidemics of the two latter years and having charge of all the city patients. He is a member of the Knox County and State Medical Societies and he and wife are members of the Methodist Episcopal Church South.

M. W. Huffaker, county surveyor, entry-taker and notary public, was born in Sevier County, Tenn., in 1833, and came to Knox County in early childhood, where he has since resided. He was reared on a farm, and educated at the public schools of the county and at Knoxville. In the year 1854 he was united in marriage to Miss M. E. Pickle, and the result of this union was the birth of nine children, seven of whom are still living. The mother of these children died in the year 1876, and in 1882 he took for his second wife Miss Mary A. Pickle, to whom one child, a daughter, has been born. James and Mary (Cunningham *nee* Huffaker) Huffaker, parents of our subject, were natives of East Tennessee, the father being born and reared in Knox County. He followed agricultural pursuits until his death in 1865. His wife's demise occurred in the year 1857. Mr. Huffaker is a member of the Masonic fraternity, and, with his family, is a member of the Methodist Episcopal Church. He took charge of his present office January 1, 1887, and has filled that position up to the present in a satisfactory manner.

Francis Kinloch Huger. Among the noted Huguenot families that came to South Carolina to escape persecution appears the name of Huger. Five patriotic brothers by that name came to this country, espoused the cause of the colonies, and rendered valuable services during the Revolutionary war. One of the brothers, Benjamin, was killed before the lines at Charleston, in 1779. He is the man who cared for the shipwrecked boy, La Fayette, and first introduced him to Washington. His son, Francis Kinloch, was an American officer, who with Dr. Erie Bollman made the daring and disastrous attempt to rescue La Fayette from the Austrian prison at Olmulz. He held the position of captain in the Revolution and colonel in the war of 1812. He also served in both branches of the South Carolina Legislature. Benjamin, the son of Francis, and the father of the subject of this sketch, was a graduate of West Point; commander of Fortress Monroe from 1841 to 1846; colonel in the Mexican war; commandant of the arsenal at Pikesville, Md., from 1854 to 1860, and major-general in the Confederate service. Francis Kinloch Huger, our subject, was born in Buford, S. C., December 5, 1845. When a young man he entered the South Carolina Military Academy, but while there the war broke out, and in 1862 he, with his class, "The Cadet Rangers," entered the Confederate service in the Sixth South Carolina Cavalry. After serving a short time as private he was promoted to the rank of second lieutenant. Soon after he was commissioned adjutant-general of the staff of Col. William Butler. In 1865 he was captured at Averysboro, N. C., and held a prisoner of war until the close. Since then he has been in the service of some of the most extensive railroad systems of this country. He began as baggage master, and is now superintendent of the East Tennessee division of the East Tennessee, Virginia and Georgia Railroad. He has been in the railroad service for twenty-two years, and has ever proved himself an able official.

Thomas W. Humes, S. T. D., librarian of Lawson McGhee Memorial Library of Knoxville, Tenn., was born in that city in the year 1815, and is the son of Thomas and Margaret (Russell) Humes. The father was a native of Armagh, Ireland, born in 1767, and came to America when a boy, locating at Morristown, Tenn., where he engaged in merchandising. He came to Knoxville in 1797, and followed the same occupation at that place; he died in 1816. The mother was born in Jefferson County, Tenn., in 1777, and died in 1854. She was married first to James Cowan, a Knoxville merchant, who died in 1799. The father and mother were both members of the First Presbyterian Church, of which the former was an elder. Our subject was reared in Knoxville, and graduated from the East Tennessee College in 1830, receiving the degree of M. A. in 1833, and then for a time was a student of Princeton Theological Seminary. In 1835 he married Cornelia Williams, of Grainger County, Tenn., born in 1817, and the fruits of this union were three children, one of whom, Andrew R. Humes, is now clerk of the United States Circuit Court, Knoxville. The mother of these children died in 1847, and in 1849 Mr. Humes married Anna B. Williams, a native of New Hartford, Conn., who was born in the year 1821. To this union five children were born, only two now living. Mrs. Humes died in 1879. In 1837, a short time after his first marriage, Mr. Humes became a member of the firm of Cowan, Dickinson & Co., merchants of Knoxville, and in 1839 he became editor of the *Knoxville Times*, the first newspaper published oftener than once a week in Knoxville. In 1840 he was also editor of the *Knoxville Register*. He was ordained a deacon of the Protestant Episcopal Church in 1845, and a presbyter at Knoxville in the following August. He became rector of St John's Church, Knoxville, in the autumn of 1846, and as such served until 1861, when he resigned. In the autumn of 1863 he was re-elected to the rectorship. He was elected president of the East Tennessee University in June, 1865, and resigned the rectorship in 1869. He continued president of the university until August, 1883. In 1869 the degree of S. T. D. was conferred upon him by Columbia College, of New York. In 1884–86 he was a missionary of the Protestant Episcopal Church in East Tennessee, and was elected to his present position in September, 1886.

Henry H. Ingersoll, attorney and president of the board of education, of Knoxville, is a native of Lorain County, Ohio. He graduated at Yale in the class of 1863; was superintendent of city schools at Kenton, Ohio, in 1863–64, and was admitted to the bar at Kenton, Ohio, in 1864, after having read law at Kenton, and also at Cincinnati, Ohio, with Hon. W. M. Ramsey. In 1864 he married Miss Emily G. Rogers, a native of Cincinnati, Ohio; to them two children have been born, one, a daughter, Mabel, still living. He located at Greeneville, Tenn., in 1865, and at once began the practice of his profession, being at that time twenty-one years of age. He resided in Greeneville until 1878, after which he located at Knoxville and has since practiced at that place, and also at Jonesboro, Greeneville, Dandridge and other places in East Tennessee. He is one of the board of directors of the Mechanics National Bank, and was judge of the supreme court commission in 1879 and 1880. He was a presidential elector on the Democratic ticket for the First District in 1876, and is now Deputy Grand Master of Masons of Tennessee. His parents, William and Semantha (Bassett) Ingersoll, were natives of Massachusetts. His father was a farmer, and also a minister of the Congregational Church; he died in 1873, and his widow in 1882.

Maj. R. C. Jackson, one of the county's most prominent and influential citizens, was born September 27, 1809, in Knox County, Tenn., and moved to Knoxville in 1813, where his early boyhood was spent. At the age of eighteen, after having filled a clerkship in the city for six years, he embarked in the general mercantile trade at Athens, Tenn. In November, 1845, he married Miss Julia Brazelton, a daughter of

Gen. William Brazelton, and to them were born twelve children, only six of whom are now living. Our subject continued merchandising at Athens until 1849, at which date he accepted the position of secretary and treasurer of the East Tennessee, Virginia & Georgia Railroad, and the additional office of general manager in 1852, filling the different offices until the road was taken charge of by the army during the war. In 1865 he was elected vice-president of the above railroad, and at the consolidation of the different branches officiated as superintendent until 1873, and as a director until 1880. In the latter year he had the misfortune to lose his wife, she dying April 13. Mr. Jackson was one of the projectors of the East Tennessee National Bank, and soon after the organization was elected president, and afterward cashier. He is at present one of the board of directors of the bank, and also of the Gas Light Company. He is a trustee of the deaf and dumb school. He resided in Knoxville until 1883, when he removed to his excellent farm, which consists of 288 acres, situated five miles north of Knoxville, where he still resides. His father, Joseph Jackson, was born in Virginia, September 4, 1781, and was reared in Petersburg, where he married Elizabeth Cardwell, and clerked in a dry goods store until they came to Knox County, about 1808. They resided in Knoxville from 1813 to 1838, after which they moved to Grainger County, where the mother of our subject died January 24, 1840. She was born March 20, 1783. Joseph Jackson afterward married a Mrs. Clowney, and returned to Knoxville, being proprietor of the Lamar House, and being also engaged in merchandising until the war. After that event, he retired from business, and died in October, 1868. The paternal great-grandparents of our subject came from Ireland and settled in Virginia, where the grandfather of our subject, Abner Jackson, was born and reared. He came with our subject's father to Knox County, but soon removed to near Franklin, Tenn., where he died.

A. N. Jackson, attorney and member of the board of public works for Knoxville, was born in Washington County, Tenn., in 1853. He was taken in infancy to Blount County, where he resided until 1877. He graduated in the law department of Cumberland University, in 1876, and then came to Knoxville the following year, where he has since practiced his profession. In 1877 he married a Miss Cox, whose nativity is Blount County, Tenn. To this union two children have been born. Mr. Jackson was elected alderman in 1884, and to his present office in January, 1886. He is a director in the proposed Elmwood Street Railroad. His father, N. T. Jackson, an attorney by profession, and a native of Washington County, was killed at Cumberland Gap while in the Confederate service. The mother, Elizabeth (Henry) Jackson, a native of Knox County, is residing at present in Blount County.

William Johnson, an enterprising farmer, was born in Knox County, Tenn., September 15, 1829, and is the son of Thomas and Martha (Rodgers) Johnson. The father was born in Blount County, Tenn., September 2, 1800, and died January 25, 1868. The mother was also a native of Blount County, born March 29, 1804, and died May 7, 1878. Both were of English descent. Our subject received his education in the common schools, and early in life engaged in farming, which occupation he has ever since followed. December 24, 1868, he married Mrs. Alexander Andes *nee* Miss Mary J. French, daughter of Jacob French; this union resulted in the birth of six children—one son and five daughters. The son and one daughter are deceased. Those living are Ida F., Julia A., Martha Alice and Pearl F. By her former marriage Mrs. Johnson had one son, J. O., and two daughters, S. Ellen and Mollie L. Mr. Johnson commenced life with very little means, but is now one of the most substantial farmers in the county. He owns over 500 acres of good land in Knox County, and is one of the most extensive stock raisers in that county. He is a Republican in politics, and a member of the Masonic Lodge.

J. L. Johnson, a farmer of the Twelfth District, and one of eight children of Allen and Matilda (Looney) Johnson, was born October 19, 1840, on the farm where he now resides. Allen Johnson was born and reared in Hawkins County, Tenn., moved to Knox County in 1839, and two years later moved to Missouri, where he remained twelve years. In 1852 he came back to Hawkins County, and afterward to Knox County, where he still lives. Mrs. Johnson was born and reared on the farm where her son now resides. She died about 1851. Absolom Looney, grandfather of our subject, moved to Knox County after he was grown. He dealt quite extensively in salt and general merchandise. When fourteen years old, our subject began working for himself, with very little of this world's goods. He first worked as a day laborer, and as soon as able purchased seventy-five acres of remarkably good land, to which he has added until he now owns 210 acres, situated four miles southwest of Knoxville. All of this was the result of his own exertion. He deals quite extensively in real estate in addition to superintending the affairs of his farm. In 1862 he married Miss Nancy Looney, who was born January 20, 1840, and who is the daughter of John and Zebella (Colman) Looney. Our subject's union resulted in the birth of seven children: Matilda (Mrs. Knott), Zebella (Mrs. Ambrose Wells), John, Mary, Artensia, Genevia and Allen. During 1862 and 1863, Mr. Johnson acted as mail carrier for the Federal Army. Gen. Robert Looney, cousin of Mrs. Matilda Johnson, was quite a prominent candidate for the gubernatorial nomination at the Democratic convention of 1886. He with Mr. Cherry and Thomas O'Conner, had the penitentiary lease for many years. Mr. Johnson is a Republican in politics, and has served his district as school director six years. He has also served as road commissioner for three years.

Jacob T. Johnson, proprietor and principal of the Knoxville Business College, was born in Overton County, Tenn., January 26, 1857. His parents, Henry D. and Margaret F. (Davis) Johnson, were born in Tennessee, where the greater part of their days have been spent, though now they live in Kentucky. The father has followed farming and merchandising, and has been quite a prominent man in local political affairs. Of their family of six children—five sons and one daughter—all except one have taught school. Our subject received his literary education at Glascow, and Edmonton, Ky., and then took a business course at Louisville, Ky. Having established Rock Spring Academy at Pekin, Tenn., at the head of which he stood two years, he took a course at the Nashville Business College, in which he was instructor for some time. He was then principal of a business college in Knoxville, and in 1885 established the Knoxville Business College. This institution graduates a large number of young men and women every year, who take the highest positions in commercial circles. Mr. Johnson is a member and clerk of the First Baptist Church.

Reps Jones, one of Knoxville's most useful and enterprising citizens, was born in Jefferson County in 1843, and at the age of ten years made Sweet Water, Tenn., his home, until the war, when he enlisted in the Confederate service as second lieutenant of the Forty-third Infantry, being soon after promoted to the first lieutenancy, in which rank he served until the close, when he came to Knoxville, and for about ten years was engaged in the pork packing business, then in the livery business until 1881, since which time he has been contracting and building, and in this way has contributed largely to the upbuilding of Knoxville. Among the many fine and substantial buildings recently constructed by him may be mentioned the Lyon's View Asylum, girls' high school and the new Knox County courthouse, all of which reflect credit to his name as a contractor. He also built the Knoxville woolen-mills, and the new Catholic Church. He employs about 125 hands during the building season, and his contracts for 1886 amounted to over $80,000. He is a director in both the old street car companies, and was at one time city alderman. He married Miss Mary Pate, of Concord, Knox County, in 1878. W. B. Jones, the father, was born in Cocke County, and married Mary Jarnagin, a native of Grainger County. He then moved to Jefferson County, where he followed merchandising until his death in 1848, his wife having preceded him in 1845. Our subject and two sisters, one being a twin sister, constitute the family. The paternal great-grandfather came from Scotland and settled in Virginia, where the grandfather was born and reared. They afterward located in East Tennessee.

Charlton Karns, secretary and treasurer of the Knoxville City Mills Company, was born in Knox County, Tenn., in 1858, and is the son of J. C. and Lorenia (Lindell) Karns. The father is a native of Knox County, born in 1833, and is at present engaged in merchandising at Adair Creek, Knox County. The mother was also born in Knox County in 1834, and is a member of the Methodist Episcopal Church, as is also her husband. Our subject was reared on the farm, situated within two miles of Knoxville, where he remained until his twentieth year, acquiring his education at Mossy Creek College, in Jefferson County. At the age of twenty he engaged with his father in the mill business at Planters' Mills, one mile north of Knoxville, where he continued for five years, and then removed to Knoxville. He then entered the employ of the Knoxville City Mills Company, becoming secretary and treasurer of the same in 1885. He is a member of the Methodist Episcopal Church, and although a young man, occupies a responsible position, and has established a good standing in business circles.

Thomas H. Kearney, M. D., one of the prominent physicians of Knoxville, Tenn., a native of Ireland, was born November 23, 1832, son of Patrick and Sophia (Apjohn) Kearney, both natives of Ireland. The father was born in 1799, and immigrated to America in 1849. He was by profession a civil engineer, and died in 1874. The mother is at present a resident of Waynesville, Ohio. Our subject was reared in his native country, and was in his seventeenth year when he accompanied his parents to this country. His medical studies began in 1855, at Cincinnati, Ohio, where he attended and graduated from the medical college of Ohio in 1858. He then served for a year as house physician at the Commercial Hospital in the above city, and next began practicing medicine at that point (Cincinnati), and continued until the spring of 1861. The civil war breaking out at that period, he entered the Federal service as medical officer on one of the gunboats of the western flotilla. After a year's service on the gunboat he was commissioned surgeon of the Forty-fifth Ohio Regiment of Infantry, a position he held until the close of the war. He returned to Cincinnati after the war, and again began the practice of medicine. He served as assistant physician of Longview Asylum for the Insane, near Cincinnati, was elected to the chair of principles of surgery in the Miami Medical College, of Cincinnati, Ohio, in 1872, and at the death of Prof. Mussey, some years later, was made professor of the principles and practice of surgery. This position he held up to his removal to Knoxville, Tenn., in 1884. He is a member of the Knox County Medical Society, of which he is now president. He was married in 1873 to Lavinia Miner, who is the daughter of the late Judge Miner, of Cincinnati. To them have been born three children, all of whom are living. Both our subject and his wife are members of the Episcopal Church.

James H. Keeling, M. D., a leading physician of Knoxville, was born in Shelbyville, Tenn., in 1849, and is the son of James L. and Charlotte (McGrew) Keeling. The father was a native of Virginia, born in the year 1800. He was a planter and trader by occupation, a member of the Presbyterian Church, and his death occurred in 1856. The mother was born in South Carolina in 1802; was a member of the Baptist Church, and died in 1873. Our subject was reared in Pulaski, Giles Co., Tenn., and attended the Pulaski High School and Giles College. He began the study of medicine in 1869 at Elkton, Giles Co., Tenn., under Drs. Bealy & Bowers, and during 1870 and 1871 attended medical lectures at the Maryland University at Baltimore, from which institution he graduated in the latter year. In 1872 he graduated from the University of Louisville (Ky.), and, after a few months spent in hospitals, returned to Pulaski, where he began practicing his profession. In October, 1879, the Doctor married Miss Jennie Dickerson, a native of Giles County, born in 1859, the daughter of Col. W. R. Dickerson. To this union was born one child. In 1882 our subject removed to Knoxville, and has since practiced medicine in that city, building up a good practice, likewise a good professional standing.

J. B. Kelley, secretary and general manager of the Knoxville Foundry & Machine Company, is a native of Barre, Worcester Co., Mass., born in 1839, and the son of Joel B. and Adaline (Billings) Kelley, both natives of Massachusetts. The former was born in 1804 and died in 1845, and the latter was born in 1813 and died in 1876. They were both members of the Unitarian Church. Our subject was reared in his native town, and, after passing three years of his life in Illinois and Minnesota, graduated from Brown University at Providence, R. I., in the class of 1862. He then passed ten years in Providence, R. I., after which, in 1870, he came to Tennessee, and located in Knoxville, where he became a member of the firm of Clark, Quaife & Co., car wheel manufacturers, and the first two years with this company were passed in rebuilding and operating the blast furnace on Stony Creek, in Carter County, Tenn. In 1874 he became associated with his present firm.

Previous to this, in 1872, he went to Providence, R. I., and was there united in marriage to Miss Hattie D. Mason, a native of Rhode Island, born in 1844, the daughter of Nathaniel and Nancy (Davis) Mason. This union resulted in the birth of five children, only two of whom are now living, viz.: J. B., Jr., born in 1873, and Lucia D., born in 1880. Mrs. Kelley died in 1883, and the following year our subject married Annie Stuart, a native of Knoxville, born in 1858, the daughter of Jacob and Margaret (Anderson) Stuart. To this union was born one child, Adeline S., in 1886.

Peter Kern, a member of the board of public works of Knoxville, and the leading confectioner of the city, was born on the Rhine October 31, 1835. While growing up he learned the shoemakers' trade, and when seventeen years of age he came to America, locating in Georgia, where he followed his trade until the breaking out of the war. In 1861 he volunteered to serve his adopted country in Company I, Twelfth Georgia Infantry (Confederate States Army). At the battle of McDowell he received a severe wound, and after sufficiently recovering was on detailed duty. In 1863 he came to Knoxville and opened a bakery, which he has continued up to the present. For a companion in life Mr. Kern chose Miss Henrietta Meyer, of Nashville, in 1864, and the fruits of this union were ten children—six sons and four daughters. Mr. Kern and wife are members of the German Lutheran Church, and he is a Democrat, although he votes for the man rather than the party. He held the position of alderman of the city of Knoxville about ten years, and is now president of the Knoxville Ice Company and of the Asylum Street Railway Company. He is an example of what a young man of energy and determination can do. Having started here a day laborer, and a stranger to our language, laws and customs, he has now become one of the wealthy men of Knoxville. He now does an extensive wholesale and retail confectionery business, which is ably conducted by his sons.

Hon. J. M. King, postmaster of Knoxville, Tenn., is a native of Roane County, of the same State, born in 1836, and reared at Athens, McMinn Co., Tenn. He was educated at Emory and Henry College, and then graduated at the Lebanon Law School in 1858, after which he located at Knoxville and practiced his profession as a member of the firm of Swan & King, afterward Swan, King & Doak, until the commencement of the war, when he enlisted in the Third Tennessee Confederate Infantry, but was afterward transferred to the Sixteenth Tennessee Battalion in 1862. In September, 1864, he was taken prisoner and confined at Fort Delaware until discharged, June 12, 1865. He then returned to Knoxville and practiced law until 1876, after which he was made chairman of the county court, and October 20, 1885, he received his appointment to the postoffice of Knoxville, of which he took charge in November of the same year. Directly after the war he married Miss Mary McCleskey, a native of Georgia, but reared in Knoxville. Six children were the result of this union, one of whom is deceased. The mother of these children died October 19, 1886. Charles L. and Julia R. (McElnee) King, the parents of our subject, are natives of Richmond, Va., and Knox County, Tenn., respectively. They reside in McMinn County, Tenn., where the father cultivates the soil. Of their family of twelve children, our subject, four brothers and four sisters, are the survivors. The grandfather, McElnee, located in Knoxville at the same time Gen. White came here. The ancestors on the King side were of Scotch-Irish descent.

James M. Kinkaid, a marble quarryman and marble dealer, was born April 21, 1827, in Rockbridge County, Va., and is the third of five children born to Isaiah and Sarah (McFarland) Kinkaid, both born and reared in Rockbridge County, Va. The father immigrated to Ohio in 1831, settling first near Dayton, and after remaining there one year moved to Miami County, where he settled seven miles north of Troy. He was a successful farmer and was highly respected by all. He died in 1873, in his seventy-ninth year. Mrs. Kinkaid died in 1836, aged thirty-three years. She was an active worker in the Presbyterian Church. After her death Mr. Kinkaid married Mrs. Sarah Miller. Our subject received very limited educational advantages. He was united in marriage to Miss Mary Ann Palmer, of Miami County, Ohio, where she was born December 31, 1827. She was the daughter of John and Margaret (Hance) Palmer. Her father was a native of Bristol, England, who immigrated to America, and settled first in New York, but finally in Miami County, Ohio. To our subject and wife were born five children: William F., Albert Horatio, Clara Bell (Mrs. E. W. Mason), John Charles and James Lawrence. The youngest two sons are bookkeepers for their father in the marble business, and also have charge of the store near their marble quarry. Mr. Kinkaid is a Republican in politics, and he and his wife and four children are members of the Missionary Baptist Church. Mr. Kinkaid followed farming and stock raising until the fall of 1872, when he moved to Troy, Ohio, and engaged in coal mining. By a complication with other parties Mr. Kinkaid lost about $100,000. He is now engaged in the cattle business in southern Kansas, which is managed by his eldest son. He also owns a very rich deposit of fine marble two miles east of Concord. James McFarland, the maternal grandfather of our subject, was a warm Abolitionist and a splendid practical business man.

Charles Kurth is a practical machinist and engineer, plumber, gas and steam fitter. His is the most conspicuous house in the above trade in Knoxville or probably in East Tennessee. It was established by that gentleman in this city May 1, 1882, and is located at No. 160 Gay Street. This building is a very extensive one, occupying an area of 25x150 feet. The exhibition of fine chandeliers, shades, gas fixtures, etc., generally contains an assortment, which for artistic workmanship and beauty of design, as well as variety and extent is unequaled in this section, and will average in value over $20,000. In addition to engineer and machinists' supplies, all kinds of plumbing, gas and steam fitting are done, and he also deals in all kinds of railroad, mining and quarry supplies. He carries a complete assortment, and makes a specialty of steam pumps, steam gauges, Hancock inspirators, injectors, jet pumps, hand mining pumps, cistern and deep well pumps, the famous American self-feeding lubricators, Pickering spring governors, asbestos, soapstone, Italian hemp and rubber packing, hose and hose trimmings, wrought iron pipe and engine and boiler trimmings of every description. Every invention or improvement made in this line is at once secured or adopted by this house, which may be implicitly relied on to perform all contracts undertaken with promptness and entire satisfaction to all concerned. The trade of this establishment is not confined to this city alone but extends throughout Georgia, Tennessee, Kentucky, Virginia, North Carolina and South Carolina and is steadily increasing, amounting now to over $50,000 per annum. Mr. Kurth was born in Germany, and came to this city four years ago, conducting his business upon an upright and liberal basis, with a thorough and practical knowledge of its every detail, and quick to avail himself of every idea promising improvement. In 1881 he married Miss Minna Engert, whose parents came from Germany a short time before her birth. To this union were born two daughters: Emma and Ida. Mr. and Mrs. Kurth are members of the Lutheran Church, and are much respected citizens.

Capt. J. K. Lones, sheriff of Knox County, was born in that county in 1842, and is one of eight children (seven now living) born to Charles and Rebecca (Johnson) Lones, both natives of Knox County, Tenn., where the mother's death occurred in 1863, and where the father is still living, engaged in agricultural pursuits. He has also been administering to the spiritual wants of his fellow men, having been a minister in the Baptist Church for many years. Our subject attained his majority on the farm, and received his education in the common schools. At the breaking out of hostilities during the late war, he enlisted in the First Tennessee Union Cavalry as private, but in June, 1862, he was promoted to the rank of second lieutenant, November, 1862, to first lieutenant, and in January, 1863, he was made captain, which position he held until the close of the war. He then returned to Knox County, and cultivated the soil until elected to his present office in August, 1886. In 1872 he married Pauline Sharp, a native of Knox County, who presented her husband with six children, four of whom are now living. Mr. Lones is a member of the F. & A. M. and G. A. R. Jacob Lones, grandfather of our subject, was a native of Virginia, and helped build the first house that was erected on the present site of Knoxville. He was captain of the State militia in the early history of the county, and died in 1860.

Hon. Edward Legg, justice of the peace of the Third Civil District of Knox County, Tenn., and one of the oldest and most prominent farmers of the district, was born in Knox County near the mouth of Big Flat Creek February 14, 1818, and is the son of Wesley and Christian (Price) Legg. The father was born in Knox County in 1797, and was the son of Edward and Polly (Grover) Legg. Our subject's grandfather was a native of England who immigrated to America when seventeen years of age, settling in Virginia, where he subsequently married. He then removed to Knox County, Tenn., and here followed farming and school-teaching as occupations, until his death in 1833. The grandmother was a native of Virginia, and died when her son Wesley was a child. Both grandparents were members of the Methodist Episcopal Church. Wesley Legg was a successful farmer, and under the old constitution held the office of constable for fourteen years. He served in the war of 1812, under Gen. Jackson, and died in 1859. His wife was born May 11, 1801, in Knox County, and was the daughter of Edward and Juda (Webb) Price, both natives of Virginia. She died in 1873. Our subject was reared on the farm, and acquired his education at Bristol, a school taught on the farm now owned by our subject. He remained on the farm with his parents until twenty-five years of age, and in 1848 was elected constable, serving eight years. Previous to this, November 30, 1843, he married Mary K. Chanaberry, a native of Knox County, born in 1817, the daughter of Peter and Mary (Epps) Chanaberry. To this marriage was born one child, George M. D., September 28, 1844, who is now a prominent merchant of Boston, Mass. The mother was a member of the Methodist Episcopal Church, and died in 1847. He was again married, November 6, 1849, to Matilda W. Harris, a native of Knox County, born April 26, 1821, the daughter of Stephen and Martha (Luttrell) Harris. Stephen Harris was a native Tennessean, a farmer, and died in 1855. The mother was born in Virginia in 1784, was a member of the Methodist Episcopal Church South, and died in 1881. To our subject and wife were born eight children: Mary, born in 1850 (now Mrs W. N. Brandon); W. E. A., born in 1852; Martha C., born in 1853 (now Mrs. A. T. Angel); Adlicia F., born in 1856 (now Mrs. W. M. Buckhart); E. P., born in 1858; Rachel M., born in 1861 (now Mrs. George Cardwell); A. J., born in 1864, and Damie T., born in 1868. The mother is a member of the Methodist Episcopal Church South, and has been totally blind for nearly four years. She nevertheless retains her health, and is able to perform light household duties. She can sew and knit and can also write letters to her children. She is an amiable and cheerful lady and a true helpmate to her husband. Mr. Legg was elected justice of the peace in 1874, and holds that office at the present time. In 1882 he was chosen to represent Knox County in the State Legislature, and served in that body with honor and credit to himself and constituents, being a member of the committee on Federal relations, claims and charitable institutions. Though a Democrat and living in a Republican district, he receives the support of both political parties and has never been unsuccessful in seeking office. Mr. Legg has followed farming all his life and has made that occupation a complete success. He is a member of the Union Baptist Church.

Frank J. Leland, vice-president of the Standard Handle Company, and one of the county's enterprising and successful citizens, is a son of J. E. and Mary E. (Crover) Leland. The father was a native of Massachusetts, and is engaged in the same business as our subject. The mother is a native of Rhode Island. Our subject was born in Windham County, Conn., August 12, 1856, and educated at the college of the city of New York. He moved to New York City when but twelve years of age. In 1874 he went to Bowling Green, Ky., and engaged in the manufacture of handles until 1881 when he came to Knoxville. He has been twice married, and by his first wife became the father of one son. In 1887 he was united in marriage to Miss May Ebbert. Mr. Leland is a member of the K. of H., of the I. O. O. F. and is a wide-awake business man.

J. F. J. Lewis, a native of Knoxville, Tenn., where he now resides, was born in that city February 13, 1830. His early education was such as the schools of that day afforded. His first business efforts, when quite young, were of the mechanical and mercantile departments. At the age of twenty-two he was admitted to the Knoxville bar to practice as a solicitor in chancery and attorney at law. His license bears the signature of two of the most distinguished judges Tennessee has produced: Thomas L. Williams, chancellor, and Ebenezer Alexander, circuit judge. Under the administration of President Buchanan Mr. Lewis was appointed postmaster at Knoxville, but resigned the office in the course of a year or two after the date of his commission. While holding that position, about 1858, he married Miss Laura A. Mitchell, a native of Alabama. Seven children were born to them, but only five survive. Soon after the presidential election of 1860 he removed to Arkansas, and made his home in Chicot County at Lake Village. There he formed a partnership for legal business with Maj. James F. Robinson and George K. Cracraft in the name of Robinson, Lewis & Cracraft. Soon after this the war paralyzed business in that country and closed the courthouses. Mr. Lewis returned to Knoxville with his family, and from that point entered the army of the Confederacy with Maj. David Sullens. At the close of the war he spent a year in Cincinnati in the wholesale hat house of Wallace and Ringel. At the urgent solicitation of his former partners he returned to Arkansas to resume the law. In 1869 the governor of Arkansas, Hon. Powell Clayton, appointed him judge of the court of probate for said Chicot County, which office he held until his final return to his native city. In 1874 he was elected clerk of the county court of Knox County, and was afterward twice re-elected, serving twelve years in the three terms. Mr. Lewis was twice elected a member of the board of mayor and aldermen in the city of Knoxville, and is now president of the board of trustees of the East Tennessee Female Institute, one of the first schools in the State. He is also Grand Master Workman of the A. O. U. W. in Tennessee. By the favoritism of the members of the order he is serving a second term, an honor conferred by unanimous vote. After the death of Hon. John L. Moses, who was the tax attorney of the East Tennessee, Virginia & Georgia Railway system, extending through four States, Mr. Lewis was appointed to that position, and now discharges the duties of the office.

J. W. Lillard, a native of Meigs County, Tenn., was born in 1832, and in youth moved to Athens, Tenn., being the first agent at that place of the East Tennessee, Virginia & Georgia Railroad. From 1852 to 1858 he was a salesman for the firm of Courtney, Tennent & Co., Charleston, S. C., becoming a member of the firm at that date (1858). After the war he severed his connection with the above firm, and for two years acted as traveling salesman for a Cincinnati firm, selling goods throughout the Southern States. At the expiration of the two years he returned to Athens, Tenn., and organized the Franklin Association Bank, which has since been merged into the First National. About the time of the organization of the East Tennessee National Bank he came to Knoxville, and assisted in the organization of the same, being made cashier soon after, which position he filled six years. He then opened a wholesale notion store, and conducted the same two years in Knoxville, since which time he has not been actively engaged in business. He was also one of the first board of directors for the Mechanics National Bank, and is at present a stockholder in the East Tennessee and the new Third National Banks. In 1869 he married Miss Martha E. Matlock, a native of McMinn County, Tenn., to whom two children have been born: John M. (deceased) and James. The paternal grandfather of our subject, Col. William Lillard, was a native Virginian, and served in the war of 1812. James, the father, was born in Virginia in 1795, and in infancy came with his parents to East Tennessee, where he married Mary Sandusky, a native of Cocke County, Tenn. He was a farmer, and died in 1879. Our subject and a twin brother were the youngest of five brothers, viz.: William C. (deceased), captain in the Mexican war; John M. (deceased), colonel of the Twenty-sixth Tennessee, Confederate Infantry, killed at Chickamauga; James, who was a private in the Third Tennessee Infantry; N. J., colonel of the Third Tennessee Confederate, now living in Meigs County. All of the above four brothers were also in the Mexican war.

John Llewellyn, farmer, was born January 19, 1836, in Morgan County, Tenn., and is the third of eight children born to William L. and Nancy (Wallace) Llewellyn, natives of Virginia and Tennessee respectively. William L. Llewellyn was born August 2, 1809, and was brought to Morgan County, Tenn., by his father, Anderson Llewellyn, when about two years of age. He was constable of Morgan County for several years, and since his removal to Knox County in 1862 has served his district as magistrate for several years. His wife, and the mother of our subject, was born about 1811 in Anderson County, where she grew to womanhood. Our subject was educated by his father, and after assisting on the farm until twenty-four years of age, married Miss Elizabeth E. Shannon, a native of Morgan County, born in 1834, and the daughter of James and Mary Shannon, citizens of Morgan County, and both of purely Irish parentage. The marriage of our subject resulted in the birth of six children: William A., Nancy Jane, John B., Newton C., Charles S. and Freeman H. Mr. and Mrs. Llewellyn and four children are members of the Missionary Baptist Church, Mr. Llewellyn being a deacon of the same. He was formerly a Whig, but is now a Democrat in politics. By his own industry and good management he has accumulated considerable property, and now owns in one body a fine farm of 225 acres of land, well cultivated and well improved. Mr. Llewellyn is giving his children good educational advantages, and he is also quite liberal in his support of all religious enterprises. He donated the land upon which the Methodist Episcopal and Baptist Churches were built near his farm, and besides gave considerable money. He is a Master Mason, and an excellent citizen.

W. B. Lockett & Co., wholesale dealers in groceries and tobacco, established their business in October, 1883. The firm is individually composed of W. B. Lockett, Sr., W. B. Lockett, Jr., J. E. Lotspeich and R. S. Hazen. W. B. Lockett, Sr., is a native of Mississippi, born in 1834. He removed to Knoxville in 1874, and there engaged in the wholesale grocery business as one of the firm of Carpenter, Ross & Lockett. Mr. Carpenter withdrawing, the firm title became M. L. Ross & Co. In 1883 this firm dissolved, and the present company formed. Mr. Lockett was married in 1860 to M. A. Ballard, of Mississippi, who bore him seven children. Both Mr. and Mrs. Lockett are members of the Third Presbyterian Church, of Knoxville. W. B. Lockett, Jr., was born in Mississippi in December, 1861. He removed with his parents to Tennessee in 1874, and secured his education at the University of Tennessee, graduating in the class of 1881. He became a member of the above firm at its organization. J. O. Lotspeich, is a native of Tennessee, born in Greene County in 1854, and the son of V. S. and Elizabeth (Easterly) Lotspeich, both natives of Tennessee. He was reared in Greeneville, and removed to Knoxville in 1872, becoming a member of the firm at its organization. He was married in 1878 to Ida S. Meek, of Jonesboro, Tenn., the daughter of C. W. and Sarah (Hale) Meek, of that place, and this union resulted in the birth of two sons. Mr. and Mrs. Lotspeich are members of the Methodist Episcopal Church. R. S. Hazen, is a native of Knox County, Tenn., born August 13, 1854, and is the son of G. M. and Mary (Strong) Hazen, both natives of Tennessee, but of New England parents. Our subject was reared in Knoxville, educated at the University of Tennessee, and became a member of the present firm at its organization. In 1882 he married A. E. Mabry, of Knoxville, and the daughter of Joseph A. and Laura (Churchwell) Mabry, both natives of Tennessee. This union resulted in the birth of two daughters. Edward Henegar, bookkeeper for W. B. Lockett & Co., was born in Charleston, Tenn., and educated at the University of Tennessee. He began with the above firm as file clerk, but was promoted to his present position.

Hon. Samuel T. Logan, judge of the criminal and circuit courts for the district of Knox, was born on the 29th of February, 1832, at Abingdon, Washington Co., Va., graduating at Emory and Henry College in 1852. He then studied law with his father, Samuel Logan, one of the first lawyers of the State, and commonwealth's attorney for many years, and was admitted to the bar in December, 1855. In January, 1856, Mr. Logan removed to Tennessee, and after practicing law about one year at Blountville located at Jonesboro, in same State. Here he continued the practice of law until 1864 in partnership with his brother, Joseph M.

Logan, at which time both removed to Knoxville and formed a partnership with Hon. Thomas A. R. Nelson, under the firm name of Nelson, Logan & Logan. This firm enjoyed a lucrative practice for several years. Mr. Logan's brother and partner died in 1869, and Judge Nelson in 1873, after which he formed a partnership with Mr. C. E. Lucky, under the firm name of Logan & Lucky. In 1882 Mr. Logan retired from the practice of the law, and in 1884 was elected State senator from the Fifth Senatorial District (composed of the counties of Anderson and Knox) by a majority of about 2,500, and in August, 1886, was elected to the present office. Judge Logan's parents were Samuel and Bethia (Talbot) Logan, both natives of Washington County, Va., where they were married in 1827. His father was elected attorney for the commonwealth of Virginia for sixteen years consecutively, first by the Legislature, and then by the people, and although a pronounced Whig, was chosen from a strong Democratic district. He died in 1855, and the mother in 1836.

A. Looney, a successful agriculturist, was born in 1817 in Hawkins County, Tenn., and when ten years old moved to Knox County, where he has since resided. His educational advantages were quite limited, and when eighteen years of age he was thrown upon his own resources. He inherited some property from his uncle, but the balance of his wealth was the fruit of his own industry. Besides a good deal of property he lost during the late war, Mr. Looney owns a first rate farm of 220 acres, well improved, and located four miles southwest of Knoxville. In 1846 he enlisted in Capt. Caswell's company and Col. Thomas' regiment, serving twelve months in the Mexican war. He was mustered out of service at New Orleans. About 1852 he married Miss Ellen Parker, daughter of John Parker, of Hawkins County, Tenn., and five children resulted from this union: Alexander, Susan, Mary (Mrs. J. G. Lones), and two who died in infancy. Mrs. Looney died in October, 1861, and July 4, 1865, Mr. Looney married Mrs. Martha Lones, formerly Miss Daniel. Mr. Looney and two daughters are members of the Missionary Baptist Church. In politics Mr. Looney is conservative, voting for principle instead of party. He is the youngest of five children born to Absolom and Nancy (Long) Looney, natives of Hawkins County, where they were reared. Absolom Looney was an accomplished scholar, a refined gentleman, and a prominent citizen of his county, which he represented in the Legislature. He was also sheriff of the county several years He was a practical civil engineer, and helped to establish the State line. He was of English descent; his grandfather, together with his twelve brothers, came to America some time before the Revolutionary war, and settled in Stanley Valley. He was killed near Knoxville by the Indians. Mr.

Looney, grandfather of our subject, was born in England, and came with his father to America. He was wounded at King's Mountain during the Revolutionary war. Our subject's father, by his second marriage, became the father of eight children. He moved to Louisiana, and here died. His son, Robert Looney, brother of A. Looney, is a well educated, highly cultured gentleman, and is at present supreme judge of the State. He is a prominent lawyer and an able jurist. He has been connected in some of the leading law suits of Tennessee and adjoining States.

Hon. James C. Luttrell, mayor of Knoxville, was born in that city in 1841. He was reared there and educated at the University of North Carolina, after which he engaged in the notion trade in Nashville, Tenn. At the breaking out of the war he enlisted in the thirty days' infantry, and then served in the Knoxville Artillery. of which he was first lieutenant, and afterward commanded a battery. At the close of the war he engaged in the hardware business in New York City for five years, and then in partnership with his brother, S. B. Luttrell, established their hardware store in this city. In 1867 he married Josephine E. Brooks, a native of this county, to whom three sons and three daughters have been born. Mr. Luttrell is a director in the Mechanics' National Bank of Knoxville, is a stockholder in three of the insurance companies, a stockholder in the Market Street Railway Company, a stockholder and director in the Bell Avenue Street Railroad Company, a director in the chamber of commerce, and chairman of committee on transportation, railroads and navigation. In January, 1886, he was elected to his second term as mayor of Knoxville, to serve two years. He is one of two sons and four daughters born to J. C. and Eliza (Bell) Luttrell. The father was a native of Knox County, born in 1811, and was a legal practitioner. He was at one time clerk of the Tennessee Legislature, and in company with Andrew Johnson, rode horseback to and from Nashville. He was county register several years, was postmaster of Knoxville under Fillmore's appointment; was comptroller of the State at the time Mr. Johnson was governor, and was also mayor of Knoxville fourteen years. After the war he was elected to the State Senate, and a short time before he was appointed special agent for the postoffice department of East Tennessee by President Lincoln. He was the first Democrat who carried Knox County in an election for several years after the war. His death occurred in Nashville, but his home was in Knoxville. The mother of our subject was of Scotch-Irish descent. Her parents located at Pittsburgh, Penn., and afterward came to Tennessee.

J. E. Lutz, senior member of the firm of J. E. Lutz & Co., dealers in boots, shoes, hats, trunks, valises, umbrellas, etc., is a native of Newmarket, Va., born in 1854, and came to East Tennessee with his parents in his youth. About 1873 he came to Knoxville, and accepted the position of bookkeeper for Alvin Barton until the present firm was formed in 1884. The firm of Dismukes & Thomas was formed, and existed one year, after which it merged into the firm of S. C. Dismukes & Co., which was after another year succeeded by the present firm of J. E. Lutz & Co., with our subject and J. C. White, of Oates, White & Co., as members. February 10, 1886, he was united in marriage to Miss Delia Armstrong, daughter of Col. R. H. Armstrong, one of Knox County's pioneers. The father of our subject, H. R. Lutz, is a native of Virginia, and is now residing on a farm near Rogersville, Tenn. He first married Sarah Andes, a native of Virginia, to whom our subject, one brother and one sister were born. The mother died in 1865, and the father afterward married Miss Mary Plecker, to whom four children have been born. Our subject's paternal grandfather was of Swiss parentage, and came from Pennsylvania to Virginia, where he died.

Hon. G. W. Mabry, a farmer of the Tenth District, was born July 21, 1823, on the farm where he now resides. He is the eldest of six children born to Joseph A. and Alice (Scott) Mabry. The grandfather of our subject, Joseph A. Mabry, was born March 19, 1796, in Westmoreland County, Va., came to Tennessee with his parents when quite young, and settled in Knox County. He was a member of the convention which framed the constitution of Tennessee, and was elected to the Legislature, serving two terms. He was a successful farmer and trader. His son, Joseph A. Mabry, was a member of the constitutional convention which met in 1870. Our subject received his education in the common schools of Knox County, and at Holston College. His father died when our subject was but fourteen years of age, and he began farming for himself shortly afterward. He married Miss J. L. Hume in 1846, and to them were born these children: Isabella (Mrs. Jerome Templeton), Maria Florence (deceased), Joseph C., George C. (deceased), Mary (deceased), Jeanette, Rowena, Margaret L., David Hume and Evelyn. Two died in infancy. Mr. and Mrs. Mabry are members of the Missionary Baptist Church, of which Mr. Mabry is a deacon. Mrs. Mabry was born in Abingdon, Va., November 8, 1825, and is the second of four children born to David and Eliza (Sanderson) Hume. Mr. Hume was born in Scotland March 9, 1794, and came to America when nineteen years of age. He was a weaver by trade. Mrs. Hume was also a native of Scotland, born in 1789, and came to America when nine years of age. Her father owned a large woolen factory where they now live in New Hampshire. Our subject is a strong Democrat. He was elected to the State Legislature in 1851 and 1853, and took quite an active part as a legislator. He presented several bills and all were passed. He was elected magistrate in 1870, and has been re-elected at each successive election since. He was chairman of the building committee during the erection of the courthouse of Knox County, and took quite an interest in all matters pertaining to the erection of that building. Mr. Mabry is a good citizen, and is of English-Irish descent.

G. L. Maloney, of the firm of Childress & Maloney, dealers in groceries at Knoxville, Tenn., is a native of Knox County, Tenn., born July 3, 1844, and is the son of James W. and Minerva E. (King) Maloney. The father, a native of Greene County, Tenn., was born February 1, 1818, and is now a resident of Knox County. The mother is a native of Knox County, and was born in March, 1817. Our subject was reared on the farm, and attended in his youth the schools of the neighborhood, and later attended Rocky Springs Academy, in Sevier County, finishing his education after the war, at Athens and the University of Tennessee, at Knoxville, and occupied the position of teacher in the preparatory department of the latter school for about a year and a half. In April, 1862, he refugeed to Kentucky, where he enlisted in the Sixth Regiment of Union Tennessee Infantry, joining Company C, Capt. R. M. Bennett. He entered as private, and serving throughout the war was mustered out of the service as first lieutenant. At the close of the Rebellion he returned to Knox County and attended and taught school for a while. In March, 1870, he entered the postoffice at Knoxville as a clerk. In 1874 he was elected clerk of the Knox County Criminal Court, and was re-elected in 1878, serving two terms of four years each. In 1886 he engaged in his present business. He is a charter member of Ed. Maynard Post, No. 14, G. A. R., of which organization he is an active member. He was married, June 8, 1868, to Sonora L. Dodson, daughter of Lazarus and Rebecca L. (Sullens) Dodson natives of McMinn County, Tenn. She was born July 31, 1852. To this union four children have been born as follows: Willie M., George E., Frank D. and James D. Both our subject and wife are members of the Methodist Church.

Rev. Francis Thomas Marron, pastor of the Church of the Immaculate Conception, Knoxville, Tenn., is a native of Ireland, born in 1843. When a child, about six or seven years of age, he immigrated with his parents to this country, and settled for a time on Staten Island, and later in New York City. His early education was acquired at St. Mary's Parochial School, Clifton, Staten Island, and at St. Mary's Parochial School, New York City. He completed his classics at the De La Salle Institute and Manhattan College, both in New York City. In 1865 he was adopted by Rt. Rev. Bishop Feehan, who had just been consecrated bishop of Nashville. The following year the Rt. Rev. Bishop sent his newly adopted candidate to St. Vincent's College, Cape Girardeau, Mo., where he completed his philosophical and theological studies. In 1871 he was ordained in the cathedral at Nashville. Father Marron's first pastoral duties were in Middle Tennessee, at Columbia, Pulaski and other points. He was placed in charge of Knoxville Parish in 1872, and this is no ordinary charge, for it not only includes the large and thrifty city of Knoxville, but all upper East Tennessee. The Catholic Church in Knoxville is in a very flourishing condition, and the church building is the largest and finest in the whole State. Father Marron is a most courageous and energetic man. He has done well for the church in Knoxville, and his people fully appreciate his services.

S. C. Martin, physician and surgeon at Campbell's Station, was born September 10, 1843, in the locality where he now resides. He is one of nine children born to Samuel and Julia Ann (Reese) Martin. The father was born in Antrim County, Ireland, about 1775, came to America when about twenty years of age, and settled in Jefferson County, Tenn. He subsequently went to Kingston, and in 1823 moved to Knox County, where he died in 1855. He was a remarkably good business man, and although he commenced life a poor man, was worth about $100,000 at the time of his death. He was a very prominent man in his time, and was considered one of the best read and most influential citizens of his part of the country. He was on quite intimate terms with men of National reputation, was well acquainted with Gen. Jackson, and was quite active in securing the reduction of the postage rates. He married a daughter of John J. Reese, of Mossy Creek, whose son, William B. Reese, was for several years one of the supreme judges. Mr. Martin's brother, Hugh Martin, came to America the same time he did, and had a son, Rev. Joseph Martin, D. D., who was a noted divine of Kentucky. Mrs. Samuel Martin, mother of our subject, was born in Jefferson County, near Mossy Creek, and died in 1854 during the cholera scourge at Knoxville. Our subject lacked one year of completing the classical course of study at Knoxville University, and made an exceptionally good record as a student. He studied medicine under Dr. Nelson, and also under Dr. McNutt of Kingston. He attended school at the Nashville Medical College, and began the practice of medicine in 1863 at Campbell's Station. He has been a very successful physician, and has a large and extensive practice. Since the death of his parents he has made his home with his sister, Mrs. Eliza Jane Nelson. Dr. Martin is a Master Mason and is a Democrat in politics.

Spencer A. Maxey, farmer, is a native of Knox County, Tenn., born March 4, 1811, and is of French lineage. He received a limited education in the common schools, and after reaching his majority chose the occupation of a farmer as a life pursuit. In 1829, however, he engaged in the distillery business and followed this for about seven years. He afterward resumed his agricultural pursuits. In 1846 he married Miss Rebecca Hommel, a native of Knox County, born May 24, 1827, and the daughter of Daniel Hommel. To them were born seven sons and two daughters, all now living with the exception of one son. Those living are Abram, born October 9, 1847, and the only one married; Franklin, born September 21, 1852; J. H., born April 9, 1855; Andrew, born October 29, 1857; John, born February 26, 1860; and William, born May 22, 1862. The daughters are Catherine, wife of J. H. Maloney, born May 21, 1850; and Sallie, born April 6, 1867, who is now at home. Mr. Maxey owns over 300 acres of land in the Thirteenth District of Knox County, and is a successful farmer. He is a Democrat in politics, and his wife is a member of the Evangelical Lutheran Church. The six sons are farmers and land holders, and all are living near the old homestead. On their land are quantities of pink and variegated pink marble, which they are now quarrying quite extensively. All the sons have received their education in the common schools and have attended higher institutions. Franklin Maxey attended the University of Tennessee during the session of 1876. James H. entered the University of Tennessee in the autumn of 1876, and continued at school for two years and a half; Andrew entered the University of Tennessee in the fall of 1877, and continued at school there for three years until the spring of 1880. William attended school at Maryville College, after which he entered the University of Tennessee, and continued there for two years; John also went to school at Maryville. Frank and James H. taught school eight years each; Andrew taught six years, and William taught two years. They and their father are extensive stock raisers, and it has been their custom for years to graze their cattle among the Smoky Mountains during the summer seasons. They are also extensive wheat and corn growers. Like their father, each son is a decided Democrat in politics.

A. L. Maxwell, president of the East Tennessee Iron and Coal Company, of Knoxville, Tenn., is a native of Saratoga, N. J., and was born February 1, 1824. He is the son of A. L. and Rachel (Stafford) Maxwell, both natives of Saratoga County, N. J., and traces his direct ancestry back to the Maxwells of Scotland and North of Ireland, and the Staffords of England, both prominent and leading families from the earliest histories of those nations to the present time; he is also a relative of the late Hon. Hugh Maxwell, of New York City. The father of our subject was born in 1789, was a railroad contractor, and died in 1862. The mother was born in 1795, and died in 1873. Both parents were members of churches—the father of the Baptist, and the mother of the Methodist. Our subject was reared in Saratoga, and acquired his education in the public schools of that town. He left home in December, 1845, going to Massachusetts, where he began life for himself as bookkeeper and paymaster for the firm of Asariah Boody & Co., the largest railroad contractors of the East at that time, the firm being composed of such men as Sidney Dillon, Amasa Stone, John Ross, Daniel L. Harris and Milton Clyde, all of whom became the leading capitalists of the United States, and constructed, as members of different firms, a majority of the railroads of New England and the early West. Our subject was married, February 1, 1845, to Harriet J. Brown, a native of Cheshire, Mass., who was born March 15, 1829, and is the daughter of Luther H. and Adaline (Mason) Brown, both natives of Massachusetts. She is a great-granddaughter of Capt. Daniel Brown, who commanded a company at the battle of Bennington during the Revolutionary war, and who had charge of a number of British officers as prisoners, quartering them at his residence. He was a prominent and wealthy citizen of that date, and an honored friend of President Martin Van Buren, and often entertained that distinguished man during his presidency. At the house of Capt. Brown was made the huge cheese, weighing nearly 1,500 pounds, which was presented to President Jefferson, the presentation being made by Elder John Leland, a noted Baptist divine. Our subject's wife is also a cousin to the wife of President Fillmore, on the Leland side. To the union of our subject and wife eight children have been born, only three of whom are living, they being Louie L., born January 30, 1855; Hattie B., born August 22, 1862, and Helen M., born April 10, 1865. He remained with the above firm until 1848, and the year following became a partner of Mr. Boody with Peter Thatcher, on track laying contracts on the Hudson River and Erie Railroads, they laying the track from New York City to Poughkeepsie, on the Hudson River Railway, and from Fort Deposit to Binghamton on the Erie Railway. In 1850 he formed a partnership with Andros B. Stone, and purchased the patent-right of Howe Truss Bridge for New York and New England. The firm dissolved in 1852. Our subject formed a partnership with A. D. Briggs, of Springfield, Mass., who afterward served for a number of years as railroad commissioner of his State. E. B. Hall and E. F. Starr, under the firm name of Maxwell, Briggs & Co., purchased the Howe Bridge patent for the Southern States, and immediately began contracting for building bridges in Virginia, Tennessee, Mississipi, Alabama and other Southern States. He located in Knoxville, Tenn., in 1852, and the first bridge he erected was the one across the Tennessee River, at Loudon, Tenn., and has since erected bridges on a large number of railroads in the Southern States. The above firm dissolved in 1855, all the members retiring, and the business was then conducted for several years by our subject alone. In 1857 he entered into a partnership with Thomas H. Callaway and George W. Saulpaw, under the firm name of Maxwell, Saulpaw & Co., and with this firm continued bridge building and masonry until the breaking out of the war. The close of the Rebellion found him in Macon, Ga., where he took the contract of rebuilding the Central Railroad of that State. He continued bridge building until 1872, when he again located in Knoxville, Tenn. In 1873 he engaged in the manufacture of car wheels, organizing the Knoxville Car Wheel Company, of which he was president until 1881, when he disposed of his interests in that company. Since that time he has had charge of the East Tennnessee Iron and Coal Company as president, and is also president of the New River Mining Company, of New York, the stockholders of both corporations embracing quite a number of the solid business men of New York, Pennsylvania, New Jersey, Georgia and Tennessee. When he came to Knoxville in 1853, he erected large machine shops in that city, and conducted an extensive manufacturing business in the way of bridge material, and subsequently became interested in foundries. This business was successfully conducted until the appearance of Gen. Burnside's army in 1863, when his machine shops, patterns, etc., were destroyed during the siege, for the destruction of which he applied to Congress for damages in the sum of $270,000, the bill for which is now pending before the Lower House, having on two different occasions passed a second reading before that body. Gen. Burnside, who, as officer in command, had personal knowledge of the destruction of the property, he having the same in his possession as a military necessity at the time, pronounced the claim valid and just. Our subject is a member of the Masonic fraternity, and has had conferred upon him thirty-two different degrees of the Southern jurisdiction, and is a member of St. Omer Commandery, No. 2, Knights Templar, of Macon, Ga., and is well known to Masons of Tennessee and Georgia. He and wife are members of the First Baptist Church of Macon, Ga., and the three daughters are members of the Third Presbyterian Church of Knoxville.

William Gibbs McAdoo was born near Knoxville, Tenn., April 4, 1820. His father was John McAdoo, a native of Jefferson County, Tenn., who married Mary A. Gibbs, a native of Knox County, and a descendant of a gallant French soldier in the French and Indian war. The paternal grandfather was of Scotch extraction, and was one of the heroes of King's Mountain. William G. received his early education in the "old field schools," and at the age of fifteen entered Union Academy at Clinton, where he remained two or three years. At the age of eighteen he became principal of that institution, and two years later took charge of Franklin Academy, in Campbell County. From 1842 to 1845 he taught school during the summer, and attended East Tennessee University during the remainder of the year. The next day after his graduation, he was elected to the Legislature from Campbell and Anderson Counties. In the spring of 1846 he enlisted as first lieutenant in Company C, Second Tennessee Volunteers, and served for one year in the Mexican war. In 1847 he went to Columbia, Tenn., and began the study of law under Judge Dillahunty. In due course of time he was admitted to practice, and in 1851 was elected by the Legislature attorney-general of the Second Judical Circuit. He was afterward re-elected by the people, and served until 1860. In 1862 he removed to Rome, Ga., where he resided until 1877, meanwhile having served as a captain in the Confederate Army, judge of the Twentieth Judicial District of Georgia, and superintendent of schools in Baldwin County, Ga. From the date of his return to Knoxville in 1877 until 1886 he filled the chair of English language and literature in the University of Tennessee. With H. C. White he is the author of an "Elementary Geology of Tennessee." In 1848 he married Miss Annie Horsley, of Columbia, who died in 1853 leaving two daughters: Kate (wife of E. F. Wiley) and Emma. In 1857 he married Mary Faith Floyd, a granddaughter of Gen. John Floyd, and daughter of Gen. Charles R. Floyd, of Camden County, Ga. She is a writer of much ability and grace and is the author of two or three romances and other publications. She also prepared a part of the chapter on literature appearing in the State history of this volume. She had previously married Randolph McDonald, who died in 1854. To this second union have been born three sons and four daughters. They are John F., Caroline B., Rosalie F. (Mrs. J. S. O'Neal), William G., Malcom R., Nona H. and Laura S.

G. C. McBee, farmer and miller, was born in Knox County, Tenn., September 12, 1840. His parents were G. C. and Sarah Bell (Love) McBee. The father was born in Knox County, Tenn., May 19, 1799, and died November 20, 1880. The mother was born in North Carolina, and died in 1870. Our subject received a good education at Strawberry Plains and is a good Greek and Latin scholar. When the late war broke out he abandoned his studies and enlisted in the Confederate Army as first lieutenant of Company D, Tennessee Infantry. Later he was changed from this position to that of a private in the cavalry, this being made on account of his having the rheumatism. At the close of the war he returned to his native county, and settled on his present homestead in the Fourth District where he has farmed ever since. In 1865, directly after the war, he married Miss N. E. Sawyers, daughter of W. S. Sawyers. Four sons and two daughters were the result of this union, viz.: W. S., born September 10, 1866; J. A., born October 6, 1868; R. L., born June 16, 1871; Sarah B., born November 22, 1873, and G. C., born May 30, 1882. Our subject owns 373 acres of excellent land, and is an enterprising and successful farmer, stock raiser and miller. He is a faithful Democrat in politics.

W. C. McCammon is a native of Knox County, Tenn., born January 5, 1837, son of Samuel and Martha B. (Cowan) McCammon. The father was born in Knox County, Tenn., May 9, 1808, and died at Nashville in 1865. He was by occupation a farmer, and served three terms as sheriff of Knox County. In 1851 he was elected State senator from Knox County and served one term, and in 1865 he was elected by a general State election to represent Knox County in the Legislature. While serving this term he suddenly sickened and died. The mother of our subject was born in Sevier County, Tenn., November 5, 1813, and died at her home in Knox County in 1876. Our subject received a fair education, and taught school for two years. He then engaged in farming, and has made this his lifetime occupation. He chose for his companion through life Miss Eliza Huffaker, daughter of Henry Huffaker. She died in 1875 leaving six children—two sons and four daughters. Previous to this our subject had served from November, 1862, to June, 1864, as a Federal soldier in the civil war. He enlisted as a private in Company B, Third Tennessee Cavalry. December 19, 1862, he was commissioned second lieutenant of Company C, Third Tennessee Cavalry, by Gov. Andrew Johnson, and was also appointed recruiting officer during the war. In 1864 he resigned his commission on account of ill health, and settled at his present homestead in the Twenty-first District of Knox County. In 1867 he was appointed deputy sheriff, and served in this capacity until 1868 when he resigned. In September, 1874, he was again appointed, and served one term under M. D. Swan. He was the nominee of the Democratic party for representative in the fall of 1876. In September, 1882, he was a third time appointed deputy sheriff, and served a term under Homer Gilmore, but refused an appointment for another term. In 1876 he married Miss Joanna E. Randles, daughter of John

Randles, and two sons were the result of this union. Mr. McCammon is the owner of more than 400 acres of land, and is a successful farmer. He is an extensive stock raiser (horses and cattle), and is the owner of some very valuable fine stock.

John N. McCammon, farmer and dairyman, was born near Knoxville, Knox Co., Tenn. He is the son of Samuel and Elizabeth (Montgomery) McCammon. The father of our subject was a prominent man in Knox County politics, and served six years as county sheriff. After being out of office some time he was re-elected to the same position and served one term. He was a man universally respected in his county, and many positions of honor and trust were given to him. He died in 1860, leaving to his family the results of a useful and successful life. Mrs. McCammon is the daughter of James Montgomery, and is now living (1887) with our subject. Both parents were natives of Tennessee. The father having died when our subject was but sixteen years of age the latter received but a limited education. At the close of the late war it became necessary for J. N. to take charge of the home farm, and this involved much responsibility but he managed the work of the farm successfully for three years, at the close of which time he removed to California. Here he made his headquarters for fifteen years while trading in cattle. He then returned to his native State and purchased the old home place which he now owns. It consists of 200 acres of fertile and well improved land situated in the Second District near Knoxville and on the Holston River. The farm contains quantities of fine limestone which the owner has extensively quarried. Mr. McCammon has been a successful farmer, and has been dairying and butchering for several years. He has never married, has never joined the church and has never entered politics, though he is entertaining, charitable, and in politics is a Democrat.

J. A. McCampbell, druggist, is a native of Knoxville, and was reared and educated in that city. In December, 1874, he established his present drug trade in the firm of Lyons & McCampbell until November, 1881, which firm was succeeded by our subject alone. He has built up an extensive retail drug trade, and employs three assistants. His paternal grandfather, Benjamin Bennett McCampbell, came from Virginia to the early settlement of Knox County, and resided here until his death. William H. McCampbell, father of our subject, was born in Knox County, Tenn., and followed merchandising until his death, which occurred in 1884. He was market master of Knoxville at the time of his death. The mother, Martha (Goans) McCampbell, was also a native of Knox County, Tenn., and still resides in Knoxville. Of their family of six children, all living, our subject is the second. He is a good citizen and an excellent business man.

C. M. McClung, senior member of the wholesale hardware firm of C. M. McClung & Co., is a native of St. Louis, Mo., born May 12, 1855, but was reared at Knoxville, Tenn. He graduated at the State University in 1874 and at Yale in 1876, after which he returned to Knoxville, and was in the employ of Cowan, McClung & Co. until he established the present firm in July, 1882. The business has grown until it is now, perhaps, the leading hardware house in Eastern Tennessee. Mr. McClung is a director and treasurer of the Knoxville Water Company, director in the East Tennessee National Bank, also treasurer and trustee of the Lawson McGhee Library. In the year 1881 he was united in marriage with Miss Annie McGhee, daughter of Charles M. McGhee, and a native of Knoxville, to whom two daughters have been born. F. H. McClung, the father of C. M. McClung, is a native of Knoxville, born November 23, 1828, and the grandson of Charles McClung, one of the early pioneers of Knoxville. F. H. is of the wholesale dry goods firm of Cowan, McClung & Co., of this city, and had resided here the greater part of his life, having been, however, engaged in the wholesale dry goods business for a few years in early life in New York and St. Louis. The mother of our subject, Eliza (Mills) McClung, was born June 2, 1833, at St. Louis, Mo., and died September 4, 1881, at Knoxville.

Maj. E. E. McCroskey, secretary and treasurer of the board of education, was born in Sevier County, Tenn., in 1839. His father, David McCroskey, was also a native of that county, and his mother, Elizabeth Rogers, was a daughter of the pioneer Baptist preacher of Sevier County. The father and mother were married in that county, and reared a family of nine children—four sons and five daughters. The mother died in 1864, and the father afterward married a Miss Trewhitt, sister of Judge Trewhitt, of Chattanooga. This marriage resulted in the birth of four children—two sons and two daughters. Grandfather McCroskey was a native of Scotland. He came to America, settled in Virginia, and finally found his way to Tennessee, being among the first settlers. Our subject is the fifth child by the first marriage. He was educated in the common schools and at Mossy Creek College. After graduating at that institution he taught school at Cleveland for some time and then went South. In 1861 he enlisted in H. W. Hilliard's Alabama Legion, and was soon promoted to adjutant on John T. Morgan's staff. Just before the battle of Murfreesboro he was severely wounded. Having sufficiently recovered he was given a military post at Mobile, and promoted to the rank of major. From Mobile he returned to Montgomery, Ala., where he constructed a fortification to withstand the advancing enemy. He participated in the last battle of the war, and near him the last man who gave his life for the confederacy fell. In 1868 Mr. McCroskey married Miss Ellen R. Chandler, and both he and wife are members of the First Baptist Church. Soon after the war Mr. McCroskey engaged in mercantile pursuits in Knoxville, and in 1872 he went into the coal trade. He has been president, secretary and treasurer of the Standard Coal & Coke Company, being now secretary of the same. In 1882 he was elected secretary and treasurer of the board of education, and has been twice a member of the board of mayor and aldermen. He is a Democrat in politics, and a Mason, having taken the thirty-second degree of that order.

J. S. McDonough, M. D., was born in Knox County, Tenn., October 24, 1830, and is the son of John and Araminta (Scott) McDonough. The father was born May 12, 1803, in the city of Baltimore, and came to Tennessee in 1825, where he engaged in farming. He died November 14, 1874. He was a nephew of Commodore McDonough, who fought the battle of Lake Champlain. The mother was born in Buckingham County, Va., August 24, 1803, and died in March, 1875. Our subject was reared in Knox County, and attended Ewing and Jefferson College in Blount County. He began the study of medicine in 1856 under Dr. B. B. Lenoir, at Lenoir's Station, Tenn., and attended the University of Nashville. In 1860 he graduated from the Atlanta (Ga.) Medical College, and began the practice of medicine at Concord, Tenn., but the Rebellion breaking out he enlisted in the Confederate Army, joining the Sixty-third Regiment of Tennessee Infantry as surgeon, and was serving under Gen. Lee at the surrender at Appomattox. In the year 1867 he married Mary L. Lenoir, a native of Loudon County, Tenn., born April 4, 1844, and the daughter of A. S. and C. F. (Welcker) Lenoir, the mother being a sister of the late Judge James M. Welcker, of the Knoxville bar, and of Judge Albert Welcker, of Cleveland, Tenn. To our subject and wife were born seven children, four of whom are living, viz.: Mary L., J. Albert, Katie W. and Maggie L.; those deceased are Laura Bell, who died at the age of one and a half years; John Henry, who died at the age of four and Fred Lenoir at the age of three and a half years. After the war Dr. McDonough returned to Knoxville, but remained only a few weeks, when he went to Memphis and there practiced his profession for a year and a half. Returning to Knoxville he resumed his practice, continuing up to the present. He and wife and two elder children are members of the Third Presbyterian Church of Knoxville.

Charles M. McGhee, one of Knoxville's most influential citizens, was born in Monroe County, and spent his boyhood on the plantation, after which he took the degree of B. A. at the State University. He owned the Peoples' Bank at Knoxville for many years, and was vice-president of the East Tennessee, Virginia & Georgia Railroad a number of years, being at the time the principal stockholder, and prominently indentified with all the transactions of that road. His first marriage was to Isabella M. White, daughter of Hugh A. M. White, who was a nephew of Hugh Lawson White; to this union was born one child, who died in infancy. His first wife dying, Mr. McGhee afterward married her sister, Cornelia H. White, who bore him the following children: Margret W. (now Mrs. Baxter), May Lawson (deceased), Annie (now Mrs. C. M. McClung), Bettie H. (now Mrs. Lieut. Tyson, of the United States Army) and Ellinor W. Mr. McGhee, in memory of his deceased daughter, built and furnished the Lawson McGhee Library at a cost of about $40,000, donating the same to the city of Knoxville. Our subject has recently made New York City his home, but spends a considerable portion of his time in Knoxville, and is still considered one of the citizens. He has been an active and efficient trustee of the State University, and was largely instrumental in procuring the renewal of that institution after the war. He was a member of the Legislature from Knox County in 1870–71. His father, John McGhee, was an able financier and a large land holder in Monroe County. His mother was the daughter of Charles McClung, and niece of Hugh Lawson White.

Green McLemore, contractor and builder of Knoxville, is the son of Green and Ellen McLemore. The father was a native of North Carolina and the mother of South Carolina. In early life both came to Tennessee and located in Knox County, where they married and passed the remainder of their days. The father was a farmer by occupation. Of their family of ten children four sons and four daughters are now living; all the sons are mechanics. Our subject was born January 26, 1839, in Knox County. He was reared on the farm and educated in the common schools. At the age of twenty he came to Knoxville, and learned the carpenter's trade under W. K. Eckles. Having worked chiefly as journeyman until 1872 he began contracting, and has gradually extended his business since. By his marriage to Miss Sarah O. Keyhill in 1869 he became the father of three sons. In 1880 Mr. Alexander Kelley joined him in the business. In connection with his trade Mr. McLemore is interested in agriculture, and owns a fine farm of 180 acres on the Holston River. Among the better buildings erected by Mr. Kelley and himself are the Hattie House, Girl's High School, First National Bank and the Knoxville Insurance Company's office. Mr. McLemore is a Republican in politics, and one of the county's best citizens.

Hon. James M. Meek. The grandfather of our subject, Adam Meek, came from Ireland and served throughout the Revolutionary war. About 1780 he located in Jefferson County, Tenn., and built the first residence in that county. He afterward followed surveying in that and adjoining counties until his death. Adam K. Meek, the father of our subject, was born in Jefferson County, and was a captain in the Indian war, being mustered in at Athens, Tenn. He was born in 1798, and has always followed agricultural pursuits. He is now residing at Strawberry Plains. His companion through life, Elizabeth (Childers) Meek, was also a native of Jefferson County, Tenn., and died in February, 1885. Our subject is a native of Jefferson County, born in 1821, and is the eldest of a family of ten children, eight of whom are now living. He graduated at Maryville College in 1850, and was admitted to the bar in his native county in 1852. He then practiced law until his election to the State Legislature in August, 1855. After serving for two years he returned to the practice of his profession, which he continued until his second election to the Legislature in 1861. In 1859 he married Miss Lizzie J. Walker, a native of Hawkins County, to whom three children have been born. In April, 1862, Mr. Meeks was taken prisoner by the Confederate forces, but was released on July 4 of the same year. He was soon after elected attorney-general for the Second Judicial Circuit of Tennessee, and upon the reorganization of the State received the appointment to the same office, serving until 1871, after which he resumed the practice of law. He was a member of the board of directors of the East Tennessee, Virginia & Georgia Railroad, representing the State from 1866 to 1869, and was interested in railroad transactions; attorney and director, from 1869 to 1883. On March 4 of the latter year he was appointed United States district attorney for the Eastern District of Tennessee, which position he filled until July 4, 1885. He is a director in the Knoxville Fire Insurance Company, and also in the East Tennessee National Bank.

James K. Meek, one of the firm of Meek & Biddle, retail dealers in dry goods, notions, millinery and dress goods, is a native of Jefferson County, Tenn. He came to Knoxville in 1878, and graduated at the State University four years later (1882). He then became connected with the firm of George & Briscoe until the firm of Barton & Meek was established in April, 1885, and this was succeeded by the present firm in September of the same year. Including the millinery and dress making department they employ about twenty assistants. In 1885 Mr. Meek chose for his companion through life Miss Lilly Baker, a native of Knoxville. Our subject is a son of James M. Meek, whose sketch will be found in another part of this work. For a young man, our subject has shown unusual business ability, and is one of Knoxville's thoroughgoing, wide-awake men.

A. Metler was born in Canton, Switzerland, December 9, 1826, and came to America in 1854. He found his way to Knoxville, Tenn., without money and without friends. While in the old country he was brought up to the dairy business in the Alps Mountains, and was master of his business. Here he hired out by the month at small wages, and by hard work and economy he managed to save up his earnings, and in three years succeeded in starting a dairy of his own, which he managed with consummate skill and judgment, and in a few years accumulated a considerable amount of money by the sale of milk and the manufacture of cheese. Shortly thereafter he established in the city of Knoxville the butchering business, thus again showing his fine business sense. He soon became the leading man in the business, and was eminently successful. He made money rapidly, and was exceedingly fortunate in his investments. He bought 300 acres of land near the city at low figures, which to-day is very valuable, being worth from $75,000 to $100,000. In 1854 he married Miss Waldburghla Frauller, by whom he had five children, three now living—two sons and a daughter. After Mrs. Metler's death our subject married Mrs. Susan Walker, and the result of this union was the birth of two children, only one now living. During the war Mr. Metler was conscripted for the Confederate Army and hired a substitute. In politics he is a Democrat, and in religion a Roman Catholic. His first wife was a Presbyterian, and his present one is a Baptist. He stands deservedly high as a citizen. Financially his credit is good in any of the banks of the city, and he is regarded as one of the most successful business men in the country.

John B. Michael, master mechanic for the East Tennessee division of the East Tennessee, Virginia & Georgia Railroad, was born in Baltimore, Md., October 3, 1850. When a mere boy both parents died, and he was reared by an uncle. His education was limited to the common schools, but by self application he succeeded in obtaining enough education for all ordinary business transactions. When only fifteen years of age he began railroad service as water boy on a construction train. A sketch of a locomotive that he made fell into the hands of Master Mechanic T. J. Hamer, who at once took John into his office. He afterward served an apprenticeship in the Philadelphia & Erie Railroad shops, and after learning his trade he held the positions, respectively, of fireman, engineer and foreman for different companies until 1885, when he was chosen foreman of the shops at Macon, Ga., for the East Tennessee, Virginia & Georgia Railroad, and soon afterward became master mechanic of the Alabama division of the East Tennessee, Virginia & Georgia. He was also general foreman of the Louisville & Nashville shops at Nashville for five years. In 1886 he was given his present position. Mr. Michael is a self-made man, and has reason to be proud of the fact.

A. H. Mitchell, an enterprising farmer, was born in Hawkins County, Tenn., in 1821. He moved to Monroe County, Ky., in 1855, where he resided four years. He then moved to Knox County, Tenn., and is living there at the present. Mr. Mitchell is a natural born mechanic. When twenty-four years old he worked at the carpenter and cabinet-maker's trade, which he followed until 1855, after which he followed agricultural pursuits. In 1859 he married Miss Parmelia A. Hall, a daughter of William Hall, who is the father of Judge E. T. Hall, of Knoxville. In 1864 Mr. Mitchell engaged in the grocery business with Mr. John Mitchell, the style of firm being A. H. & J. Mitchell, and followed this occupation very successfully for one year. He also traveled very extensively through the United States in his younger days. He owns a good farm of 180 acres located nine miles north of Knoxville, all well improved and well cultivated. Mrs. Mitchell died in 1872, and our subject took for his second wife Miss Eliza Crippen in 1874. She is the daughter of William and Dicy (Tyndle) Crippen. William Cribben was sheriff of Knox County six years, constable ten years, and was a farmer by occupation. Mr. Mitchell is a Democrat in politics, casting his first presidential vote for Zachary Taylor, and his wife is a member of the Methodist Episcopal Church South. He was the fifth of ten children born to John and Martha (Lyon) Mitchell, both of whom were born and raised in Hawkins County, Tenn. The father was of English and the mother of German descent. Mr. Solomon Mitchell, grandfather of our subject, was a soldier in the Revolutionary war, and our subject's father was a soldier in the war of 1812. The latter was justice of the peace of his district for twenty-five years. He was one of the county commissioners while the present courthouse was being built, and held various other offices of the county and district in which he lived. About 1833 he was appointed by the State Legislature as entry-taker of what is now known as "Symm's Survey."

Joseph R. Mitchell, president of the People's Bank, of Knoxville, Tenn., was born at Rogersville, Hawkins Co., Tenn., in 1824. His grandfather, Richard Mitchell, was of Scotch-Irish descent. He was a member of the convention which met at Knoxville, January 11, 1796, and at the age of seventeen was clerk and private secretary of Gov. Blount, by whom he was appointed county court clerk of Hawkins County in 1790, and held the position until 1815. Richard and his wife united themselves to the Presbyterian Church, and were baptized at Rogersville when at the advanced age of eighty-two and ninety-two years respectively. The parents of our subject, Stokley and Alice G. (Rogers) Mitchell, were natives of Rogersville, where they were married and resided until their deaths in 1861 and 1873 respectively. The father was county court clerk of Hawkins County from 1815 to 1845. He was also clerk of the House of Representatives several terms, and filled the position of cashier and president of the Nashville Bank and the Bank of Tennessee. Our subject is the eldest of a family of six sons and five daughters, nine of whom are still living. He remained in his native place until 1857, then soon after came to Knoxville to accept the position of bookkeeper in the Ocoee Bank, of which he afterward became cashier. This position he filled until 1865, when he established the general brokerage and banking house of J. R. Mitchell & Co., which was merged into the Knoxville Depository, and afterward the People's Bank. In 1845 he wedded Miss Eliza C. Messengill, a native of Grainger County, to whom six sons and seven daughters were born—seven children now living.

John M. Montgomery, farmer, was born August 16, 1835, in Roane County, Tenn., where he grew to manhood. In 1869 he moved to Arkansas, settling near Fort Smith, and afterward moved to Loudon County, Tenn., and from there to Knox County in 1875, where he has since resided. He is the eldest of eight children born to Josiah and Martha M. (Watson) Montgomery. The father was born January 12, 1811, in Roane County, Tenn., where he passed the remainder of his days. He died April 29, 1868. He was a very efficient minister in the Missionary Baptist Church, particularly so as a revivalist and class organizer. The mother of our subject was born May 21, 1811, in Roane County, where she has since lived, and although seventy-six years of age is very healthy and active, but quite deaf. She is a devoted member of the Cumberland Presbyterian Church. Her parents, John and Martha Watson, came from North Carolina and settled in Roane County at a very early day. Our subject acquired a good practical education at the family fireside, and taught four different sessions of school. October 5, 1862, he enlisted in the Sixty-third Tennessee Infantry, and was for a while sergeant of his company. He was wounded quite severely at the battle of Chickamauga, and this rendered him unfit for duty a short time. He was mustered out in 1865, and returned to Loudon County, where he rented a farm and engaged in agricultural pursuits. This occupation he has since followed. November 28, 1867, he married Miss Mary J. Wilkerson, who was born May 6, 1845, and who is the daughter of M. W. and Mary E. (Hardin) Wilkerson. To Mr. and Mrs. Montgomery were born these children: Ida Lee, William Austin, Hattie Miller, John Chester, Mary Annie, Martha Elizabeth and Dartha Eva. Mr. and Mrs. Montgomery and three elder children are members of the Cumberland Presbyterian Church. In politics Mr. Montgomery is a Democrat, and cast his first presidential vote for John C. Breckinridge. His paternal grandparents, Josiah and Mary (Lewis) Montgomery, came from Virginia early in life, and his grandfather, Josiah Montgomery, was a soldier in the war of 1812.

Mark Morel, farmer of the Eleventh District, was born in Switzerland, and came to America in 1857, settling first at Knoxville. He is the third of five children born to Charles S. and Catherine Morel. Our subject received his education in the common schools of Switzerland, and at the age of sixteen began working for himself, with but the clothes he wore. He first followed farming, afterward blacksmithing, then railroading, then carpentering, and is now engaged in agricultural pursuits again. He is a natural mechanic, being able to make most anything out of wood or iron. Mr. Morel has been remarkably successful as a farm manager, and owns 304 acres of land, well improved, which is located seven miles west of Knoxville. In 1867 he married Miss Susan Ferguson, a daughter of James and Mattie Ann Ferguson, and the result of this union was the birth of seven children: Charles, Louisa, James, Anna, Mary, Sarah and Samuel (deceased). Mr. Morel is a Republican, and a member of the Missionary Baptist Church. April 18, 1862, he enlisted in Company D, Sixth Tennessee Infantry, and served until the close of the war.

J. B. Morris, a successful farmer of the Nineteenth District, and one of seven children born to Joseph and Rachel (Waters) Morris, first saw the light of day July 29, 1827, in Ashe County, N. C. He immigrated to Tennessee with his parents in 1832, and settled in Knox County, where he has since resided. The father of our subject was born in North Carolina, as also was his wife. He was a soldier in the war of 1812, and died in the year 1842, aged fifty-two years. His wife followed him in 1875. Our subject acquired his education mostly after he became grown. When seventeen years of age he apprenticed himself to learn the saddler's trade, which he continued to follow until 1865, after which he engaged in farming. During the late war he assisted considerably in furnishing the Confederate Government with supplies. Mr. Morris began life a poor man, but by industry and good management he has made money rapidly. In the fall of 1864 he married Mrs. Margaret J.

Nelson, formerly Miss Marley, a native of Knox County, and the daughter of John and Elizabeth (Ayers) Marley. Two children were the fruits of our subject's marriage: Joseph Robert and John Dickenson. Mr. Morris is a Democrat in politics, and cast his first presidential vote for Millard Fillmore. He is a Master Mason. His parents were of English descent, and his paternal grandmother lived to the remarkably advanced age of one hundred years, being quite active up to the time of her death. Mr. Morris is the discoverer of the only sure cure for hog cholera now known in the United States. The remedy has been quite severely tested for the past nine years, and has proved eminently successful in all instances.

Hon. John L. Moses (deceased), who was tax attorney for East Tennessee, Virginia & Georgia Railroad, and a prominent resident of Knoxville, was a son of John F. and Mary (Pearson) Moses, both natives of New Hampshire and both of English descent. The father was a wool merchant by occupation, carrying on the business quite extensively. He was a man who stood high in the estimation of the people, as was evinced by the public positions he held. Several times he occupied a seat in the State Legislature, and was one to cast an electoral vote for the last Whig candidate for the presidency. His union with Miss Pearson resulted in the birth of seven children. After her death he married Abbie C. Boyd, who bore him three children. Our subject was born in Exeter, N. H., May 9, 1822, and passed his early life in his native town, surrounded by the best of educational advantages. After attending the Phillips Exeter Academy he went to Waterville College, in that State, and graduated in 1841. He soon after came to Knoxville, and he and his brother, James C., decided to establish a church of the faith of their ancestors. Though both were quite young, and neither a church member, they organized the First Baptist Church in the city, and this church has grown to be one of the strongest churches here. After reading law a short time our subject engaged in journalism for several years. He then followed mercantile pursuits until elected cashier of the Bank of Knoxville. From 1855 Mr. Moses was connected with railroad service as president of Tennessee State Line; secretary, treasurer and superintendent of the Knoxville & Ohio, and was, up to the time of his death, assistant secretary; secretary and treasurer of Coal Creek & New River. For several years he was tax attorney for the East Tennessee, Virginia & Georgia Railroad, and was also secretary and treasurer of the Coal Creek Consolidated Coal Company; president of the Tennessee Deaf and Dumb School, having held that position twenty-four years. For a number of years he was judge of the county court, and president of the board of trustees of the University of Tennessee.

In 1847 he married Miss Susan Williams, whose father was an early settler of Knoxville, and commanded a regiment at the battle of Horse Shoe Bend. He was also a United States Senator. By her he became the father of seven children, five now living—four sons and one daughter. Mrs. Moses died in 1877. Both were members of the Baptist Church. Mr. Moses was a Democrat in politics. He was a kind father, an excellent citizen, and his death, which occurred April 2, 1887, was universally regretted.

Thomas L. Moses, principal of the Tennessee Deaf and Dumb School at Knoxville, was born near Knoxville on December 13, 1849, and is the son of Hon. John L. and Susan (Williams) Moses. Our subject was educated at Knoxville and at Exeter (N. H.) High School. Soon after leaving school he became a teacher of the Deaf and Dumb School, and in this capacity continued about ten years. In the year 1871 he took for his companion through life, Miss Katie Teasdale, daughter of Rev. T. C. Teasdale, of Columbus, Miss., and the fruits of this union were three children, two of whom are now living—a son and daughter. In 1883 Mr. Moses was chosen principal of the Deaf and Dumb School, and has filled that position satisfactorily and ably from that time to the present. He was a member of the board of education of the city schools for a period of nine years, and is now a member of the board of directors of the Y. M. C. A. Both he and wife are active workers in the First Baptist Church, he being superintendent of the Sunday-school.

Frank A. Moses, cashier of the People's Bank of Knoxville, was born in Knox County in 1845, and completed his education at the State University in 1861. In May, 1862, he enlisted in the Sixty-third Tennessee Confederate Infantry, and was afterward promoted to the rank of first lieutenant. At the close of the war he returned to Knoxville, and engaged in the hardware trade until 1871. In 1870 he married Miss Elizabeth Mitchell, a native of Hawkins County, and the daughter of Joseph R. Mitchell, whose sketch appears elsewhere in these pages. The fruits of this union were one son and one daughter. In January, 1875, Mr. Moses was elected clerk of the Legislature and House of Representatives, and in the fall of the same year assumed the duties of corresponding clerk of the People's Bank. In May, 1877, he engaged in journalism as business manager of the *Knoxville Tribune*, which position he filled until July, 1880. In the fall of 1877 he was appointed a member of the railroad assessors of Tennessee. In 1881 he returned to the People's Bank as bookkeeper, and in May, 1886, was elected cashier. His parents, James C. and Susan W. (Baker *nee* Park) Moses, were natives of New Hampshire and Tennessee respectively. The father followed journalism from

1838 to 1849, after which he engaged in the hardware trade until his death in 1870. He was one of the trustees of the State University, and for a number of years was president of the board of trustees of the Deaf and Dumb Asylum. He was founder of the First Baptist Church of Knoxville, and was the first member baptized in that faith in Knoxville (1842). The mother is still living. She had three children by a previous marriage, all still living, and our subject is the third of eight children born to her second marriage, six of whom are still living. The paternal grandparents of our subject were of Welsh descent, and the maternal of Scotch-Irish.

John W. Moulden, farmer, son of Maj. William and Nancy (Johnson) Moulden, was born in Jefferson County, Tenn., September 28, 1836. His father, born in Henry County, Va., December 11, 1798, was of English descent, and was quite a prominent citizen of Knox County. He took considerable interest in public affairs, and although he commenced life with no other capital than willing hands, died comparatively wealthy. He drove the first spike in the East Tennessee & Virginia Railroad, in whose incorporation he was a stockholder and director. He was a director in the Tennessee State Bank at Knoxville before the war. He was for a long time justice of the peace, was a member of the Methodist Episcopal Church, and died at his home in Knox County March 24, 1886. The mother of our subject was born in Washington County, Va., February 10, 1800, and was of English descent. She died at her home in Knox County, at the age of eighty-three years. She was also a member of the Methodist Episcopal Church, and was a most excellent woman. Our subject was educated at Strawberry Plains, Jefferson Co., Tenn., and engaged in farming on the Holston about two miles below Strawberry Plains. In 1860 he married Miss Almeda McMillan, and to them were born six children, only four now living: Belle M. (Mrs. Caldwell); John, who is with McMillan & Treadwell, of Knoxville; Nannie E., who is at home with her father, and Fred T., who is with his sister, Belle, attending school at Strawberry Plains. In 1887 our subject married Miss Anna Lee Boyd of Atlanta, Ga. He is a member of the Methodist Episcopal Church, and a Democrat, although he votes for principle and not for party.

Hon. E. F. Mynatt, one of Knoxville's most promising young lawyers, was born in Knox County, Tenn., February 22, 1858. He secured his education in this county, and at the age of nineteen, commenced reading law with Hon. W. L. Ledgewood, of Knoxville, Tenn., and was admitted to the bar on the day he was twenty-one years old. He practiced his profession alone until the spring of 1887, when he became a member of the firm of Caldwell & Mynatt. Mr. Mynatt rose rapidly in his profession, and in a very short time, after having been admitted to the bar, took rank among the best lawyers in East Tennessee. His forte is criminal law; he has great power before a jury, and is called all over East Tennessee, in important criminal trials. Mr. Mynatt has never sought political honors, but in 1886 the people of Knox County took him up, and elected him to the Legislature of 1887, where he served with great distinction, making, it is said, one of the ablest representatives Knox County has had since the war. He was faithful to every trust, and looked well to the interest of his people standing upon the floor of the House of Representatives, for five hours' fight against the passage of the revenue bill of 1887, but the bill passed by one vote. Hon. E. F. Mynatt was the youngest man Knox County has elected to represent them in the Legislature, since 1852. Joseph A. Mynatt, the father of our subject, was born in 1828, and has always resided in Knox County, where he followed agricultural pursuits. Melvina (Ally) Mynatt, mother of E. F. Mynatt, is also a native of Knox County. Richard Mynatt the paternal grandfather, came to Knox County in the early settlement of that county. The Mynatt family is among the oldest families of Knox County.

J. C. Mynatt, a farmer of the Seventh District, was born November 4, 1821, on a farm where he has since resided. He is the tenth of eleven children born to John and Frances (Clark) Mynatt. Mrs. Mynatt was the widow of Mr. Gist by whom she had three children: Joshua H. (deceased), Spencer C. (deceased), who was commander of a vessel which was engaged in the battle of Vera Cruz during the Mexican war. Shortly after the battle he took the yellow fever, died, and is buried at Vera Cruz. He was a graduate at West Point, a prominent man and a splendid soldier. His grandfather, Spencer Clack, and brother, John Clack were signers of the first constitution of the State of Tennessee, which was made at Knoxville in 1796. Mrs. Mynatt's third child was Barthella (Mrs. Flint, deceased). Elizabeth Haven, John Mynatt's first wife, bore him eight children. She was born February 7, 1777, and he July 31, 1780, in Virginia. He came with his father to Knox County when seven years of age, and settled in Grainger County, near Clinch Mountain. He died April 23, 1867. All the Mynatts living in the United States are descendants of William Mynatt, who came from England to America before the Revolutionary war. J. C. Mynatt's uncle, William Mynatt, was aid-de-camp under Gen. Cocke during the war of 1812. John N., father of the subject of this sketch, lived with and was supported by his son, J. C. Mynatt. The latter was married to Miss Frances W. Hall

December 1, 1841. She is a daughter of William and Nancy (Nelson) Hall. Her brother, M. L. Hall, was judge of the criminal court sixteen years, and another brother, E. T., was judge of the circuit court eight years. M. L. Hall served as clerk of the circuit court for many years and as clerk of the Federal court for several years. He is now a prominent attorney of Knoxville, as is also his brother, E. T. Hall. Eight children were the result of our subject's marriage: Oliver C., William B., John Hall, Flavius, Josephus, Cynthia F. (deceased), Mark Donel (deceased) and Major Clack. Mr. and Mrs. Hall are members of the Missionary Baptist Church; Mr. Hall joined in February, 1840, and since that time has continued an active Christian worker. Mr. Mynatt has been deacon of the church for about twenty years. He had two sons in the Federal Army, and was a stanch Union man. He began life as a poor man, but by untiring industry and good management accumulated quite a fortune, besides giving his children excellent educational advantages. Mr. Mynatt is a Democrat in politics, and cast his first vote for the Whig candidate of 1844. Mrs. Mynatt's grandfather and mother, Hall, came from North Carolina to Tennessee at a very early day, and her maternal grandparents came from Virginia to Tennessee also at a very early day. All of our subject's ancestors, as far back as they have knowledge, were members of the Baptist Church. J. C.'s father and grandfather each served the Baptist Church of his neighborhood for many years as deacon. Our subject and brother, Dr. B. K. Mynatt, are the only children living of the father's family. The latter, Dr. B. K., is a graduate of the Nashville Medical College and is quite a prominent and successful physician in Rhea County.

J. H. Nave, farmer, was born June 10, 1820, within two miles of where he now resides. He is one of eight children born to John and Mary (Morrison) Nave. John Nave was born in Rockingham County, Va., near Green Brier. His father came to Tennessee at quite an early day, settled first in Blount County, and was a native born German. John Nave was a soldier in the war of 1812 under Gen. Jackson, and was a much respected citizen. Our subject's educational advantages were very limited. At the age of seventeen he began working for himself at $4 per month. March 23, 1843, he married Miss Margaret Gray, who bore him six children: Mary A. V. (deceased), Andrew H. (a graduate of West Point Military Academy, and is now captain in the regular army located at Houston, Tex.), Susan J. (deceased), Margaret E. (Mrs. Joseph Nelson), Isabella B. (deceased) and Alice C. (deceased). Besides giving his children a farm a piece, our subject owns eighty-nine acres of splendid land seven miles west of Knoxville. All this was accumulated by his own exertion. Mr. Nave is a Democrat in politics, and a member of the Presbyterian Church. Mrs. Nave died April 29, 1864, aged thirty-seven. She was an earnest worker in the church, and was respected by all. Mr. Nave's grandmother, Mary Marshall, died in Illinois in 1840, aged ninety years.

M. Nelson, senior member of the firm of M. Nelson & Co., wholesale and retail clothiers, of Knoxville, Tenn., is a native of that city, and was born in 1817, being the son of Mathew and Martha (Cannon) Nelson. The father was born in Virginia in 1778, and came to Tennessee when a young man. He was elected to represent Roane County in the State Legislature in 1813, and while serving in that body was elected treasurer of East Tennessee, which position he held until 1827, having during that time charge of and the sale of all the public lands of that section of the State, and was made at different times defendant in large land suits. In one instance a rich North Carolina syndicate purchased large tracts of lands in East Tennessee in a fraudulent manner, and Mr. Nelson refused to sign the necessary papers to make good the title. An effort was made to bribe him, but he was to honorable, and an immense amount of litigation followed, in which he came off victorious. The lands were re-sold, and his fees amounted to over $13,000, which he refused to accept, his reason for so doing being that he had fought the syndicate for a principal, and that, should he accept the fees accruing from the sale of lands he wrested from them, his actions would be construed by them as having been prompted by a desire of gain. In 1845 he was elected, and served two years as treasurer of Tennessee. During his official career he was also engaged in merchandising. He died full of honors in 1853. The mother was born in North Carolina in 1785, and came with her parents to Tennessee in her youth; she died in 18——. Our subject was reared in Knoxville, and educated at the old Knoxville College, which at that time stood on the left side of Gay Street opposite the H—— House of to-day. At the age of sixteen years he engaged as clerk in the mercantile house of McClung & Hazen, of Knoxville, which position he held for about five years, and then removed to Pulaski, Tenn., where he became a member of the firm of Morgan & Nelson, merchants. Two years later he returned to Knoxville and engaged in the dry goods business, and in 1875 began dealing in clothing and carpets. He was married in 1855 to R. A. McGauhey, of Athens, Tenn., who was born in 1833, and is the daughter of John McGauhey. To them two sons have been born as follows: M. M., born in 1856, and Hugh B., born in 1868; both of whom are connected with their father in business.

Thomas A. R. Nelson, attorney-general for the district of Knox, is a native of Washington County, Tenn., born in August, 1848, and at the age of fifteen came to Knox County. He received his education at the university, after which he studied law with his father; was admitted to the bar in 1872, and began the practice of his profession. He was city alderman during 1876-77 after which he received a four years' appointment as commissioner of the claims under the United States Government, and at the expiration of this time resumed his legal practice, which he followed successfully until elected to fill his present office in August, 1886, for a term of eight years. He and two sisters are the surviving members of a family of five children born to Thomas A. R., Sr., and Ann (Stuart) Nelson, natives of Roane and Washington Counties, Tenn. The father was born in 1812, and afterward moved with his parents to Washington County, Tenn. He was married in that county, and soon afterward came to Knox County. He was attorney-general of the First Circuit many years, was presidential elector, was twice a member of Congress, was one of President Johnson's council in his impeachment trial, and was elected to the supreme bench of Tennessee in 1870, which position he resigned in 1872 to resume the practice of law. His wife died in May, 1850, and he afterward married Mary Jones, who is still living, and by whom five children were born, all living. The father was counsel of the East Tennessee, Virginia & Georgia Railroad many years, and died August 24, 1873. He was of Scotch-Irish descent.

D. D. Nicholas, president of the Gem Marble Company at Concord, was born September 10, 1841, at Gomer, Ohio. He is the fourth of five children born to James and Mary (Jones) Nicholas. The father was born September 10, 1810, in Butler County, Ohio. In 1833 he moved to Allen County, Ohio, where he still resides. He was justice of the peace of the district where he resides for fifty-three years, and is still holding the office. He was a son of James Nicholas, a native of Cardingshire, Wales, who came to America in 1797, settling first in Beula, Penn., but afterward moved to Ohio in 1800, and settled in Butler County of that State. The mother of our subject was born in Montgomeryshire, North Wales, in 1810, and came to America in 1817, settling in Butler County, Ohio. Our subject received his education in the common schools of Allen County, Ohio, also at Lebanon (Ohio) Normal School, and Nelson's Business College, Cincinnati, Ohio. In 1867 he was elected county surveyor of Allen County, Ohio, and held that office twelve years. He was elected city engineer of Lima, Ohio, in 1868, and held that office up to 1882. Mr. Nicholas, with several other gentlemen, all of Ohio, formed a partnership under the name of The Lima & East Tennessee Marble Company, with Mr. R. Mehaffey, president, of the Merchant's National Bank, of Lima, Ohio, and D. D. Nicholas as general superintendent. From a small beginning they increased the average capacity to many car loads per month, shipping marble to all parts of the country. The quarry produces some of the finest marble in the country. In 1878 Mr. Nicholas married Miss Flora E. Cunningham, of Lima, Ohio, the daughter of James and Martha (Kennedy) Cunningham. To Mr. and Mrs. Nicholas were born two children: Nellie and Mary. In 1885 the Gem Marble Company was organized, with D. D. Nicholas as president. From a beginning the Gem Marble Company has increased, until their present monthly capacity averages twenty car loads. Mr. Nicholas is also connected with two other marble companies, known as the Buckeye Marble Company, of which he is president and director, and the National Marble Company. He is prominently connected with several other of the most substantial business firms of Ohio and Tennessee. Mr. and Mrs. Nicholas are members of the Presbyterian Church, and Mr. Nicholas is a Democrat in politics. He was candidate for the State Legislature from Knox County, Tenn., on the Democratic ticket in 1886, and helped cut down the usual majority of 1,700, to something less than 1,000. In 1862 Mr. Nicholas enlisted in Company F, One Hundred and Eighteenth Ohio Volunteer Infantry, and served until the close of the war. He was wounded at the battle of Resaca, and excepting the time lost during the healing of his wound, was in all the battles and severe skirmishes in which his regiment took part.

James O'Conner, the leading saddler and harness manufacturer of Knoxville, was born January 27, 1835, at Halifax C. H., Va. His father, John O'Conner, was born in Virginia, where he died in 1854, being seventy-two years of age. He was a wheelwright by trade, and was a soldier in the war of 1812. The mother of our subject, Rebecca (Powell) O'Conner, was also born in Virginia, and died there in 1882, being over eighty years of age. Of their family of eleven children, five are now living—four sons and one daughter. Grandfather O'Conner was a native of the Emerald Isle, and came to America soon after the Revolutionary war. Our subject was educated in the old field schools, and at the age of eighteen went to Lynchburg, Va. to learn his trade. During the war he was purchasing agent, in his line, for the Confederate Government, traveling over a principal part of the South. In 1868 he began his present business in Knoxville, commencing as a day laborer he gradually arose until now he runs an extensive establishment requiring from 75 to 125 hands. In 1872 he married Miss Mary S. Price, a native of the same village as himself. Three children were the result of this union—two sons and one daughter. Mr. O'Conner is a Democrat in politics, and he and wife are members of the First Baptist Church. He is a reliable and prominent man, and is well respected by all who know him.

Ogden Bros. & Co., booksellers, stationers, printers and binders, have their business situated at 145 and 147 Gay Street, Knoxville, Tenn. The firm of Ogden Bros. was established about 1871, and existed until 1883, when it was succeeded by Ogden Bros. & Rule. It thus continued for two years, when it merged into the present firm, which consists of the two Ogden brothers, S. R. and Alfred, T. H. Robinson and Samuel Hensell. The Ogden brothers are natives of Wellington, Ohio. S. R. came to Knoxville in 1871, and established the business of which he has since been the principal. Alfred Ogden is now a resident of Brooklyn, N. Y. Mr. Robinson is a native of England, where he received his education. He came to Knoxville in 1883 and associated himself with the Ogdens. Mr. Hensell came to Knoxville from West Virginia about 1875, and accepted a clerkship with the firm of which he became a member April 1, 1886. The firm employs about thirty assistants, and keeps one traveling salesman regularly on the road. The amount of business transacted annually is about $100,000. They furnish all the stationery supplies for the East Tennessee, Virginia & Georgia Railroad, and also for the K. of H., delivering the blank books, stationery, etc., for the above named order at St. Louis, Mo.

R. G. Osborn is a woodworkman by trade, and for many years has been an employe of Burr & Terry, of this city. He became a member of the U. O. of .G. C. soon after the organization of the order in Knoxville, and is now treasurer of Hope Commandery, No. 2, member of the finance committee of the Grand Commandery, and member of the committee on laws and grievances of the Supreme Commandery. He was born in Monroe County, Tenn., in 1831, but has resided in Knoxville since infancy. December 27, 1855, he married Miss Sarah J. Beal, a native of Rogersville, Tenn. His father, James Osborn, was a native of Virginia, born in 1799, and came to Tennessee when fifteen years of age. He located a few years after marriage in Monroe County, after which he came to Knox County, where he died in 1877. The mother, Sabella (Helsley) Osborn, was a native of Greene County, Tenn. She was born in 1804, and is still living in Knoxville. Our subject is the fourth of eleven children born to his parents, all living with the exception of one sister.

John F. Parker, farmer of the Third Civil District of Knox County, Tenn., is a native of that county, born in 1842, and the son of F. S. and Mary B. (Coker) Parker. The father was a native of North Carolina, where he was born in 1811. He came to Tennessee when a young man and located in Knox County, where he followed farming until his death, which occurred about 1857. The mother was a native of Tennessee, born in 1817, and is a member of the Baptist Church. She is now residing with her son, whose farm is situated six and one-half miles from Knoxville. Our subject was reared on the farm, and attended Spring Place Academy. He has made a decided success of farming, which occupation he has followed all his life, and is regarded as one of the substantial and enterprising men of the district. He was married in 1871 to Miss P. C. Ross, who presented him with one child, H. D., who was born in 1873. The mother died in 1877, and in 1879 Mr. Parker married Miss Jennie Roberts, of Knox County, who was born in 1861. The fruits of this union were three children, viz.: Howard R., born in 1880; Loyd C., born in 1882, and Hugh F., born in 1885. Both Mr. and Mrs. Parker are members of the Spring Place Baptist Church.

Col. M. L. Patterson was born in Stokes County, N. C., in Oct., 1827, and was reared on a farm. In his seventeenth year (1844) he had the misfortune to lose his left arm by the first portable threshing machine that came to his native State. In 1847 he moved to Washington County, Tenn., where he attended the common schools a few months. He then completed his education at Clear Springs Academy, and taught school about three years in Washington and adjoining counties. In 1853 he went West and spent two years. He then returned to Tennessee, and filled two terms as circuit court clerk of Greene County. Soon after the commencement of the war he acted as captain and commissary officer of Gen. Spears' brigade, but on the organization of the Fourth Tennessee Infantry he was elected first lieutenant and regimental quartermaster, from which he was promoted to major and then to lieutenant colonel, serving until March, 1865, when he resigned and accepted the appointment as clerk of the supreme court for the Eastern Division of Tennessee, which he held until September, 1870. In 1866 he married Miss Nettie E. Slemons, a native of Paris, Ill., to whom two children have been born: Edgar and Orton. Edgar died in his tenth year. In October, 1870, he was appointed clerk and master of the chancery court, at Knoxville, and reappointed in 1876, serving until October, 1882. He was the youngest of nine children, three of whom are living, born to James and Mary M. Patterson, both natives of North Carolina. The father remained in his native State until 1861, when he moved to Indiana, and there died in 1869. He was a participant in the war of 1812, and at the time of his death was in his eighty-sixth year. His wife died in 1857.

A. C. Payne was born in Knox County, Tenn., March 28, 1837, and is of English and Dutch descent. He received a limited education, and early in life turned his attention to farming. At the breaking out of the late war he left home, went to Kentucky, and here offered his services to the Federal Government. On account of a deformed hand he was rejected. He then went to Nashville, Tenn., where he was employed by a sutler, and remained at this place until February, 1865, when he moved to Pulaski, Giles Co., Tenn., and was at that point when the war closed. He then came to Knox County, Tenn., and in 1865 formed a partnership with E. W. D. Wrinkle in mercantile pursuits. In 1874 our subject married Miss Susan Slatery, daughter of John Slatery. Four children were the result of this union, only one now living, named Laura; she was born January 23, 1877. Mr. Payne followed mercantile pursuits until 1875, when he and his partner, in connection with this, also engaged in farming. They now own 375 acres of Knox County land, and have it well improved. Mr. Payne is a Republican in politics, and a good citizen.

R. S. Payne, president of the East Tennessee National Bank, a native of Davidson County, Tenn., was born in 1844. He was reared and educated in Davidson County, and at the commencement of the war enlisted in the Second Tennessee Infantry, with which he served until 1863, when he was placed on Gen. Morgan's staff, but at the death of Morgan he was placed on Breckinridge's staff, a short time after which he acted as first lieutenant of Capt. Gracey's artillery. He was engaged in the wholesale hat trade in New York City from 1866 to 1868, then located at Knoxville in the same trade, which he continued until 1885, since which time he has been a member of the firm, McTeers, Payne, Burger & Hood. In 1879 he married Miss Bettie Dismukes, a native of Davidson County, to whom three sons and one daughter have been born. Mr. Payne was elected mayor of Knoxville in 1882, and served about one year. He was elected director and vice-president of the East Tennessee National Bank shortly after its organization, and April 14, 1884, he was elected president, which position he still fills. He is a director in the Knoxville Gas Light Company, and stockholder in the Knoxville Woolen Mills, East Tennessee Insurance Company, Island Home Insurance Company, and has taken an active part in all worthy enterprises for the upbuilding of Knoxville. He is a member of the Masonic fraternity. R. S. Payne (Sr.) and Sarah C. (Lewis) Payne, the parents of our subject, were natives of Davidson County, Tenn., and North Carolina respectively. They were married in Sumner County, Tenn., and the father followed merchandising in Nashville and Springfield until his death at the latter place. The mother's death occurred in Sumner County. Our subject was the second of the family, which consisted of himself and three sisters, all deceased but himself.

W. H. B. Prater, farmer of the Eleventh District, was born July 4, 1842, in Blount County, Tenn. He is the second of four children born to William and Mary Blair (Leeper) Prater. The father was born July 22. 1811, in Roane (now Loudon) County, Tenn. He was a very enthusiastic farmer, as well as a very enterprising and successful one. He was killed by being thrown from a horse. Benjamin Prater, grandfather of the subject of this sketch, was born and reared near Lynchburg, Va., and afterward moved to North Carolina, and from there to Tennessee, settling on French Broad River, where he married Miss Nancy Lane. He began life by splitting rails, and by his remarkable energy, enterprise and excellent practical ability accumulated quite a fortune. He and wife were of Scotch descent. The mother of our subject was born August 7, 1815, and is the daughter of Hugh B. and Malinda (Saunders) Leeper, natives of Pennsylvania and Georgia respectively. She is still living, is quite active, and enjoys excellent health. She has a remarkably good memory for dates and historical facts, reads considerable, and carries on quite an extensive correspondence. After the death of her husband she married John W. Lee, a native of Virginia, and a relative of Gen. Robert E. Lee. Our subject secured his education at Knoxville University, at the University of Lexington, Ky., and Ewing and Jefferson College. He enlisted in Hugh L. McClung's battery in the spring of 1862, and was discharged at Loudon in 1863. He was in part of the siege at Vicksburg, Miss., and took part in all the battles and severe skirmishes in which his regiment was engaged. He married Miss M. G. Lee in 1867. She was born August 6, 1850, and is the daughter of John W. and Elizabeth (Akers) Lee. The result of our subject's marriage was the birth of seven children: Mary Ellen, William Walter, Hugh Leeper, James Gaines, Roddy Clifford, Ernest and Bessie Lee. Mrs. Prater died June 16, 1886. She was a member of the Presbyterian Church. Mr. Prater has always followed agricultural pursuits. He now owns a fine farm of 700 acres of land, on the Kingston Pike, and 100 in Blount County. He is a Democrat in politics, and cast his first vote for Horace Greeley.

G. W. Prater, farmer, was born September 15, 1846, in Blount County, Tenn., and is the third of four children born to William and Mary B. (Leeper) Prater. The father was born July 22, 1811, in Roane County, Tenn., where he grew to manhood. When twenty-seven years of age he moved to Blount County, Tenn., where he followed the occupation of a farmer and trader, and where he accumulated considerable property. He was colonel of the State Militia, and was a man highly respected by all. He was passionately fond of stock raising and trading, loved company, and delighted in fishing and hunting. The mother was born in Shelby County, Tenn., August 7, 1815, and moved with her parents to Blount County, where she was reared and married; she is still living. Our subject received a fair education in the common schools of Blount County, and subsequently attended Union and Jefferson College. In 1863 he went to Kentucky, and located near Lexington. Later he came back to Blount County, where he remained until 1868, and then removed to Knox County. In the fall of 1869 he removed to California, but in the fall of 1870 returned to Knox County, where he has since resided. He received some property from his father, but the late war and the freshet of 1867 destroyed about all he then had. He now owns 670 acres of good land. October 10, 1872, Miss Elizabeth Brooks became his wife. She was born September 23, 1850, and is a daughter of Gen. James A. and Margaret A. (McMillen) Brooks. To Mr. and Mrs. Prater were born seven children: Hattie W., Tracy W., Mary B., Joseph B., George W., Frederick B. and Bob. Mr. and Mrs. Prater are members of the Southern Presbyterian Church, he being a deacon of the same. He is a Democrat in politics. He began life as a stock dealer, and followed this business until 1863. From that date until 1865 he handled goods from Nashville to Lexington, Ky., and from 1865 to the present has cultivated the soil.

A. S. Prosser, attorney at law, was born in Pennsylvania, December 4, 1838, and reared on a farm until fifteen years of age. He then attended the public schools of Johnstown, Penn., where he received his education, after which he moved to Illinois. April 19, 1861, he enlisted in the Tenth Illinois Infantry, with which he served in the commissary department until 1864, at which date he was transferred to the Second Tennessee United States Cavalry, as first lieutenant. He was mustered out July 9, 1865, at Nashville, and remained there until February, 1866, after which he located at Knoxville, and entered the law firm of Maynard & Washburn, which title was afterward changed to Washburn & Prosser, and continued as such until January, 1870, since which time he has practiced alone, and is one of the leading members of the bar. He is a director in the Central Guarantee Life Association, and a stockholder in the Knoxville Gas Company. In 1869 he was attorney-general, *pro tem.*, of the State. In 1875 he married Lizzie, daughter of Judge George Brown, a native of Monroe County, to whom one child—Brown, has been born. Our subject is the third of a family of four sons, all still living, born to David and Rachel (Williams) Prosser, natives of Wales, where they were married. They came to America in 1832, and located near Harrisburg, Penn., where they remained until 1837, after which they moved to Johnstown. The mother died in 1842, and the father afterward married Mariah Kenton, a native of Bedford County, Penn., to whom eight children were born (two deceased). The father of our subject was the first man to open out a coal bed in western Pennsylvania. His death occurred in November, 1884. T. E. Prosser, M. D., brother of A. S. Prosser (our subject), is one of the young physicians of Knoxville. He is a native of Pennsylvania, and attended the high school of Johnstown. In 1883 he began the study of medicine, and in 1884 entered Bellevue Hospital Medical College, at New York City, from which he graduated in 1886. He returned to Johnstown, Penn., where he practiced his profession until he removed to Knoxville, Tenn. He is a medical director of the Central Guarantee Life Association, of Knoxville, and is a young physician of rare promise.

Dr. James Gettys McGready Ramsey, was born in Knox County, Tenn., on March 25, 1797. His paternal grandfather was Reynolds Ramsey, who, with his parents, came from Scotland. On the passage across the ocean the mother was drowned. The remainder of the family settled at New Castle, Del. Reynolds Ramsey married Naomi Alexander and located on Marsh Creek, in York County, Penn. They had three or four sons and one daughter. The eldest son, Francis A., was born May 31, 1764. Early in life he came west, stopping in Washington County, N. C. Soon after he came to Tennessee, took an active part in forming the State of Franklin, and became one of the leading actors in those troublous times. On April 7, 1789, he married Peggy Alexander, of Mecklenburg, County, N. C., and settled on Little Loudon Creek, where, on March 26, 1791, their first son, William B. A., was born. They then removed to Knox County, where three more sons: J. M. A., Samuel G. and J. G. M., were born. In July, 1805, the mother died, and the next year Col. Ramsey married Mrs. Ann Fleming. She also preceded him to the grave, and he married Mrs. Margaret Humes in 1820. He died November 13, 1820. The subject of this sketch received the rudiments of an education from a private teacher, and in 1809, with his brother William, was sent to the Ebenezer Academy, where they remained until 1814. They were then sent to Washington College, where they graduated. In 1817 James entered the office of Dr. Joseph C. Strong, of Knoxville, and two years later he entered the medical department of the University of Pennsylvania. On August 1, 1820, he opened an office in Knoxville, and on the 1st of March, following, he married Peggy Barton, daughter of Capt. John and Hannah Crozier. He continued to live at Knoxville until 1823, when he removed to the Forks, where he named his home Mecklenburg. From that time until the war, although actively engaged in his profession, he was prominently identified with railroad and banking enterprises, and found time to prepare his history of Tennessee. He was a man of great energy and activity, both mental and physical. During the war he was among the most extreme secessionists. Upon the Federal occupation of East Tennessee his house, with all its contents, was burned, and he was compelled to seek safety within the Confederate line. With his wife he remained in North Carolina until 1870, when he returned to Knoxville, where he died in 1884. Mrs. Ramsey, a most estimable and intelligent lady, is still living, at the advanced age of eighty-five years. Twelve children were born to them, only six of whom are now living. William W. died in California during the gold excitement there. Arthur C. was mortally wounded at the battle of Piedmont, during the war. Two daughters also died during the war. John C. died since the war. Those living are Frank A., Robert M., J. G. M., Mrs. Davidson Alexander, Mrs. E. A. R. Breck and Mrs. M. J. Dickson.

Maj. Robert B. Reynolds, farmer of the Twelfth District, was born November 11, 1811, on Flat Creek, Knox Co., Tenn., and is the third of eight children born to John and Barbara W. (Frazier) Reynolds. John Reynolds was a native of Ireland, and came to America with his father when ten years of age. The father settled first in Harrisburg, Penn., and three years later moved to Hawkins County, Tenn., where he remained one year; he then moved to Knox County, and here died. John Reynolds was major of a battalion under Gen. James White in the Creek Indian war of 1812, and served in many campaigns against the Indians prior to that year. He lost his health from exposure during this war, and was an invalid sixteen years. He died in 1835, aged sixty-four years. Our subject acquired a good English education in the common schools and under private tutors. When twenty-two he studied law under George W. Churchwell, of Knoxville; was admitted to the bar, and in a short time gained quite a reputation as an able lawyer and jurist. He was elected attorney-general by the Legislature in 1839, having jurisdiction over six counties, and held this office six years. In 1846 he was appointed assistant quartermaster by President J. K. Polk, which position he held about eight months, and then was promoted to the position of paymaster with the rank of major. At the close of the Mexican war he was reappointed paymaster for the regular army, and held this office until 1861, when he resigned. He was then appointed to the same position in the Confederate Army with the same rank, but did not accept the position. After the close of the war he spent four years in Virginia, Illinois, Missouri, and then returned to Knox County, where he has followed agricultural pursuits. He owns a good farm of 230 acres well improved and well cultivated, and situated five miles west of Knoxville. In 1875 he married Miss Mary Kennedy, daughter of George B. and Myra J. Kennedy, who bore him five children: Mary B., Robert B., John P., Ida L. and Claude E. Mr. Reynolds is a Democrat in politics. His wife is a member of the Methodist Episcopal Church.

Charles E. Ristine, M. D., physician of Knoxville, Tenn., was born in Abingdon, Va., in December, 1845, and is the son of J. C. and Susan (Elliott) Ristine, the former being a native of New Jersey, and the latter of Virginia. The father was born in 1810, and was a coach maker by trade. The mother was born in 1811 and died in 1878. Our subject was reared in Knoxville, and acquired his early education at the East Tennessee University. He began the study of medicine in 1866 under Dr. L. L. Coleman at Nashville, Tenn., and in 1867–68 attended the old University at Nashville. He next attended the University of Pennsylvania at Philadelphia, from which institution he graduated in 1880. The same year he married Mary Alice Peach, a native of Nashville, who died in 1875. In 1880 he married Ella McKinney, of Nashville, who was born in 1856. To this union one child was born, who is now six years of age. Both our subject and wife are members of the Methodist Church South. After marriage he practiced for one year at Coal Creek, Anderson Co., Tenn., and then for eleven years in Nashville, three years of which time he was professor of physiology in the medical department of the University of Tennessee. He next removed to Knoxville, where he has since resided, practicing his profession with success. He is a member of the Knox County and State Medical Societies.

Russell H. Roberts (deceased) was born on Big Flat Creek, Knox County, Tenn., October 22, 1823, and during his life was one of the enterprising and successful farmers of the Third Civil District, of that county. He was the son of Maj. Andrew and Jane (Kelley) Roberts. The father was a native Tennessean, born in 1796, and served as major of the militia under Gen. Jackson during the war of 1812. He died in 1860. He was the son of Henry Roberts, who immigrated to Tennessee at an early date. The mother of our subject was born February 18, 1801, and was the daughter of Joseph and —— (Woods) Kelley, natives of Virginia; she died in 1876. The subject of this sketch was reared on the farm, attended the common district schools, and followed farming as an occupation. He married Nancy Meek, of Knox County, March 3, 1846, who was born December 1, 1824, and who is the daughter of Joseph and Rebecca Meek. Joseph Meek was a native of Knox County, Tenn., born June 1, 1788, and died October 14, 1851. He was a soldier in the war of 1812, and was the son of John and Jane (McCutcheon) Meek, both natives of Virginia, who were married June 15, 1770. John Meek was the son of James and Ann Meek, who had six children as follows: Damie, Mary, John, Samuel, Elizabeth and Martha. Rebecca Meek, mother of Mrs. Roberts, was born in Knox County May 7, 1792, and died April 19, 1870. She was the daughter of Col. John and Rebecca (Crawford) Sawyers. John Sawyers was an officer of the Revolutionary war. Rebecca (Crawford) Sawyer's parents were massacred by the Indians. Our subject was a successful farmer, and a member of Washington Presbyterian Church, of which he was a deacon. He died April 9, 1874. To the union of our subject and wife eleven children were born, five of whom are dead, as follows: Joseph A., born January 21, 1847, died August 10, 1881; Henrietta E., born December 3, 1848, died October 10, 1874; Rebecca J., born September 19, 1850 (now Mrs. Jacob Slair, of Knox County); Narcissa R., born December 27, 1852, and died April 12, 1861; John B., born February 27, 1855, who was married August 29, 1883, and is now living with his mother; William F., born December 7, 1856, now of Kansas; Henry L., born November 25, 1858; Gains S., born November 3, 1860, now a teacher at New Market Academy, Tennessee; Ellen C., born October 25, 1862, died May 30, 1880; Robert L., born May 17, 1865, now of Kansas, and an infant, born in 1868, and died same day of birth unnamed. Mrs. Roberts is a member of the Washington Presbyterian Church, of which all her children are also members and her son, John, an elder.

P. A. Roberts, of the firm of Roberts & Bros., liverymen, of Knoxville, Tenn., is a native of Knox County, born July 13, 1833, and the son of Henry G. and Rebecca (Harris) Roberts, both natives of Tennessee. The father was born in 1808, and followed farming successfully during life. He died in 1864, leaving a name noted for honesty and industry. The mother was born in 1809, and is now living in Knox County. Our subject was reared on the farm, and acquired his education in the neighboring schools, finishing the same at Walnut Grove Academy, in the Fourth Civil District. He removed to Chester, S. C., in 1860, where he engaged in the livery and sale business. In December, 1861, he returned to Knoxville, and on the 15th of that month enlisted in the Confederate Army, joining Company D, Second Regiment of Tennessee Cavalry, organized at Cumberland Gap. He was with the regiment at the battles of Fincastle, Tenn., Stephensville, Ky., Richmond, Ky., and was then with others detached on special duty and sent to Tennessee. Returning to Kentucky, he participated in the fight at Perryville. He was at Chickamauga, and in the retreat to Atlanta, Ga. He was mustered out of service at Sugar Creek Church, North Carolina, in May, 1864, and then returned to Chester, S. C., where he entered the livery and sale business, which he continued for seven years. He next removed to Greene County, Tenn., where he remained for three years, and again returned to South Carolina. Later he removed to Knoxville, opened his present business, and has been a resident of that city ever since. He became a member of the Felix K. Zollicoffer Camp, No. 3, Confederate Veterans of Knoxville, in 1886, of which he served as officer of the day. He is an extensive dealer in stock, and is regarded as one of the substantial citizens of Knoxville.

James Rodgers, M. D., one of the leading and the oldest practicing physician of Knoxville, Tenn., was born in that city July 2, 1818. He is the son of Thomas and Annie (Patton) Rodgers, both of whom are natives of East Tennessee, the former of Washington County, and the latter of Knox County. The father was a useful mechanic, living an honorable life, and dying in the year 1870. The mother, a most worthy woman, died about the year 1821, leaving our subject, an infant of tender age, to the mercy of the world. Reared and educated in the city of Knoxville, our subject completed his education in the University of Tennessee, and in the year 1840 began the study of medicine under the direction of Dr. J. Morrow, of Knoxville, and during 1842-43 took lecture courses in the medical department of Transylvania University, at Lexington, Ky. Thereupon he returned to Knoxville, began practicing his profession, and has thus continued until the present. He served several times as president of the East Tennessee Medical Society (now the Knox County Medical Society), and is a member of the American Medical Association and the American Public Health Association. He is also a member of the East Tennessee Lodge, No. 34, I. O. O. F., and served as Grand Master of the State. In 1870 the University of Tennessee voluntarily conferred upon him the degree of M. D. In 1843 he was united in marriage to Miss Rosina, daughter of Daniel McMullen, the latter a native of Ireland. This lady was born in Knoxville in the year 1830, and has presented her husband with ten children, nine of whom are yet living, as follows: Thomas, Isabella, James, Samuel R., Charles E., Anna, Wallace D., Hugh M. and Lillie. Our subject and wife are members of the Second Presbyterian Church, of which he is an elder.

Dr. W. A. Rodgers, practicing physician of Knox County, Tenn., merchant of Graveston and farmer, was born in Knox County, Tenn., August 30, 1820. He is the son of John and Rebecca (Patton) Rodgers, both natives of Virginia, and of Scotch and English descent respectively. Our subject received his primary education in the common schools, and subsequently attended the Knoxville schools. About 1840 he began the study of medicine, and in 1843 he began practicing in McMinn County, where he continued two years. He then removed and located near Graveston, Knox Co., Tenn., where he continued the practice of his profession up to the breaking out of the late war. November 4, 1847, he married Miss Ann Clapp, daughter of Daniel Clapp, and to this marriage were born two sons, and a daughter named Margaret, who is deceased. The sons are named Samuel and John. In August, 1861, our subject became assistant surgeon in the First Tennessee Regiment, and later was promoted to surgeon of the Third Tennessee Regiment. After the war he returned to his home at Graveston, where, in connection with farming and mercantile pursuits, he has practiced his profession ever since. He has a farm of 175 acres of well improved land in Knox County, and is an excellent citizen. Our subject was appointed examining surgeon for the pension department at Knoxville. He is a Republican in politics.

L. H. Rogan, assistant superintendent and one of the directors of the Knoxville Foundry and Machine Company, is a native of Washington County, Va.; was born in 1819, and is the son of Daniel and Catherine (Crawford) Rogan. The father was a native of Ireland, and the mother of Pennsylvania. Our subject was reared in Sullivan County, Tenn., and acquired his education at the schools of that county. He came to Knoxville in 1858, engaged in the foundry and machine business, and in 1870 founded the business of which he is now assistant superintendent and director. The firm at that time being L. H. Rogan & Co. was next Rogan & Kelley, and in 1878 became incorporated under the above name. He was married in 1836 to Margret Cloud, a native of Tennessee, who was born in about 1818, and died in 1877. To the above union four children were born, three of whom are living. In 1880 our subject married Nancy Trout, a native of Knox County, who was born in about 1844. He is a member of the Presbyterian Church.

Thomas M. Rolen, of the firm of Rolen & Hill, Co-operative Stove Company, of Knoxville, Tenn., was born in Knox County, Tenn., December 3, 1844, and is the son of George and Hila (Clawson) Rolen. The father was born in Virginia in 1812, came to Tennessee when a boy, and is at present a farmer of Knox County, Tenn. The mother was born in North Carolina in 1822, and both she and her husband were members of the Methodist Episcopal Church. Our subject was reared on the farm and attended the neighborhood schools. In the spring of 1863 he left home to avoid the Confederate conscript law; went with his brother on foot and in secret to Somerset, Ky., where he joined the First East Tennessee Scouts, under the command of Maj. John Black. That organization being unable to secure recognition under that name by the Federal government, it was subsequently mustered into service in June, 1863, as the Eleventh East Tennessee Cavalry Regiment, United States Troops, our subject being a member of Company C. In March, 1865, the Eleventh and Ninth Cavalry Regiments were consolidated at Camp Contonement Springs, Tenn., and he became a member of Company I, of the Ninth Cavalry. In February, 1864, he was captured at Camp Wiremon, Lee County, Va., was taken to Richmond, Va., and held as a prisoner of war for some time, in Castle Thunder and Belle Island, and after some time he was exchanged for and returned to his command at Cumberland Gap; was mustered out of the service at Knoxville, Tenn., September 5, 1865, and remained on the farm until the fall of 1867, when he became traveling agent for Cruze & Adney, Knoxville, Tenn., manufacturers of stoves and tinware, and traveled in this capacity until the fall of 1878, when he became a member of the firm of Havey, Rolen & Co., manufacturers of stoves and tinware. In 1880 the firm changing to Rolen, Sevy & Co., in 1887 the firm changing to Rolen & Hill, Co-operative Stove Co. Mr. Rolen is a member of Ed. Maynard Post, No. 14, G. A. R., of Knoxville, and of East Tennessee Lodge, No. 34, I. O. O. F. On June 3 he married Miss Carrie Sparkes, a native of Tennessee, born in 1852, and the daughter of Jacob Sparkes. To this union were born three children. Mr. Rolen is a member of the Methodist Episcopal Church, and his wife is a member of the Methodist Episcopal Church South.

M. L. Ross, president of the Chamber of Commerce, vice-president of the Mechanics' National Bank, and senior member of the wholesale grocery firm of M. L. Ross & Co., is a young man thirty-six years of age, a native of Anderson County, Tenn., and one of two survivors of a family of three children born to James and Mary Martin Ross. The father was a native of Virginia, of Scottish descent, and prior to the marriage to the mother of our subject was united in marriage to a Miss Slover, who bore him five children, two of whom are now living, viz.: John S. and G. W. Ross. After her death he was married to Miss Mary Martin, who still survives him. He was an officer under Col. Kirkpatrick during the war of 1812, and afterward followed merchandising for upward of fifty years. He died in 1869. He was frequently in the Legislature and State Senate for ten or twelve consecutive terms. He was an intimate and warm friend of John Bell, Zollicoffer, James K.

Polk and Andrew Johnson. The mother of our subject is a native of Roane County, Tenn., and now resides in Knoxville. M. L. Ross secured only a fair education at Emory and Henry College, Virginia, having to leave the college on account of the death of his father in 1869. Taking charge of a store in Anderson County, he managed it successfully for a few years, but possessed of indomitable energy he sought out a larger field, and in 1871 came to Knoxville, where he formed a co-partnership with Maj. D. A. Carpenter to carry on the wholesale grocery business under the firm name of Carpenter & Ross, who did a prosperous business until 1879, when the firm was changed to its present style of M. L. Ross & Co., who have built up an extensive trade in five or six States. Mr. Ross is commonly called Martin, is a director in the Knoxville Car Wheel Company, Knoxville Fire Insurance Company, the Protection Fire Insurance Company, Knoxville Street Railroad Company, Knoxville Provident Company, and Knoxville & Western Railroad Company, also a Knight Templar. In 1870 he married Miss Ellen Carey, daughter of Hon. William Carey, of Caryville, Campbell Co., Tenn., to whom three children have been born, two now living: Mary Martin and William Carey Ross.

Michael F. Rourke, plumber and dealer in steam heating apparatus and gas fixtures, Knoxville, Tenn., was born in Ireland in 1844, and in 1861 he immigrated to America and located in New York City. At first he was employed to sweep a store, but afterward learned the plumber's trade and worked at this until 1871. He afterward worked in Chicago, St. Louis, Memphis, Cincinnati, and finally, in 1879, came to Knoxville. Having saved his earnings he invested them in plumber's supplies, and took as partner a contractor and builder who failed, ruining both. These were hard times for Mr. Rourke. Finding himself in debt, and with nothing to go on he redoubled his efforts and soon began to rise again, becoming one of the leading plumbers of the South. To him was intrusted the mammoth task of fitting up the East Tennessee Insane Asylum. In 1875, while in Cincinnati, he was united in marriage to Miss Mary McDonough, who presented him with five children—one son and four daughters. As a business man Mr. Rourke has been quite successful, and now has a good store house, stock and other property.

Hon. William Rule, editor-in-chief of the *Knoxville Journal*, stands in the front rank of Tennessee journalists. He was born in Knox County in 1839, and passed his boyhood days on the farm, but before reaching the years of manhood he left the parental roof and entered the newspaper office of Parson Brownlow, who was then publishing the *Knoxville Whig*. He soon became Brownlow's trusted friend, and remained with him through all the days of strife preceding the war, and they ever after remained fast political friends. In 1858 Mr. Rule married Lucy A. Maxey, a native of Knox County, and to them were born six children. After Brownlow's departure from Knoxville in 1862, our subject enlisted in the Sixth Tennessee Union Infantry, commanded by Col. Joseph A. Cooper, and soon became adjutant of the regiment, which position he held until the close of the war, sharing in all the battles of the Army of the Cumberland. At the close of hostilities he returned home, and was the same, year elected county court clerk, and after being re-elected resigned in 1870 to re-enter journalism. He edited the *Chronicle* until 1875, when Gov. Brownlow, whose term as United States senator had just expired, purchased an interest in the paper, and the weekly edition from this time took the name of the *Whig and Chronicle*. The paper was thus edited until Brownlow's death and then by our subject alone until 1882, at which date he sold out, and soon after, with Mr. S. Marfield, began the publication of the *Daily Journal*. In 1873 he was elected mayor of Knoxville, and a municipal committee waited upon the President and secured a special order by which he was allowed to serve (although without salary) and remained in the Government service, he having previously been appointed special agent of the postoffice department. He was the same year appointed postmaster of Knoxville, which position he retained until 1880, when he was a delegate to the national Republican convention, and during the same year entered the race for Congress, but met the fate of many other editors who fearlessly uphold their views by their pen, and afterward enter the political field. Frederick Rule, father of our subject, was born in Knox County in 1817, and resided in that county until his death in 1874. The mother, Sarah E. (Brakebill) Rule, was a native of Blount County, Tenn., and died in 1883. William was the first-born of six children, five of whom are still living.

W. L. Russell, a merchant at Concord, was born January 11, 1832, in Blount County, Tenn. When sixteen years of age he came to Knox County, where he has since lived. He is the fifth of seven children born to John H. and Annie (Gillespie) Russell. John H. Russell was born in Knox County, January 3, 1796, where he grew to manhood. He then went to Blount County, where he resided until his death in August, 1878. He was a successful farmer and a remarkably energetic and enterprising man. His wife was born near Little River in Blount County, where she was reared, and where she married John H. Russell. She died August 3, 1841. W. L. Russell received his education in the common schools of Blount and Knox Counties. At the age of sixteen he began working for himself as clerk in a general store. At the age of twenty he became a member of the firm of M. & R. Russell, of Campbell Station, which partnership existed about seven years. After this he came to Concord, and became a member of the firm of Pate & Russell. Mr. Pate retired in 1878, since which time Mr. Russell has been a member of the firm of W. L. Russell & Co., and of Cox & McNutt. In May, 1868, he married Miss Dannie J. Evans, a daughter of Daniel and Elizabeth (Harrison) Evans. Her father was born in North Carolina, and reared in Cocke County, Tenn., where he died in September, 1845. He was a successful farmer. Her mother, Mrs. Evans, was born in Jefferson County on the French Broad River, and died in June, 1863. They were both of Scotch-Irish descent. To our subject and wife were born nine children: Frank P. (deceased), Joseph E., John P., Lizzie Kate, Linda A., Anna M., Margaret A., William L. and Dannie E. (deceased). Mr. and Mrs. Russell are members of the Presbyterian Church. He was previously a Whig, but since the war has voted the Democratic ticket and is now in full accord with the Prohibition party.

D. R. Samuel & Son. D. R. Samuel, senior member of the above mentioned firm, is a native of South Wales, England, born in 1832. In 1854 he married Mary Bynon, a native of Carbondale, Penn., born in 1835. He came to Knoxville in 1872, and founded the present manufactory. He was one of the organizers of Market Square Street Railway Company, of Knoxville, of which he is vice-president. He was also one of the founders of Pilgrim Congregational Church, of which he and wife are members. W. B. Samuel, junior member of the above firm, was born at Pittston, Penn., in 1856, and remained there until his sixteenth year, acquiring his early education in the local schools. He attended the University of Tennessee, at Knoxville in 1873-75, and in 1878 graduated from Eastman's College, Poughkeepsie, N. Y. He became a member of the above firm in 1877, and has since occupied the position of superintendent and bookkeeper. In 1881 he wedded Mary P. Tustin, a native of Baltimore, Md., and the daughter of John D. Tustin, a commission merchant of Philadelphia. To this union were born two sons and one daughter: Philip, born in 1883; Joe, born in 1885, and Ruth, born in 1887. Mrs. Samuel is a member of the Pilgrim Congregational Church. In the board of enterprise, organized in 1884, which organization accomplished great and lasting benefit to Knoxville, Mr. W. B. Samuel was chairman of the committee of manufacturers, the duties of which office he discharged in a satisfactory manner. He is a member of East Tennessee Lodge, No. 34, I. O. O. F., and for four years represented it in the Grand Lodge.

E. J. Sanford, vice-president of the East Tennessee National Bank, president of the Knoxville & Ohio Railroad, and a member of the wholesale drug firm of Sanford, Chamberlain & Albert, is a native of Connecticut, where he was reared and educated. He came to Knoxville in 1853, and engaged in the lumber trade until the commencement of the war. In 1860 he married Miss Emma Chavanes, to whom ten children have been born, six still living—three sons and three daughters. Edward T., the eldest son, is a graduate of the University of Tennessee, and is now attending the Harvard Law School. At the breaking out of the war our subject joined a company for the Union Army, which went to Kentucky, where many of them enlisted, but owing to bad health Mr. Sanford returned to Connecticut. He returned to Knoxville in 1883, with Burnside's Army, and established his wholesale drug house in 1864 under the firm name of E. J. Sanford & Co., which company existed until 1872, when the present firm was formed. They employ four traveling salesmen, and in volume of trade rank among the largest drug firms of the South. At the death of Maj. O'Conner Mr. Sanford was elected president of the Mechanic's Bank, but after its establishment upon a firm basis, dissolved his connection with that bank, though requested by every director not to do so. In 1882, he was elected vice-president of the East Tennessee National Bank, which position he now holds. He has been one of the directors of the Kentucky & Ohio Railroad about ten years, and was elected president in 1886. He is the only director of the East Tennessee & Georgia Railroad, residing in Tennessee if not in the South. He is president of the Coal Creek Mining & Manufacturing Company and of the Knoxville Woolen Mills, and has been, for a term of years, president of the board of education for the Knoxville city schools. His parents, John W. and Altha (Fanton) Sanford, are natives of Connecticut, and still reside on the homestead of our subject's grandfather in Connecticut at the ripe old age of eighty-seven and eighty-eight years respectively.

R. H. Sansom, assistant postmaster of Knoxville, Tenn., was born at Round Rock, Williamson Co., Tex., September 8, 1854, and is the son of Richard and Mrs. Mary Agnes Sansom. The father was born October 28, 1828, and was the son of Dr. D. N. Sansom, of Columbia, Tenn. He died June 13, 1880. The mother was born July 3, 1831, and is the daughter of Matthew D. Cooper, and sister of ex-United States Senator Henry Cooper (deceased). She is now a resident of Georgetown, Williamson Co, Tex. Our subject was reared until his sixteenth year in Texas. He then came to Tennessee, and attended the Montgomery Bell Academy, at Nashville. After this he went to Columbia, Tenn., where he acted as deputy clerk and master of the Maury Chancery Court, under his uncle, D. B. Cooper. He next practiced law for a number of years in Columbia, and then located at Washington City, where he was extensively engaged in contracting in partnership with Messrs. D. B. Cooper and J. W. Whitthorne. September 3, 1876, he wedded Loulie, youngest daughter of the late Gen. Felix K. Zollicoffer. She was born February 8, 1856, at the old Zollicoffer homestead, at Nashville. In January, 1881, he removed to Knoxville, and entered the firm of Frierson & Morgan, marble dealers. At the dissolution of that firm he became a member of the Crescent Marble Company, of Knoxville, of which he had practical charge until November, 1885, and yet retains stock in the same. He was appointed to his present position in November, 1885. He is a member of Felix K. Zollicoffer Camp, No. 3, Confederate Veterans, and is Grand Master of Oriental Lodge, No. 453, F. & A. M., of Knoxville. He is also Second Lieutenant Commander of Knoxville Consistory No. 10, and also Generalissimo of Cour de Leon Commandery No. 9, K. T., of Knoxville. He and Mrs. Sansom are members of the First Presbyterian Church.

H. Schubert, owner and proprietor of the beautiful and popular Schubert's Hotel, situated at the corner of Cumberland and Gay Streets, was born in Germany, in 1842, and came to New York City in 1857. He remained there three years, then came to Nashville, Tenn., and engaged in the restaurant and retail liquor business until 1865, after which he continued in the same business two years in Chattanooga, and in Grainger and Union Counties. In 1872 he came to Knoxville, where he continued the same business until May 10, 1875, when he opened out the nucleus of his present model hotel. By 1880 he found his patronage increasing to such an extent that additions were made to his already large building, but he again found himself inadequate to accommodate his rapidly increasing number of guests. In December, 1885, he completed the hotel as it is at present. The building is three stories high, fronts 80 feet on Gay Street and 150 feet on Cumberland, and possesses all the conveniencies of modern architectural improvements. In 1869 he married Hannah Furner, a native of Union County, to whom one son, A. A. N. Schubert was born; he is still residing with his father. The death of Mr. Schubert's life companion occurred in October, 1886. She was a member of the First Baptist Church. Our subject's parents, A. and D. (Alexander) Schubert, were both natives of Germany, where the mother still lives and where the father died in 1875. Our subject was the eldest of six children, four still living—one in Chicago, one in Australia, one in Berlin and our subject in Knoxville, Tenn.

Dr. John R. Scott was born in Boyle County, Ky., near Danville, July 6, 1828, and is the son of Col. C. C. and Elizabeth B. (Westerfield) Scott. The father was a native Virginian, and of Irish descent. The mother was born in Pennsylvania, and was of French-German descent. They were early settlers in Kentucky. Our subject graduated at Franklin College, Tennessee, in 1848 and studied medicine at Athens, Ala., from 1851 to 1854, and was licensed to practice in the latter year. In 1856 he began practicing in Union County, Tenn., and continued there until 1857, when he returned to Athens, Ala. Here he remained until 1862, when he was employed as surgeon at Post Hospital, Strawberry Plains, and remained there until 1863. December 6, 1865, he married Miss Callie Shropshire, and to them were born these children: C. C., R. L., J. L., N. R., D. H., E. A. and M. A. In 1863 our subject came to Union County, Tenn., where he remained until 1870, since which time he has practiced at Graveston, Tenn., where he owns 175 acres of land. He has been United States examining surgeon for Union County, Tenn., is a Democrat in politics and a Master Mason, Graveston Lodge, No. 321. He is a relative of Gen. Winfield Scott and Charles Scott, ex-governor of Kentucky. He has written both prose and poetry for the local press, and is the author of medical works which he has not yet finished.

Frank A. R. Scott was born in Knox County in 1827, and has always resided in this county. He began operating a linseed oil mill in 1850, and a tannery in 1851, both at the present location of the Knoxville Leather Company. He sold the entire property in 1853, the tannery then being run by an incorporated company until the close of the war, when it was purchased by our subject and his present partner, John S. Van Gilder. They manufacture all kinds of leather, and consume about 6,000 hides annually. In 1857 he wedded Miss Margaretta F. Deaderick, a native of Knoxville, to whom eleven children have been born. Our subject's grandfather, James Scott, of Scotch-Irish descent, located in Knox County about 1820. He established a carding and fulling mill which in all probability was the first mill established in Tennessee. The father of our subject, James Scott, Jr., was born in 1797, and operated the mill mentioned above in connection with farming. His death occurred in 1838. The mother of Frank A. R. Scott, Eliza J. (Ramsey) Scott, was a sister of Dr. Ramsey, the author of "Annals of Tennessee." Her death occurred in 1858. Of her family of five children all are still living. Two of her sons were in the Confederate Army—one was wounded at Chattanooga and the other at Shiloh.

James N. Seaton, farmer, was born April 3, 1815, in the locality where he has since resided. He is the second of eleven children, two now living—his elder sister and himself—born to James and Elizabeth (Love) Seaton. The father was born February 27, 1788, and died in 1853. He served as magistrate for about twenty years, giving universal satisfaction. He was an elder in the Presbyterian Church for many years, was a very efficient and successful school teacher, took an active part in all public affairs, and was a highly respected citizen. His wife, Elizabeth (Love) Seaton, was born about 1793 in Lancaster County, Penn., and was brought by her parents to Tennessee some time before the celebrated Cavett massacre. Her father, Mr. John Love, was a highly respected man, and an elder in the Presbyterian Church. He lived to a ripe old age. He had but one son, who moved to McMinn County, and was a prominent citizen; he died in 1882. James N. Seaton, our subject, received his education in the common schools of the Tenth District. He assisted his father on the farm until twenty-one years of age, when he married Miss Rachel Craig, who died in 1849. His second wife was a Miss Caroline Wills, who bore him four children: Mary (Mrs. Thomas Fox), Caroline D. (deceased), Sophronia J. and an infant deceased. Mrs. Seaton died March 29, 1857, and in October, 1857, he married Miss Margaret C. Good, and to this union were born five children: Kate, Emma, Susan, James, Robert and one who died in infancy. Mrs. Seaton died November 2, 1881, and February 8, 1883, Mr. Seaton married Mrs. Sarah Louesa McCampbell, formerly Miss S. L. Bond, the daughter of George and Eliza (Swan) Bond. Mrs. Bond died in 1869, but Mr. Bond is still living, ninety years old, and is still comparatively hale and hearty. He has been a ruling elder in the Presbyterian Church for about sixty years. Our subject began life a poor man, but now has a good farm of 400 acres, well improved, and located one mile north of the State road. His land is very valuable for the excellent marble which is to be found on it. It is considered one of the largest and best veins of marble to be found in Eastern Tennessee. Mr. and Mrs. Seaton and children are members of the Presbyterian Church, of which Mr. Seaton has been deacon and elder for over twenty years. Mr. Seaton is a Democrat in politics, and was captain and adjutant for several years of the State militia. He is a man of very rugged constitution, is seventy-two years old, and has never taken any medicine except for rheumatism, with which he is occasionally slightly afflicted. He is one of the county's very best citizens.

J. F. Sharp, a successful agriculturist of the Eighth District, was born May 15, 1853, in Claiborne County, Tenn., and came to Knox County in October, 1882. He is the eldest of four children born to William and Elizabeth (Mason) Sharp, both of whom were born and reared in Claiborne County, where they are now living. The father is one of the most successful farmers of the locality in which he resides and was a Master Mason. Our subject was educated in the common schools of Claiborne County. He remained with and assisted his father on the farm until he was twenty-four years of age, when he married Miss Mary Condray, a daughter of John and Carley Condray. They were highly respected citizens; both died in the year 1874. Five children were the fruits of our subject's union, viz.: Minnie May, Elmer, Parris (deceased), Amy and Condray. Mr. Sharp is a Democrat in politics, casting his first presidential vote for Samuel J. Tilden, and he and Mrs. Sharp are members of the Baptist Church, of which he has been clerk of the sessions three years. He has a good farm of 100 acres of land, well improved and cultivated, and is considered an excellent citizen by all his acquaintances.

Paris M. Shell, farmer of the Third Civil District of Knox County, Tenn., was born on Beaver Creek, Knox County, November 3, 1841, and is the son of Christian and Susan (Shell) Shell. The father is a native of Montgomery County, Va., born in 1811, and is the son of Jacob Shell, also of Virginia. Christian Shell came to Tennessee about 1838, and located in Knox County, but subsequently removed to Sweet Water Valley, McMinn County, where he is now engaged in farming. He is a member of the Presbyterian Church. His wife was a native of Tennessee, born in Knox County about 1818, and was the daughter of John and Nancy (Persley) Shell; she died in 1880. John, the maternal grandfather of our subject, was a native of Tennessee, and served in the campaign of removing the Cherokee Indians from their reservation. Our subject was reared in McMinn County and acquired his education at Mouse Creek and at Maryville. At the age of twenty-two years he enlisted in the Federal Army, joining Company I, One Hundred and Fifteenth Indiana Regiment of infantry enlisting for six months and serving nine. He was in the neighborhood of Knoxville during the siege of that city, and was with his regiment at the engagements of Blue Springs and Walker's Ford on Clinch River. He was mustered out of service in February, 1864, and returned to McMinn County, where he followed farming. October 20, 1868, he married Lucy J. Cole, daughter of Sampson and Nancy J. (Anderson) Cole, and to this union were born two children: Lula E., born July 15, 1869, and died March 13, 1873, and William T., born September 22, 1870, and died October 25, 1872. October 14, 1874, he married M. Crippen, a native of Knox County, born September 13, 1847, and the daughter of William and Dicy (Tindell) Crippen, both natives of Tennessee. William, the father, was born in

1811 and died in 1872. He was a son of James and Martha (Hall) Crippen, the former being a native of Virginia, and the latter of North Carolina. Dicy, the mother, was born in 1811, and is the daughter of Samuel and Zillah (Parker) Tindell, both of whom were natives of North Carolina. She makes her home with her son, P. M. Shell. To our subject and wife were born five children, viz.: Sanford C., born March 4, 1876, and died June 18, 1876; Albert E., born August 19, 1877, and died May 1, 1880, and Lina B. born December 23, 1878. Two children died in infancy. The mother is a member of the Methodist Episcopal Church. In 1875 Mr. Shell removed to Knox County, where he has established himself as an enterprising and worthy citizen.

Lazarus C. Shepard, trustee of the deaf and dumb school at Knoxville, is a son of Sueton and Dymah A. (Hurd) Shepard, natives of Connecticut, where they are now peacefully sleeping. Their family consisted of eight children—three sons and five daughters. Our subject was born June 2, 1816, in Connecticut, where he grew up and received a limited education. He then followed the trade of his father, which was that of a carpenter, and for some time ran a car shop and sash and blind factory. In 1837 he married Miss Emily E. Strong, who presented him with five children, three now living—two sons and a daughter. Both sons were Confederate soldiers in the late war. In 1854 Mr. Shepard came to Knoxville, and in connection with two partners, opened car works which were burned during the war. After that event he engaged in the rolling mill business for a time and then turned his attention to the manufacture of furniture and undertaking, which he has followed ever since. Mrs. Shepard died in 1882. Mr. Shepard and all the children are members of the Protestant Episcopal Church, of which he is also senior warden. For about eight years he has been magistrate, and he also filled the position of alderman for some years in Knoxville. He is president of the Knoxville Building Loan & Association, treasurer of the Masonic lodge and of the I. O. O. F. lodge, and is secretary and treasurer of the Knox County Humane Society. He is one among the old and highly respected citizens of Knoxville.

Philo B. Shepard, chief of the Knoxville Fire Brigade, was born in 1841 in Bridgeport, Conn., and is the son of L. C. and Emily (Strong) Shepard, both natives of Connecticut, but since 1853 citizens of Knoxville, the father being senior partner of the firm of Shepard, Mann & Johnston. Our subject grew to manhood in Knoxville, and was educated in the University of Tennessee (then known as East Tennessee University), which institution he continued in up to the war. He connected himself with the Fifth Tennessee Cavalry, Confederate States

Army, at the formation of that regiment at the commencement of the war. He remained with this regiment, serving in various capacities until early in 1862, when he was ordered on duty at Loudon in connection with the hospitals, in which capacity he served until the Kentucky campaign, when he connected himself with the Texas and Arkansas Brigade, during which campaign he occupied various staff positions. On the return of the army from Kentucky he was compelled, on account of disease contracted during the campaign, to retire from active service. He then engaged in business in Loudon until the evacuation of East Tennessee by the Confederates, when he was carried to Augusta, Ga., where he remained until Gen. Longstreet started the advance on Knoxville. He then connected himself with the Georgia Brigade of Cavlary as assistant adjutant-general, in which capacity he served until Longstreet raised the siege, after which he served in the ordnance department. On the return of the army to Georgia he was commissioned first lieutenant, and assigned to Company K, Sixth Georgia Cavalry, in which capacity he served until nearly the close of the war, when he was ordered to Augusta, Ga., as assistant provost-marshal, and this position, as he says himself, was the most trying of the war, as he was always on duty. After the close of the war he removed to Mobile, Ala. (the sentiment against ex-Confederates being very strong in East Tennessee), and engaged in the commission business. In 1867 he moved to Selma, Ala., where he engaged in the life insurance business, and later in agricultural implements and machinery and planting. January 8, 1868, he was married to Miss Lou Coleman, of Dallas County. In 1876 he removed to Knoxville and established a steam laundry, whlch business he followed until 1880. He then engaged in business in Lebanon, Tenn., for one year, when he moved to Arkansas, and engaged in the agricultural implements and machinery business until 1882, when on account of the sickness and subsequent death of his mother he returned to Knoxville, Tenn., since which time he has been connected with the firm of H. G. Mead & Co. He was elected to his present position March 26, 1886, a position to which he is peculiarly adapted, having been connected with fire departments since his eighteenth year. In December, 1885, he organized Felix K. Zollicoffer Camp, Confederate Veterans, of which he is First Lieutenant Commander. Both he and wife are members of the Episcopal Church.

Prof. J. W. Sherman, teacher and farmer, was born at Jonesboro, Washington Co., Tenn., December 22, 1840, and is the son of James and Emily (Chadwich) Sherman. The father was a native of North Carolina, and of English descent. The mother was born in Germany.

Our subject received his education at Maryville, Blount County, and also at Bethany College, West Virginia. He then took an extra course at the State University, at Lexington, Ky., and while there taught the primary department in the Woodland school of the university. He afterward took charge of Rice's Academy, in Garrard County, Ky., where he remained two years, and then came to Tennessee. In 1872 he married Miss Cordelia M. Reeder, daughter of Hon. Alexander Reeder, of Knoxville. The fruits of this union were six children, the eldest of whom (a son) died in infancy. Those living are Alzada Tennessee, Linnie Belle, Mary Effie, Emma Hazel, and the youngest (a boy) is named John Thomas Wentforth. After our subject's marriage he engaged in farming, and this, in connection with teaching, has been his occupation through life. In September, 1886, he took charge of the Walnut Grove Academy, where he is at the present time. He is the owner of 120 acres of land in the Sixteenth District, a part of it good timbered land.

Isaac Sherrod, a native of Knox County, Tenn., was born June 5, 1842, and is the son of Jonathan and Charlotta (Bales) Sherrod. The father was a native Tennessean, born December 25, 1813, and died in the year 1854. The mother was born in the same State in 1812, and died in 1860. Our subject was educated in the country schools, and in 1862 was united in marriage to Miss Elizabeth Pittille, who bore him seven children—two are married, one is in the Walnut Grove school, two are at home, and two are deceased. In 1880 our subject took for his second wife Miss Margaret Howell, a native of Knox County, born March 25, 1845, and this marriage resulted in the birth of five children. Our subject is an energetic, wide-awake farmer, and his fine farm of 165 acres situated on Holston River, in the Sixteenth District, is well cultivated and well improved. Mr. Sherrod is a Republican in politics, and one of the county's best citizens.

William Shinpaugh was born in Roane County near Loudon County, Tenn., July 16, 1818, and is the youngest of three children born to Henry and Elizabeth (McDaniel) Shinpaugh, natives of North Carolina. Their parents came to Knox County about 1770, where Mr. and Mrs. Shinpaugh were married. Of their children none are living except our subject. Henry Shinpaugh served three years in Capt. Steward's company, and three years after the war he died from the effects of exposure during that struggle. Our subject attended school only about twelve months in his life. When about nineteen years old he married Miss Sallie Letsinger, who was born in June, 1825, and was the daughter of John and Joanna (Buckaloo) Letsinger. Her father was a very successful farmer, and died in 1881. To Mr. and Mrs. Shinpaugh were born these children:

Hugh, John (deceased), Calvin, James, George, William, Alexander, Joanna (Mrs. W. Young), Elizabeth (Mrs. Young) and Sallie (Mrs. E. E. Duncan). Mr. Shinpaugh is a Republican in politics, and he and Mrs. Shinpaugh are members of the Methodist Episcopal Church South. Mr. Shinpaugh came from Roane to Knox County about 1833, and settled first in Hardin Valley. He came to Hind's Valley about 1860. He has always followed farming, and has been quite successful.

J. W. Shipe, one of the leading farmers of the Third District of Knox County, Tenn., was born in that county and district on February 26, 1830, and is the son of Henry W. and Deborah (Scaggs) Shipe. The father was a native of Virginia, and was born in 1797, his father being a native of Pennsylvania and his mother of Maryland. Henry W., the father, came to Knox County in 1807, at a time when there were but few settlers here, and the country was a wild and unbroken forest and canebrake. He followed farming, and served in the war of 1812 with Gen. Jackson, and was at the battle of New Orleans. He enlisted when but eighteen years of age, and was in Gen. Coffee's command. He was a member of the Baptist Church for over forty years, and died November 9, 1879, on his ninetieth birthday, leaving a name universally respected for upright and honest dealing. Deborah, the mother, was born in Knox (now Union) County, of English parentage, in 1796, and died in 1871. She was also a member of the Baptist Church. Our subject was reared on the farm, and attended the neighborhood schools. When about eighteen years of age he left home and learned the tanner's trade. Two years later he went out to California, where he remained for three years and six months, spending the time in mining for gold and lumbering. He returned to his home in Knox County January 30, 1857, and has since resided in the county, following farming as an avocation, making a success of the same, being now one of the most highly respected citizens of the district. He joined the Union Baptist Chuch in 1861, and three years later was elected deacon of that church, which office he holds at present. He was married, July 1, 1857, to Ruth C. Crippen, a native of Knox County, who was born August 8, 1833, and is the daughter of William P. and Dicy (Tindell) Crippen. Her father served as sheriff of Knox County for six years, and was a well-known and highly respected citizen, he dying December 13, 1872. To this union nine children have been born, eight of whom are living, as follows: George W., born April 2, 1858; Apolinia E., born August 18, 1859; William H. McC., born July 11, 1862; Martha E., born August 9, 1861, and died August 14, 1861; Joseph F., born April 14, 1864; Charles Russell, born August 11, 1866; James C., born February 11, 1868; Alvin B., born February 2, 1871, and John D., born June 4, 1873. The wife and four children are members of the Union Baptist Church.

W. H. Simmonds, secretary and treasurer of the Knoxville Fire Insurance Company, is a son of Cyrus Simmonds, a native of Virginia, who chose his wife from one of North Carolina's fair daughters. In 1830 they moved to West Tennessee, and reared a family of five children —two sons and three daughters. One of the sons, Dr. James H. Simmonds, was a surgeon of a Florida regiment during the late war. The father was a merchant by occupation, and accumulated a large fortune, which was swept away by the war. The parents are now living with our subject, and both are in their eighty-fifth year. Our subject was born in West Tennessee in 1836, and received his education at West Tennessee College. In 1856 he went to Nashville to engage in mercantile pursuits. In 1858 he married Miss Lillie, daughter of Col. W. B. A. Ramsey, and to them were born three children—one son and two daughters. In 1861 Mr. Simmonds was appointed commissary by Gen. Bragg, which position he held until the close of the war. He then returned to Nashville and began merchandising, first as a member of the firm of Dodd & Simmonds, and afterward of the firm of W. H. Simmonds & Co. In 1872 he came to Knoxville, and since that time has been engaged in merchandising, in real estate and in insurance business. He was elected secretary and treasurer of the Knoxville Fire Insurance Company in 1880, and he also holds the position of secretary and treasurer of the Powell Land & Kaolin Company, and president of the Mechanic's Building and Loan Association. He is a Mason, and he and wife are members of the Third Presbyterian Church.

Jesse Simpson, farmer, is the son of Jesse, Sr., and Mary (Giffin) Simpson. The father and mother are both natives of Virginia, and of English descent, their ancestors being natives of New England. The father was the son of John Simpson. Our subject was born in Virginia; his education was very limited, and obtained in the rude and primitive log schoolhouses of early times. He assisted his father on the farm until twenty-two years of age, after which he was engaged for a short time in cabinet-making, and then began trading on the Tennessee River. In 1836 Miss Margaret Coker, daughter of Charles Coker, became his wife, and two children—a son and a daughter—were born to this marriage; the son died when a year old, and the daughter, Mary Sophia, is the wife of B. S. B. Love. Mrs. Simpson died in September, 1840, and in May, 1842, Mr. Simpson took for his second wife Miss Mary J. Anderson, daughter of James and Anna Anderson. This marriage resulted in the birth of two sons and four daughters: Margaret C., Joseph Alexander, Sarah Elizabeth, David La Fayette and Delilah Jane and Telitha Ann (twins). Since about the time of our subject's first marriage, he has followed farming. He owns 160 acres of land on the opposite side of the Tennessee from Knoxville, all well improved and well stocked. He, his wife, and all the children are members of the Baptist Church, he having been deacon in the same for more than thirty-five years. He is a Republican in politics.

J. A. Smith, agriculturist of the Eighth District, was born December 11, 1822, in Grainger (now Union) County, Tenn. He came to Tennessee in September, 1882, and settled where he now resides. He is one of seven children born to Josiah and Nancy (Stanley) Smith. Josiah was born in Virginia, came to Tennessee with his father when a boy, and settled in Union County, Tenn., north of Maynardville. He was a successful farmer, and much esteemed citizen. He died about 1836, aged fifty-five years. He was a soldier in the Creek Indian war under Gen. Jackson. The mother of our subject was born and reared in Union County, Tenn. Both parents were of English descent. Harbord Smith, grandfather of our subject, moved from Tennessee to Alabama at a very early day, where he died. He was a very successful and practical business man, and accumulated considerable property. When about twenty years of age our subject married Miss Emily Ann Buckner, a daughter of Ezra and Elizabeth (Duncan) Buckner, highly respected citizens of their locality. To our subject and wife were born twelve children: William E., Nancy B. (deceased), Mary E. (Mrs. Harris), Pernina C. (Mrs. Hamilton), Margaret B. (deceased), Joseph W., Pauline C. (Mrs. McPhetsidge), James, Hugh L. (deceased), Penelope T. (Mrs. McDowell), John L. (deceased), Laura L. and Oscar D. Mr. Smith is a stanch Republican in politics, casting his first presidential vote for J. K. Polk, and he and family are members of the Missionary Baptist Church, of which he has been deacon for over thirty years, and has only missed attending church two times in thirty-two years.

B. L. Smith, senior member of the firm of Smith & Bondurant and a prominent business man, is the son of John A. and Lucy P. (Williams) Smith, both natives of Virginia. The father was cashier of the Farmers' Bank, at Richmond, and died in 1864. The mother is still living, and makes her home with her son, B. L. Our subject, the only living child of his parents, was born in Virginia in 1846 and while growing up acquired a good education. Toward the close of the war he served two years in the Richmond Howitzers, and after the final surrender of the South moved to Virginia, where he remained until 1870. He then came to Tennessee. Two years later he located at Knoxville, and became a member of the present firm, being dealers in meat and shippers of produce. In 1877 he married Miss Bell Stover who bore him six children. Mr. Smith has been secretary and treasurer of Mabry Bell Avenue & Handle Street Railroad Company since its first organization. He is a Democrat in politics, and inherits English blood from both father and mother.

J. Allen Smith, president of the Knoxville City Mills, is the son of Burgess and H. W. (Jordan) Smith, and a native of Georgia, born in 1850. He was reared in Elbert, Ga., where he acquired his education at the public schools. He began life for himself in 1868 as clerk in a wholesale house at Atlanta, Ga. In 1871 he removed to Knoxville, Tenn., where he engaged in the grain business. In 1878 he was united in marriage to Miss Lillie Powell, who was born in Knoxville in 1855, and is the daughter of Columbus Powell. The result of this union was the birth of two children; the first, a girl, died at the age of two years. Mr. Smith founded the Knoxville City Mills Company in 1881. It began as a private enterprise, but grew in importance until in 1884 it was deemed advisable to enlist others in the building and equipping of the handsomest and most substantial plant of the kind in East Tennessee. In this year the company was organized under a charter and began their work. Mr. Smith was elected president of the company, which position he holds at the present time. The position is more important by virtue of the recent consolidation of the firm of J. Allen Smith & Co., the largest provision and grain merchants in the place, with the Knoxville City Mills Company, increasing their capital to $100,000. At this time they are erecting a large grain elevator to accommodate increasing trade. He and his wife are members of the Methodist Episcopal Church South.

W. T. Smith, farmer, was born in Knox County, Tenn., December 7, 1829, and is the eldest of eight children born to John T. and Nancy A. (Golston) Smith. The father was born in Rockbridge County, Va., and came to Knox County with his father, William Smith, in 1801. He died in 1874. William Smith, grandfather of our subject, was a native of Ireland, and came to the United States, settling first in Virginia, but afterward came to Knox County in 1811. He was a good farmer and an excellent financier. He died in 1853. Our subject received his education in the common schools of Knox County and at Ewing and Jefferson College. At the age of twenty-one he left the parental roof, and soon married Miss Lucinda E. Doak, born August 14, 1829, the daughter of H. and E. Doak. To Mr. and Mrs. Smith were born twelve children: Samuel L., Harvey (deceased), Laura Ellen (Mrs. C. G. Ninney), James B. (deceased), Lizzie, Sidney, Eugene, Luther, Sophia, Adelia (Mrs. H.

D. Boyd), Maggie and Arthur. Mr. Smith since the dissolution of the Whig party has voted the Democratic ticket. He was elected magistrate in 1870 and served eleven years. Mr. Smith has a fine farm of 350 acres in the Tennessee Valley, on which is an excellent marble quarry that yields a greater variety of fine marble than any other quarry in the State. Mr. and Mrs. Smith are members of the Presbyterian Church.

Robert Snead, M. D. (deceased), was born in Washington County, Va., December 20, 1820, and is the son of Henry and Jane (Kesner) Snead. The father was born in Halifax County, Va., in 1792, and died in Washington County of the same State in 1864. The mother was also a native of Virginia, born in 1796 and died in the year 1833. While young our subject had very poor educational advantages, but he worked hard and accumulated sufficient money to enter Emory and Henry College, Virginia. He would alternately attend college, work on the farm and teach school. He never completed his collegiate course, and took up the study of medicine, studying with his uncle in Virginia. When he became competent to practice his profession he removed to Dandridge, Tenn., where he lived and studied with another uncle. He afterward took a trip South in search of a location, but returned to Strawberry Plains, Jefferson Co., Tenn., and here located. Later he entered the Louisville (Ky.) Medical College, graduated from this institution, and then returned to Strawberry Plains, where he practiced his profession until his death, which occurred in 1882. While driving some cattle he was kicked by a horse, and lived but eight weeks after this accident. To his marriage to Miss Malinda Bryan in 1852 was born one child, a daughter who lived but four short years. Mrs. Snead was born in Tennessee January 16, 1827, and is the daughter of Hon. Allen Bryan, who was a member of the State Legislature of Tennessee at the time Knoxville was the capital of the State, and also after it was removed to Nashville. Dr. Snead was a wise and skillful physician, a man of marked and decisive character, and his death was a sad blow to his companion through life.

Joseph W. Sneed, city attorney, was born in Knox County in 1854, and has resided here since with the exception of a few years during the war, when he went with his parents to Georgia, and there remained a few months, when he returned to Knoxville, and from here went to Salem, N. C., Liberty, Va., and Atlanta, Ga. In 1867 he located again in Knoxville. He attended the State University in 1870 and 1871, and was admitted to the bar in 1875. In January, 1874, he took for his life companion Miss Lizzie D. Williams, a native of this county, who bore him two sons and three daughters, one daughter deceased. After being admitted to the bar our subject practiced alone until the present firm of Williams & Sneed was formed in 1883. He was city alderman in 1884-85, and January 1, 1886, he was elected city attorney. His parents, M. H. and Eliza D. (Williams) Sneed, were both of English descent, and natives of Davidson and Greene Counties, Tenn., respectively. In 1843, soon after their marriage, they moved to Greene County, where the father was admitted to the bar, and practiced in partnership with Judge McKinney a short time. He then came to Knoxville, and was here practicing at the time of his death. He represented his district in Congress in 1856-57, and was in the Confederate Congress. He died September 18, 1869, and the mother September 7, 1873.

George L. Snyder, farmer and dairyman, was born in Blount County, Tenn., April 28, 1856, and is the son of Col. George W. and Elizabeth (Slaughter) Snyder. Our subject attended the Maryville Normal School for four years, and the Grant Memorial University at Athens, Tenn., for two years. At the age of twenty-one he began teaching school, and followed this occupation alternately with attending college up to 1883, since which time he has followed farming. In 1882 he married Miss Fannie Pelleaux; she died in March, 1884, leaving one son, Roy Sankey. In 1886 he married Mrs. Sarah Jones, *nee* Miss Sarah Massey. She was born in North Carolina April 12, 1835, and came to Tennessee, where in 1875 she became the third wife of John A. Jones, a native of Sevier County, Tenn., born January 28, 1815, and died at his home near Knoxville August 17, 1884. He was a farmer, a lifetime member of the Baptist Church, and a kind and faithful husband and father. To the above marriage were born two sons: Charles D. and Frank J., and one daughter, Anna B.

R. A. Sterling, chairman of the county court of Knox County, was born in that county in 1842, was reared on a farm, and educated at the common schools of the county. In 1866 he went to California, where he engaged in the lumber trade until 1870. He then returned to Knox County, and embarked in the mercantile trade at Ebenezer, in which he is still interested. He was constable of his district in 1866; was elected justice of the peace of the Eleventh District in 1879, to fill an unexpired term, then in 1882 he was re-elected for a term of six years, and in January, 1882, he was elected chairman, and re-elected in January, 1886 and 1887 In 1874 he married Mrs. R. L. Morris, *nee* Walker, a native of the county, and a daughter of James and Isabella (Swan *nee* Gillespie) Sterling, natives of Knox and Blount Counties respectively. The mother's death occurred in 1849. She had three children by her first husband, one now living, and three by her union with the father of our subject, all of whom are living. The father is still living, and is a resident of Ebenezer, Knox County.

Nathan Stern, dealer in clothing and gents' furnishing goods, was born in Bavaria, in 1842, and when nineteen years of age came to New York City, where a brother and sister had preceded him. Here he worked at his trade (tinners') until 1863, when he came with his brother to Tennessee, and located in Knoxville, where they established a general merchandise store, of which our subject became a partner in 1864. The business was then carried on under the firm title of M. & N. Stern, until 1878, they having merged it into a clothing store in 1867. In 1878 they dissolved partnership, and our subject conducted the business alone until 1882; it then took the firm name of N. Stern & Co., until 1885, since which date he has again been the sole proprietor. In 1877 he married Miss Minnie Gump, a native of Philadelphia, to whom two daughters have been born. A brother of our subject's paternal grandfather, was a general in the French war, under Napoleon Bonaparte, and the maternal grandfather, Haas, was at the head of the commissary department for the French Army. The father of our subject, Joseph Stern, was a man of considerable wealth, and led a retired life in Brooklyn, N. Y., from 1868 until his death in 1883. He was also in the war of 1812, being then but a youth. He married Leanora Haas, a native of Hesse Darmstadt, whose death occured in 1865. Of the eleven children born to this marriage, five of whom are living (all in the United States), our subject is the tenth.

Joseph Churchill Strong and Gideon Hazen Strong, brothers, are farmers and stock raisers at McMillan, Knox Co., Tenn. J. C. was born September 20, 1841, at Shelbyville, Tenn.; G. H. was born October 5, 1850, at McMillan, and are the sons of Joseph Churchill Strong, M. D., born in Knoxville, Tenn., December 25, 1808. He married Sophronia, daughter of John A. and Nancy (Stone) Morrs, at Shelbyville, Tenn., September 25, 1832; she was born February 17, 1817. Their children are Prof. Robert Nilson, John Morrs, Martha Jane (wife of W. O. Monday), Charles Ready and Horace Strong, all now deceased; Joseph Churchill and Gideon Hazen Strong, of McMillan; Benjamin Rush, Mary Hazen (wife of J. W. Borches), William Erwin and Albert Newton Strong, all of Knoxville. Joseph Churchill Strong, M. D., lived at Knoxville until 1826. He then went to Shelbyville, Tenn., where he engaged in selling drugs and practicing medicine until 1847. He then removed to McMillan, Tenn., where he lived the remainder of his life, a practicing physician and farmer. He was noted for his generosity and kindness. He attended to the sick of the poor as well as of the rich. He was a great reader and thinker. He kept a record of things in general of each day for many years. He died at McMillan, Tenn., December 27, 1878. His wife Sophronia also died at McMillan, Tenn., November 20, 1867. The grandfathers of our subjects are Joseph Churchill Strong, M. D., born at Bolton, Conn., October 3, 1775 (he married Catherine, daughter of William Neilsom, at Hot Springs, N. C., December 6, 1804. She was born November 25, 1785, and died May 13, 1810), who was the son of Juda Strong, born in Bolton, Conn., November 28, 1738; who was the son of Dr. David Strong, of Bolton, Conn., born December 15, 1704, and died January 25, 1801; who was the son of John Strong, of Windsor, Conn., born December 25, 1665, and died May 29, 1749; who was the son of John Strong, Jr., of Windsor, Conn., born in England in 1626 and died February 20, 1698; who was the son of Elder John Strong, of Taunton, Somersetshire, England, born in 1605; who was the son of Richard Strong, born in the county of Caernarvon in 1561, and died at Taunton in 1613. Elder John Strong, of Taunton, moved to London and afterward to Plymouth. Having strong Puritan sympathies he sailed from Plymouth for the New World March 20, 1630, in the ship "Mary and John," Capt. Squeb, and arrived at Nantucket, Mass., about twelve miles south of Boston, Sunday, May 30, 1630. He died April 14, 1699, aged ninety-four. The grandfather of our subjects, Joseph Churchill Strong, married Jane Kain for his second wife, May 23, 1811. She was born January 30, 1788, and died October 3, 1846. He entered the United States Navy as assistant surgeon, under John Adams' administration, where he continued until the sale of the navy by Jefferson in 1801. He was aboard the frigate "Trumbull" the day she was sold, and often said pleasantly that he came near being sold with her, as the auctioneer offered her with all her contents to the highest bidder. He settled at Knoxville, Tenn., in 1804, where he became eminent in his profession. In 1816 he became a member of the First Presbyterian Church of Knoxville, and afterward became an elder in the same. He died November 3, 1844. Our subjects received a common-school education, and have devoted most of their lives to farming and stock raising. They own a farm of 1,000 acres in the Eighteenth District on the Holston River; through it passes the East Tennessee, Virginia & Georgia Railway. The land is fertile, and is well improved. Their dwelling is handsome and commodious, and is supplied with hydrants, whose aqueduct is a natural spring a quarter of a mile away, and a force pump, operated by water power, forces the water through the dwelling in bath room, water closet, etc. In the way of fine stock they imported from Holland some Holstein cattle that are very fine. These brothers have always been closely associated together in their pursuits, and although they commenced with very little capital, have succeeded in accumulating considerable wealth. June 7, 1877, G. H. married Miss Elizabeth Brice, daughter of N. B. Brice. She was born in Knox County February 11, 1858, and by her marriage became the mother of Ralph, born September 3, 1878, died August 16, 1882; Mary Eliza, born February 8, 1882; Sophronia, September 25, 1884; Gideon Rush, February 26, 1887. Both our subjects are members of the Masonic fraternity.

Alex. Summers, editor-in-chief of the Knoxville Daily *Tribune*, is a native of Knox County, Tenn., born in 1856, and a graduate of the University of Tennessee in the class of 1876. He taught school in the county part of the time while procuring his education, and after graduating continued that occupation a short time. In 1878 he accepted the position as reporter for the Atlanta *Daily Post*, of which he afterward became assistant editor. In August, 1880, he, in connection with Messrs. Bean & Wallace, began the publication of the Knoxville *Daily Tribune*, successors to Frank Q. Moses & Co. He was at first city editor and afterward editor-in-chief. In 1881 he was united in marriage to Miss Kate Smith, who has presented him with one son, named Norman. Mrs. Summers was reared in Atlanta, Ga. George W. Summers, father of our subject, was born in Knox County in 1822, and has always resided in the county. He is at present residing in the Thirteenth District, where he was justice of the peace many years, and where he was also county surveyor eighteen years. The mother, Mary (Johnson) Summers, is also a native of Knox County. Our subject is the eldest of a family consisting of himself and four sisters, all still living. His paternal great-grandparents came from England and located in Virginia, where the grandfather, Thomas Summers, was born, and there in the early settlement of Knox County, located and afterward died.

J. A. Swan, county trustee, is a native of Knox County, born in 1857, and the only son of a family of six children born to W. H. and Mary A. (Seaton) Swan. The father is also a native of Knox County, born in 1817, and is now a resident of Knoxville. He was justice of the peace of Knox County from 1848 to 1856, and then deputy sheriff six years. He was sheriff two years, tax collector two years, and county court clerk a short time in the year 1864. He was then city recorder from 1866 to 1867, after which he filled an unexpired term of over a year in the criminal court clerk's office. He was city tax collector one year, and in 1878 was elected county trustee. He was re-elected in 1882, but resigned in 1884, our subject succeeding him. The mother of our subject was also a native of Knox County, and died in 1880. Our subject was reared and educated in Knox County, completing his studies at the University in 1877. In 1878 he acted as deputy trustee under his father, whom he succeeded in 1884, and has filled the office since that date. In 1878 he married M. J. Partin, a native of Arkansas, who bore her husband two children: Clarence L. and Anna Belle. Mr. Swan's paternal grandparents were born and reared in Tennessee, and came to Knox County in the early part of the present century.

Charles A. Sweet, superintendent of the Brookside Mills, Knoxville, Tenn., is a native of Rhode Island, born in 1860, and the son of Charles J. and Mary J. (Whipple) Sweet, both natives of Rhode Island, now residing in Knoxville, Tenn. Charles A. attended the public schools, and was to study medicine, but contracted the measles which settled in his eyes, and his physicians assured him that unless he gave up his studies he would become blind. He then began work in the cotton-mill at Killingly, Conn., where his father was agent, and went through all the different departments, and for three years acted as overseer of carding. At the age of twenty he accepted a situation as superintendent in a small yarn mill of 6,000 spindles, which position he held for one year and a half, and was then tendered the situation of superintendent of the Lippitt Mills, Phenix, R. I. He held this situation for three years, and then resigned to come to Knoxville to assist his father in starting the Brookside Mills of Knoxville. While at Lippitt Mills Charles A. was known as the boy superintendent, being the youngest superintendent in the State.

R. R. Swepson, president of the Knoxville Gas Light Company, is a native of Virginia, and came to Knoxville in December, 1866. He was president of the First National Bank until it closed in December, 1872. In July, 1884, he became a member of the firm of Briscoes, Swepson & Co., of which he is still a member. In September, 1876, he was elected president of the Knoxville Gas Light Company, and is the principal stockholder of the company which was organized in 1856. He is also stockholder in the Island Home and East Tennessee Insurance Companies, Coal Creek Mining & Manufacturing Company and Poplar Creek Mining Company. Our subject is the third child, and the only surviving member of a family of seven children born to William M. and Ann E. (Redd) Swepson, both of whom were natives of Virginia, Mecklenburg and Prince Edward Counties respectively. They both died in the former named county. Our subject's ancestors were of Scotch descent, and settled in Princess Anne County, Va.

Jacob Tarwater, farmer, was born in Knox County, Tenn., April 29, 1830, and is the son of William and Judia (Childres) Tarwater. The father was born in Blount County, Tenn., February 14, 1790, and died at his home in Knox County September 21, 1857. The mother was born in Sullivan County, Tenn, April 20, 1794, and also died at her home in Knox County, October 28, 1866. Our subject received a limited education in the country schools, and early in life began cultivating the soil. In 1855 he married Evaline French, a native of Knox County, Tenn., born July 19, 1828, and the daughter of George French. She is of German descent, and an earnest worker in the Methodist Episcopal Church. Although they have had no children of their own, six orphan children have been reared by them, thus clearly showing Mr. Tarweather's charitable, benevolent nature. He has ever been a zealous Republican, and was a strong Union man during the late war. He has been an earnest and energetic farmer, and though he commenced the occupation of farming without capital he has accumulated wealth and is the owner of 375 acres of Knox County land. He has never held any civil or political office.

E. A. Taylor, D. D., pastor of the First Baptist Church, of Knoxville, Tenn., is a native of Louisiana, born October 16, 1853, the son of A. B. and E. C. (Fluker) Taylor, both natives of Louisiana. The father was a physician by profession, and served as a general in the war between the United States and Mexico. He died in 1855. The mother was born in 1830, is still living, and is the daughter of Col. Robert Fluker, an officer in the war of 1812. Our subject was reared in Natchez, Miss., where he acquired his early education in the primary schools. Desiring to prepare himself for the ministry, he entered and graduated from Mississippi College (Baptist), and followed this with a two years' course at the Baptist Theological Seminary, at Louisville, Ky. His pastoral duties began at Grenada, Miss., in 1878, where he took charge of the Baptist Church of that place, and continued as pastor for four years. During that period, however, he was given a vacation in order to travel through Europe, and visit Palestine and other points in the East. His duties in Grenada were pleasant and very successful. He removed from that place to Knoxville, Tenn., and took charge of the First Baptist Church, succeeding as pastor Rev. C. H. Strickland, D. D. The membership of this church numbers 700, being one of the largest and most important of that denomination in the State. The pastorate of our subject has been very successful, the membership increasing under his charge at an average rate of eighty per annum. Among the incidents pertaining to the prosperity of the church under his management is the erection of the present handsome church edifice on Gay Street, the corner-stone of which was laid in June, 1886, and which, when completed, will cost about $30,000 exclusive of the ground on which the building stands, the money for the payment of which has already been raised. Our subject was united in marriage, in 1882, to Miss Maggie Jordan, a native of Tennessee, born May 26, 1862, and the daughter of E. L. Jordan, Esq., one of the wealthiest and most influential citizens of Murfreesboro, Tenn., and president of the First National Bank of that city. He is also the oldest (in point of service) director of the Nashville, Chattanooga & St. Louis Railroad. The result of our subject's marriage was the birth of two children, viz.: Eugene A., Jr., born in 1883, and E. Leland, born in 1885. In 1887 he preached the baccalaureate sermon for Carson College, University of Tennessee, and Mississippi College, and received the title of D. D. from the first named college, in his thirty-third year.

O. P. Temple was born in Greene County, Tenn., in 1820, near old Greeneville College. His father, James Temple, was a farmer and surveyor. He was the son of Mazer and Mary (Kennedy) Temple. Maj. Temple moved from Pennsylvania to North Carolina in 1766, and here resided until 1786, when he settled in Greene County, Tenn. He took an active part in the battle of King's Mountain, and was a man of considerable property and high standing. His wife was a relative of Gen. Daniel Kennedy, of Tennessee, and aunt of Gen. Thomas Kennedy, of Kentucky. On the maternal side our subject's mother, Mary Craig, was the daughter of Robert and Jane Innis Craig. Robert Craig served throughout the Revolutionary war as a captain in the Pennsylvania forces, and at one time commanded the body guard of Gen. Washington. He was distinguished for his gallantry and daring. After the war he moved to South Carolina, where he married Jane Innis Burns, daughter of John Burns, also a Revolutionary soldier, who moved to Greene County, Tenn., about 1795. Our subject was reared on a farm, which he assisted in cultivating during the summer and going to school during the winter. He lived within one mile of Greeneville College, and his early educational advantages were good. In 1838 he went to Tusculum College, where he passed three years. He then spent three more years at Washington College, then in a flourishing condition under the presidency of the brilliant young teacher and pulpit orator, A. Alexander Doak. Here he graduated in 1844. He was immediately offered a professorship in the college, which he declined. Soon after this he commenced reading law, and obtained license as a lawyer in 1846, and settled in Greeneville, Tenn. In 1847, one month before the election, he became a candidate for Congress against Andrew Johnson, in a district Democratic by about 2,000 majority; a hot canvass followed, resulting in reducing the majority of Johnson so low that it was regarded at the time as a defeat for him although he was elected. This race gave

Temple a notoriety throughout the State. In 1848 he moved to Knoxville, where he has ever since resided, following his profession until the last six years. In 1851 he married Miss S. C. Hume, of Blount County, a beautiful young lady of great attractions. Their only child, Miss Mary B., is a young lady of finished education. In 1860 Mr. Temple was the Bell and Everett elector for the Knoxville district, and as such was very active, making speeches, etc. In 1861 he was earnest and outspoken in his opposition to secession, and glories in the fact to this day that he was a Union man. After the war he returned to his profession, and in 1866, without the slightest knowledge or solicitation, was appointed chancellor, which position, after three weeks' hesitation, he finally accepted and held for twelve years, having in that time been twice elected by overwhelming majorities. In 1878 he voluntarily declined becoming a candidate for re-election, and returned to the bar. About 1867, when Judge Milligan left the supreme bench of Tennessee for a position in the court of claims at Washington, the vacant position was tendered to Mr. Temple, which he promptly declined, preferring to remain as chancellor. In 1874 he was appointed by President Grant a member of the board of visitors to West Point. In 1881 he was appointed postmaster at Knoxville, which position he accepted as a convenient way of retiring from his profession. He held this office for four years, and discharged its duties in a faithful and efficient manner. Since retiring from that position he has devoted his time to his own private affairs and to certain public trusts, among these the most important is, his connection with the University of Tennessee as a trustee. He is at this time president of the board of trustees, and chairman of the farm and experimental station committee. He has for many years been an active and leading member of the board, and many of the reforms introduced in the university originated with him. He is thoroughly alive with the spirit of progress and development, especially in the direction of scientific and industrial education and training. He is a descendant from Scotch-Irish ancestors, and is a member of the Presbyterian Church.

Jerome Templeton, of the law firm of Washburn & Templeton, was born in Bradley County, Tenn, but reared in Chattanooga. He graduated at Cumberland University in 1871, after which he taught the Loudon High School at Loudon, Tenn., three years, and in the meantime read law. He was admitted to the bar at Loudon, and soon began practicing at Sevierville where he remained until 1881, when he located at Knoxville, the present firm being formed in May, 1882. The firm is counsel for the Knoxville Insurance Company, Mechanics' National Bank, Knoxville Car Wheel Company, Knoxville Gas Company, and also, for five years, has represented the Rugby colony. Mr. Templeton married Miss Belle Mabry, eldest daughter of Col. G. W. Mabry, of Knox County, in 1873. Mr. Templeton is a Master Mason, and a successful, enterprising citizen. He is the second of five children born to Allison and Mahala (Cunningham) Templeton, all living with the exception of one son, who was killed in the Peach Tree Creek fight near Atlanta. The father of our subject was a native of Rhea County and devoted his entire life to the ministry in the Cumberland Presbyterian Church. He never missed preaching a single Sunday during the war. His death occurred in Texas in June, 1882. The mother of our subject was a native of Monroe County, Tenn., and died February 22, 1861.

The firm of Cone, Shields & Co., wholesale grocers and manufacturers of tobacco, of Knoxville, was organized in 1885, and is composed of H. Cone & Sons, of Baltimore, Md., and J. T., Jr., and J. S. Shields, of Knoxville. J. T. Shields, Jr., is a native of Grainger County, Tenn., was born in 1860, and was reared in that county and educated at the University of Tennessee. After leaving college he became a member of the firm of Coffin, Shields & Co., and in 1885 of the present firm. J. S. Shields was born in Grainger County in 1863, and like his brother was educated at the University of Tennessee. Upon leaving college he traveled for two years for the firm of Coffin, Shields & Co., and then became a member of the present firm. Judge J. T. Shields, father of our subjects, was born in Grainger County in 1825, and is one of the leading lawyers of East Tennessee, practicing only before the supreme bench. In 18— he was appointed by Gov. Porter to a place on the supreme bench, and later was appointed a member of the court of referees of the supreme court. He is now a resident of Bean's Station. The mother of our subjects was Elizabeth Simpson, who was born at Rodgersville, Tenn., in 1827.

James W. Trent, manufacturer and dealer in tobacco, was born in Henry County, Va., October 15, 1834, and is the son of William B. and Sallie W. (Garrett) Trent, natives of Virginia and North Carolina, and of Welsh and French descent respectively. Our subject received his education in the common schools, and his first pursuit in life was that of a tobacconist. In 1854 he married Miss Mary E. Mitchell, a native of Virginia, born April 5, 1837, of Irish-French descent, and a member of the Methodist Episcopal Church South, to which she has belonged since twelve years of age. To the marriage of our subject were born seven children: William L., whose sketch is found below; C. F., who is a merchant of Knoxville; Mollie T., wife of John F. Davis, of Knoxville; J. R., who is traveling salesman for his father's business in tobacco; Bettie Lee; Flora B., and Samuel, who died when only two years of age.

In 1858 our subject removed from Virginia to Alabama, where he manufactured and dealt largely in tobacco until the fall of 1866, when he removed from Alabama to Tennessee, and settled on his present farm, which is located a few miles below Strawberry Plains, Jefferson County, Tenn. Here he established a factory, and engaged in his present business. In January, 1885, his son, William L., became a partner in the business, and ever since the firm has been J. W. Trent & Son. Early in life Mr. Trent became a member of the Methodist Episcopal Church South, and for the last twenty-six or twenty-seven years has been a steward of the same. He is a Royal Arch Mason, and a Democrat in politics. His son, William L., was born in Franklin County, Va., January, 21, 1855, received his primary education in the common schools, and subsequently attended Hiwassee College, where he graduated in May, 1876. He taught school for two years, and in September, 1878, entered the Cumberland University Law School, and graduated in June, 1879. The following September he located at Knoxville, and practiced law for two years, after which he was for one year business manager of the *Knoxville Republican*, and after the consolidation of the *Republican* and *Chronicle* he was the business manager of the *Daily and Weekly Chronicle*, whose editor was Henry R. Gibson. At the end of one year he abandoned journalistic pursuits on account of ill health, and removed from Knoxville to his father's home near Strawberry Plains, Tenn. In 1880 he married Miss Sallie E. Thompson, of Jefferson County, Tenn., daughter of William and Martha M. Thompson, and niece of James L. Thompson, of the United States Army. To this marriage has been born one child, a son, named James. William L. Trent is a Republican in politics, and he and wife are members of the Methodist Episcopal Church South.

Dr. W. W. Tydeman, a prominent practitioner of Knoxville, Tenn., and one of the pioneers of the homœopathic school of medicine of that city, is a native of England, born in 1824. He immigrated to America in 1869, and located in Knoxville in 1872, where he began practicing his profession, and although almost unknown in the city at that time, the school he represented has since grown into knowledge and standing. Our subject has succeeded in building up a good practice, and established a good name in the profession. He is at present senior member of the firm of Tydeman & Caulkins, the junior member being Douglas Caulkins, who is a native of Duchess County, N. Y., and who was born December 15, 1857. He received his education at Athens, Tenn., where he began the study of medicine in 1879. He then attended Rush Medical College, of Chicago, in 1882–83, and later graduated from

Hahnemann College, Philadelphia. He then married Miss Lucie Tydeman, daughter of his partner, in 1886. To this union a daughter, Edith, was born January 5, 1887. Mrs. Caulkins was born on Jamaica Island, West Indies, and is of English parentage.

Maj. J. H. Wagner, United States pension agent for the Southern States, at Knoxville, Tenn., was born at Mountain City, Johnson County, Tenn., January 14, 1841, and is the son of M. M. and Mary S. (Fyffe) Wagner. The father was born in Tennessee, February 15, 1801, is a farmer and merchant, and a resident of Mountain City. The mother was a native of North Carolina, born February 16, 1807, and is still living. Both parents are members of the Baptist Church. Our subject was reared in Mountain City, where he acquired his early education, later attending school at Boon's Creek Academy, Washington County, Tenn. At the breaking out of the war he had not finished school. In August, 1862, he went through the lines to the Federal Army at Cumberland Gap, but did not immediately enlist, but joined his uncle in Missouri, where he remained until the following spring. He then went to Nashville and made an ineffectual attempt to join the Fourth Regiment of Tennessee Volunteer Infantry, then being organized. He applied to Gov. Johnson for a permit to reach the camp of the regiment, but it was refused on account of the stringent orders existing in regard to parties going nearer to the front. He then went North to await developments, and here learned of the organization of the Thirteenth Regiment of Tennessee Cavalry, at Camp Nelson, Ky., and in December, 1863, joined Company E, of that regiment. A little later he was promoted to major of the same. In 1865 he was elected from the regiment to the State Legislature, and after serving the first session resigned, and returned to his home in East Tennessee, where he engaged in mercantile pursuits, continuing the same until about 1883. October 2, 1886, he was appointed to his present position. June 18, 1874, he was united in marriage to Sallie K. White, of Live Oak, Fla., who was born in Tennessee, February 4, 1852, and who is the daughter of Col. John F. White. To this union have been born six children, only four of whom are living: Mary, born May 18, 1875; Mathias M., born December 23, 1879; Joseph Cleveland and George Hendricks (twins), born July 8, 1884, the day the Democratic Convention met in Chicago and nominated Cleveland and Hendricks for President and Vice-President. Our subject is a member of the Masonic fraternity, and his wife of the Methodist Episcopal Church South.

W. P. Washburn, attorney, of the firm of Washburn & Templeton, was born in Massachusetts in 1830. He was reared in that State, and graduated at Amherst College in 1851. In 1856 he came to Knoxville, and was admitted to the bar in 1857, since which time he has resided and practiced his profession here. The firm of which he is a member was formed in May, 1882. In 1864 he married Mrs. Minnie Leonard, *nee* Brown, whose death occurred in 1877. He afterward married Mrs. Edward Maynard, *nee* Harper, to whom two children have been born, one of whom is still living. Mr. Washburn is vice-president of the Knoxville Gas Light Company; secretary of the Knoxville Car Wheel Company, and director in the Mechanics' National Bank and Knoxville Fire Insurance Company. Our subject and a brother, John H., constituted the family born to Rev. Royal and Harriet (Parsons) Washburn, natives of Vermont and Massachusetts. The father was a minister in the First Congregational Church of Amherst, and died there in 1833. The mother afterward married Hon. David Mack, who died about 1859; she died in 1876. His brother, John H., is is vice-president and secretary of the Home Fire Insurance Company, of New York City.

J. W. Weatherford, of the firm of Middleton & Weatherford, brickmakers and contractors, is a son of William and Charity Weatherford, natives of Virginia and North Carolina respectively. On coming to Tennessee they settled in Sullivan County, where the father followed the shoemaker's trade. Their family consisted of twelve children—eight sons and four daughters. The father afterward moved to Knoxville, and here he sickened and died. In 1848 his widow and younger children also came to Knoxville. Of the children, two served in the Mexican war, two in the Federal and one in the Confederate Army. Our subject was born in Sullivan County in 1835, and at an early age began in a brickyard as an off-bearer. During the war he was in the railroad service, and at its close he returned to Knoxville. In 1865 Mr. Weatherford married Miss Lizzie Vincon, of Knoxville, and both he and his wife are members of the Methodist Episcopal Church South. In 1866 our subject and Mr. Middleton started a brickyard, without a dollar. Their outfit was a horse and a mud-mill for which they were in debt. Now they make their bricks by steam power, turning out a daily product of 30,000 bricks. For twenty-one years Mr. Weatherford has been in that business, and though he started with nothing, has succeeded in accumulating a nice property.

David H. Weaver, proprietor of the Knoxville Pottery & Pipe Works, was born in Boyd County, Ky., June 29, 1839, and is the son of George C. and Eliza M. (Hogan) Weaver. The father is a native of Pennsylvania, where he married and became the father of two children, both deceased. After the death of his first wife he moved to Kentucky, and here met and married Miss Hogan, who presented him with seven children—five sons and two daughters. Both parents are living in Knoxville, and although seventy-three years of age the father still works at the potter's trade. Our subject learned the trade of his father in early life, and followed this until 1862, when he volunteered in Company F, One Hundred and Fortieth Pennsylvania Infantry, Federal Army. At the battle of Chancellorsville a ball cut off his right forefinger and wounded his left hand severely. As soon as able for duty he was appointed assistant postmaster at Point Lookout, holding that position until the close of the war. In 1865 he married Miss Mary E. Emery, a native of Ohio, and to them were born six children—one son and five daughters. In 1869 Mr. Weaver came to Knoxville, and the following year purchased his factory, which he has operated successfully ever since. He is a Republican in politics, and he and his wife are members of the Methodist Episcopal Church. He is a Mason and for ten years has been secretary of the lodge.

William M. Weber, druggist of Broad and Crozier Streets, was born in western New York April 19, 1840. His parents, P. S. and Maria (Norton) Weber, were natives of New York. Both parents are now deceased. When only thirteen our subject began working for himself. He had received his education at South Bend, Ind., and soon afterward took an apprenticeship in a drug house, where he continued until 1861. He then volunteered in Company G, Fifteenth Indiana Infantry, and was in the Western Virginia campaign, coming South with Gen. Buell's army, and afterward under Rosecranz. At Shiloh he became first lieutenant and subsequently quartermaster of his regiment, holding that position until the close of his service. He was offered the position of post quartermaster at Loudon, Tenn., but declined on account of the expiration of his time. He was mustered out at Indianapolis in 1864. He was superintendent of the military post at Paducah, Ky., until its disorganization, after which he engaged in the drug business at Louisville, Ky. In 1884 he came to Knoxville, and has been dealing in drugs ever since. In 1869 he married Miss Sarah Carpenter, of Kentucky, and four children were the result of this union—one son and three daughters. Both he and wife are members of the Christian Church. He is a Mason and a member of the G. A. R.

T. A. West, M. D., city physician of Knoxville, Tenn., was born in Knox County of that State, near Graveston, in 1841, and is the son of Edward and Arminda (Roberts) West, both natives of Tennessee. The father was born in the year 1818, and the mother in 1821. They are now residing in Knox County, and the mother is a member of the Presbyterian Church. Our subject was reared in Knox County until fifteen years of age, when he went to Jefferson County, Tenn., and in 1859 began the study of medicine under Drs. Rodefer and Blackburn at New Market, Tenn. He attended medical college in New York City, and in 1862 began the practice of his profession near Graveston, Tenn., with Dr. L. M. Mynatt. He next removed to Dandridge, Jefferson County, where he practiced his profession for three years. He then went to Georgia and remained here ten years, after which he returned to Knox County. In 1884 he came to Knoxville, and in January, 1886, was elected city physician, and re-elected in 1887. He was married June 22, 1862, to Miss Sallie B. Mitchell, a native of Dandridge, Tenn., born in 1840, and the daughter of Maj. Berry Mitchell. Four children were the result of this union—three sons and one daughter. The eldest and youngest sons are engaged in the drug business in Knoxville. Dr. and Mrs. West are members of the Third Presbyterian Church of Knoxville.

Hon. W. O. White, of the firm of Chapman, White, Lyons & Co., wholesale and manufacturing druggists of Knoxville, Tenn., was born in Cleveland, Bradley Co., Tenn., March 14, 1843, and is the son of William H. and Caroline (Townsend) White. The father was born in Tennessee in 1808, was a merchant, and died in 1848. The mother was born in 1825 in Vermont, and is residing in Cleveland. Our subject was reared on a farm near Cleveland, and acquired his education at the schools of that place. In December, 1862, he went to Louisville, Ky., where he enlisted in the Federal Army, joining Company E, Fourth Regiment of Tennessee Union Cavalry, Capt. C. D. Champion. He served as private for nine months, and was then promoted first lieutenant and regimental quartermaster. In May, 1864, he was promoted captain of Company I, Fourth Tennessee Regiment Cavalry, and commanded the same until the close of the war. In the charge at the battle of Franklin, Tenn., in the Hood campaign, he was wounded by a blow from a musket. After the war he engaged in business in Cleveland. In 1867–68 he represented Bradley County in the State Legislature, and in 1869 removed to Knoxville, where, for a year, he was in the service of the United States revenue department. He next became a member of the firm of Hawkins, Butt & Co., stove and tinware dealers, and in 1880 became a member of the present firm. He is a member of Coeur de Leon Commandary, No. 9, K. of T. of Knoxville. He was married in 1871 to Lute Lynn, who was born in Sullivan County, Tenn., March 14, 1843, and is the daughter of Joseph Lynn. To them have been born three boys. Both our subject and wife are members of the Fourth Presbyterian Church of Knoxville.

John Wieland, farmer and fruit-grower of the Twelfth District, was born July 15, 1817, in Frederick County, Md., and immigrated to Montgomery County, Ohio, in 1837. In the spring of 1869 he came to Knox County, Tenn., where he has since resided. He is the second of eight children (five of whom lived to be grown) born to Barnherd and Elizabeth (Bechtol) Wieland, natives of Virginia and Maryland, respectively. Mr. Wieland was a life-long farmer, and he and wife were of German descent. John Wieland's grandfather, Barnherd Wieland, was born and reared in Wurtenburg, Germany. He came to America shortly after the Revolutionary war and settled in Frederick County, Md. Our subject received his education in the subscription schools of Maryland, and at the age of twenty-two began working for himself. He inherited $1,500 but the balance of what he is now worth was accumulated by his own exertions. He owns a fine farm of 410 acres, all well improved, and located four miles northwest of Knoxville. Besides the land above mentioned he has given considerable to his children. September 15, 1844, he married Miss Margaret Fudge, a daughter of Jacob and Elizabeth (Potter) Fudge, and to them were born eight children. Mrs. Wieland was a member of the Lutheran Church, and died January 1, 1865. Mr. Wieland is a member of the same church and is a Republican in politics, casting his first presidential vote for William Henry Harrison. Since the death of his wife Mr. Wieland has made his home with his children.

J. C. J. Williams, United States district attorney, is a native of Knox County, Tenn., born September 8, 1847, and reared on a farm until sixteen years of age, securing the rudiments of an education by attending the country schools in the winter season. He then attended school at Princeton, N. J., two years, after which he studied under a private tutor at home one year. At the age of twenty he began to study law in Knoxville, where he was admitted to the bar in October, 1868. In November, 1873, he married Miss Anna Hazen, a native of Knox County, Tenn., to whom five children have been born—four daughters and one son. The mother of these children died February 3, 1885. In 1873 Mr. Williams was appointed district attorney for the district of Knox, then, in August, 1874, he was elected to the same position, holding the office until March 2, 1878, when he resigned. Previous to this, in 1872, he was defeated for the office by twenty-four votes, and his competitor afterward resigning gave him his appointment in 1873. He was the Democratic candidate for criminal judge in 1878, for the State Senate in 1882, and Knox County representative in 1884. July 3, 1885, he was appointed United State district attorney, which appointment was conferred July 26, 1886, against the bitter opposition of the Republicans in East Tennessee. Mr. Williams still continues the practice of law in connection with his official duties. The Williams' family, ancestors of our subject, came to America from Wales and settled in Halifax previous to the Revolutionary war, in which the great-grandfather was a colonel. The grandfather was a colonel under Gen. Jackson at the battle of Horseshoe in the war of 1812. He came to Knox County, Tenn., at the beginning of the present century, and married a daughter of Gen. James White, who was of Scotch-Irish descent. The grandfather was eight years in the United States Senate, and then was defeated in 1823 by Gen. Jackson. The parents of our subject, John and Rhoda (Morgan) Williams, were natives of Knox County, and resided here until their deaths. The father represented Knox County several times in the Legislature, and was the Democratic candidate for Congress in 1867, being defeated by Horace Maynard. His death occurred April 21, 1881, and the mother died March 2, 1867.

C. M. Woodbury, secretary and treasurer of the Standard Handle Company, of Knoxville, was born in Alexandria, Va., April 15, 1853. His father, Gen. Daniel P. Woodbury, was a native of New Hampshire. He was a man of fine mathematical attainments. He is the author of a work entitled, "Theory of the Arch," and other mathematical works used in the leading colleges. He constructed Fort Jefferson, on Tortugas Island, and opened Cape Fear and James Rivers. During the war he rendered excellent service as chief engineer in the pontoon department of the Army of the Potomac; he died in 1864. The mother of our subject was born on Governor's Island, N. Y., and was the daughter of Col. Thomas Childs, of Mexican war fame. Of the six children born to this union, four are now living—two sons and two daughters. The other son, Thomas Childs Woodbury, is a lieutenant in the United States Army. Our subject was educated on Long Island and at Adelphia Academy, of Brooklyn. At the age of seventeen he engaged as clerk in a New York house, and remained there thirteen years, rising in the meantime from the lowest to the highest position in the house. In 1879 he married Miss Mary S. Nicoll, of Long Island, by whom he has three sons. He and his wife are members of the Protestant Episcopal Church. In 1881 he moved to Knoxville, and organized and started the Standard Handle Company, an establishment which sends its products directly to foreign countries, as well as all over the United States, and enjoys a reputation second to none in this line of manufacture.

W. W. Woodruff, of the wholesale hardware firm of W. W. Woodruff & Co., is a native of Kentucky, born in 1840, and was reared and educated in his native State. At the breaking out of the late war he enlisted as captain of Company D, Thirteenth Kentucky Infantry, United States Volunteers, with which he served throughout the war. He then located at Knoxville, and established the wholesale hardware firm of which he is senior member. In 1865 he was united in marriage to Ella T. Connelly, a native of Frankfort, Ky., to whom eight children have been born, six still living. Mr. Woodruff is one of the board of trustees for the deaf and dumb asylum, and president of the Standard Coal and Coke Company, vice-president of the Knoxville and the Protection Fire Insurance Companies. He is a director of the East Tennessee National Bank, and also a director of the Knoxville Car Wheel Company.

Nathan S. Woodward, business manager for James O'Conner & Co., was born in Knoxville, July 19, 1844, and in that city received his education. At the age of seventeen he entered the express service as a messenger, and step by step he rose to agent, and finally to assistant superintendent of the office from Lynchburg, Va., to Selma, Ala., and Atlanta, Ga. In 1882 he assumed the duties of his present position. His father, Alexander Woodward, was a native of Virginia. He was a man of good literary attainments, although acquired without the assistance of school or teachers, and was a physician by profession. About 1842 he came to Knoxville and took for his second wife Miss Mary, sister of David Sullins, D. D. Of this marriage our subject is the only son. He has a family of three children—one son and two daughters—born to his union with Miss Annie Peed. Mrs. Woodward is a native of Knoxville, and an earnest worker in all the movements that tend to elevate the social and moral standing of the community. She has been treasurer of the Woman's Missionary Society in Holston conference since its organization, and is also an active worker in the Methodist Episcopal Church South. Mr. Woodward is a Knight Templar; is a member of the Masonic order, and has held the position of Senior Warden, Deputy Grand Master, Grand Master of the State, and is now Grand Captain General Knights Templar Tennessee.

John D. Wrinkle was born in Knox County, February 15, 1845, and is the son of John and Sophia (Wrinkle) Wrinkle. The father was born in Knox County, Tenn., in 1806, and died at his home in Knox County in 1881. The mother was born in Knox County in 1812, and at present is living with her sister in Missouri. The father was of Dutch extraction, and the mother of Scotch-Irish. They both became members of the Baptist Church early in life. The father was ever a zealous Democrat. Our subject received a limited education in the common schools, but by observation and study has become a well informed man.

He is a Democrat, but takes no part in politics more than to cast his vote in favor of his party. He has always been a farmer and has been quite successful in that occupation. He has also followed stock raising on his fine farm of 500 acres. To his marriage to Miss Margaret A. I. Bowman in 1870 were born five children, the eldest is deceased. Those living are two girls, Maggie and Burton, and two boys, Samuel and W. Grover Cleveland. Mrs. Wrinkle was born in Knox County, Tenn., November 14, 1849.

Thomas E. Wrinkle, a successful farmer, was born in Knox County, Tenn., December 9, 1854, and is the son of John and Sophia (Wrinkle) Wrinkle. (For further particulars of parents see sketch of John D. Wrinkle.) Our subject received his education in the common country schools, and while yet quite youthful turned his attention to agricultural pursuits. Miss Evaline Hines became his wife in 1879, and to this union were born three children, one dying when quite young. The two living are Virgie May and Hattie Evaline. The mother died May 26, 1885. In 1886 Mr. Wrinkle married Miss Kate Slatery, a native of Knox County, born February 6, 1862. One child, Allen A., was born to this union November 27, 1886. Our subject is a young and energetic farmer and owns a farm of 125 acres of land well improved and very productive. He is and always has been an uncompromising Republican.

Col. Isham Young, chairman of the board of public works for Knoxville, was born in Roane County, Tenn., in 1838, and was reared in that county until the commencement of the war, when he enlisted in the First Tennessee Infantry, United States Army, and at the organization was elected orderly sergeant, from which he was promoted in a few months to first lieutenant of the same company (I), and February, 1862, assumed the duties of captain until April 15, 1863, when he was appointed lieutenant-colonel of the Eighth Tennessee Infantry. August 16, 1863, he was commissioned with two others, to organize the Eleventh Tennessee Cavalry, and October 21 of the same year he was mustered in as colonel of the same. Previous to the war, in 1858, he wedded Miss Margaret C. Atkinson, a native of Roane County, to whom three children have been born. December, 1864, Mr. Young located at Knoxville, and was connected with the East Tennessee, Virginia & Georgia Railroad, from July, 1865, until April, 1882, and in January, 1886, was elected to his present position. He is a member of the Masonic fraternity. His father, Freemoton Young, is a native of Roane County, Tenn., born in 1813, and still resides there. He was at one time trustee of that county. Lucinda (Evans) Young, mother of our subject, was also a native of Roane

County, and died there October 27, 1885. Of their family of eight children, six are now living.

A. Ziegler, of the firm of Metler & Ziegler, was born in Germany in 1844, and came to America in 1866, locating soon after at Knoxville, where he has since been successfully engaged in the meat trade. He followed the butcher's trade with Ignaz Fanz one year, and then became a member of the firm of Schneider & Ziegler, where he coutinued until 1872, when the present firm was formed. The same year he took for his life companion Miss Eliza Metler, daughter of the senior member of the firm. The result of this union was the birth of six children, two of whom are deceased. The parents of our subject were born in Germany, where the mother still resides, and where the father died about 1863.

INDEX

Prepared by
Colleen Morse Elliott
Fort Worth, Texas

KNOX COUNTY, TENN.

Abernathy, S. 833
Abongphohigo (Indian) 816
Adair, John 801,808,810,
  839,875,890,892
Adkins, E. W. 814
Adkinson, J. W. 838
Adney, G. W. 855
Adney...1037
Aiken, H. M. 868,909
  Martha 909
  Mary 909
  Thomas 873
  William A. 909
Akers, Elizabeth 1029
Akin, G. W. 856
Albers, A. J. 868
  G. W. 855,868
  R. J. 853
Albert...1041
Alexander...829
  Miss D. 1042
  Mrs. Davidson 1032
  Dicks 826
  E. 844
  Ebenezer 812,824,995
  Naomi 1031
  Peggy 1031
Alldredge, Margaret 940
Allen...856,917
  John M. 860
  Martha 924
  Rebecca 917
Allison, A. 835
  Alexander 870
  R. D. 826
Ally, Melvina 1021
Ambrose, J. F. 889
Anderson...853,855
  Anna 1050
  Eliza 937
  Isaac 821,875,886,891,
    895
  James 800,809,821,826,
    855,1050
  Joseph 815
  Joseph R. 951
  Margaret 991
  Mary J. 1050
  Nancy J. 1045
  Robert M. 821,971
  W. A. 814
  William E. 820,821
Andes, Alexander 987
  George S. 852
  J. O. 987
  Mary J. 987
  Mollie L. 987
  Sarah 1001
  S. Ellen 987
Andrews, Abigail 926
  Amelia 926
  Jonathan 926
Angel, A. T. 995
  Blanch 910
  Julia E. 910
  Martha C. 995
  Martha G. 909
  Samuel 909
  Samuel P. 909
  Samuel P., Jr. 910
  S. P. 856,889
  William P. 910
Annan, R. 852
Anthony...842
Apjohn, Sophia 989

Armistead, Ed. 845
Armstrong, Aaron 892
  A. C. 916
  Alice G. 959
  Ann Eliza 911
  Delia 1001
  D. P. 811,843,844
  James 839,890
  James M. 838
  Joshua 894
  Mary 916
  Moses A. M. 911
  R. H. 830,1001
  Robert 800,809
  Thomas N. 911
Arnold, M. D. 851
  Thomas D. 820
Asbury, Daniel 884
Ashby, H. M. 835
Atchley, William D. 838
Atkin, George 886
  J. H. 856
  Samuel T. 887
  S. T. 856,857,861
Atkins...856
  J. H. 873
  S. T. 860
Atkinson, Margaret C. 1071
Ault...885
  Albert H. 911
  Bettie Lee 911
  Charles L. 911
  Cyntha C. 911
  Cyntha J. 911
  Frederick 886
  Harvey 845
  Henry A. 911
  James W. 911
  J. K. 911
  Lena May 911
  Lizzie 911
  Margaret 911
  Margaret D. 911
  Mary 911
  Martha 911
  Michael 911
  Rachel 911
  Robert B. 911
  William G. 911
Aurin, John 905
Ausmus, William 838
Austin, Miss E. L. 881
  Emily L. 880
Averill, John T. 950
  Nellie 950
Axely, James 885
Ayers, Elizabeth 1018
Ayres, R. O. 889

Bachman, Nathan 896
Badget, Robert 948
Badgett, Barckley Majors
  912
  B. F. 912
  Burwell F. 912
  Cassandria E. 912
  Charles 912
  Clementine 912
  Drucilla 913
  Eglentine 912
  Elizabeth Wallace 912
  Eliza J. 964
  Eliza Jane 912
  Florence C. 912
  James 913

Badgett, Josephine M. 912
  Lucy 912
  Lucy A. 912
  Mary 912
  Nannie V. 912
  Ransome 913
  Ransome N. 912
  R. D. 912
  Rebecca 912
  Rebecca J. 912
  Roberta C. 912
  S. E. 913
  Sophira 913
  Susan Reeder 912
  Susie R. 912
  William C. 912
Bain, John 894
Baird, Alexander, Jr. 881
Baker...901
  Harvey 921
  Leonidas 870
  Lilly 1013
  Maggie A. 921
  Susan W. 1019
  William 811,905
  William J. 870,871
Balch, Hezekiah 890
Bales, Charlotta 1048
Ball, Nicholas 805
Ballard...806
  J. H. 913
  Lucy B. 914
  Miss M. A. 998
  Sallie A. 913
  Thomas 914
Banks, Abigail 926
  Harriet B. 926
  Thomas 926
Barker, E. S. 856
  F. 860
  J. H. 860
  S. 856
Barnard, J. D. 819
Barnes, A. A. 868,869,914
  Hannah 914
  Henry 914
  Louisa T. 914
  Lou Lyon 914
  Mary Rolfe 914
  Nathan 885
  Susan Wallace 914
Barry, Hiram 814
  I. E. 856
Barshall, Henrietta 968
Bart, J. C. 905
Barton...1013
  Alvin 1001
  Isaac 898
Baryar, John P. 838
Bassett, Semantha 985
Bates, W. H. 888
Baugh, W. H. 898
Bauman, Joseph L. 894
Baumann, Catherine 915
  Ella K. 915
  J. F. 915
  William 915
Bayless, Herman A. 916
  Herman G. 916
  J. C. 838
  John C. 916
  Mary 916
  Rosa 916
Bays, H. W. 887
  W. W. 887

Baxter, John 833,846,915
  John K. 915
  Margret W. 1012
  Mary 915
  William M. 915
Beach, John P. 864
Beal, Lucinda 910
  Sarah J. 1026
Bealy...990
Beaman, Blanche 916
  Clarence 916
  Ernest Andrew 916
  F. C. 916,917
  James Garfield 916
  Maggie 916
  Mary J. 916
  Orin C. 916
  Rebecca 917
  Ruth 916
  Timothy 917
Bean, Alonzo 834
  Joseph H. 872
Beard...803
  Hugh 808
  James 799,806
Bearden...855
  B. F. 814
  Elizabeth Trigg 968
  Marcus D. 814
  M. D. 812,838,844,848,
    869,874
  Richard 842
  R. M. 835
Bechtol, Elizabeth 1068
Bell...856
  Eliza 1000
  John 1037
  Joseph 886
  Samuel 826,844,874
  W. M. 856
Bellue...901
Bennett, R. M. 1002
  Rufus M. 838
Benton, Thomas H. 825
Benziger, J. W. 869
Bergrath, J. 905
Berkley, Charles H. 865
Berry, James O. 837
  John M. 838
  Sophia A. 929
Berwanger...855
Betterman, W. J. 917
Betterton, Charlotte 917
  J. N. 855,917
  Thomas 917
  Zephana 917
Biddle...855,1013
Biemans, J. L. 905
Billings, Adaline 990
Bince, R. 838
Bird...856
  J. W. 958
Black, Jane 944
  John 1037
  Joseph 815
Blackburn...1067
  Robert G. 889
Blackwell, J. E. 836
  J. E. S. 844
Blain, Sarah W. 965
Blair, A. A. 833,834
  James 809,897
Blake, Adam B. 917,918
  Alice E. 918
  Anna Porter 918
  Eliza A. 918
  Emily W. 918
  James K. 918
  Jane M. I. 918
  John 917
  John T. 918
  Margaret J. 918
  Martha E. 918

Blake, Martha J. 918
  Mary 917,918
  Mary A. 918
  Mary Jane 918
  Nancy E. 918
  Robert B. 918
  Samuel A. 918
  Samuel M. 918
  William H. 918
Blakeley, Frances 924
Blang, Joseph A. E. 838
  J. S. A. 814
Blaufield...855
  J. 856
Bleakley, Alexander 899
Blount...802
  Mary C. 841
  William 815,936
  Willie 819
Boggle, Jonathan 816,817
  William 883
Boldman, Jane 963
Bolli, Edward 925
  Eliza 925
Bollman, Erie 984
Bond, Catherine J. 919
  Eliza 919,1044
  Elizabeth 919
  George 919,1044
  Hugh M. 919
  Isaac 919
  Isaac H. 919
  Isabella C. 919
  James A. 919
  Martha 919
  Mary 919
  Mary Eliza 919
  Sarah 919
  Sarah L. 919
  S(arah) L(ouisa) 1044
  Stephen F. 919
Bondurant...856
Boody, Asariah 1005
Booth, Z. 842
  Zach. 843
Borches, ...851
  J. W. 852,867,1055
  Mary Hazen 1055
Bosworth...847
  Nathaniel 847
Bounds, Cynthia J. 911
  Francis H. 838
  Thomas 816
Bowen...842
  William 843
  William R. 811
  W. R. 814
Bowers...990
Bowlus, L. H. 814
Bowman...799
  Elizabeth 920
  E. W. 885
  Isabella 920
  James W. 920
  J. N. 978
  John C. 920
  Joseph S. 920
  Margaret A. I. 1071
  Mary 920
  Pressure M. 978
  Samuel 920
  S. G. 868,920
  W. P. 920
Bowyers, Luke 809
Boyce, George 833
Boyd...845,856,859,883
  Abbie C. 1018
  Adelia 1052
  Alice E. 922
  Anna 921
  Anna Lee 1020
  Bell 830
  D. W. 921

Boyd, Edwin T. 922
  Elizabeth 921
  Freddie M. 922
  H. D. 1053
  Henry D. 922
  Isabella R. 920
  James S. 921,814
  J. M. 921
  John 873
  John L. 922
  John M. 870,879,921,947
  John R. 963
  John Wilson 921,922
  Lavenia 962
  Lavinia J. 922
  Lorenia 972
  Maggie A. 921
  Mahulda J. 922
  Mamie F. 922
  Minnie A. 922
  Samuel B. 823,874,920,
    921
  Samuel E. 951
  S. B. 859,866,921,951
  S. B., Jr. 860
  Susan H. 921
  Thomas 897,921
  Thomas A. 922
  William J. 922
Boyle, Andrew 815
  Samuel 815
Boyles, Hezekiah 899
  John 899
Bradbury...806
Bradford, William 833,834
Bradley, Ailcy 923
  Archlers 923
  Charlton W. 923
  Clarence 923
  Evaline 923
  George 923
  H. L. 922,923
  John 923
  Malinda 923
  Margaret C. 923
  Marshall 923
  Maynard 923
  Nancy 923
  T. J. 923
Braeker, D. M. 902
Brakebill, Catherine 946
Brakehill, Sarah E. 1039
Brakeville, Annie 945
  John 945
Brandau...855
Brandon, Mary 995
  W. C. 838,869
  W. N. 995
Branner, Benjamin 846
  George M. 846
  H. B. 875
  John R. 846,866
  Joseph 846
  William A. 846
Brazelton, Julia 985
  William 834,951,986
Breazeale, D. W. 819
Breck, Mrs. E. A. R. 1032
Breckenridge...968
  John C. 972
Breckinridge, Catherine S.
  931
Brice, Elizabeth 1057
  N. B. 1057
Briggs...849
  A. D. 1005
Briscoe...1013
  Daniel 851,866,923,924,
    951
  Kate C. 923
  Martha 924
  P. J. 851,924
Briscoes...1058

Brock...982
  Pearson 815
Brooks...856
  C. A. 924
  Catherine 924
  Elizabeth 924,1023
  Fannie J. 950
  Frances I. 924
  Gertrude 924
  Harriet O. 924
  Isaac J. 924
  James A. 1030
  J. M. 874
  Joseph 816
  Joseph A. 950
  Josephine E. 1000
  Lawson L. 924
  Lawson S. 924
  Lelia W. 924
  Lewis F. 924
  Margaret A. 1030
  Minerva J. 924
  Moses 800,816
  Paulina T. 924
  Robert 891
  Robert N. 924
Brother, H. M. 908
Brown...855,856
  Adaline 1005
  C. H. 858,869
  Daniel 1005
  Frances 924
  George 824,854,1030
  H. 876
  Harriet J. 1005
  Hugh 817
  H. V. 904
  Jane 936
  J. T. 924,925
  Joseph 896
  Joshua 924
  Lizzie 1030
  Luther H. 1005
  Margaret 944,952
  Martha J. 925
  Mary 911
  Minnie 1065
  P. B. 856
  Pink Lawson 925
  William 819
Brownlee...856
Brownlow...960
  James P. 837
  Mary 909
  Parson 1038
  W. G. 833,889,872
  Wm. G. 888
Bruce, A. C. 904
  Jane 966
Bryan, Allen 1053
  Malinda 1053
Buchanan, A. 904
  James 912
Buckaloo, Joanna 1048
Buckhart, Adlicia 995
  W. M. 995
Buckner, Elizabeth 1051
  Emily Ann 1051
  Ezra 1051
  S. B. 828
Buffat, Alfred 925,926
  Charles A. 925
  E. 946
  Edward F. 925
  Elise B. 926
  Eliza 925
  Ernest 926
  Flora F. 926
  P. F. 925
  Samuel T. 926
  Sylvia 925
  Walter D. 926
  William E. 926

Bullard, Joseph A. 901
Bunch, McD. J. 827
  Samuel 825
Burden, William 815
Burger...1028
  C. 852
  V. 856
Burkhart, M. T. 837
  T. J. 814
Burks, John 869
Burlson, G. B. 869
Burns, Jane Innis 1060
  John 1060
Burnside...828
  A. E. 948
Burr...861.1026
  Amelia 926
  George H. 926
  Harriet B. 926
  Moses 926
Burroughs, J. J. 836
  W. H. 836
Burrow, Martha G. 909
Butler, William 984
Butt...1067
  Frank M. 927
  J. R. 854,898
  J. R., Jr. 926,927
  J. R., Sr. 926
  Laura 927
  Leannah T. 926
  Will L. 927
Button, W. H. 856
Byerley, Charles S. 927
  Elizabeth 927
  Henry E. 927,928
  James 927,928
  James W. 927
  Luo L. 927
  Martha A. 927
  Mattie Pearl 928
Bynon, Mary 1040
Byram, Ebenezer 803
Byrne...845

Cage, Lucy 943
Caldwell...855
  A. 868
  Alfred 812
  Belle M. 1020
  George 809
  Samuel A. 894
Callan, F. J. 856
Callaway, Charlotte 917
  Thomas H. 1006
Calloway, John 814
  S. 883
  Thomas H. 865,866
Camp, E. C. 866
  Henry 866
  Mary W. 948
Campbell, Alexander 890
  Andrew W. 816
  Anna E. 928
  David 801,808,810,811,
  815,842,844,873
  George W. 817,819,842
  James 890,893,928
  James "Scotch Jimmy" 842
  James R. 928
  J. B. 869
  John 928
  Lucy 928
  M. Linda 928
  R. H. 814
  Thomas B. 928
  T. R. C. 928
  William A. 928
Cannon, Elbert J. 837
  Martha 1023
Cardwell, Elizabeth 986
  George 995
  Rachel M. 995

Carey, Ellen 1038
  James 802
  John 816
  William 1038
Carhart, H. B. 852
  W. B. 852
  W. E. 852
Carmichael, Alexander 841
  Bettie 942
Carnes, William D. 876
Carpenter...853,998
  C. L. 854
  D. A. 858,867,875,928,
  929,1038
  Malinda E. 928
  Sarah 1066
  Sophia A. 929
  William S. 928
Carr...840
  James K. 982
  Mary E. 982
Carrick, Samuel 890,891
Carriger, Arthur Lee 930
  John 930
  John H. 930
  J. Sterling 930
  Margaret 930
  Michael 930
  Musidora 930
  Vandalee 930
Carroll...828
  W. H. 827
Carter...856
  Aurelia A. 932
  Caleb 816
  Catherine 965
  Charles B. 933
  E. E. 932
  Elizabeth 931,932
  E. R. 932
  Gertrude 932
  James 929,979
  James E. 834
  James M. 931
  James Madison 932
  J. D. 834,894
  Jennie Minnie 932
  Jodie Cleveland 932
  Julia 932
  J. W. 834
  Miss L. E. 927
  Lucinda 933
  Margaret Ann 932
  Martha M. 933
  Mary 932,982
  Mary Alice 932
  M. B. 931
  Nannie 932
  Peyton 856,933
  Rebecca 931
  Robert Lee 932
  S. P. 832
  T. W. 898
  Walter H. 933
  W. H. 932
  W. R. 814,869,932,933
Carson, Emma F. 931
  James F. 931
  James Green 931
  Joseph 930
  Katie W. 931
  Rachel 931
  William W. 930,931
Casey, Joel 819
Casteel, William 805
Caswell...859,920,999
  William 859
  Wm. R. 826
Cate, A. M. 838
  Charles 947
  Deborah Ann 947
  Elizabeth 947
Caulkins, Douglas 1063

Caulkins, Edith 1064
   Lucie 1064
Cavanaugh, William 815
Cavett, Alexander 804
Cawood, Daniel 856
Chadwich, Emily 1047
Chamberlain...941,1041
   Frederick W. 934
   Harper L. 934
   H.S. 857
   Kate E. 934
   Leander 933
   Susannah 933
   W. P. 933
Chamberlin, W. P. 853,865
Champion, C. D. 1067
Chanaberry, Mary 994
   Mary K. 994
   Peter 994
Chandler, Ellen R. 1011
   Mary 932
Chapman...1067
   E. R. 865
   J. E. 853
   Thomas 814
Charlton, C. W. 871,888
Chavanes, Emma 1041
Cherry...988
Childers, Elizabeth 1013
   James 899
Childres, Judia 1058
Childress, John 886
   Lennes 945
Childs, Rowland 899
   Thomas 1069
Chisolm, John 807,809,840,
   841
Christian, Ann E. 934
   Carrie V. 934
   Charles B. 934
   Frank H. 934
   Henry 934
   Jane 934
   John W. 934
   Katie 934
   Lorinda 934
   Mary H. 934
   Walter L. 934
   William T. 934
Churchwell, George W. 823,
   1032
   Laura 998
   William M. 823
   W. M. 833,869
   Wm. M. 845,868
Clack, John 1021
   Spencer 1021
Claiborne, W. C. C. 819
Clapp, Alvira Cornelia 935
   Ann 1036
   Daniel 1036
   H. 813
   Henderson 935
   H. M. Brownlow 935
   James 838
   James S. 935
   Linwill Foyd 935
   Lucinda 935
   Lurina E. 935
   Martha Elizabeth 935
   Mary A. 935
   Mary E. 935
   Nicholas 935
   Orlena M. 935
   Pherba 935
   Pherba E. 935
   Rachael Minerva 935
   Richard R. 935
   R. La Fayette 935
   Rufus Solomon 935
   Sarah Jane 935
   Solomon 935
   Solomon Conrad 935

Clapp, William Joseph 935
   William R, 935
Clark...857,990
   Edwin 983
   Frances 1021
   Harvey 858
   Hattie C. 983
   H. W. 858
   Mary 983
   Mary Payne 914
Clawson, Hila 1036
Clayton, Powell 996
Cleveland, Eli 899
Cloninger, J. 905
Cloud, Margret 1036
Clowney, Mrs....986
Clyde, Milton 1005
Clyman, John E. 868
Cobb, Martha E. 918
   Mary A. 918
   P. A. 835
Cocke...1021
   John 819,820
   John E. 936
   Musidora 930
   Walter M. 936
   William 817,819,936
   William E. 936
Cockrum, Lavicy 947
Coffin...806
   Charles 835
Coffman, Leanah T. 926
Coker, Charles 1050
   Margaret 1050
   Mary B. 1026
Cole, Alexander 816,937
   Eliza 937
   Eva 938
   James 937
   Laura 937
   Lucy J. 1045
   Martha J. 937
   Nancy J. 937,1045
   Sampson 1045
   Sampson D. 937
   Samuel 937
Coleman, James H. 838
   L. L. 1033
   Lou 1047
Collier,Alice 937
   Clio Brown 937
   Ivy McBath 937
   Jane 936
   M. B. 936,937
   Robert Hoyal 937
   Thomas 936
   Thomas Carl 937
Collum, R. N. 834
Colman, Zebella 987
Compton, Charlotta 976
   Miss D. 976
   William 976
Condon, Bridget 938
   John 938
   Kate E. 939
   Margaret M. 938
   Martin J. 853,938,939
   Michael J. 853
   Mike J. 938
   Paul A. 938
   S. P. 855,938
   Stephen P. 853
Condroy, Carley 1045
   John 1045
   Mary 1045
Cone, C. 852
   H. 1062
   M. A. 852
Congdon, Samuel 865
Conley, Abraham 817
   Silas 817
Connelly...969
   Ella T. 1070

Conner...807
   Almeda N. 940
   Emily A. 940
   George W. 940
   James 800,839,940
   John Tate 940
   John W. 814,940,941
   Joseph 940
   Joseph Wesley 941
   Katie R. 941
   Louisa 940
   Margaret 940
   Mary 940,957
   Mary S. 940
   Sallie 939
   Sarah 957
   Sarah A. 940
   Susan 940
   S. Y. 939,940
   Thomas 940
   W. A. A. 812,940
   William 939,957
   William P. 940
   Zerada E. 941
Conway...842
Cooley...855
   Andrew J. 941
   Bettie 942
   Elizabeth 942
   Emma J. 954
   Fleming B. 941
   James L. 894
   J. L. 941,942
   Laura A. 941
   Lucy 941
   M. O. 904
Cooper, D. B. 1042
   Henry 1041
   Joseph A. 838,942,1039
   Lenora A. 966
   Mary Agnes 1041
   Matthew D. 1041
   S. H. 966
   W. R. 942
Coram...901
Cornick, Simpson 858
Cosby, James 799
Cottrell, Adam T. 838
   A. T. 814
   Josephine M. 912
   Louisa T. 912
   Mary 975
   Samuel 912
Coulter, John 815
Council, Jordan T. 827
Councill, Jesse 899
Courier, Martha E. 969
Courtney, John 899
Cowan...1010
   A. G. 826
   James 840,841,941,984
   James H. 811,843,874,
   876,877
   J. D. 851
   J. H. 842,844,896
   Margaret 984
   Martha B. 1008
   Nathaniel 840,842,875
   Samuel 840,841
Cox...883,986,1040
   Curd 957
   George H. 905
   George W. C. 814
   Sallie 939
   Sarah 957
Cozby, James 805,808,809,
   810,890,892
Cracraft, George K. 996
Craig, David 808,809
   James 893
   Jane Innis 1060
   J. J. 844,863
   John J., Jr. 864,942,743

Craig, John J., Sr. 864, 943
  J. W. 897
  L. E. 861,862
  Lucy 943
  Mary 1060
  Rachel 1044
  Robert 1060
  William 812,814
Craighead, John 843,848, 893
  Robert 810,842,890,891
  Thomas 896
Cranton, Lucretia 981
Crawford, Amanda 943
  Anderson 937
  Barnes 943
  Bessie 943
  Catherine 1036
  Jean B. 943
  John H. 970
  Josiah 885
  Lennis 943
  Martha J. 937
  Mattie 943
  Nancy J. 937
  Rebecca 1034
  Samuel B. 943
  Sarah 937
  Saxton 943
  Sophia E. 974
Creeg, C. C. 906
Crippen, Dicy 1015,1049, 1045
  Eliza 1015
  James 1046
  M. 1045
  Martha 1046
  Ruth C. 1049
  William 1015,1045
  William P. 1049
Crippin, William P. 814
Crittenden, G. B. 827
Crockett, Joseph H. 827
Crookshank, Annie 972
  Lavenia 962
  Lorenia 972
  Roxie 962
  Thomas 962,972
Cross, Ann A. 944
  Britton 944
  Charles W. 839
  Frank 944
  Jane 944
  John H. 943,944
  Mary 944
  William 944
Crover, Mary E. 995
Crozier, A. R. 868
  C. W. 871
  Elizabeth J. 947
  Hannah 1032
  J. H. 797
  John 841,842,843,875, 876,877,892
  John H. 819,822,828,846
  Lenora 973
  Peggy Barton 1032
Cruse, A. B. 944
  Arthur Temple 945
  Charlotta E. 945
  Chester Ellis 945
  Jacob A. 945
  John M. 945
  Lucy Jane 945
  Margaret 944
  Margaret E. 945
  Nancy E. 945
  Sarah Evaline 945
  W. W. 944,945
Cruze...855,856,1037
  Catherine 946
  C. C. 945

Cruze, Clifford 946
  Edna 946
  Elizabeth 945
  Esther 946
  Isabella 946
  James 945,946
  James H. 945
  J. H. 946
  John 854,946
  John W. 868
  J(ohn) W., Jr. 945,946
  J. W., Sr. 945,946
  Lennes 945
  Margaret 945,946
  Rachel M. 945
Cullen, J. C. 856
Culverhouse, J. L. 869
Cumming, James 888
Cummings, D. H. 833
Cunningham, Alexander 809
  Charlotta 976
  Flora E. 1025
  James 816,1025
  Mahala 1062
  Martha 1025
  Paul 839
Cunnyngham, Jesse 884
Cuquel, N. 856
Currey, Richard O. 871
  R. O. 870
Curtis, H. W. 856
  J. L. 868

Daily, W. C. 889
Dana...829
Daniel, Martha 999
Daniels...855
Danner, W. C. 836
Dardis, James 842,873
  Thomas 819,842
Daughtry, Josiah B. 886
Davenport, Randall 899
David, A. 856
Davidson, John 969
Davis...842,877
  Albert 946,947
  Anna E. 928
  B. O. 887
  D. D. 906
  Deborah Ann 947
  E. J. 866,906,951
  James 947,963
  Jasper 947
  Jefferson 910
  John 825,877
  John F. 1062
  J. R. 852
  Lavicy 947
  Margaret F. 988
  Marian 947
  Mollie T. 1062
  Nancy 963,991
  Taylor 947
  Thomas 906
Deaderick...843
  C. 947
  David 947
  David A. 814,893
  Elizabeth J. 947
  J. C. 848
  Margaretta F. 1043
  Rebecca 947
Dean, J. R. 878
Dearmond, David F. 812
  Richard 803
De Armond, Columbus 911
  David 911
  D. F. 910
  Dowe 911
  James 911
  Marian 911
  Rhoda 910
  Richard I. 910

De Armond, Sarah 910
  William 911
Deaton, Spencer 838
Deery, James A. 869
De Groat, William 858
Dempster...859
Denison, Joseph 826
De Pue...946
  C. W. 854,889
  Zilpha 982
Dew, J. R. 902
Dickerson, Jennie 990
  W. R. 990
Dickinson...843,985
  P. 851,867
  Perez 833,876
Dickson, Mrs. M. J. 1032
Dillon, Sidney 1005
Dismukes, Bettie 1028
  S. C. 852,1001
Dixon...845
  James 885
Doak...991
  A. Alexander 1060
  E. 1052
  H. 1052
  H. M. 833
  Samuel 810,815,894
  Samuel H. 895
  William 810
Dodson, Lazarus 1002
  Rebecca L. 1002
  Sonora L. 1002
Doherty...803
Don Carlos, Mary L. 977, 978
  William Carter 977,978
Donelson...798
Donnell, George 897
Dooley, I. E. 852
Dorsey, Elizabeth 956
Dortch, N. 825
Dorton, Mary 964
Double Head 804
Doughty...832
  Adelia 948
  Benjamin 948
  Elizabeth 948
  George W. 948
  James A. 948
  J. H. 868
  Mary W. 948
  Sarah A. 948
Douglass, Hiram 897
  J. E. 878
Dow, S. B. 853,868
Dowell, Malinda 923
  Wm. T. 888
Doyle, J. T. 812
Drake, Amanda 949
  Charles M. 949
  Nellie 950
  W. W. 979
Dreher, W. D. 979,980
Duke, Lucy B. 914
Dulaney, J. E. 833
Duncan, E. E. 1049
  Elizabeth 1051
  Fannie J. 950
  J. C. 950
  Sallie 1049
  Stephen 841
  Thomas 903
Dunlap, Ephraim 819
  Hugh 806,839,821
  Hugh G. 821,894
  James T. 821
  R. G. 826
  Richard G. 821,894
  William 811,814
  William C. 821
  Wm. C. 894
Dunn, W. W. 838,869,870

Durham, J. M. 889
   Vandalee 930
Dyer, Calvin M. 837

Eager, George B. 901
Easterly, Elizabeth 998
   George 905
Ebaugh, Rachel 979
Ebbert, May 995
Eckardt, E. W. 856
Eckle, Mattie 943
Eckles, William K. 812
   W. K. 1012
Edes...866
Edgar, Isabella W. 978
Edge, Benjamin 885
Edington, Catherine J. 952
   Fanny 952
   James 952
   J. M. 864
   Margaret 952
   R. H. 874,952
   Thomas D. 838
Eldridge, David 952
   Elizabeth 952
   Maudie 953
   Osie 953
   Sallie 953
   T. C. 862,952,953
Elkin, George 885
Elliott...845
   Margaret 930
   Susan 1033
Ellis, J. H. 838
Elmore, E. A. 897
Elwell...877
Emery, Mary E. 1066
Emmerson, Thomas 817,819,
   873,874,875
   Joseph 905
Emory, Talton 906
Engert, Minna 993
English, Georgianna 959
Epps...856
   Armenia 953
   Mary 994
   Richard 953
   William 953
Ernest, James H. 951
   Kate C. 923
Esperandieu, Fred 869
Estabrook, Joseph 878
Evans, Amanda 949
   Daniel 1040
   Dannie J. 1040
   Elizabeth 1040
   Emma 953
   John 808
   Lucinda 1071
   Lucy 941
   P. H. 953
   Rebecca 953
   S. P. 814,867,953,954
   Walter 950
   W. H. 864,960

Fanton, Altha 1041
Fanz, Emma J. 954
   Ignaz 838,863,869,870,
   954,1072
Farmer, Alvira Cornelia
   935
   A. P. 935
Farragut...830
Fatio, P. 870
Faulkerson, Samuel V. 960
Faulkner, Abraham 960
   Lucy 912
Feehan...1003
Ferguson, Arch. 868
   James 1017
   Mattie Ann 1017
   Susan 1017
Ferrero...828

Findley, Theodosia A. 878
Finley...803
   John 899
Finnegan, M. J. 905
Finnie, Rachel 931
Fisher, Amelia 954
   Daniel 954
   Ella 954
   F. L. 867,951,954
Fiske...845
Fizer, Mary 954
   S. L. 954
   Tennie 955
   W. H. 954
Flagg, Henry G. 837
Flanders, John C. 856
Flanniken, Samuel 810
Fleming, David 889
   Ann 1031
   John M. 833,871,872
Flenniken, B. P. 955
   E. H. 955
   Elizabeth 956
   John Howell 955
   Malissa Ann 955
   Mary Adaline 955
   Samuel 956
   S. W. 855
   Wallace 955,956
   William B. 955
Flint, Barthella 1021
   F. F. 832
Floyd, Charles R. 1007
   John 1007
   Mary Fiath 1007
Fluker, E. C. 1059
Foot, Joseph I. 893
Ford, James P. 956
   Joseph 956
   Orlena 956
   Susan 956
   W. B. 814,956
   William 835
Formwalt...886
Fouche, Charles 858
Fowler...949
   Elbert S. 957
   Elizabeth 956
   Fanny 956
   James A. 957
   John 956
   John W. 957
   J. W. 812,956
   Louisa J. 957
   Mary 957
   Nancy E. 957
   Samuel 956
   Samuel P. 957
   Sarah E. 957
   William P. 957
Fox, Ann Galbraith 958
   Austin 957,962
   Charlotta B. 957
   Daisy Adelia 957
   David N. 957
   Etta J. 957
   John 957
   Joseph O. 957
   J. W., Jr. 958
   J. W., Sr. 958
   Louisa Ellen 957
   Margaret 957,962
   Mary 1044
   Mollie T. 957
   Thomas 1044
   William M. 957
   W. M. 957
Frauller, Waldburghla 1014
Frazier, Adra 958
   Alice 958
   Angus 958
   Barbara W. 1032
   Benjamin 894

Frazier, Beriah 979
   Gustavus 958
   Henry 958
   Ida 958
   James 958
   J. T. 887
   Margaret 958
   Sarah 958
Freeman, John 899
   Mary 961
French...843,884
   A. G. 813
   Elizabeth 958
   Evaline 1059
   George 958,1059
   George D. 887
   Jacob 959,987
   Jacob Dexter 959
   J. L. M. 887
   Lilly 959
   Lizzie C. 879
   Mary Adaline 955
   Mary J. 987
   Sarah 959
   Sarah Opha 959
   Susan M. 959
   Urban Alexander 959
   W. B. 951,959
   W. H. 958,959
Frierson...1042
Fristoe, Robert 898
Frizzell, John 868
Fryar, Sarah 919
   William 919
Fyffe, Mary S. 1064
Fudge, Elizabeth 1068
   Jacob 1068
   Margaret 1068
Fulcher, W. C. 875
Fulkerson, A. 833
   Alice Armstrong 959
   Alice G. 959
   Floyd Hurt 959
   Frank 834
   Georgianna English 959
   James 960
   Mrs. James L. 960
   James L. 959
   James Lyons 959
   J. V. 868,959,960
   Lula 959
   Lula Oldham 959
   Margaret Virginia 959
   Thomas Oldham 959
Funck, Charles M. 960,961
   Henry 961
   J. Cora 961
   Rosina 961
Furner, Hannah 1042

Gage, W. A. 870
Gahagan, Julia J. 975
Gaines, M. M. 843,874
Galbraith...883
   W. A. 868
Galbreath, Lorinda 934
Gallaher, CarrieSue 962
   Charles 962
   David C. 961,962
   Effie J. 962
   George 961,962,972
   George B. 962
   George H. 961
   James 973
   John F. 961
   Joshua J. 961,962
   Lucy A. 961
   Margaret 962
   Mary 961,962,972,973
   Permelia 962
   Robert H. 961,962
   Roxie 962
   Sallie E. 961

Gallaher, Sallie P. 934
  Sarah 961,962
  Sarah R. 971
  Sophronia 962
  Thomas 962
  Thomas J. 961
  William 961.962
  William B. 961
  William N. 961
  Willie R. 962
Gallatin, W. A. 893
Galyon, J. A. 902
  J. R. 870
Gamble, A, M. 838,839
  John M. 842
  Robert 815
Gammon...855
  Ed. 834
  J. P. 894
Garrett. Sallie W. 1062
Gass, Ewing 962
  J. M. 962,963
  Nancy 963
  Parmelia 962
Gauley, Elizabeth 952
Gaut, Jane 963
  John 963
  J. W. 856,880,963
  Lutitia 963
  Mary 963
  Robert 963
George...1013
  Bettie 964
  Charley Kelso 964
  Eliza J. 964
  Isaac Wright 964
  James 856
  J. L. 964
  Joe Leath 964
  J. W. 964
  Mary 964
  Milton Heiskell 964
  Samuel 964
  S. H. 852
Geiger, C. 862
Getaz...813,861
Gettys, R. P. 862
Gibbons, William E. 854
Gibbs, Daniel 935
  George W. 819
  John 965
  Lucinda 935
  Mamie 965
  Mary A. 935,1007
  Nicholas 810
  Orlena M. 935
  R. J. 935
  Sarah W. 965
  W. C. 908
  W. F. 814,965
  W. W. 835
Gibson...799
  Catherine 965
  Fanny 965
  Fanny M. 965
  Henry R. 941,965,1063
  H. R. 825,872
  Nellie 965
  Woolman 965
Giffin, Mary 1050
  Nancy 970
  Samuel Benton 970
  William 970
Gilbert, George 883
  John A. 856
Gillam, James 803
  Thomas 803
Gillenwater, E. E. 888,889
Gillespie, Annie 1039
  Clementine 912
  Cowin 912
  H. C. 835
  Isabella 1054

Gillespie, Thomas 800,802, 890,892
Gilliam, Deveraux 800,890
Gilmore, Homer 814,1008
Gilson, Catherine J. 966
  Daniel 966
  Daniel F. 966
  Emma C. 966
  Horace M. 966
  Jane 966
  Jessie C. 966
  John R. 966
  Joseph W. 966
  Lenora A. 966
  Mary C. 966
  Mary M. 966
  Nancy J. F. 966
  Nettie G. 966
  Samuel H. 966
  Sarah Mack 966
  S. L. 838,966
  Thomas W. 966
Gist, Barthella 1021
  Frances 1021
  Joshua H. 1021
  Spencer C. 1021
Glenn, Frank A. 967
  George W. 967
  John W., Jr. 967
  John W., Sr. 967
  Lula 967
  Mary 967
  Mary J. 967
Goans, Martha 1009
Godby, Emma 953
Goddard...884
  Ann 920
  John 920
  Mary 920
Goforth, Alexander 834
Golston, Nancy A. 1052
Good, Margaret C. 1044
Goodall...856
  T. T. 862
Goodhart, B. 870
Goodheart, Briscoe 932
Gooding...855
  Charlotta 968
  C. J. 967,968
  George 968
  Martha 968
Goodrich, William 846
Goodwin, Jacob 979
  Margaret 979
Gossett, Calvin 826
  C. B. 814,965
  V. F. 814,838
Gounds, William 897
Gracey...1028
Graham, L. B. 833
  William 903
Grainger, Mary 841
Gratz, L. A. 870
  Elizabeth Trigg 968
  Henrietta 968
  L. A. 869,968
  Sol 968
Graves, Henry 886,887
  Peter 899
  Samuel W. 860
Gray, Bridget 938
  Isa E. 881
  John 819
  Margaret 1022
  William 809
Gredig...945
  A. 854,868
Green, Caroline C. 930
  Elizabeth 920
  James 884
  Jesse 884
Greer, Andrew 825
  Annis 968

Greer, David 819
  J. M. 855,968,969
  John 968
  Joseph 810,815,885
  Martha E. 969
  Moses, Jr. 856
Gregg, Abraham 969
  Katie 969
  Nathan 969,970
Griffin, G. W. 901
Grigsby, J. W. 907
Groner, Catherine J. 952
  Margaret 952
  Wilson 952
Grover, Polly 994
Gump, Minnie 1055
Gurley, Tennie 955
Guthrie, James 897

Haas, Leanora 1055
Hackett, John 810
Hailey, O. L. 901
Hale, Sarah 998
Hall, Cynthia F, 1022
  E. B. 1005
  Elijah T. 824
  E. T. 1015,1022
  Flavius 1022
  Frances W. 1021
  H. W. 856
  John 837,971
  John Hall 1022
  Josephus 1022
  J. S. 855
  Major Clack 1022
  Major Learoy/M. L. 970, 971
  Mark Donel 1022
  Martha 1046
  Martha J. 925
  M. L. 824,1022
  N. R. 904
  Oliver C. 1022
  Parmelia A. 1015
  R. L. 814
  Robert 971
  Sarah 971
  S. W. 855
  Thomas 898,970,971
  Thomas D. 811
  W. A. B. 855
  William 925,971,1015, 1022
  William B. 1022
Halmark, George 899
Hamer, T. J. 1014
Hamilton...949
  Francis 898,899
  Joseph 808,809
  Pernina C. 1051
  Samuel 833
  William 808
Hammons, Willis 899
Hamstead, H. C. 908
Hamsted, H. C. 927
Hance, Margaret 992
Hancher, J. K. 905
Hand, G. W. 856
Haney, John 886
Hannah, Andrew 815
Hannifin, P. 855
Happersett, Reese 893
Harbert, Sallie W. 976
Hardin, Adelia 973
  Alice Florence 973
  Amanda 973
  Amos 971,972,973
  Amos G. 973
  Ann E. 934
  Annie 972
  Charles L. 972
  Cynthia A. 973
  Ernest M. 972

Hardin, Ernest M. 972
   George B. 972
   G. G. 971,972,973
   James 972,973
   James B. 973
   J. J. 972
   John G. 934,971,972
   Joseph 973
   Laura 973
   Lavenia S. 972
   Lenora 973
   Lurinda G. 973
   Major W. 973
   Malinda H. 973
   Mary 972,973
   Mary B. 973
   Mary E. 1017
   Matilda C. 972
   Nancy 973
   Robert 812
   Robert John 973
   R. W. 973
   Sallie B. 972
   Sallie R. 934
   Sarah 973
   Sarah J. 973
   Sarah Jane 973
   Sarah R. 971, 972
   Tennessee 972,973
   Thomas 971
   Willie M. 972
Harp, Micajah 806
   Wiley 806
Harper...1065
   Kate E. 934
Harrill, Emaline 974
   G. M. 974
   J. S. 974
   Mattie 974
   Sophia E. 974
Harris, Daniel L. 1005
   Isham G. 920,970
   J. J. 932
   Joe 974,975
   Jugie 975
   Martha 994
   Mary E. 1051
   Matilda W. 994
   Mrs. R. C. 974
   Rebecca 1034
   Miss S. J. 932
   S. K. 974
   S. T. 867
   Stephen 994
Harrison, Elizabeth 1040
   W. A. 894
Hart, F. 855
   Joseph 809
Hartley, B. J. 812
Hartranft...828
Harvey, L. 870
   R. B. 826
Hascall...828
Hausch, Rosina 961
Havely, I. B. 844
Haven, Elizabeth 1021
Havens, Rebecca 980
Havey...1037
Hawkins...1067
   H. C. 868
Hayes, George 816
   R. B. 881
   R. Y. 869
Haynes...852,856
   D. M. 861
   Elizabeth 959
   Jordan 959
   Susan 956
   Susan M. 959
Haynie...842,885
   John 886
Hays, Nancy 970
Hazen...1023

Hazen, A. E. 998
   Anna 1068
   Asa 852
   Flem. 953
   Gideon M. 848
   G. M. 811,843,874,998
   Mary 998
   R. S. 853,998
Heald, T. H. 865,866
Heckle, John 905
Heiskell, Bettie 964
   Caroline 964
   F. S. 877,960
   Julia J. 975
   Milton Y. 964
   S. G. 975
   William 877,964,975
Helms, William 899
Helsley, Sabella 1026
Henderson, James 827
   Margaret 952
   Orlena 956
   W. A. 879
Henegar, Edward 998
Henley, David 841
Henninger, John 886
Henry, Elizabeth 986
   Isabella 946
   John R. 896
   P. H. 889
   William 809
Hensell, Samuel 1026
Henson...852
   Alexander 905
   Charles C. 976
   Clementine B. 976
   Mrs. D. 976
   D. R. 976
   Ida B. 976
   John 975
   John G. 976
   L. C. 976
   L. W. 976
   Mary 975
   Mary J. 976
   Matilda B. 976
   M. T. 975,976
   Nathan H. 976
   Sarah M. 976
   Vilanto 976
   William 976
   William L. 976
Herrell, Nancy E. 957
Herrick, Henry 878
Hickey, David 977
   Fanny 977
   James 873
   Rhoda 977
Hicks, J. F. 976
   Sallie W. 976
   Thomas H. 976,977
Higgleton, William 895
Hill...1037
   Adele 977
   C. C. 855'
   Cecile L. 977
   Charles Willard 977
   Charlotta 977
   J. Willard 977
   O. F. 977
Hilliard, H. W. 1010
Hillsman, J. 900
   John 814,842,875
   M. 902
Hinch, Rhoda 910
Hindman, Samuel 816
Hines, A. D. 978
   A. D. C. 977,978
   Evaline 1071
   George Washington 978
   Isaac 977,978
   Isaac B. 978
   John M. 978

Hines, Mary L. 977,978
   Millie E. 978
   Nancy C. 978
   Nancy E. 945
   Pressure M. 978
   Rhoda 977
   Robert 911
   Samuel B. 978
   Sarah 910
   William 977,978
Hodge, Mrs. A. N. 856
Hodges, Mary 918
Hogan, Eliza M. 1065,1066
Holden, J. W. 889
Holman, J. H. 875
   John H. 864
Hommel, Daniel 1004
   Rebecca 1004
Honk, L. C. 941
Hood...828,1028
   Annis 968
   E. Lyman 906
   Isabella W. 978
   Margaret 979
   Mary 964
   Nathaniel 978
   R. N. 874,964
   S. P. 978,979
   W. H. 852
Hooper, Robert 886
Hope...856
   Mrs. B. 973
   Daniel L. 979
   D. J. 979,980
   Elizabeth 979,980
   Hattie 980
   James 973
   Jane 934
   John W. 979,980
   Mary E. 979
   Rachel 979
   Sarah 973
   Thomas 979
Horne, Amanda 980
   George 980
   J. F. 855
   John F./J. F. 980
Hornor, John S. 943
Horsely, Annie 1007
Horton, H. T. 881
Houk, L. C. 872
House, Sam 867
Houser, George 905
   Lydia 905
   Sarah 905
Houston...826
   Robert 809,810,814,815,
     875,877,891
Howe...859
Howell, Adam Daniel 981
   Azalee T. 981
   Donald Henry Luther 981
   Elizabeth 956
   James Benjamin 981
   James H. 980
   John Mc. 981
   Louisa Rebecca 981
   Margaret 1048
   Martha E. 981
   Minerva 981
   Rebecca 980
   Robert S. 981
   Sallie D. M. 981
   W. H. 980,981
   William H. 981
   William S. 877
Hoxsie, J. B. 951,981
   Lucretia 981
   Reynolds 981
   Zilpha 982
Hoyt...849
Huffacre, George 802,803
Huffaker, Eliza 1008

Huffaker, Henry 1008
  James 983
  Justus 885
  Mary 983
  Mary A. 983
  Mrs. M. E. 983
  M. W. 983
Huddleston...855,856
  Harry L. 982
  John F. 982
  L. 901,902,982
  Mary 982
  Mary E. 982
  O. W. 982
  T. L. B. 839
Hudgings, Edward 982
  Hattie C. 983
  J. C. 982,983
  Mary 982
Hudiburgh...886
Hudiburg, A. S. 814
Hudiburgh, J. L. 855
  Thomas 898,899
Huger, Benjamin 983
  Francis Kinloch 983,984
Hughes, M. J. 871
Hume, David 1001
  Eliza 1001
  Miss J. L. 1001
  Miss S. C. 1061
Humes, Andrew R. 903,984
  Anna B. 984
  Cornelia 984
  Margaret 984,1031
  Thomas 816,842,873,875,
    876,893,984
  Thomas W. 707,804,831,
    833,842,844,878,879,
    881,903,984
  T. W. 903
  W. T. C. 835
Hunt, Thomas 900
  William 869
  W. M. 827
Hunter...960
  John 846
  Robert 846
  Sophira 913
Hurd, Dymah A. 1046
Hutchinson, Anderson 873
Huwald, G. A. 836,837
Hyden, J. A. 831,888

Ingersoll, Emily G. 985
  Henry H. 985
  H. H. 867,868,936
  Mabel 985
  Semantha 985
  William 985
Ingles, W. C. 960
Inglis, Thomas 816
Ish, John 815

Jack, James 892
  Jeremiah 799,800,808,
    809,810,890
  John F. 819
Jacks, N. G. 904
Jackson...842,865,960
  Abner 986
  A. G. 843,845
  A. N. 986
  David G. 835
  Elizabeth 986
  Joseph 986
  Joseph S. 826
  Julia 985
  "Mudwall" 831
  N. T. 986
  R. C. 866,867,873,951,
    985,986
  Richard C. 951
Jacobs, S. D. 874,877

Jacobs, S. T. 843
Jacques, Joseph 874,875
Jaques, Joseph 951
Jaurolman, R. D. 889
Jarnagin, John 834
Jarnigan, Mary 988
Jeffrey, Jeremiah 816
Jenkins, B. A. 866,951
  P. F. 869
  W. 856
Jett...855
  Sarah M. 976
Johns, T. 856
Johnson...856
  Allen 987
  Andrew 929,948,1008,
    1038,1060
  Artensia 987
  A. S. 904
  Fanny 952
  Genevia 987
  Henry D. 988
  Ida F. 987
  Jacob T. 988
  J. L. 987
  John 885,987
  Joseph 899
  Julia A. 987
  Laura A. 941
  Margaret F. 988
  Martha 968,987
  Martha Alice 987
  Mary 987,1057
  Mary J. 987
  Matilda 987
  Michael 816
  Nancy 1020
  Pearl F. 987
  Rebecca 931,993
  Robert 837,870
  Thomas 987
  V. Q. 833
  William 898,987
  Zebella 987
Johnston...970
Jones...859
  Anna B. 1054
  A. S. 881
  Charles D. 1054
  C. W. 812
  Egbert 945
  Frank J. 1054
  J. B. 902
  John 825,906
  John A. 1054
  John H. 857
  Mary 954,967,988,1024
  Reps 988
  Sam 828,831
  Sarah 1054
  W. B. 988
  William E. 834
Jordan, E. L. 854,1060
  H. W. 1052
  Maggie 1060
Justice, Moses 815

Kain, Jane 1056
  John 819
  W. C. 836
Karnes, Charlton 859
  H. L. 861
Karns, Charlton 989
  J. C. 989
  Lorenia 989
  Margaret 911
  T. C. 907,908
Karr, Matthew 803
Keane, Joseph S. 905
Kearney, Lavinia 990
  Patrick 989
  Sophia 989
  Thomas H. 989,990

Kearns, John 808
Keith, J. H. 887
Keeling, Charlotte 990
  James H. 990
  James L. 990
  Jennie 990
  J. H. 868
Keener, W. B. 854
Kellar, T. W. 898
Kelley, Adaline 990
  Adeline S. 991
  Alexander 809,1012
  Annie 991
  Hattie D. 991
  Jane 1033
  J. B. 990
  J. B., Jr. 991
  Joel B. 990
  Joseph 1033
  Lucia D. 991
Kelly, H. A. 855
  H. E. 855
  J. B. 858
Kelso, Caroline 964
Kemp, Sterling 899
Kennedy...855
  Daniel 1060
  George B. 1033
  James 848,918
  Jane M. I. 918
  John 819
  John M. 894
  Martha 1025
  Martha A. 918
  Mary 1033,1060
  Myra J. 1033
  Robert 918
  Samuel B. 823,826
  Thomas 1060
  William 848
  William S. 811,893
Kennon...901
Kenton, Mariah 1031
Kern, Henrietta 991
  P. 856
  Peter 863,905,991
Kerns, Pherba E. 935
  W. R. 935
Kerr, John 816
Kesner, Jane 1053
Keyhill, Sarah O. 1012
Kimbrough...901
  Duke 898
King...803,842
  Amanda 973
  Charles L. 992
  Elizabeth 921
  James 843,870,874,877,
    887
  J. B. 834
  Jeremiah 961,973
  J. M. 991,992
  Joseph L. 846,874,877
  Julia R. 992
  Mary 961,973,992
  Minerva E. 1002
  Nancy 970
  Richard 895
  Robert 842,843,844,877
  S. L. 838
  William 883
Kinkaid, Albert Horatio 992
  Clara Bell 992
  Isaiah 992
  James Lawrence 992
  James M. 992
  John Charles 992
  Mary Ann 992
  Sarah 992
  William F. 992
Kinsloe...871
Kirkman, John 915
  Mary 915

Kirkpatrick...1037
  R. L. 878
  Robert 816
Knaffl, Lucy 946
  Dr. R. 953
  Rudolph 853
  Sallie 953
Knox, Henry 840
Knott, Matilda 987
Kohlhase, C. 856
Kountz, Sarah 959
Kuhn, John 835
Kurth, Charles 993
  Emma 993
  Ida 993
  Minna 993
Kyle, A. A. 833

Lackey, W. W. 833
Lacy, Hopkins 809,818
La Fayette...983,984
Lamar, G. B. 865
Lamb, Rufus 833
Lane, Nancy 1029
Lanes, Charlotte 957
Langford, N. C. 835
Large, Elizabeth 979
Larue...855
Lauderdale, David 825
Lavender, John 846
Lawrence, J. H. 876
Lawson, Fanny 956
Lea, Luke 819,842
  Pryor 820,821
  William 816
  William L. 838
Leadbetter...832
Ledgerwood, Ailcy 923
  Evaline 923
  J. L. 838
  William 923
  W. L. 838
Ledgewood, W. L. 1020
Lee, Charles 961
  Elizabeth 1029
  John W. 1029
  Malinda 1029
  Miss M. G. 1029
  Robert E. 1029
  Sallie E. 961
Leeds...849
Leeper, Elizabeth 931
  Hugh B. 1029
  James M. 931
  Malinda 1029
  Mary Blair 1029
  N. E. 931
Leftwich...837
Legg, Adlicia F. 995
  A. J. 995
  Christian 994
  Damie T. 995
  Edward 994
  E. P. 995
  George M. D. 994
  J. E. 995
  Martha C. 995
  Mary 995
  Mary K. 994
  Matilda W. 994
  Polly 994
  Rachel M. 995
  W. E. A. 995
  Wesley 994
Leland, F. J. 860
  Frank J. 995
  John 1005
  Mary E. 995
  May 995
Lenoir, A. S. 1011
  B. B. 1011
  C. F. 1011
Leonard, Minnie 1065

Lester, Henry D. 922
  Mahulda J. 922
  Malinda 922
Letsinger, Joanna 1048
  John 1048
  Sallie 1048
Lewis...852
  J. D. J. 869
  J. F. J. 814,941,995,996
  Laura A. 996
  Mary 1017
  Rosa 916
  Sarah C. 1028
  T. D. 857,863
  Thomas D. 870
  William 835
  W. T. 951
Leyden...829
Lichtenwanger, J. 855
Liddy, John 809
Lillard, James 997
  Jasper W. 951
  John M. 997
  J. W. 996,997
  Martha E. 997
  Mary 997
  N. J. 997
  W. H. 868
  William 997
  William C. 997
Lindell, Lorenia 989
Lindsay, Moses 844
Lindsey, Isaac 885
  Robert 847,893
  William 843
Little...982
Littleford, Miss...877
Llewellyn, Anerson 997
  Charles S. 997
  Elizabeth E. 997
  Freeman H. 997
  John 997
  John B. 997
  Nancy 997
  Nancy Jane 997
  Newton C. 997
  William A. 997
  William L. 997
Lloyd, Elizabeth 947
  J. L. 901
Lobenstein, A. 855
Locke, E. C. 853
  Ella 954
Lockett, M. A. 998
  W. B., Jr. 853,998
  W. B., Sr. 853
Logan...971
  Bethia 999
  Joseph M. 998
  Samuel 998,999
  Samuel T. 998,999
  S. T. 824
Lones...848
  Amanda 943
  Catherine J. 966
  Charles 993
  Jacob 994
  Jacob K. 837
  J. G. 999
  J. K. 814,993,994
  Martha 999
  Mary 999
  Pauline 994
  Rebecca 993
Long, Frank 905
  Henry 905
  Jacob 905
  John B. 825
  John P. 893
  Nancy 999
  Peter 905
Longmire, E. E. 839

Longstreet...828
Looney, A. 999
  Absolom 987,999
  Alexander 999
  Ellen 999
  John 987
  Martha 999
  Mary 999
  Matilda 987
  Nancy 987,999
  Robert 987,1000
  Susan 999
  Zebella 987
Lord...846
Lotspeich, Elizabeth 998
  Ida S. 998
  J. E. 998
  J. O. 853,998
  Ralph 885
  V. S. 998
Loudenslager, Amelia 954
Love, Ann Eliza 911
  B. S. B. 1050
  C. R. 855
  Elizabeth 1044
  John 814,1044
  Joseph 814,891
  Mary Sophia 1050
  R. 951
  Robert 799
  Samuel 811,814,819,900
  Sarah Bell 1007
Low, Aquila 899
  S. D. W. 897
Loward, Henry 899
Lowry, John 819
  William 808
Loyd, J. J. 855
Lucas, George 886
Luckey, C. E. 867
Lucky, C. E. 999
  Seth J. W. 824
Luttrell...885
  Amanda 980
  Eliza 1000
  James C. 836,854,874,875,1000
  James C., Jr. 980
  James C., Sr. 980
  J. C. 814,867,1000
  Joseph W. 927
  Josephine E. 1000
  L. E. 927
Lutterell, Lewis 811
Luttrell, Martha 994
  Martha A. 927
  S. B. 812,854,867,875,951,1000
Lutz, Delia 1001
  H. R. 1001
  J. E. 856,1000,1001
  Mary 1001
  Sarah 1001
Lynn, Joseph 1067
  Lute 1067
Lyon, Louisa T. 914
  Martha 1015
  Mary Payne 914
  Miss...943
  Thomas C. 914
  William 914
Lyons...826,1009,1067
  Daniel 869
  Thomas C. 826,865
  Thomas L. 825
  William 869
  W. L. 853

Mabry, Miss A. E. 998
  Alice 1001
  Belle 1062
  David Hume 1001
  Evelyn 1001

Mabry, George C, 1001
  G. W. 813,1001,1002, 1062
  Isabella 1001
  J. A. 868
  James 808
  Jeanette 1001
  J. L. 1001
  Joseph A. 998,1001
  Joseph C. 1001
  Laura 998
  Margaret L. 1001
  Maria Florence 1001
  Mary 1001
  Rowena 1001
Mack, David 1065
  William 845,896
Malcolm, J. B. 898
Maloney, Catherine 1004
  Frank D. 1002
  George E. 1002
  George L. 814,870
  G. L. 838,1002
  James D. 1002
  James W. 1002
  J. H. 1004
  Minerva E. 1002
  Sonora L. 1002
  Willie M. 1002
Manifee, John 810,886
Maniner, P. A. 866
Mann...856
  E. B. 869
  George 806
Marfield...872
  S. 1039
Marley, Elizabeth 1018
  John 1018
  Margaret 944
  Margaret J. 1018
Marrell, Isaac 969
  Katie 969
Marron, Francis Thomas 905, 1002,1003
Marshall...856
  Mary 1023
  S. W. 957
Marston...923
Martin, Cassandria E. 912
  C. N. 912
  Eliza Jane 1003
  Hugh 1003
  J. H. 896
  J. J. 902
  Joseph 801,1003
  Julia Ann 1003
  Mary 1037
  Samuel 1003
  Sarah A. 948
  S. C. 1003
  William 836
Maskall, C. F. 856
Mason, Adaline 1005
  Clara Bell 992
  Elizabeth 1044
  E. W. 992
  Hattie D. 991
  Nancy 991
  Nathaniel 991
  Susan H. 921
Massey, Sarah 1054
Mathes, A. A. 895
Matlock, Martha E. 997
Matthews, Jeremiah 808
  L. C. 856
Maury...828
Maxey, Abram 1004
  Andrew 1004
  Catherine 1004
  Franklin 1004
  J. H. 1004
  John 1004
  Lucy A. 1039

Maxey, Rebecca 1004
  Sallie 1004
  Spencer A. 1004
  William 1004
Maxwell, A. L. 846,849, 858,864,865,869,1004, 1005
  A. N. 868
  Harriet J. 1005
  Hattie B. 1005
  Helen M. 1005
  Hugh 1005
  Louie L. 1005
  Rachel 1004
Maxey, Mrs. S. 905
Maynard...1030
  Ed 949
  Edward 838,910
  Mrs. Edward 1065
  Horace 825,845,878,914, 1069
Mayo, D. R. 855
Mays, J. F. B. 901
McAdoo, Annie 1007
  Caroline B. 1007
  Emma 1007
  John 1006
  John F. 1007
  Kate 1007
  Laura S. 1007
  Malcolm R. 1007
  Mary A. 1007
  Mary Faith 1007
  Nona H. 1007
  Rosalie F. 1007
  W. G. 797
  William G. 823,1007
  William Gibbs 1006,1007
McAfferty, William 858
McAffrey, J. M. 861
McAffry, James M. 869
  Terence 848
  Thomas 827
McAnally, D. R. 878
McBath, Alice 937
  Caroline 937
  J. R. 868
  Robert 937
  Sallie 937
  William 937
  W. R. 814
McBee, G. C. 1007,1008
  J. A. 1008
  N. E. 1008
  R. L. 1008
  Sarah B. 1008
  Sarah Bell 1007
  W. S. 1008
McCafferty, Ella K. 915
McCallum, Lurinda G. 973
McCampbell, Benjamin Bennett 1009
  J. A. 855,1009
  James 811
  John 896
  Martha 1009
  Robert 811
  Sarah 971
  Sarah Louesa 1044
  Solomon 886
  William H. 1009
  Wm. A. 895
McCammon, Eliza 1008
  Elizabeth 1009
  Joanna E. 1008
  John N. 1009
  Martha B. 1008
  Samuel 814,1008,1009
  W. C. 1008,1009
  William 814
McClanahan, E. G. 869
McClellan...841
  Geo. B. 844

McClellan, George B. 944
  John 810,844
  M. S. 852
  M. W. 826
McCleskey, Mary 992
McClung...943,1023
  Annie 1010,1012
  Charles 808,809,810,814, 836,840,841,842,877,894, 1010,1012
  C. J. 851,867
  C. M. 854,866,867,951, 1010,1012
  Eliza 1010
  E. S. 835
  F. H. 851,941,1010
  Franklin H. 951
  H. 843
  H. L. W. 835
  Hugh L. 814,846,876,1029
  James 894
  M. 843
  Matt 851
  Matthew 844,877,894
  P. M. 868
McCollum, J. R. 834
McCombs, Thomas 870
McCorry, Thomas 873,875
McCoy...846,856
  W. C. 902
McCroskey...848
  David 1010
  E. E. 866,868,881,1010, 1011
  E. J. 898
  Elizabeth 1010
  Ellen R. 1011
McCrum...855
McCullen, John 873
McCulloch...847
  J. S. 882
  Thomas 808
McCully, George 894
McCutcheon, Jane 1034
McDaniel, Elizabeth 1048
  T. P. 855,904
McDaniels, T. P. 859
McDonald, A. 894
McDonaugh, A. A. 904
McDonough, Araminta 1011
  Fred Lenoir 1011
  J. Albert 1011
  John 1011
  John Henry 1011
  J. S. 1011
  Katie W. 1011
  Laura Bell 1011
  Maggie L. 1011
  Mary 1038
  Mary L. 1011
McDowell, Penelope T. 1051
McElnee, Julia R. 992
McElrath...843
McFarland...803
  James 992
  John 804
  Sarah 992
McGauhey, Miss R. A. 1023
McGhee, Annie 1010,1012
  Bettie H. 1012
  Charles 904
  Charles M. 865,1010, 1011,1012
  C. M. 865,866,867,951
  Cornelia H. 1012
  Ellinor W. 1012
  Isabella M. 1012
  John 1012
  Lawson 975,1010,1012
  Margret W. 1012
  May Lawson 1012
McGlothen, Charles 889
McGoffey, C. D. 880

McGonegal, Floyd 898
McGowan, J. P. 828
McGrew, Charlotte 990
McIntire, John 815
McIntosh, Donald 870,874,
   877
McKee, John 819
McKendree, William 885
McKinney...823
   Ella 1033
   Samuel 849,871,951
McLain, Mary 940
McLaws...829
McLemee...840
McLemore, Ellen 1012
   Green 1012
   Sarah O. 1012
McMahan, M. B. 846,847
McMillan,...855,856
   A. 843,877
   Alex 953
   Almeda 1020
   Andrew 844
   E. E. 852
   John 852
   Margaret M. 938
   David 825
McMillen, Margaret A. 1030
McMullan...843
McMullen, Daniel 1035
   James P. 894
   Robt. B. 893
   Rosina 1035
   W. B. 864
McNairy, John 815
McNamee, Peter 841
McNew, Mattie 974
McNott, George 875
McNulty, F. 852
McNulty...851,853
McNutt...883,1003,1040
   George 800,808,810,839,
   890,892
   James 877
   William 819
   W. J. 854
McPhetsidge, Pauline C.
   1051
McTeer, C. E. 852
   Joseph T. 867
   J. T. 852,867
McTeers...1028
Mead, H. G. 855,1047
   W. S. 857,881
Meade, Everard 904
Meek...855,941
   Adam 799,1012
   Adam K. 1013
   Ann 1034
   C. W. 998
   Damie 1034
   Elizabeth 1013,1034
   Ida S. 998
   James 1034
   James K. 1013,1014
   James M. 866,867,1012,
   1013
   Jane 1034
   J. M. 951
   John 1034
   Joseph 1034
   Lilly 1013
   Lizzie J. 1013
   Martha 1034
   Mary 1034
   Nancy 1034
   Rebecca 1034
   Samuel 1034
   Sarah 937,998
Meeks, William 809
Mehaffy...859
Nehaffey, R. 1024
Merryman, Malinda E. 928

Messengill, Eliza C. 1016
Metler, A. 1014
   Eliza 1072
   Susan 1014
   Waldburghla 1014
Meyer, Henrietta 991
Meyers, Archibald 838
   J. H. 896
Middleton...1065
Miller...979
   Adam 905
   James 841
   John 806,833
   M. M. 833
   Pleasant M. 819,842,876
   Samuel 841
   Sarah 992
   Sarah Jane 935
   William 935
   W. M. 855
Milligan...1061
Milliken...901
   James 816
   Thomas 816
Mills, Eliza 1010
Miner, Lavinia 990
Minnis, J. B. 855
Mitchell...855
   A. H. 1015
   Alice G. 1016
   Berry 1067
   Eliza 1015
   Elizabeth 1019
   Elizabeth C. 1016
   John 1015
   John B. 877,1014,1015
   Joseph R. 846,1015,1016,
   1019
   J. R. 866,879
   Laura A. 996
   Martha 1015
   Mary E. 1062
   Parmelia A. 1015
   Richard 1015,1016
   Sallie B. 1067
   Samuel 815,819
   S. D. 960
   Solomon 1015
   Stokley 1016
Mixter...866
Mizner, H. S. 860
Moffett...849
   H. P. 827
   John S. 864
Molton, M. C. 826
Monday, Martha Jane 1055
   W. O. 1055
Monserrat, G. H. 828
Montgomery...826,833
   Dartha Eva 1017
   Elizabeth 1009
   Hattie Miller 1017
   Ida Lee 1017
   James 1009
   Jefferson E. 896
   John 798
   John Chester 1017
   John M. 1016
   Josiah 1016,1017
   Lemuel P. 825
   Martha Elizabeth 1017
   Martha M. 1016
   Mary 1017
   Mary Annie 1017
   Mary J. 1016
   William Austin 1017
Moore, C. J. 855
   D. 856
   Kate E. 939
   W. A. J. 902
   William 894
Morel, Anna 1017
   Catherine 1017

Morel, Charles 1017
   Charles S. 1017
   James 1017
   Louisa 1017
   Mark 1017
   Mary 1017
   Samuel 1017
   Sarah 1017
   Susan 1017
Morgan...1023,1042
   Calvin 842,843,844,847,
   873,876,877
   Calvin G. 842
   Gideon 896
   John H. 942
   John T. 1010
   R. 842
   Rhoda 1069
   Rufus 848,873
Morman, J. 871
Morris...826
   J. B. 1017,1018
   John Dickenson 1018
   Joseph 1017
   Joseph Robert 1018
   Margaret J. 1017
   Rachel 1017
   Mrs. R. L. 1054
Morrison, Mary 1022
Morrow, Charles 812,814
   J. 1035
   James 826
   Robert 865
   Samuel 846
   William 847,868
Morrs, John A. 1055
   Nancy 1055
Morse, Miss...877
   William 847
Morton, P. A. 927
Moses, Abbie C. 1018
   Elizabeth 1019
   F. A. 866
   Frank A. 872,1019
   Frank Q. 1057
   James C. 845,901,1019
   John F.1018
   John L. 812,846,901,
   996,1018,1019
   Katie 1019
   Mary 1018
   Susan 1019
   Susan W. 1019
   Thomas L. 1019
Moss...949
   Arnold 899
Moulden, Almeda 1020
   Anna Lee 1020
   Belle K. 1020
   Fred T. 1020
   John 1020
   John W. 1020
   Nancy 1020
   Nannie E. 1020
   William 1020
Mowbray, William 903,904
Mullet, A. B. 875
Munson, Spencer 868
Murphy, Adelia 948
   A. E. 838
   James A. 948
Murwin, Abigail 926
Mussey...990
Mustard, J. C. 863
Myer, Catherine 924
Mynatt, B. K. 1022
   E. F. 1020,1021
   Elizabeth 1021
   Frances 1021
   Frances W. 1021
   H. L. W. 814
   J. C. 1021,1022
   John 811,1021

Mynatt, John N. 1021
  Joseph A. 1021
  L. M. 1067
  Melvina 1021
  Richard 1021
  W. C. 874
  William 1021
  William C. 820,877

Naill, John 892
Nave, Alice C. 1022
  Andrew H. 1022
  Isabella B. 1022
  J. H. 1022,1023
  John 1022
  Margaret 1022
  Margaret E. 1022
  Mary 1022
  Mary A. V. 1022
  Susan J. 1022
Neal, Nicholas 816
Neely, James 809
Neilsom, Catherine 1056
  William 1056
Nelson...886,1003
  Ann 1024
  Charlotte 957
  David 842,873,957
  Eliza Jane 1003
  H. O. 859
  Hugh B. 1023
  John R. 822
  Joseph 1022
  Louisa Ellen 957
  M. 812,855,877,1023
  Margaret E. 1022
  Margaret J. 1017,1018
  Martha 1023
  Mary 1024
  Mathew 1023
  M. M. 1023
  Nancy 925,971,1022
  R. A. 1023
  Suthy 957
  Thomas A. R. 845,999,
    1023,1024
  Thomas H. 892
Netherland, Harriet 920
  John 833,920
Newell, Samuel 808,809,814
Newhouse, C. B. 883
Newman, C. S. 853
  Cullen 853
  Curtis 853
  Henry B. 814
  James 836
  J. E. 869
  S. 856
  Tazewell 827
Newport, Richard 898,899
Nicholas, D. D. 951,1024,
  1025
  Flora E. 1025
  James 1024
  Mary 1024,1025
  Nellie 1025
Nicholl, F. B. 838
  Josiah 842
Nicholls, John 841
Nichols, Katie R. 941
Nicoll, Edward 860
  Mary S. 1069
Ninney, C. G. 1052
  Laura Ellen 1052
Ninny, Patrick 817
Nisonger, James A. 862
North, J. W. 858
Norton, Maria 1066
Norwood, Nicholas 886

Oates...1001
  E. T. 860
Oats, Roger 805
Oats, Sarah 961
Ochs, Julius 812,869
Ogden...848,856
  Alfred 1026
  S. R. 1026
  Titus 840
Oglesby, Joshua 885
O'Keefe, John 838
Oldham...960
  Georgianna 959
  Lula 959
  Thomas E. 894,959
  William 847
O'Neal, J. S. 1007
  Rosalie F. 1007
O'Conner, James 861,1025,
  1026,1070
  Mary S. 1025
  Rebecca 1025
  Thomas 836,861,988
Ore, James 841
Orr, G. J. 967
  Mary J. 967
Osborn, James 1026
  Martha 909
  R. G. 1026
  Sabella 1026
  Sarah J. 1026
Outlaw, Alexander 808,809,
  818
Owen, Hattie 980
Owens, H. J. 855

Palmer, John 992
  Margaret 992
  Mary Ann 992
Pancoast, Joseph 950
  William H. 950
Parham, E. N. 889
  Thomas 838
Park, C. W. 848
  James 811,842,843,844,
    873,874,875,877,892,
    893,895
  Susan W. 1019
  William 842,843,873,
    875,893
Parke, John G. 828
Parker, Ellen 999
  F. S. 1026
  Harriet A. 878
  H. D. 1027
  Howard R. 1027
  Hugh F. 1027
  Jennie 1027
  John 999
  JohnF. 1026,1027
  Loyd C. 1027
  Mary B. 1026
  P. C. 1027
  R. H. 887
  Robert 816
  W. H. 869
  Zillah 1046
Parks, H. W. 839
  Rebecca 953,854
Parsons, Charlotta 977
  Enoch 819
  Harriet 1065
  Peter 819
Partin, M. J. 1058
Passavant...905
Pate...883,1040
  Ann A. 944
  John F. 944
  Margaret 944
  Mary 988
Pates, John 803
Patrick, James 864
  William 864
Patterson, Edgar 1027
  James 1027
  John 815

Patterson, Mary M. 1027
  M. L. 814,1027
  Nettie E. 1027
  Orton 1027
  W. R. 832
Pattison, William 885
Patton, Annie 1035
  Isaac 892
  Jacob 891
  Rebecca 1036
Patty, Obed 899
Paul, F. M. 872
Paxton. James W. 868
  John 833,870,871
  John W. 868
  Joseph W. 870,871
Payne...855
  A. C. 1028
  Bettie 1028
  J. K. 877
  John K. 879
  Laura 1028
  R. S. 852,866,867,875,
    951,1028
  Sarah C. 1028
  Simpson 826
  Susan 1028
Peach, Mary Alice 1033
Pearson, Mary 1018
Peed, Annie 1070
  Elizabeth 924
Pelleaux, Fannie 1054
Penland, N. A. 876
  Nobel A. 892
Pepper...883
Perkins, W. J. 832
Perry, W. C. 855
Persley, Nancy 1045
Peters...859,923
  G. W. 902
Phagan, John 825
Pickens, William C. 838,
  839
Pickle, Jonathan 958
  Margaret 958
  Mary A. 983
  Miss M. E. 983
Pierce, I. A. 889
Pigeon, Charles D. 893
Piper...845,920
  A. M. 874
  Julia E. 910
  Lucinda 910
  William 910
Pitman, Charles 864
Pittille, Elizabeth 1048
Plecker, Mary 1001
Plumlee...845
Poe, O. M. 830
Polk, James K. 1038
  J. K. 1032
Porta, Eliza 925
Porter, James 819
  Joseph A. 894
  J. S. 897
Post, Esther 946
  F. H. 862
  Joseph 946
  S. T. 862
Potter...828
  Elizabeth 1068
Powell, C. 845,854,867
  Lillie 1052
  Rebecca 1025
  Thos. J. 874
  T. J. 845
Powers...855
  S. T. 982
Prater, Benjamin 1029
  Bessie Lee 1029
  Bob 1030
  Elizabeth 1030
  Ernest 1029

Prater, Frederick B. 1030
  George W. 1030
  G. W. 1029,1030
  Hattie W. 1030
  Hugh Leeper 1029
  James Gaines 1029
  Joseph B. 1030
  Mary B. 1030
  Mary Blair 1029
  Mary Ellen 1029
  M. G. 1029
  Nancy 1029
  Miss N. E. 931
  Roddy Clifford 1029
  Tracy W. 1030
  W. H. B. 1029
  William 1029
  William Walter 1029
Price, A, J. 860
  Christian 994
  Edward 994
  Juda 994
  Mary S. 1025
  R. N. 888
  T. R. 860
  William N. 838
Prichard, M. B. 865
Pride, Benjamin 809
Prosser, A. S. 869,870,
  1030,1031
  Brown 1030
  David 1031
  Lizzie 1030
  Mariah 1031
  Rachel 1031
  T. E. 1031
Pruett, M. 816
Putnam, W. C. 869

Quaife...857,990
Quarles, R. 826
Quincy...862

Raht, J. E. 951
Ramage,..856
  W. J. 869,870
Ramsey, Ann 1031
  Arthur C. 1032
  Eliza J. 1043
  F. A. 799,814,817
  Francis A. 810,815,870,
  885,890,894,1031
  Francis H. 875
  Frank A. 871,1032
  G. B. 836,837
  James Gettys McGready
  1031,1032
  J. G. M. 807,814,845,
  846,870,890,892,894,
  1031,1032
  J. M. A. 1031
  John C. 1032
  Lillie 1050
  Margaret 1031
  Naomi 1031
  Peggy 1031,1032
  Reynolds 1031
  Robert M. 1032
  Samuel G. 814,875,892,
  894,1031
  W. B. A. 807,814,823,
  844,874,894,1050
  William B. A. 1031
  William W. 1032
  W. M. 985
Randles, Joanna E. 1008
  John 1009
Rankin, William 799
Ray...901
Rayl...845,921
  J. A. 849,879,880
  Jesse A. 951
Reagan, William 802

Redd, Ann E. 1058
Reed, E. A. 866
  Fanny M. 965
Reeder, ...912,965
  Alexander 814,1048
  Cordelia M. 1047
  Eliza Jane 912
  Z. 900
Reese, James 809
  John J. 1003
  Julia Ann 1003
  William B. 817,877,1003
Reeve, F. A. 832,880
Reid, Abraham 899
Reis, George L. 857
Reynolds, Barbara W, 1032
  Claude E. 1033
  Ida L. 1033
  John 1032
  John P. 1033
  Mary 1033
  Mary B. 1033
  Robert B. 1032,1033
Rhea, Archibald 896
  Archibald, Jr. 890
  Archibald, Sr. 800,890,
  892
  John 809,816,818
  Mary 919
  R. M. 851
  William 815
Rhoades, George T. 904
Rhodes, A. G. 856
Ricardi...845
Rice, Luther 899
Richards, D. 857
  David 906
  David C. 906
  David J. 906
  D. C. 951
  Elizabeth 980
  J. 857
  Joseph 906
  Richard 885
  W. J. 857
Richardson...861
  Jugie 975
  J. W. 975
Richie, Thomas 816
  William 816
Ringel...996
Ristine, Charles E. 1033
  Ella 1033
  J. C. 869,1033
  Mary Alice 1033
  Susan 1033
Ritter...856
Roady, P. D. 870
Roane, Archibald 809,818
Robards, Israel 901
Roberts, Andrew 1033
  Arminda 1066
  E. C. 838
  Ellen C. 1034
  Gains S. 1034
  Henrietta E. 1034
  Henry 1033
  Henry G. 1034
  Henry L. 1034
  J. 886
  James 877
  Jane 1033
  Jennie 1027
  J. G. 838
  John 837
  John B. 1034
  Joseph A. 1034
  Narcissa R. 1034
  P. A. 856,1034,1035
  Rebecca 1034
  Rebecca J. 1034
  Robert L. 1034
  Russell H. 1033,1034

Roberts, Samuel 842,843
  T. J. 856
  William F. 1034
Robertson, Emaline 974
  R. D'S. 881
Robinson, Dick 948
  J. A. 927
  James F. 996
  T. H. 1026
  W. C. 838
Robison, Thomas 816
Rockhold, Harriet 920
  Mary 919
  William 920
Rodefer...1067
Rodgers, Ann 1036
  Anna 1035
  Annie 1035
  Charles E. 1035
  Hugh M. 1035
  Isabella 1035
  James 868,870,871,1035
  James M. 883
  John 1036
  Lillie 1035
  Margaret 1036
  Martha 987
  Rebecca 1036
  Reuben B. 822
  Rosina 1035
  Samuel 1036
  Samuel A. 824
  Samuel R. 823,971,1035
  Sophronia 962
  S. R. 813
  Thomas 811,1035
  W. A. 1035,1036
  Wallace D. 1035
  William 871,897,962
Rogan, Catherine 1036
  Daniel 1036
  L. H. 858,868,1036
  Margret 1036
  Nancy 1036
Roger, Cecile L. 977
Rogers, Alice G. 1016
  Elijah 898
  Elizabeth 1010
  Emily G. 985
  George 959
  John 835
  William H. 888
Rohel, A. 966
  Emma C. 966
Rolen, Carrie 1037
  George 1036
  Hila 1036
  Thomas M. 1036,1037
  T. M. 855
Rolfe, Hannah 914
Rollings, Mrs. C. F. 856
Rollins, T. G. 845
Roney, S. C. 851
Rose, D. M. 861
Ross, Ellen 1038
  George W. 864,875
  G. W. 1037
  James 1037
  John 1005
  John M. 864
  John S. 1037
  Martin 1038
  Mary Martin 1036,1037
  M. L. 853,867,998,1037,
  1038
  P. C. 1027
  William Carey 1038
Rotach...860
Roth, George W. 869
  Lewis 894
Roulstone, George 807
Rourke, Mary 1038
  Michael F. 1038

Rouser, U. A. 868
Rowley, M. 876
Rowntree, J. T. 855
Rudder, A. A. 905
Rule...884
   Frederick 1039
   Lucy A. 1039
   M. A. 889
   Sarah E. 1039
   William 814,839,868,872,
   874,889,1038,1039
Russell...883
   Andrew 897
   Anna M. 1040
   Annie 1039
   Dannie E. 1040
   Dannie J. 1040
   Frank P. 1040
   George 897
   John H. 1039
   John P. 1040
   Joseph E. 1040
   Linda A. 1040
   M. 1040
   Margaret 984
   Margaret A. 1040
   Nancy 1034
   R. 1040
   Thomas 888
   Thomas H. 889
   William L. 1040
   W. L. 1039,1040
Ruth, Albert 881
Rutherford...847
   C. 838,855
   Martha 911
   Rachel 911
Ryan, A. J. 905

Sammon, R. 856
Sample, J. C. 852
Samples...803
Samuel, D. R. 860,1040
   Joe 1040
   Mary 1040
   Mary P. 1040
   Philip 1040
   Ruth 1040
   W. R. 860,1040
Sanders...828
Sanderson, Eliza 1001
Sandusky, Mary 997
Sane, Joseph 905
Sanford, Altha 1041
   Edward T. 1041
   E. J. 853,862,865,866,
   867,951,1041
   Emma 1041
   John W. 1041
Sansom, D. N. 1041
   Loulie 1042
   Mary Agnes 1041
   R. H. 868,1041,1042
   Richard 1041
Saulpaw, George W. 812,1006
Saunders, Malinda 1029
Sawyer, Miss R. C. 974
Sawyers, James 871
   John 808,810,875,1034
   Miss N. E. 1008
   Rebecca 1034
   W. S. 1008
Saxton, H. N., Jr. 860
Saylor, John W. 908
   J. W. 926
Scaggs, Deborah 1049
   Eli 899
Scarborough, W. B. 855
Schaad...860
Schaffer, Jacob M. 905
Schaidt, J. George 905
Schneider...1072
   J. C. 855

Schneider, W. A. 855
Schirman, L. W. 870
Schubert, A. 1042
   A. A. N. 1042
   D. 1042
   H. 856,1042
   Hannah 1042
Scott...859
   Alice 1001
   Araminta 1011
   Callie 1043
   A. C. 1043
   Charles 1043
   D. H. 1043
   E. A. 1043
   Edward 817,819,842,971
   Elizabeth B. 1043
   Eliza J. 1043
   F. A. R. 847,848,894
   Frank A. R. 1043
   I. N. 856
   James 847,848,1043
   J. L. 1043
   John R. 1043
   M. A. 1043
   Margaretta F. 1043
   N. R. 1043
   R. L. 1043
   T. S. 896
   Winfield 1043
Scruggs, Parmelia 962
Seaskind, A. 855
   S. 855
Seaton, Caroline 1044
   Caroline D. 1044
   Elizabeth 1044
   Emma 1044
   James 1044
   James N. 1043,1044
   J. N. 919
   Kate 1044
   Margaret C. 1044
   Mary 1044
   Mary A. 1057
   Rachel 1044
   Robert 1044
   Sarah L. 919
   Sarah Louesa 1044
   Sophronia J. 1044
   Susan 1044
Seawell, Benjamin 819
Seay, T. S. 855
   William 886
Selden...855
Sessler, Mary 983
Sevier...801
   John, Jr. 819
Sevy...1037
Seymour, C. 881
Shackleford, J. M. 828
Shannon, Elizabeth E. 997
   James 997
   Mary 997
Sharp, Amy 1045
   Andrew 913
   Condray 1045
   Drucilla 913
   Elizabeth 1044
   Elmer 1045
   J. F. 1044,1045
   Pauline 994
   Mary 1045
   Minnie May 1045
   Parris 1045
   Sinai 913
   William 1044
Sharpe, William 816
Shelby, Evan 798,801
Shell, Albert E. 1046
   Christian 1045
   Jacob 1045
   John 1045
   Lina B. 1046

Shell, Lucy J. 1045
   Lula E. 1045
   M. 1045
   Nancy 1045
   Paris M. 1045
   P. M. 1046
   Miss R. 935
   Sanford C. 1046
   Susan 1045
   William 935
   William T. 1045
Shepard...849,856
   Dymah A. 1046
   Emily E. 1046
   Lazarus C. 1046
   L. C. 857,869
   Lou 1047
   Philo B. 1046,1047
   Sueton 1046
Shepherd...846
   P. B. 870
Sheridan...862
Sherman, Alzada Tennessee
1048
   Cordelia M. 1048
   David A. 876
   Emily 1047
   Emma Hazel 1048
   James 1047
   John 941
   John Thomas Wentforth
1048
   J. W. 1047,1048
   Linnie Belle 1048
   Mary Effie 1048
Sherrell, Margaret 945
Sherrod, Charlotta 1048
   Elizabeth 1048
   Isaac 1048
   Jonathan 916,1048
   Margaret 1048
Shetterly, J. M. 856
Shields, Elizabeth 1062
   John 864
   J. S. 852,1062
   J. T., Jr. 852,1062
Shinpaugh, Alexander 1049
   Calvin 1049
   Elizabeth 1048,1049
   George 1049
   Henry 1048
   Hugh 1049
   James 1049
   Joanna 1049
   John 1049
   Sallie 1048,1049
   William 1048,1049
Shipe, Alexander 933
   Alvin B. 1049
   Apolinia E. 1049
   Charles Russell 1049
   Deborah 1049
   George W. 1049
   Henry W. 1049
   James C. 1049
   John D. 1049
   Joseph F. 1049
   J. R. 908,926
   J. W. 1049,1050
   Martha E. 1049
   Martha M. 933
   Ruth C. 1049
   William H. McC. 1049
Shropshire, Callie 1043
Shughrue...855,967,968
Simmonds, Cyrus 1050
   James H. 1050
   Lillie 1050
   W. H. 867,874,894,1050
Simmons, C. N. 862
Simpson, David LaFayette
1051
   Delilah Jane 1051

Simpson, Elizabeth 1062
  Jesse, Jr. 1050,1051
  Jesse, Sr. 1050,1051
  John 1050
  Joseph Alexander 1050, 1051
  Margaret 1050
  Margaret C. 1050
  Mary 1050
  Mary J. 1050
  Mary Sophia 1050
  R. R. 873
  Sarah Elizabeth 1051
  Telitha Ann 1051
Singleton, John 894
  Robert 894
Skaggs, Elizabeth 927
Slair, Jacob 1034
  Rebecca J. 1034
Slatery, John 1028
  Kate 1071
  Susan 1028
Slaughter, Elizabeth 1054
Slemons, Nettie E. 1027
Slocum, J. W. 855
Slover, Miss...1037
Smart, James R. 981
  Minerva 981
Smith...855,856
  Aaron 899
  Adelia 973,1052
  Arthur 1053
  Birton 837
  Bell 1052
  Burgess 1052
  E. Kirby 828
  Emily A. 940
  Emily Ann 1051
  Eugene 1052
  Frank M. 908
  Guy 825
  Harvey 1052
  Hugh L. 1051
  H. W. 1052
  J. A. 1051
  J. Allen 856,859,1052
  James 1051
  James B. 1052
  John A. 1051
  John H. 903
  John L. 1051
  John T. 1052
  Joseph W. 1051
  Josiah 1051
  Kate 1057
  Kirby 836
  Laura Ellen 1052
  Laura L. 1051
  Lillie 1052
  Lizzie 1052
  Lucinda E. 1052
  Lucy P. 1051
  Luther 1052
  Maggie 1053
  Margaret B. 1051
  Mary 917,982
  Mary E. 1051
  Matilda C. 972
  Nancy 1051
  Nancy A. 1052
  Nancy B. 1051
  Nathaniel 825
  Oscar D. 1051
  Pauline C. 1051
  Penelope T. 1051
  Pernina C. 1051
  Pherba 935
  Samuel L. 1052
  Sidney 1052
  Sophia 1052
  S. P. 907
  Stephen H. 814
  Thomas A. 838

Smith, William 1052
  William E. 835,1051
  W. P. 854
  W. S. 812
  W. T. 1052
Snapp, J. K. 826
Snead, Henry 1053
  Malinda 1053
  Jane 1053
  Robert 1053
Sneed, Eliza D. 1054
  Joseph W. 1053,1054
  Lizzie D. 1053
  M. H. 1054
  W. H. 825
Snyder, Catherine 915
  Elizabeth 1054
  Fannie 1054
  George L. 1054
  George W. 1054
  Roy Sankey 1054
  Sarah 1054
Sommerville, John 841
Somerville, Mary 948
Sommers, Louisa T. 912
Sparkes, Carrie 1037
Spears...1027
Spence...855
  John F. 878,889
Spencer, Elizabeth 924
Squeb...1056
Stafford, Rachel 1004
Staley, W. B. 825
Stamps,..859
Stanfield, A. 825
Stanley, Nancy 1051
Starr, E. F. 1005
Staub...856
  Peter 858,874,875
Steel, John 816
Steen...856
Stephens, Alexander H. 910
  Benjamin 817
  J. V. 898
Stephenson...813,861
  W. R. 869
Steptoe, Zephana 917
Sterling, Isabella 1054
  James 1054
  R. A. 813,1054
  R. L. 1054
Stern, Joseph 1055
  Leanora 1055
  M. 1055
  Minnie 1055
  Nathan 1055
Stevenson, R. J. 860
Stewart, J. W. 870
Stine, L. H. 904
Stinnett, Vilanto 976
Stone, Amasa 1005
  Andros B. 1005
  John 809,842
  Nancy 1055
Stout, George 816
Stover, Bell 1052
Strickland, C. H. 901,1059
Stringfield, Thomas 888
Strong, Albert Newton 1055
  Benjamin Rush 1055
  B. R. 867
  Catherine 1056
  Charles Ready 1055
  David 1056
  Elizabeth 1057
  Emily E. 1046
  Gideon Hazen 1055
  Gideon Rush 1057
  Horace 1055
  Jane 1056
  John 1056
  John Morrs 1055
  Joseph C. 870,874,876,

Strong (continued)
  Jos. C...877,892,893, 1031
  Joseph Churchill 1055
  Juda 1056
  Martha Jane 1055
  Mary 998
  Mary Eliza 1057
  Mary Hazen 1055
  Ralph 1057
  Richard 1056
  Robert Nilson 1055
  Sophronia 1055,1057
  William Erwin 1055
Stuart, Ann 1024
  Annie 991
  Jacob 991
  Margaret 991
  Thomas 825
Sturgis, F. E. 896,914
  Lou Lyon 914
Sturn, C. 905
Sullens, David 996
  Rebecca L. 1002
Sullins, D. 833
  David 1070
  Mary 1070
Sullivan, Dennis 965
  Mamie 965
  M. D. 812
Summers, Alex. 1057
  Alexander 872
  C. R. 924
  George W. 1057
  Harriet O. 924
  Kate 1057
  Mary 1057
  Norman 1057
  Thomas 1057
Swan...991
  Anna Belle 1058
  Catherine 919
  Clarence L. 1058
  Eliza 919,1044
  Isabella 1054
  J. A. 814,1057,1058
  James 919
  J. D. 827
  Mary A. 1057
  Mat. 958
  M. D. 814,1008
  M. J. 1058
  Moses M. 811,814
  W. H. 814,1057
  William 823,877
  William G. 874
  William H. 814
Swearinger, Richard 834
Sweepson...923
Sweet, Charles A. 1058
  Charles J. 1058
  C. J. 863
  Mary J. 1058
Swepson, Ann E. 1058
  R. R. 851,1058
  William M. 1058

Tadlock, A. B. 874
Talbot, Bethia 999
Tarr, Elizabeth 942
Tarwater, Evaline 1059
  H. C. 814,872,889
  Jacob 1058,1059
  Judia 1058
  William 1058
Tate. J. O. 825
  John 898
Tatham, William 818,819
Tauxe, Sylvia 925
Taylor, A. B. 1059
  E. A. 901,1059,1060
  E. C. 1059
  E. F. 904

Taylor, E. Leland 1060
  Elizabeth 948
  Eugene A., Jr. 1060
  Franklin W., Sr. 951
  F. W., Sr. 867
  J. D. 833
  John 896
  Luther 885
  M. 856
  Maggie 1060
  N. G. 833
Teasdale, Katie 1019
  T. C. 1019
Tedford, Catherine J. 919
  H. 919
  Isabella C. 919
Temple, A. O. P. 824
  James 1060
  Mary 1060
  Mary B. 1061
  Mazer 1060
  O. P. 1060,1061
  S. C. 1061
Templeton, A. 897
  Allison 1062
  Belle 1062
  Isabella 1001
  Jerome 1001,1061,1062
  Mahala 1062
Terry...861,1026
Thatcher, Carey 873
  Peter 1005
Thomas 999,1001
  D. 857
  Ellis 826
  J. E. 826
  J. L. 851
  Lytton 852
  Robert D. 906
  Thomas 906
Thompson...891
  Ailcy 923
  John 923
  Martha M. 1063
  Sallie E. 1063
  Samuel H. 885
  William 819,1063
Thornburg, D. G. 832
Thornburgh...855
  Russell 837
  T. T. 839
Tiel, Edward 806
Tillery, Eglentine 912
  S. L. 912
Tillman, Lewis 904
Tindall, Jeremiah 886
Tindell, Charles 940
  Dicy 1045
  Mary 940
  Samuel 1046
  Zillah 1046
Tipton, Malissa Ann 955
  William C. 955
Todd, S. J. 870
Tomes, Charles 903
Tompkins...855
Toms...856
Townsend, Caroline 1067
  J. B. 878
Tracey, William R. 837
Treadwell...855,1020
Trent...856
  Bettie Lee 1062
  C. F. 1062
  Flora B. 1062
  James 1063
  James W. 1062,1063
  J. R. 1062
  Mary E. 1062
  Mollie T. 1062
  Sallie E. 1062,1063
  Samuel 1062
  William B. 1062

Trent, William L. 1062, 1063
Trewhitt...1010
  Thomas L. 839
Trice, James 899
Trigg...971
  E. C. 833
Trimble, James 817,819,842
  William 815,816
Trout, A. W. 924
  Gertrude 924
  Nancy 1036
Trower, James 885
Truman, H. P. 856
Tunnell, John 812
  Robert 899
Tunstall, T. B. 826
Turner, J. L. 838
  John 837
Tustin, John D. 1040
  Mary P. 1040
Tuttle, S. S. 866
  W. R. 857,870
Tydeman, Lucie 1064
  W. W. 1063,1064
Tyndle, Dicy 1015
Tyson, Bettie H. 1012

Underwood, Margaret 958

Valentine, W. H. 888
Vance, Zebadee 960
Vandyke, Richard 834
Van Gilder, John S. 845, 847,867,874,1043
  S. 861
Vanuxem...845
Vaux, William 903
Vestal, Robert 837
Vickars, Laura 927
Vincon, Lizzie 1065

Wagner, George Hendricks 1064
  J. H. 1064
  Joseph Cleveland 1064
  Mary 1064
  Mary S. 1064
  Mathias M. 1064
  M. M. 1064
  Sallie K. 1064
Wagoner...885
Walker, Miss B. 973
  David 816
  Elijah 962
  F. M. 833
  George 816
  James 186
  Joseph H. 846
  Lizzie J. 1013
  Margaret 957,962
  M. H. 852
  Miss R. L. 1054
  Sarah 962
  Susan 1014
  West 898
  William 825
Walkinshaw, James A. 924
  Paulina T. 924
Wallace...843,943,996
  Campbell 865,896
  James W. 872
  Joel 802
  Nancy 997
  Oliver 816
  William 808,834
Waller, Catherine 931
  H. A. 833
  J. L. 833
  William S. 930
Ware, Thomas 884
  W. G. 856
Washburn...1030,1061

Washburn, Harriet 1065
  Hugh 817
  John H. 1065
  Minnie 1065
  Royal 1065
  W. P. 867,1064,1065
Washburne, W. P. 896
Waterhouse, Euclid 865
  Richard 826,827
Waters, J. S. 900
  Rachel 1017
Watson, John 1016
  Martha 1016
  Martha M. 1016
Watts, John 804
Weatherford, Charity 1065
  J. W. 1065
  Lizzie 1065
  William 1065
Weaver, David H. 1065,1066
  Eliza M. 1065
  George C. 1065
  Mary E. 1066
Webb, John 847
  Juda 994
Webber, Mary S. 940
Weber, Maria 1066
  P. S. 1066
  Sarah 1066
  William M. 1066
  W. M. 855
Weeks, Frances I. 924
  Ira W. 924
Welch, Mary E. 979
Welcker, A. G. 824
  Albert 1011
  Miss C. F. 1011
  James M. 824,1011
Weldon, Joseph 815
Wells...802
  Ambrose 987
  Daniel 965
  R. P. 896
  Zebella 987
Wenning, J. 856
  L. 856
Wesson, Isaac 924
  Minerva J. 924
  Tobitha 924
West, Arminda 1066
  Edward 1066
  J. D. 855
  Sallie B. 1067
  Samuel B. 897
  T. A. 1066,1067
Westerfield, Elizabeth B. 1043
Whatcoat...885
Wheeler...829
  F. M. 889
Wheless...846
Whipple, Mary J. 1058
Whitaker...845
White, A. M. 843
  Andrew 819
  Caroline 1067
  Cornelia H. 1012
  George B. 811,814,846, 874,878,893
  H. C. 1007
  H. L. 826
  Hugh A. M. 844,846,896, 1012
  Hugh L. 815,817,819,823, 836,842,877,886
  Hugh Lawson 1012
  Isabella M. 878,1012
  James 799,800,802,805, 808,809,810,820,825,833, 839,848,874,890,892, 1032,1069
  J. C. 860,1001
  John F. 1064

White, L. 875,876
   Lute 1067
   Margaret H. 878
   Moses 827,848,872,893
   Sallie K. 1064
   Samuel A. 814,874
   William H. 1067
   W. O. 853,1067
Whitehead, Floyd L. 913, 914
   Sallie A. 913
Whiteside, Jenkin 819
Whitlow, J. H. 855
   J. H. 917
   Zephana 917
Whitson...842
Whitthorne, J. W. 1042
Whitton, S. D. 839
Willand, Barnherd 1068
   Elizabeth 1068
   John 1068
   Margaret 1068
Wightman...887
Wilcox, C. C. 866
   J. Cora 961
   M. C. 865,866,877,908
Wiley, E. F. 1007
   Henry S. 865
   Kate 1007
Wilkerson, Mary E. 1017
   Mary J. 1016
   M. W. 1017
Wilkinson, John 819
Willet...970
Willey, Susannah 933
Williams...849,853,855,938
   Anna 1068
   Anna B. 984
   "Cerro Gordo" 831
   Cornelia 984
   E. 843
   Eliza D. 1054
   G. R. 856
   James 843
   J. C. J. 894,1068,1069
   John 819,921,825,842, 1069
   John T. 948
   L. E. 905
   Lewis 821
   Lizzie D. 1053
   Louisa 940
   Lucy P. 1051
   Mary 948
   M. W. 848,864
   N. B. 905
   N. W. 819
   Permelia 962
   Rachel 1031
   Rebecca 947
   Rhoda 1069
   Robert 804
   Susan 1019
   Thomas L. 817,819,821, 971,995
   W. E. 856
   W. S. 876
   William 843,856
Willis, E. D. 838
   Samuel G. 895
Wills, Caroline 1044
Winkle, Isabella 920
   J. D. 920
Wilson, 829
   Anna 921
   Elizabeth 924
   Frank 970
   George 875
   James P. 924
   J. L. 834
   Rhoda 977
   Thomas 886
Wood, H. B. 827

Wood, John 841
   Mary 963
   Richard 898,899
Woodbury, C, M. 860,1069
   Daniel P. 1069
   Mary S. 1069
   Thomas Childs 1069
Woodruff...945
   Ella T. 1070
   W. W. 853,866,867,880, 901,1069,1070
Woods...1033
Woodward, Alexander 1070
   Annie 1070
   J. 870
   Mary 1070
   Nathan S. 1070
   N. S. 868
Wool...826,914
Woolfolk, L. B. 901
Wordworth, W. W. 951
Worsham, W. J. 833,855
Wright, J. P. 882
Wrinkle, Allen A. 1071
   Burton 1071
   Evaline 1071
   E. W. D. 1028
   Hattie Evaline 1071
   John 1070,1071
   John D. 1070,1071
   Kate 1071
   Maggie 1071
   Margaret A. I. 1071
   Samuel 1071
   Sophia 1070,1071
   Thomas E. 1071
   Virgie May 1071
   W. Grover Cleveland 1071
Wyley, E. F. 865
   Samuel Y. 893

Yarnell, Daniel 886
   Michael 886
   Sarah E. 957
Yeager...855
York, Margaret C. 923
Youmans, T. J. 856
Young, A. L. 855
   Alex 974
   D. K. 853
   Elizabeth 1049
   Emaline 974
   Isham 1071,1072
   J. P. 854
   Lucinda 1071
   Margaret C. 1071
   W. 1049
   Joanna 1049

Zachary, C. 838
Zachery, Sinai 913
Zbinden, D. H. 855
Ziegler, A. 1072
   Eliza 1072
Zimmerman,..853,938
Zollicoffer...827,1037
   Felix K. 870,917,1042
   Loulie 1042

#

www.ingramcontent.com/pod-product-compliance
Lightning Source LLC
Chambersburg PA
CBHW020057020526
44112CB00031B/207